KU-534-116

UNDER SAIL
Equipment for the Serious Sailor

EQUIPMENT FOR THE SERIOUS SAILOR

UNDER SAIL

Edited by

TONY MEISEL

Illustrated by

PETER MILNE

A QUARTO BOOK

First published in Great Britain 1982 by
NAUTICAL BOOKS
Macmillan London Ltd
4 Little Essex Street
London WC2R3LF

Produced and prepared by
Quarto Marketing Ltd.
212 Fifth Avenue
New York, New York 10010
USA

Editor: Bill Logan
Designer: Ken Diamond
Design Assistant: Susan Newman

ISBN 0-333-32883-3
Printed and bound in Hong Kong.

TABLE OF CONTENTS

UNDER SAIL
Equipment for the Serious Sailor

INTRODUCTION

Going to sea, whether for a day or a month, around the buoys or across oceans, is not a matter for haphazard planning. The fun, excitement and challenge we sail for can rarely be found on a badly kept boat. Proper preparation and topflight equipment are essential. Leaky bilges, frayed lines, chafed sailcloth and wheezing winches don't make for comfortable or confident sailors. In the days when sailing ships ruled the waves, there was many a pleasure sailor who'd taken his apprenticeship in the hard school of commercial sailing. Even the less experienced could count on a wise bosun to advise him or experienced sailors to assist him. Now, not only are the old skills hard to find but new technologies have changed the face of yachting.

The advice we offer you in *Under Sail* is a distillation of old salts' wisdom and new designers' skills. The authors have all experienced enough wet nights in gale force winds, enough lonely midocean passages and enough heart-stopping tacking duels to say, with some authority, what works and what doesn't. In our professions too—whether as designers or journalists—we have kept a close watch on the new technologies. Thus, we approach you with both trepidation and pleasure: Trepidation because all of our knowledge and experience together can but offer a compilation of recommendations which the reader's own experience must prove or disprove. Pleasure because we are arrogant enough to enjoy sharing what we know.

A yacht is judged by the soundness of its construction, the quality of its fittings and equipment and its speed and seaworthiness. Construction is the province of the builder, and other than minor strengthening, the owner can do little to correct bad building. Speed and seaworthiness derive from the basic conception and design of the yacht. If the designer has done his job well, and the builder has followed suit, the rest is up to you.

Every fitting, from mast truck to underwater transducer, must function flawlessly and smoothly if the yacht is to be considered "ready for sea". Whether you are racing, cruising, daysailing or circling the globe, the efficiency and safety of your voyage depends on robust quality for success. A lot of mediocre gear passes over chandlery counters yearly. For the serious sailor, it just will not do.

Inappropriate fitments are sometimes the result of ill-conceived production economies. One thinks of the astronaut who said he felt less than comfortable knowing he was about to blast off in a craft contracted for by competitive bidding. Often, too, the weight-paring requirements of racing or the mismatching of gear to boat results in a hideously inefficient sailing craft. The sea knows no half measures, offers no compassion, makes no compromises. If one block cannot stand the strain and fails, you may lose the entire rig. If one seacock malfunctions, the vessel may founder. The importance of high-quality equipment cannot be stressed too much. Buying the best will be an economy in the long run. Assuming your yacht is the biggest expense after your home, can you afford not to?

Under Sail is a showcase for the best and the brightest sailing equipment. Herein, you will find expert advice on everything with which you might choose to equip your boat. We will tell you not only what is best, but why. You will find lists of suppliers, detailed explanations and recommendations. No one is trying to curry favor with manufacturers or advertisers. As a result, you'll get the kind of specific advice never obtainable in a magazine.

However, *Under Sail* is *not* a catalog! Our specific advice is accompanied by carefully thought-out discussions of equipment purpose and use. We are trying not to sell you anything, but to tell you what is best for any particular application. Furthermore, most of the fittings discussed are available worldwide. The authors have gone to great pains to make this book useful for sailors everywhere.

In the following text, you will meet a motley and distinguished crew:

David Vietor/Sails: President of Ratsey & Lapthorn Sailmakers. Experienced offshore racer. Sailmaker for America's Cup contender, *Clipper.*

Roger Marshall/Deck Gear and Rigging: Distinguished naval architect and yacht designer for Sparkman & Stephens. Design professor at Roger Williams College in Rhode Island. Graduate of Southampton University.

Don Sharp/Propulsion Systems: Contributing editor at *Boating* magazine. Author of articles on every aspect of marine engines, propellers, transmissions, electrical equipment and installations. Extensive practical experience.

Jeff Neuberth/Steering Systems: Design veteran of three America's Cup campaigns. Project director in 1977 for *Courageous* and *Independence.* Writer for *Yachting* magazine. Author of *The Yachtsman's Guide to Rigging.*

Manfred Meisels/Navigation and Electronics: Recognized marine electronics expert. Contributing editor at *Yachting.*

Doug Schryver/The Bosun's Locker: Associate Editor at *Boating.* Experienced sailor, naval architect and boatbuilder.

Tony Meisel/Editor, Below Decks, Safety Gear and Clothing: Former editor at *Motor Boating & Sailing* and the Nautical Book Club. World-travelling sailor.

All of us have endeavored to produce not only an extensive review of our respective equipment areas, but an overview of the theory and practice of seamanship and proper yacht design. As I mentioned before, *Under Sail* is not a catalog; rather, it is the distilled opinions and experience of seven seasoned and knowledgeable men of the sea. You may not agree with everything we say, but you can be sure our judgments are based on long hours at the helm, in the bilge and up the rigging. If it works well, you'll find it in *Under Sail.*

Tony Meisel
New York

Chapter 1

SAILS

Until the middle of the nineteenth century, flax was woven into tough, heavy, baggy and reasonably long-lasting sail-cloth. It propelled the world's square riggers and fore-and-aft vessels—well when sailing off the wind, reasonably on a reach, but rather badly to windward. The flaxen cloth tore, sagged, stretched and misbehaved, though it was kept aloft by the ministrations of the sailmaker and the care of captain and crew.

Cotton made its mark in 1851, when the vessel *America* saw fit to drop in at Cowes and astonished the yachting world by beating the best British sailors for the Hundred Guinea Cup. After the races, the British were fast to copy the lines of the American hull. Certainly her fine entry and clean run played their part, but the flatter, more shapely, fitted cotton sails won the day. From then on, until the middle of the twentieth century, cotton sails remained the norm.

In the 1890s, Nat Herreshoff devised the modern mode of cutting sailcloth, with the panels running at right angles to the leech—the cross-cut (or horizontal-cut) sail as we know it today. This method of stitching the cloth resulted in a sail which would better hold its shape, free of the bunching and puckering so prevalent with traditional cuts.

All cloths are woven by aligning one set of threads—the *warp*—vertically on the loom, while another set of threads— the *weft*—are woven over and under the warp threads. This process means that the weft threads are generally less prone to stretching than the warp. The cross-cut method aligns the weft threads parallel to the sail's leech, thus placing the most stable threads along the line of highest loads. For this reason a cross-cut sail is generally less liable to bunching and bellying than an old vertical-cut sail.

Nevertheless, even cross-cut sails were prone to stretch, especially in damp and rainy weather, and great care had to be taken to break them in. Furthermore, they were still subject to deterioration from mildew and rot, and demanded more time in maintenance than you spent sailing.

Beginning in the 1950s, sailmakers learned to use synthetics for sailcloth. What makes a polyester shirt so hard to wear is the same thing that makes polyester sails so good: low porosity. Just as the shirt refuses to let any wind through to your skin, so the sail catches more of the wind that strikes it. First nylon, then Dacron (Terylene) came into general use. Nylon proved too stretchy for anything but spinnakers, but Dacron had among its properties stability, strength, resistance to rot and the ability to hold its sewn-in shape. Using the new materials, master sailmakers like Ted Hood in Marblehead and Jeremy Howard-Williams in Cowes began to fashion sails which easily outran the competition, much as *America* had run away from the fleet at Cowes a hundred years earlier.

Here were sails which didn't need breaking in, didn't stretch appreciably and could be cut for reasonably constant camber (degree of curvature). Also, a Dacron sail could withstand much greater ranges of wind than cotton, and with the general acceptance of the masthead rig, yachts could beat to windward with greater efficiency, at higher angles of attack and in heavier conditions of sea and wind.

Nylon, meanwhile, became the norm for spinnaker cloth for much the opposite reasons that Dacron managed so well for mainsails and headsails: Nylon's higher stretch helps to absorb the shocks the unsupported sail takes as the boat bounces downwind and means that a lighter weight cloth can be used, helping to keep the spinnaker aloft.

Nevertheless, no single sail will do for all the conditions a yacht encounters. Different cloth weights and cuts will be

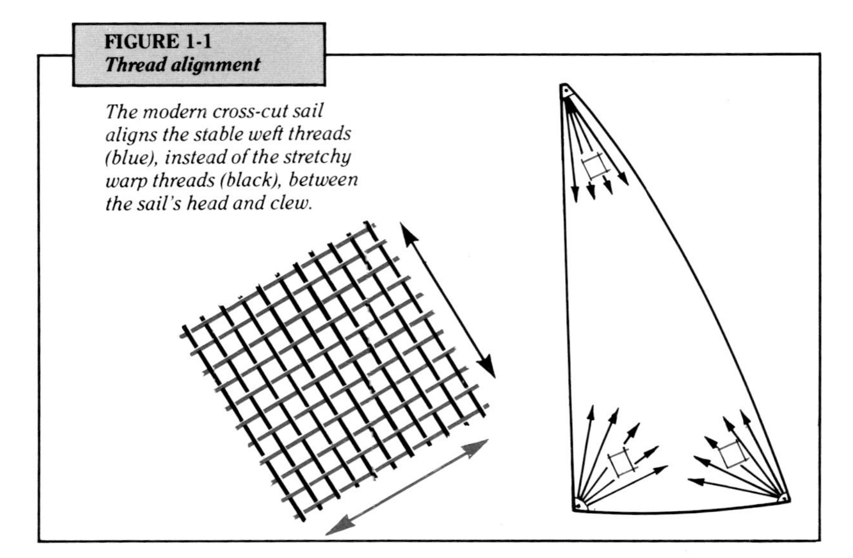

FIGURE 1-1
Thread alignment

The modern cross-cut sail aligns the stable weft threads (blue), instead of the stretchy warp threads (black), between the sail's head and clew.

appropriate for varying winds. How many sails you carry will depend on the sailing you do. In racing, a large crew is taken for granted. Furthermore, boat, rig and sails have probably been designed as a unit (at least if you are really serious about your racing). Thus, you will have a much larger inventory and the personnel to change sails with the slightest variance in wind conditions. Serious racers will carry from 15 to 20 sails for offshore work, exclusive of the main. In all likelihood, there will be a sail for every conceivable condition and every point of sail.

Cruising sailors, on the other hand, will be aboard with far fewer crew, and will be less determined to achieve maximum boat speed. After all, you're out there to enjoy it. Also, simply to save space, a cruiser will carry a much smaller inventory of softer, more adaptable cloth.

SOURCES

How do you ensure good quality sails for your boat? Foremost, realize that a good set of sails is really the result of close collaboration between owner and sailmaker. Quality sailmaking is custom manufacturing. A lot of the success of a good sail comes from the experience of the firm designing and manufacturing it, but the sails are still one of the most critical performance areas over which you can exercise some control. To ensure quality sails it is important that the sailmaker completely understand the customer's needs. The selection of the correct fabric still requires an empirical understanding which goes beyond mathematical analysis. What Ted Hood said when he first entered the sailmaking business 30 years ago still holds true: "A sail is only as good as the cloth from which it's made." It's also only as good as your sailmaker's understanding of your boat's needs.

Still, there are a few ways to ensure you get the best possible service. Word of mouth recommendations are as good as anything in a field that is a craft and likely to remain so, but try to find out why people recommend the sailmaker they do. Many lofts specialize in a certain type of sails: racing, cruising or dinghy. A few makers survive by making sails only for a given one-design class! If you sail a coastal cruiser, you may be disappointed to find a recommended sailmaker suggesting you use more than half a dozen headsails. He's probably a racing specialist, less familiar with your particular needs.

Certain internationally franchised sailmakers—like Hood, North and Horizon—are well known for their fine racing sails. Hood also has a reputation for making dependable cruising sails, but distance cruisers may go to their own specialists, lofts which may take a week or 10 days to painstakingly complete a sail that less careful manufacturers would turn out in a few days.

If you're an average coastal cruiser, however, you will do best to pick a local sailmaker with a proven track record making your kind of sails. It's far better to have your craftsman a few miles down the road, than across an ocean. Even if you can save 20 percent by having sails made in Hong Kong, think of the difficulty of getting satisfaction if you should have complaints. The local sailmaker, on the other hand, is more accessible and has a reputation to protect.

When you visit a prospective sailmaker, ask to see the loft. If he or she will take the time to show you around and explain the advantages of the shop, chances are you'll get the same personal service when it comes to designing your sails. Don't be afraid to ask specific questions. Does the loft use only first-quality cloth? (Some use seconds or cheaper-grade fabric.) Are the seam threads sewn in a contrasting color, making wear easier to spot? How long have the workers been with the firm? A reputable sailmaker shouldn't be embarrassed by such questions. Belligerent responses often mean that the salesman has something to hide.

Your sailmaker, once chosen, should ask some basic questions:

What kind of boat have you?
What do you use it for?
Where do you sail?
How large an inventory will you carry?
How many crew are usually aboard?

Do you race to the International Offshore Rule (IOR) or any other rule?

How much do you wish to spend?

Sail weight and inventory will be conditioned by the kind of sailing you do, the conditions you are likely to encounter and the restrictions imposed by the rules of your class. An offshore racer may carry as many as 15 headsails. A coastal cruising boat gets along with four or five. The size of crew is also important. A husband and wife cruising team may not have the muscle power to haul in a 170 percent genoa in moderate air, while an offshore racer will have the deck gorillas and the winches needed.

If you race to a rule, your sails will have to be cut to the provisions of that rule, placing limits on inventories, percentage overlaps, spinnaker area and hoist limits. Rules were created to equalize the chances of different size boats. The International Offshore Rule, for example, penalizes high aspect ratios and encourages large headsails at the expense of smaller mains. The genoas are usually constructed so as to overlap the main by about 50 percent. Larger overlaps incur increasing penalties. IOR boats use many spinnakers and running sails, though their girths are also limited. Whether to take the penalty in exchange for improved performance is a matter for you and your sailmaker to decide.

FIGURE 1-2
Using the wind's force

A sailboat depends on its keel's resistance to sideforce to keep it moving forward while sailing to windward. Only a relatively small part of the total wind force is converted into forward motion.

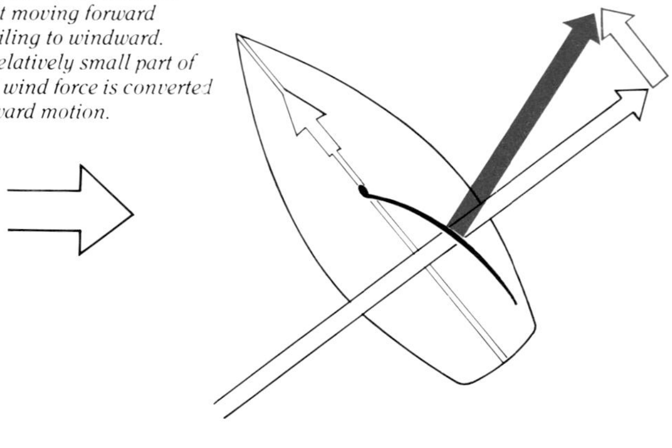

Your sailmaker must try to wring the maximum sail out of the rule for your particular boat. This is sophisticated stuff, and your knowledge of the rule must be as thorough as possible. A good introduction to IOR rules is contained in Wallace Ross's *Sail Power.*

How much you spend depends mainly on the depth of your pocketbook. Nevertheless, there are ways to economize wisely. Headsail reef points can make one sail do double duty. Careful cloth selection—finding just the right weight and finish to provide good power over the widest range of wind velocities—can do the same; but extra heavy-duty workmanship—triple-stitching and hand-finishing—can be expensive. Do you really need it for the type of sailing you are undertaking? Only ocean racers and blue water cruisers need costly refinements.

Your sailmaker may also offer new technologies that promise cost reductions: glued seams, ultraviolet inhibitors and the like. The glued seam makes for a smoother airfoil and thus reduces turbulence, but the durability of the bond has yet to be proven. Ultraviolet inhibitors have been shown, in tests, to slow cloth deterioration effectively. If your sails are improperly constructed however, no amount of peripheral technology can help them.

HOW SAILS WORK

A sail is an airfoil, much like the wing of an airplane. Unlike a wing, however, a sail uses the air as *both* a support and a source of power. Adjusting, or trimming, a sail correctly helps give it the shape to extract maximum power from the wind, but a certain amount of shape must be built into the sail to encourage the formation of that efficient form. The object is to give the sail maximum lift (forward force) with minimum drag. When you consider that the wind almost always—except in a downwind run—strikes the sail from the side, you can imagine how complex sail geometry can become.

The optimum lift/drag ratio is a direct function of the amount of camber in any sail, camber being the degree of curvature in the body of the sail. Boats whose hull designs discourage lateral motion can take more powerful sails than other boats. A boat with a wide, deep keel (which helps reduce leeway) can use more powerful sails than can boats with smaller keel areas. Likewise, boats with greater dynamic stability (or beam) can afford more power from their sails than narrower boats or those with slack bilges. Just the right amount of power from the rig is necessary for good performance. Pointing is a function of the forces on the keel. Without sufficient sideforce, the keel cannot achieve proper lift. If there's too much sideforce, the boat wastes energy trying to right itself.

The sail designer specifies the amount of camber and its distribution in order to provide the power appropriate for any given yacht design. A shapely sail is every bit as important as a strong sail. If you consider a sail to have three vertical sections—the leading edge *(entry),* the middle *(body)* and the leech *(exit)*—it is possible to ascertain the shape criteria necessary for a good sail. The entry should be rounded enough to enable you to steer the sail. With too flat an entry, the sail will break aft too suddenly and lose drive. Flat entries, for example, will cause a spinnaker to collapse very quickly and almost without warning. The flatter and finer the entry, the more likely the sail is to stall. In a seaway this condition occurs when the sail and its luff telltales jump around quickly, first on the windward then on the leeward side of the sail.

The body of the sail should be full enough to provide the horsepower capable of moving the boat well on the points and in the strengths of wind for which the sail is designed. If a sail is too full for the conditions, it will quickly overpower the boat. Too flat a sail will not move the boat well enough. When a crew changes a full #1 genoa for a flatter #2 genoa, without recognizing that the flatter sail will produce less power and consequently less apparent wind, the wind drops suddenly, requiring a change back to the #1 genoa. The crew had failed to realize that most of that wind speed was being made by the boat itself.

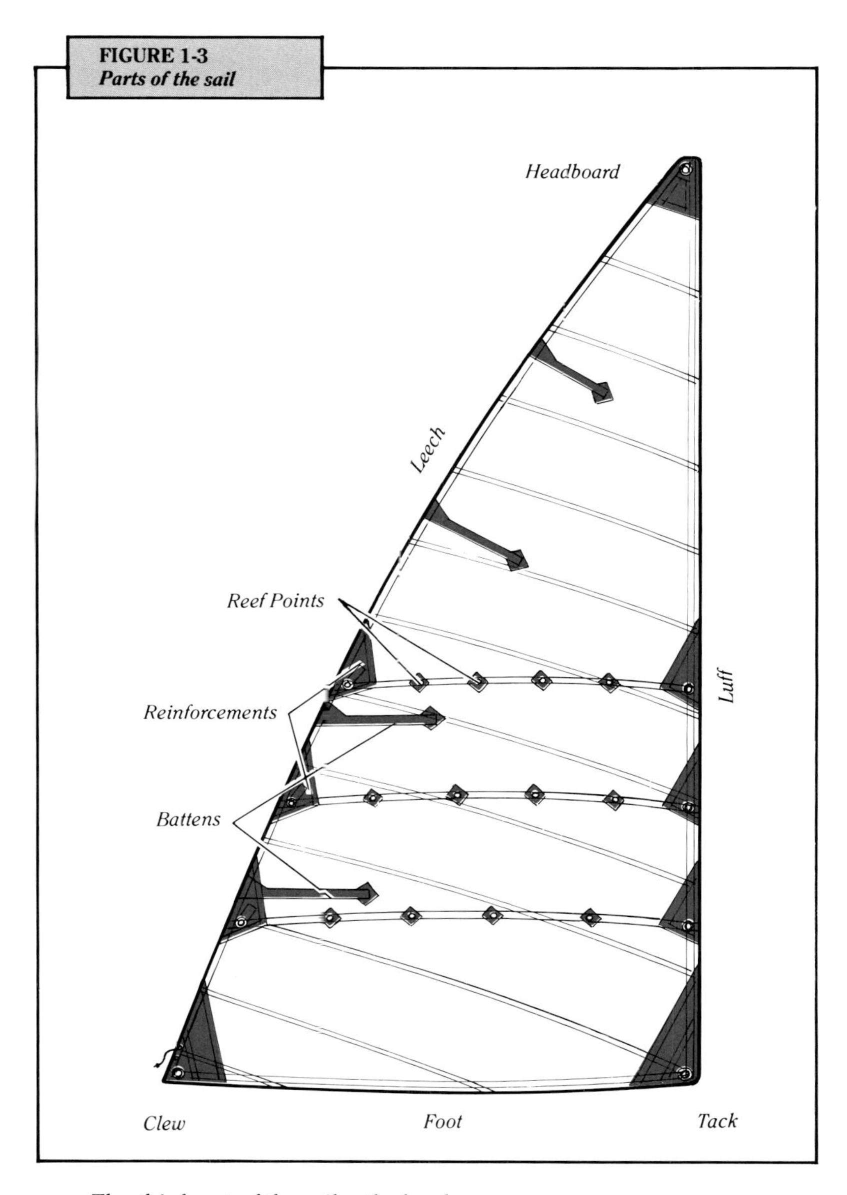

FIGURE 1-3
Parts of the sail

The third part of the sail—the leech—is an equally important aspect of its shape. Any sail should have a smooth transition from the body to its exit. Too full a leech will overpower a boat very quickly. If a headsail leech is too full, for example, it will direct a lot of flow into the main, causing backwinding. This is quite noticeable on a long narrow boat like a 12-meter where the headsail overlaps the main with reasonable proportions, not the 170 percent or more of an IOR sail plan. The more closed the slot between the two sails becomes, the slower the boat will go, due to turbulence. The crew tries to improve the situation by

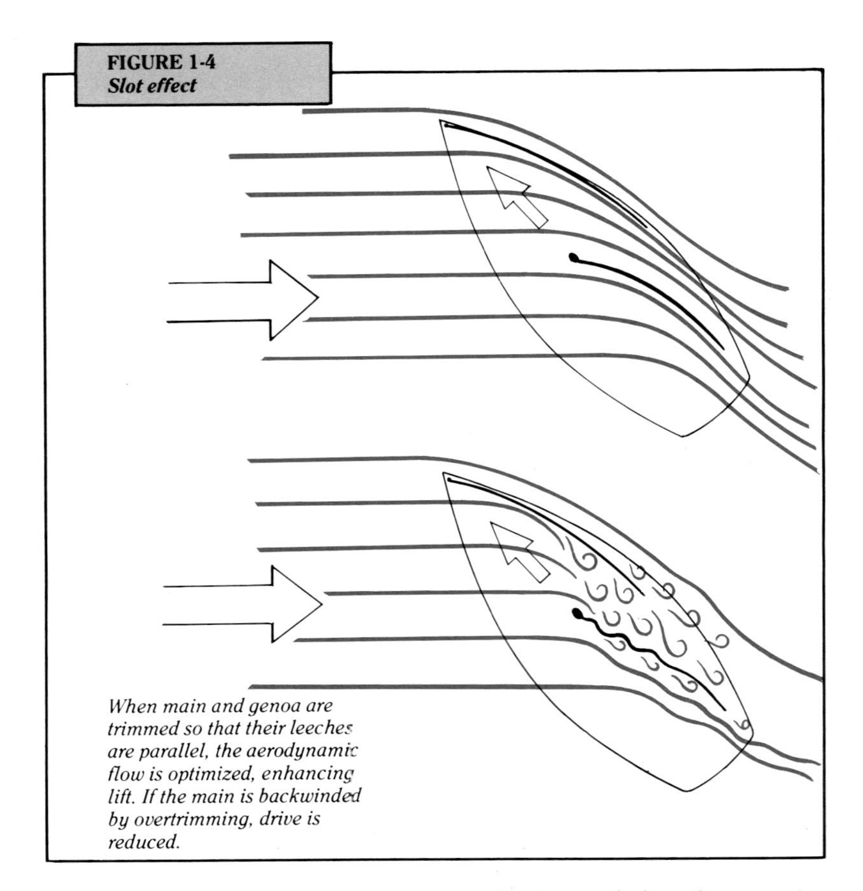

FIGURE 1-4
Slot effect

When main and genoa are trimmed so that their leeches are parallel, the aerodynamic flow is optimized, enhancing lift. If the main is backwinded by overtrimming, drive is reduced.

trimming the headsail, but doing so increases sideforce and slows the boat still further.

The more rounded the leech sections in both the main and genoa, the more weather helm the yacht develops. Where the airflow cannot exit the aft section smoothly, the effect is the same as when you bear away in a breeze with everything overtrimmed. Sideforce is greater, so the boat increases its heeling angle and slows dramatically at the same time.

SAILCLOTH

Translating the desired shape into materials which are inherently stretchy is the perennial challenge for the sailmaker. A sail fabric must withstand loads which increase by the square of the wind velocity. A light genoa built for use in 4 knots of true wind must withstand quadrupled loadings if the true wind speed is doubled.

The fabric selected for any sail largely determines the wind ranges it can work in. Heavier fabrics can withstand higher loads, but in any given cloth weight there can be a number of different styles with different characteristics determined by the finish of the cloth.

A 6.5-ounce Dacron cloth, for example, comes in three different finishes. The first is a soft nonresinated finish specially designed for easy handling and withstanding tough ocean passages. Its tensile strength makes it durable. The second finish is a resin (melamine-based) which is driven into the structure of the fabric to reduce slippage of the yarns and control stretch. This finish alone can occur in gradations from medium to very firm, all of which influence tear resistance, stretch and ease of handling—the harder finishes being more easily damaged. The third finish is a very tough polymer resin applied directly to the surface of the fabric, producing an extremely stiff cloth with a minimum of stretch. Its drawback is loss of durability and tear resistance. The harder finishes are, in general, sought by the racer, who needs the most rigid airfoil possible to give his boat maximum power. For him, the lowest stretch cloth is absolutely necessary. An offshore cruiser, on the other hand, would probably prefer easily handled sails built from a more supple fabric.

As can be seen, a 6.5-ounce fabric can be produced with many modifications. The sailmaker must choose the correct fabric weight, and the finish best suited for each type of sailing. On page 17 is a cloth selection chart showing the weight of fabric generally used for an average 38-foot yacht under different wind conditions. Your naval architect can choose the weights appropriate for your boat.

The most significant new development in cloth is Mylar. Like Dacron, Mylar is a polyester, but with a different molecular structure enabling it to be extruded in sheets of film. Consequently it has no thread lines, and will stretch uniformly in any direction. Bonded with a cloth scrim, Mylar will reduce stretch to negligible amounts.

Introduced first on the race course, Mylar composites may represent as great a transition as the postwar change to Dacron

TABLE 1-1
***Cloth Weight and Wind Speed*[1]**

True Wind	Cloth Weights		Apparent Wind	
(in knots)	*Upwind*	*Downwind*	*Up*	*Down*
0-8	3·4	0·5	0-11	0-5
8-15	4·5	0·75	11-19	5-12
16-22	4·5	0·75	19-26	13-18
22-30	6·0	1·5	26-35	19-25
30-35	7·2	2·2	35-40	25-29

[1]Assuming a 38-foot cruiser.

In some respects it could be even greater, since for the first time in the history of sailmaking one is dealing with nonwoven material. The absence of thread lines will dramatically alter the traditional layout patterns now seen in all sails.

Along with this development, improvements in adhesives may eventually cause the sewn seam to disappear. Mylar seams acquire their strength from being glued together. Spreader patches, for example, can now effectively be stuck rather than sewn onto a sail.

SAIL INVENTORY

Most of today's auxiliaries, whether racing or cruising yachts, tend to be either sloop or cutter rigged. There are still a number of yawls and ketches being built, but except for the addition of a mizzen these rigs do not pose any unusual inventory problems.

Any sloop or cutter needs at least one large overlapping headsail, along with the main, in order to perform adequately in light to medium air. Backing up the large headsail will generally be a #2 genoa and #3 genoa along with a working jib or some other smaller headsail. For reaching, many yachts carry a double head rig consisting of a high-clewed reacher and staysail. Spinnakers have long been the most popular running sails.

While the above sails do not make up any specific inventory, they isolate the principal categories of sails: mainsails (and mizzens), headsails (genoas and working sails), staysails and spinnakers. Depending upon individual need, the number of sails carried can vary from a full racing complement of some 22 sails to one consisting of a large headsail, working jib and main. Recommended sail inventories appear on pages 18-19.

THE WELL-CONSTRUCTED SAIL

The best possible sail fabric is useless until it has been laid out and put together, so as to produce a finished sail capable of taking a great deal of use and even abuse without failure. Rarely is anyone really prepared to hoist the correct sail immediately in changing conditions. A little latitude in the actual construction of a sail is advisable. Panel alignment and shape must be appropriate. All seams, hanks and boltropes should be well secured, and the equipment for raising and lowering sails should be dependable and efficient.

Since it is woven, sailcloth must be cut to minimize or control stretch. However the sail may be cut, its panels will usually be tapered. The seam shaping (called *seam dilation*) along the edges of a panel—generally in the shape of an arc—is simply a way of stressing a sail by varying the widths across a panel of sailcloth. If the panels at the edge of a sail are less wide than those in the middle, the edges when under tension will load up before the greater widths in the middle. Seam dilation gives the sail much of its shape and, in so doing, influences its aerodynamics.

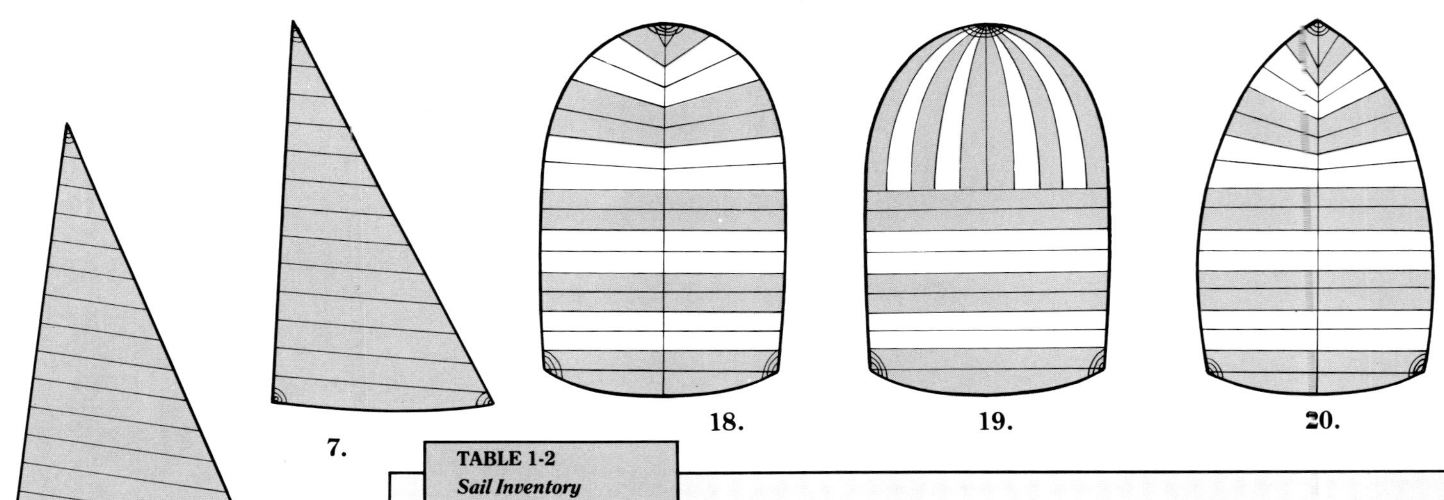

6.

7.

18.

19.

20.

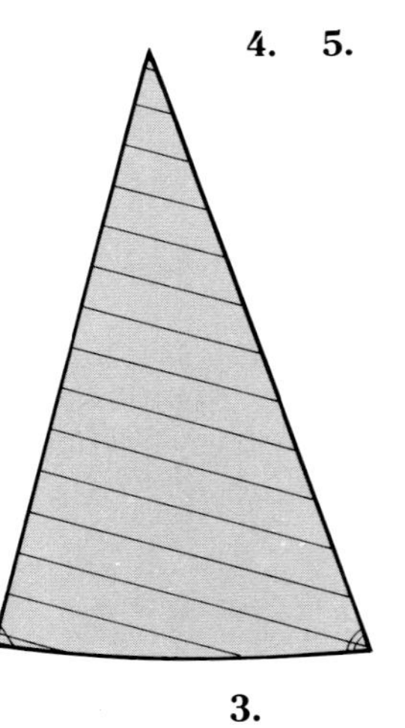

4. 5.

3.

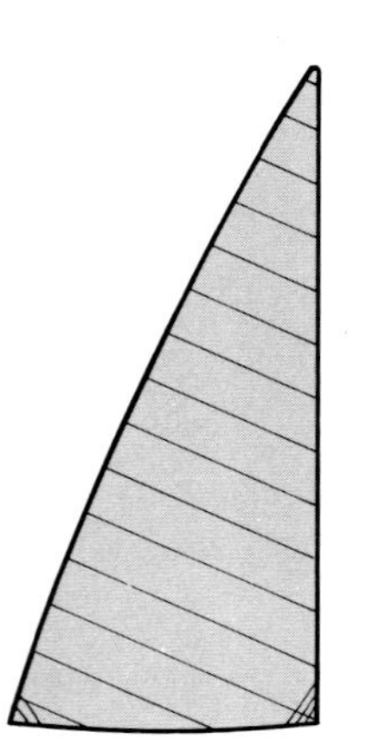

1.

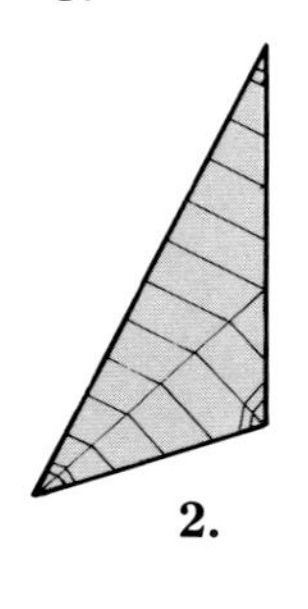

2.

TABLE 1-2
Sail Inventory

· This table contains suggested inventories for cruisers, coastal cruisers and racers in all size ranges.

LOA (in feet)	TYPE	1. Main	2. Storm Trysail	3. Light Genoa	4. Light #1 Genoa	5. Medium #1 Genoa	6. Heavy #1 Genoa	7. #2 Genoa
18-25	Coastal	•		•				
	Offshore	•	•	•				
	Racer	•	•			•		
26-30	Coastal	•		•				
	Offshore	•	•	•		•		
	Racer	•	•		•			•
31-35	Coastal	•		•		•		
	Offshore	•	•	•				•
	Racer	•	•	•		•	•	•
36-40	Coastal	•		•		•		
	Offshore	•	•	•		•		•
	Racer	•	•			•	•	•
Over 40	Coastal	•	•	•		•		
	Offshore	•	•	•			•	
	Racer	•	•		•	•	•	•

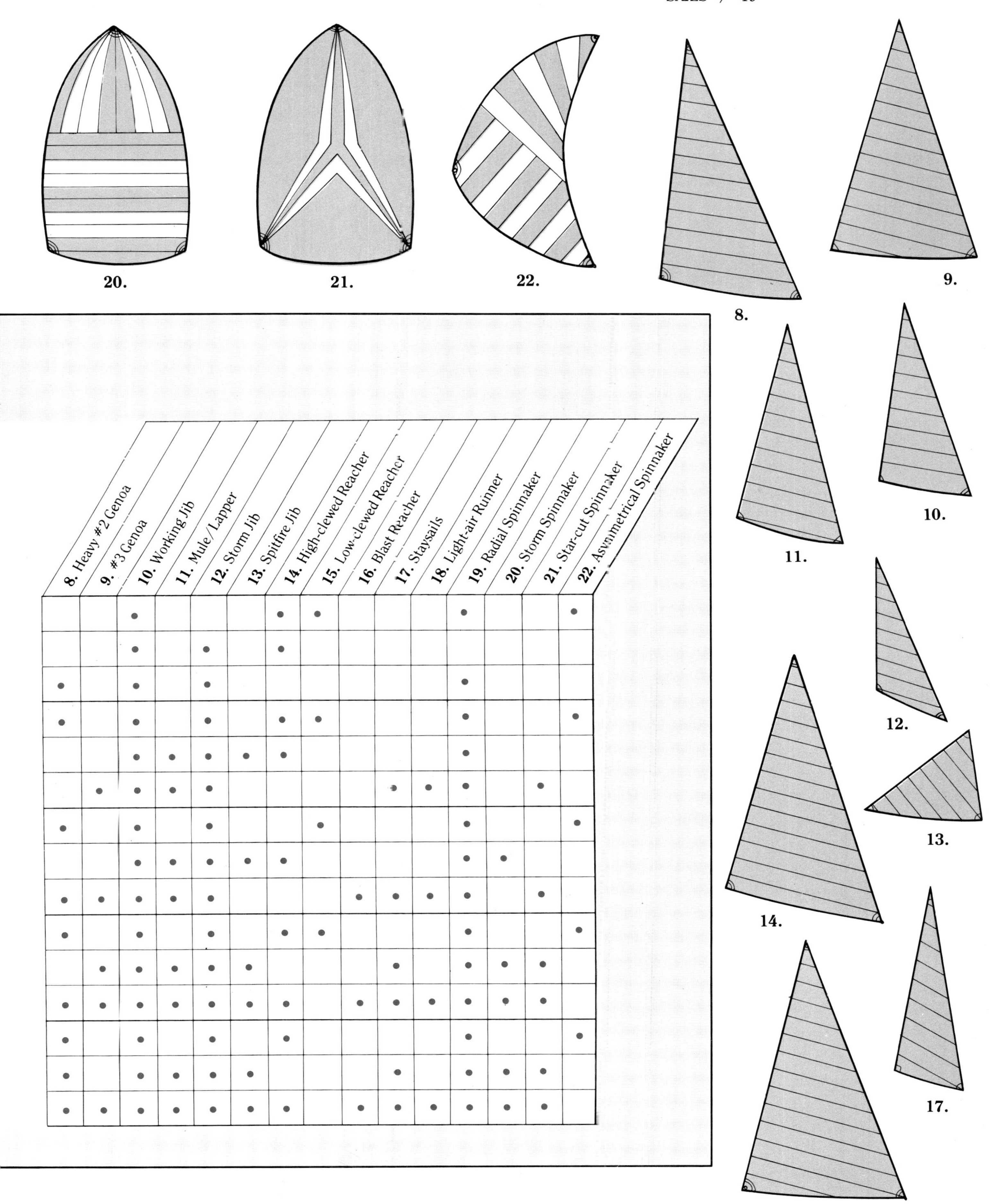

8. Heavy #2 Genoa	9. #3 Genoa	10. Working Jib	11. Mule/Lapper	12. Storm Jib	13. Spitfire Jib	14. High-clewed Reacher	15. Low-clewed Reacher	16. Blast Reacher	17. Staysails	18. Light-air Runner	19. Radial Spinnaker	20. Storm Spinnaker	21. Star-cut Spinnaker	22. Asymmetrical Spinnaker
		•				•	•				•			•
		•		•		•								
•		•		•							•			
•		•		•		•	•				•			•
		•	•	•	•	•					•			
	•	•	•	•					•	•	•		•	
•		•		•			•				•			•
		•	•	•	•	•					•	•		
•	•	•	•	•				•	•	•	•		•	
•		•		•		•	•				•			•
	•	•	•	•	•				•		•	•	•	
•	•	•	•	•	•	•		•	•	•	•	•	•	
•		•		•		•					•			•
•		•	•	•	•				•		•	•	•	
•	•	•	•	•	•	•		•	•	•	•	•	•	

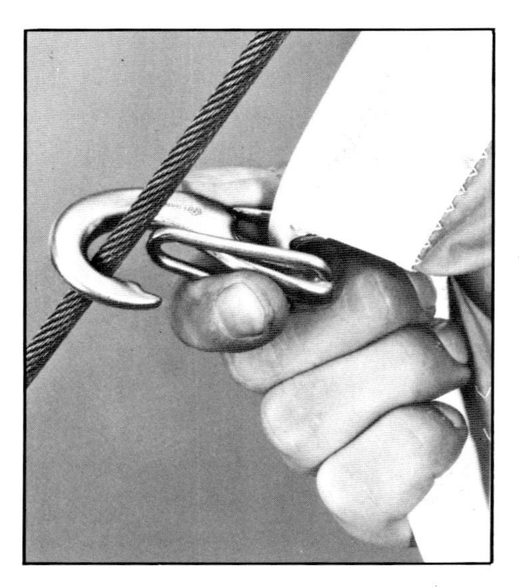

The Wichard luff hank allows one-handed attachment of foresails to stay.

No matter how carefully its panels may be cut and joined, a sail will not be durable unless its edges are equally well made. The edges must be protected from chafe and wear. On a genoa's leech and foot the best quality sails are furnished with either an external tape or tabling sewn down along the edge. Within the tape there should be leech and foot lines—serving both as vital controls and as reinforcement for the unsupported edges of the sail. Along the luff, heavier duty tapes should enclose either a rope or wire, to which the hanks are seized. At the three corners, the reinforcing patches should be large, with enough layers so that the pressed rings can be firmly seated. Any space between the fabric and the ring can allow water to seep beneath the ring, eventually corroding it.

Headsails

Most headsails today are cross cut rather than miter cut. This means that the cloth panels are laid perpendicular to the leech of the sail. Such a cloth layout has the advantage of letting the panels meet the luff at the same angle so that the entire luff will react uniformly under tension.

The modern masthead rig's principal source of power is the foretriangle. Consequently, for varying wind strengths, it needs a fair number of headsails. This inventory is customarily broken down into a light genoa (a full area sail) along with a heavy genoa. These are followed by successive stepdowns to a #2, #3 and/or #4 genoa. The weights of these sails will range generally from 4- to 6-ounce Dacron.

The most common luff system for headsails used to be a wire luff hanked to a headstay. In the past decade, wire has been replaced by rope enclosed in tape. This makes for a stretchy luff whose tension can be varied by the halyard. It is also easier to handle and provides better draft control. The stretchy rope luff replaced the traditional wire luff, while still retaining the advantages of hanks. Like hanks, a rope luff allows you to keep the sail attached to the headstay when you lower it.

In the last five years the grooved luff foil has revolutionized the racing headsail. Instead of hanks, this system uses a boltrope which slides up and down in a grooved foil. The first of these to become widely used was the Hood Seastay, followed shortly by Stearn Sailing Systems' Twinstay.

FIGURE 1-5
Grooved luff

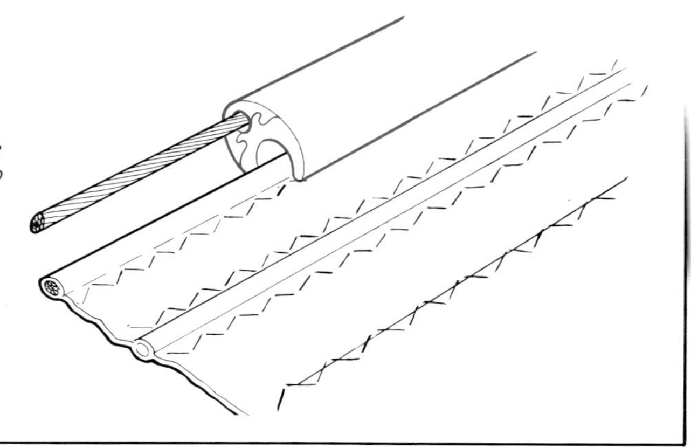

The luff wire of the headsail is fed into the groove of an extruded headstay foil, making for a cleaner entry and less luff sag, because the foil is rigid and leaves no gap between stay and sail.

FIGURE 1-6
Grooved foil systems

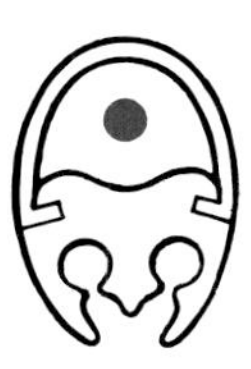

Left to right: 1. single groove; 2. foil fits into sleeve over headstay, allowing for quicker removal; 3. twin grooves allow one headsail to be raised as the other is lowered; 4. grooves fore and aft allow two sails to be boomed out for running.

and Hood Yacht Systems' Gemini foil. The last two added a second groove, allowing the sailor to change genoas without going baldheaded during the change. A further benefit of all the systems is the cleaner aerodynamic entry for the leading edge of the airfoil. Also, since the foil is smooth (as opposed to the serrations of a wire forestay), a spinnaker slides off more easily and therefore is less likely to wrap.

Although first developed for racing yachts, the grooved forestay has proven to be a boon for the cruising sailor. Until recently, most roller furling headsails were free flying with a 1 × 19 wire luff tensioned between the genoa halyard and a deck-mounted drum just aft of the stem. It took a great deal of halyard tension—more than many halyard winches could stand—to control sag. The grooved forestay solves this problem, because it is more rigid than a wire stay. Since the luff has adequate support, it becomes possible to reef a larger sail in heavier weather. Also, the grooved

Right: Roller-reefing genoa reefed down to storm-jib size. Left: The Hood Seafurl system's furling/reefing drum.

headstay itself makes for easier sail changes and permits the sail to be removed easily for repairs and maintenance.

In terms of sail construction, the only addition a roller furling/reefing genoa needs is a suncover along the leech and foot to protect the sail when it is left furled on the headstay for long periods of time. The best protective material is either Acrylon or Sunbrella.

For very light air locales, you should carry a reacher in addition to the usual complement of headsails. Made of nylon or very light Dacron, it is really an adaptation of the old gollywobblers seen on schooners. Let it be as large as you can handle, cut high in the foot to catch the air and sheeted to a block attached to the stern rail or the end of the boom. This is a cloud of a sail, and must be light enough to stay full in the slightest zephyr.

Mainsails and Mizzens

Mainsails are unique since they are used in all winds from 0 to 60 knots. Consequently, a well-designed main must be built to withstand a wide range of loadings, though it does have the benefit of being the only sail supported on two of its three sides. The support is not secure, however, unless the sail is solidly attached to it.

The traditional, and still most common, method of attaching the luff and foot to the spars is with slides, either shackled on or seized on with twine or tape. Some lateral play must be permitted; otherwise, particularly if shackles are used, the slides may snap off. A boltrope, however, can alleviate the point loading which occurs with slides.

Mainsails are designed to be reefed, and the most popular method today is slab, or "jiffy," reefing. Here one should be sure that the clew patches are made heavy enough to take the strain of reefing lines. Very often it is advisable to secure the leech reef with webbing or braids for additional reinforcement. The slab-reefing boom is designed to allow large sections or panels of the sail to be pulled down onto the boom. There should be at least two lines at each end of the boom to facilitate reefing and unreefing. These lines may run inside or outside the boom. On an offshore cruising boat the external systems are preferable since they make for less chafe and easier replacement of lines. For racing boats or day sailers, the reefing lines should be led inside the boom, reducing the chance of their catching on deck fittings and also cutting windage. Other details to look for on the sail are leech lines exiting at all of the reef patches, large reef diamonds and well-reinforced batten pockets.

Battens do two things: They help maintain the roach's aerodynamic curve, and they keep the leech of the sail from fluttering. The fiberglass battens supplied

FIGURE 1-7
Roller furling/reefing jib

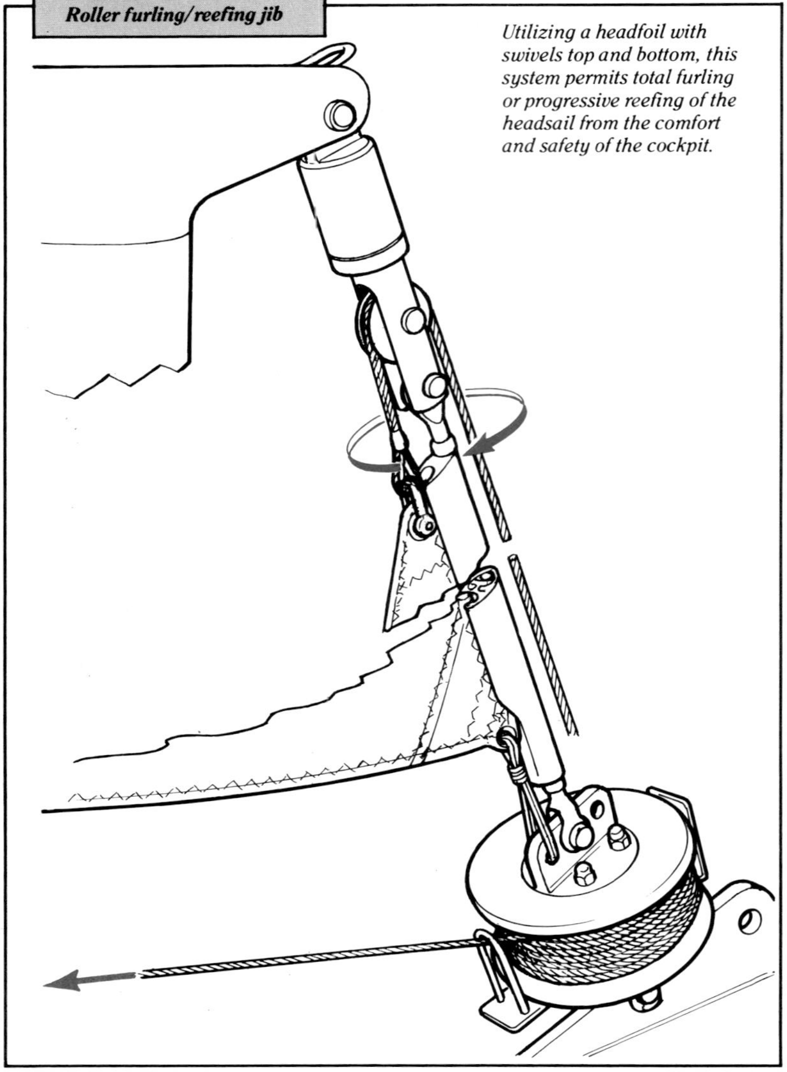

Utilizing a headfoil with swivels top and bottom, this system permits total furling or progressive reefing of the headsail from the comfort and safety of the cockpit.

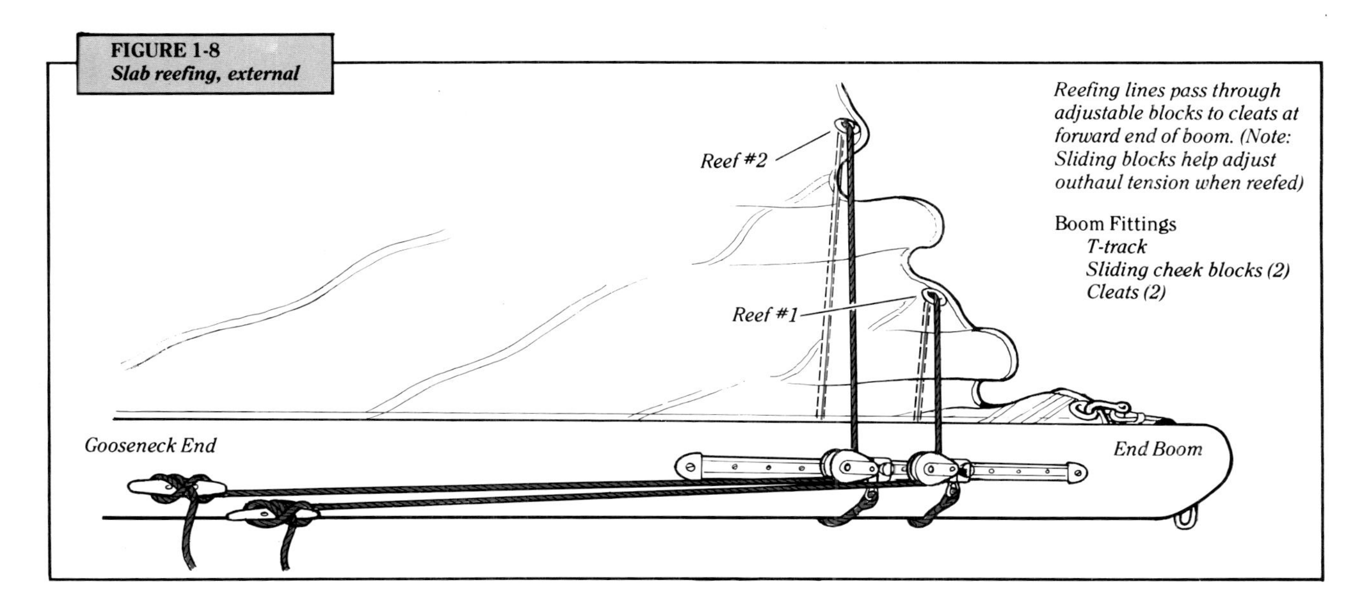

FIGURE 1-8
Slab reefing, external

with sails must be capped with a softer material, like PVC, to prevent chafing. Wooden battens are prone to splintering and cannot be furled on the main boom without running the risk of warping. In design terms, mains with the largest roaches are supplied to racing sailors looking for every bit of area. These roaches can be as much as 60 percent of the batten length, while roaches for cruising mains average around 35 percent. Large roaches should, however, be carefully designed. When a roach is more than half as long as its battens, the whole edge of the sail may have a tendency to seesaw.

Mainsails—like genoas—have profited from recent innovations. A number of cruising designs now employ mains with hollow leeches to do away with the troublesome roach and batten-pocket areas. The loss in area is not enough to materially affect performance, while the easier trimming and reduced maintenance represent a valuable gain.

Another significant development is Hood Yacht Systems' Stowaway mast. This system has already proven itself in the 1980 Observer Single-handed Transatlantic Race (OSTAR) on board Phil Weld's trimaran *Moxie*. It is nothing more than a roller

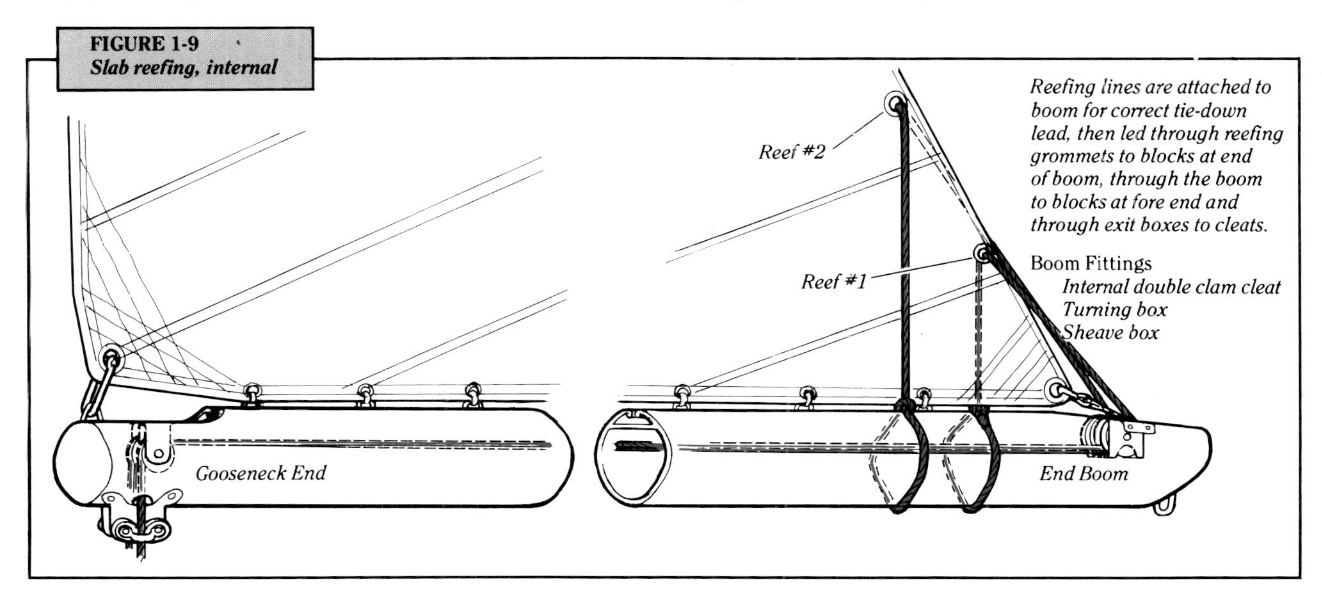

FIGURE 1-9
Slab reefing, internal

Right: Though the sail is by Hood, the mainsail furling gear is by Stearn. The whole sail rolls up behind the mast, allowing infinitely adjustable reefing.
Left: Clew attachment for the furling main.

furling sail rolled up into the spar itself. The easy handling which this system provides is perhaps its most valuable asset, but the protection afforded to a sail furled inside the spar is another good reason to use it.

Mizzens act very much like mainsails; in fact, they are designed as mini-mains. They should be cut flatter since they must operate in the very disturbed air caused by the flow aft from the main. A blue water cruiser will generally use a heavier mizzen than its day racing counterpart, because it may sail under jib and mizzen alone, in heavy weather.

Staysails

Once staysails were, as the name suggests, jib-like sails hanked to an extra stay. The spinnaker staysail, genoa staysail, banana staysail and tallboy are all variants on the traditional type. Recently, a new type of staysail—called a "big boy" or "blooper"—has been developed to provide extra power on downwind runs when the true wind is at least 10 knots. Unlike the others, it is a free-floating sail tacked near the bow.

The kind of staysail determines how its luff will be finished. If it is designed to hank onto an inner forestay, the luffs should be stretchy rope. If the sail is free-floating, the best system is a sleeve fitting over the luff wire. The wire and sleeve help you control the luff tension more easily on such a delicate, hard-to-handle sail.

Spinnakers and Twins

With exception of the big boy and twins, most running sails are spinnakers. Since a spinnaker is entirely free-flying, its design requires a compromise between a sail full enough to support itself and one that is flat enough to project well for superior performance. The fuller the sail, the more stable it is; the flatter the sail, the less stable but faster it will prove.

In the last decade the most popular constructions have been the radial head and the tri-radial (or star-cut) head. These two configurations simply align the thread lines of the nylon along the load lines of the sail. This alignment produces a very strong sail with a greatly extended range compared to the older cross-cut layouts. It can also be cut flatter, so the sails can be used up to a close reach, powering a yacht with more lift and greater speed. Nylon is used to make spinnakers because of its elasticity and resilience. The stretchiness of nylon greatly increases its tear resistance, while its lightness and low porosity help it stand up in the lightest breezes.

Flying and trimming a spinnaker is usually approached with great trepidation. Most of the horror stories associated with sailing relate to a spinnaker broach of one kind or another. Many years ago the large ketch *Mir* lost her mainmast after a spectacular broach just before the finish of the Transpacific Race off Diamond Head. The only thing left to do was to sail backwards across the line with the mizzen spinnaker.

One of the drawbacks of a spinnaker for a small crew is the gear necessary to fly it. The spinnaker pole is generally cumbersome and requires the addition of a number of sheets and guys. The asymmetrical spinnaker does away with all of this gear, since its unequal luffs can be tacked directly to the stem without the use of a pole. Bent on in this fashion, the spinnaker operates as a free-flying reacher/drifter, and does not need any of the paraphernalia associated with the racing spinnaker. Used strictly for cruising, they are far hardier than conventional spinnakers and can be flown even by singlehanders. Be careful of area, though; if they're too large, they can overpower the boat; if too small, they provide no advantage over a large genoa. Marketed originally by Ulmer Sails with the name Flasher, this type of sail is really just an updating of the old delivery trick of tacking a chute directly to the stem of the boat.

Another very popular running rig is twin running sails. These are an excellent way of making good time on passage sailing before a trade wind. They avoid the constant trim required of a spinnaker, and can be kept flying in stronger winds. They can be reefed very quickly by letting both clews fly forward. A typical twin will have higher clews than normal and an area usually about 66 percent of the largest headsail.

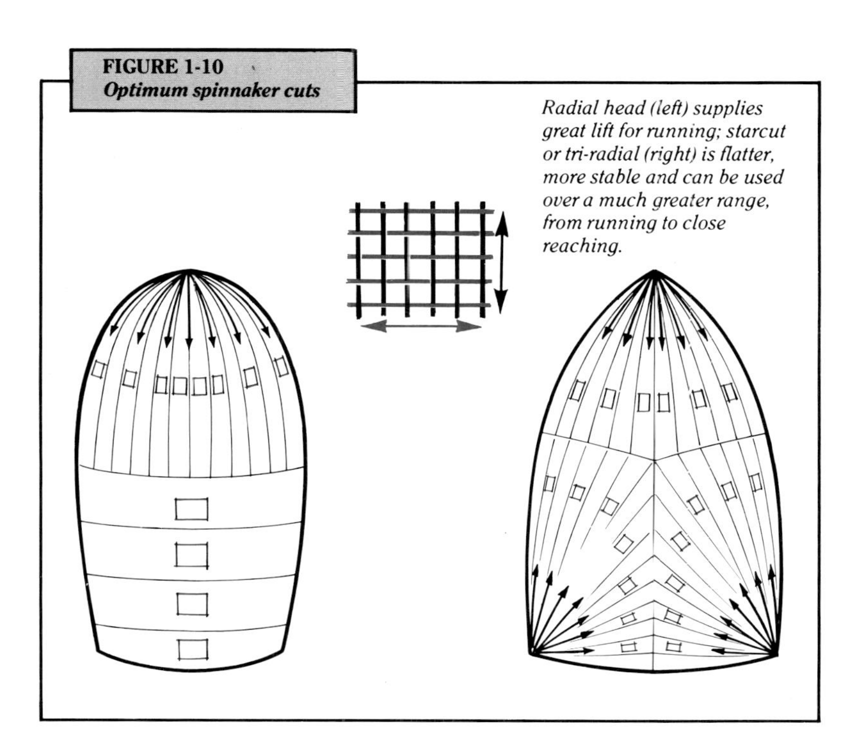
FIGURE 1-10
Optimum spinnaker cuts

Radial head (left) supplies great lift for running; starcut or tri-radial (right) is flatter, more stable and can be used over a much greater range, from running to close reaching.

Built of Dacron, twin running sails have long been a favorite of offshore voyagers.

Storm Sails

Storm sails may be called upon to save your life and vessel. They are rarely unpacked, lying damply in the bilge or sail lockers in hopes that they may never be used. Nevertheless, in terms of safety, these are perhaps the most important sails aboard.

The requirement for a storm sail is simple: it must be able to take a boat safely to windward in storm conditions. This means that strong construction techniques like double-reinforced tapes, triple-stitching and wider seams are mandatory. Leech and foot lines are also necessary in order to control any flogging which may occur along the edges of a sail. In wind speeds of 50 knots or more, it is very easy for a sail to flog itself to pieces.

The storm trysail is a very seamanlike sail since it does away with the need for a boom in dangerous storm conditions. It can still be set even if the boom is broken. The sail should always be at least the same weight as the mainsail, with an area no larger than about 35 percent that of the fully hoisted main. It should have a hollow leech, to avoid the use of battens. A little stretch is not a problem; it's even beneficial when the wind is really howling. A trysail is usually made with a miter cut, so that the cloths are at right angles to both the leech and foot.

The storm jib should be just as strong as the trysail and should be cut with a reasonably high clew to keep the sail out of the water. The higher clew also allows the sail to be sheeted further aft on the same track used for the other headsails.

One new development is the introduction of bright orange sailcloth to enhance the visibility of a small yacht in stormy conditions. It is also wise to have some kind of identification on the trysail itself: either the yacht's racing numbers or her name.

FIGURE 1-11
The well-made trysail

A storm trysail is rarely used, but when it is, it must withstand the most horrible abuse. Seams should be triple stitched, tabling doubled and sheets and downhaul permanently spliced in.

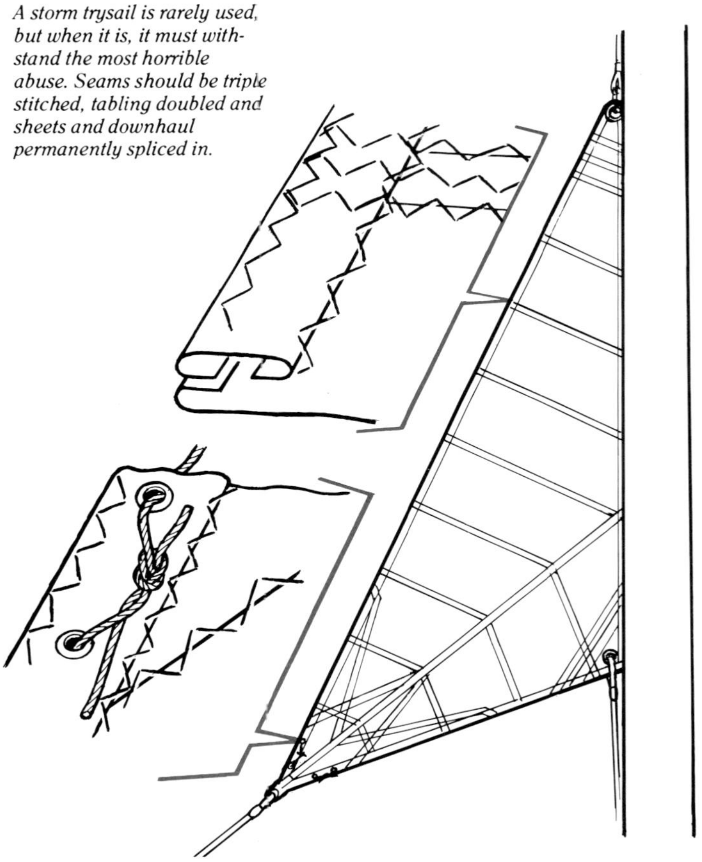

SAIL CARE

The care of a good set of sails is almost as important as any maintenance a sailor has to do. There are a few basic rules which should be followed. (Repair is dealt with in Chapter Eight.)

At the beginning of the sailing season, the entire rig should be checked over carefully for areas that might cause chafes and tears. Inspect all standing rigging for broken wires, and tape the spreaders. Be sure turnbuckles, particularly cotter pins, are also taped. Any deck gear which might have sharp edges or projections, such as cleats, ventilators and window frames, should be filed smooth. Furthermore, the rig should be set up to match the bend which your sailmaker has anticipated. Aluminum spars are very often not stayed as tightly as they should be. Both mains and jibs can be made too full by a reverse bend in the spar caused by a slack headstay or backstay.

To keep a sail clean and the cloth in good condition, wipe down the standing rigging. Aluminum spars pick up an oily dirt that is almost impossible to remove from Dacron.

Modern synthetic materials have reduced to a fraction the time need for drying and airing, but certain precautions should be taken. Sailcovers are a must. There have been cases where gases from factories have done serious damage to synthetic sails. It is just as important to protect the thread in the seams from rotting. Consequently an owner should be sure his sail lockers are well ventilated, and should be careful that when the sails are sent below, they are as dry as possible.

New developments in finishing and weaving will lessen maintenance. For example, silicone finishes applied directly to the yarn make a sail virtually impervious to water and salt. Ultraviolet inhibitors added to the yarn before the weaving process help to protect sails and seams from ultraviolet degradation. Cruising sailors—who need maximum durability from their sails—may find UV inhibitors most useful.

Chapter 2

RIGGING AND DECK GEAR

The days of wood and manila, deadeyes and lanyards, plow steel and wire splices are gone. Unless you sail a gaff cutter or Friendship sloop, you'll find little evidence of centuries of marine tradition. More likely, your yacht gleams with stainless steel, aluminum and multi-colored synthetic cordage; its working parts are filled with needle bearings, exotic metals, Delrin, tufnol, lithium grease and devices and materials unheard of as little as a generation past. The economics of sailing is much like the economics of television sets and automobiles. Round picture tubes and solid rubber tires have gone by the board. Lignum vitae blocks and flax sails have followed the same path.

Nevertheless, much of the postwar boom in sailing and the greatly increased efficiency and safety of the modern yacht are due to developments in rigging and hardware. New alloys, lighter weight and streamlined design have all contributed to stronger and more effective hardware and fitments.

What you *need* for your yacht depends on what type of sailing you do. For Grand Prix racing, nothing but the best will do. This rarefied realm of sailing is beyond the reach of most of us, though we may benefit from its developments. However, it is essentially a battle of money, and the man with the most will have the most efficient machine.

For those of us who fit out off the shelf of our local chandlery, the optimum assortment of cleats, fairleads, chocks, tracks and travellers, blocks and winches, turnbuckles, rails, anchoring gear, lights and rigging must be chosen with care. And, the choice is well-nigh endless, though too much gear is just as bad as too little.

Of course, only trial and error will provide the answer, but it is usually best to err on the side of caution and not riddle the deck with new holes. Improvise first, then make your mistakes.

MASTS

On the majority of yachts sold today, the mast comes with the boat and the owner has very little choice in the selection of the sparmaker. Often, all the buyer can really do is to specify whether he wants a tapered or untapered mast. The tapered mast reduces windage and, just as important, it bends to give the racing sailor optimum performance. Tapered masts are made in a variety of ways, but each is custom-built for the individual yacht. They are, thus, quite expensive. An untapered mast, being a standard section, is easier to fit and replace.

A good mast is one that does its job properly and effectively without bending unduly, ripping the sails or shredding halyards. Care should be taken when assembling the mast to ensure that sharp edges are filed down. Some spar makers use self-tapping screws to hold exit boxes and fittings into the mast. Unfortunately these screws can shred internal halyards. It is much better to weld or rivet such fittings to the mast.

The height of the mast is determined by the designer. He will be guided by design ratios like sail-area-to-wetted-surface and sail-area-to-displacement. Once he has calculated the optimum sail area to propel the boat, the next step is to decide on the length of the base of the sail-area triangles —a fairly easy procedure because the foretriangle will usually not be longer on the base than the distance from the mast to the bow. Your designer will then suggest a specific ratio between the foretriangle and mainsail, based on the kind of sailing that you do and where you sail. Thus, having found the foretriangle's base length and knowing the total required area, he can establish the mast height. This step is usually completed fairly early in the design process.

Next, your designer calculates the stability of the yacht and decides upon the type of rig—masthead or fractional—and the number of shrouds and spreaders to be used. The advantage of a masthead rig is its simplicity. You may need a larger inventory of headsails to cope with changing conditions, but the rig needs few adjustments while under sail. The fractional rig, on the other hand, is more easily adjustable because it allows the mast to bend. This demands a greater number of rig controls, but because the fractional rig uses a proportionately smaller foretriangle, it needs a smaller inventory of headsails. You can easily shorten sail by reefing the mainsail. Choice of rigging configurations (shrouds and spreaders) will be discussed below (see page 32).

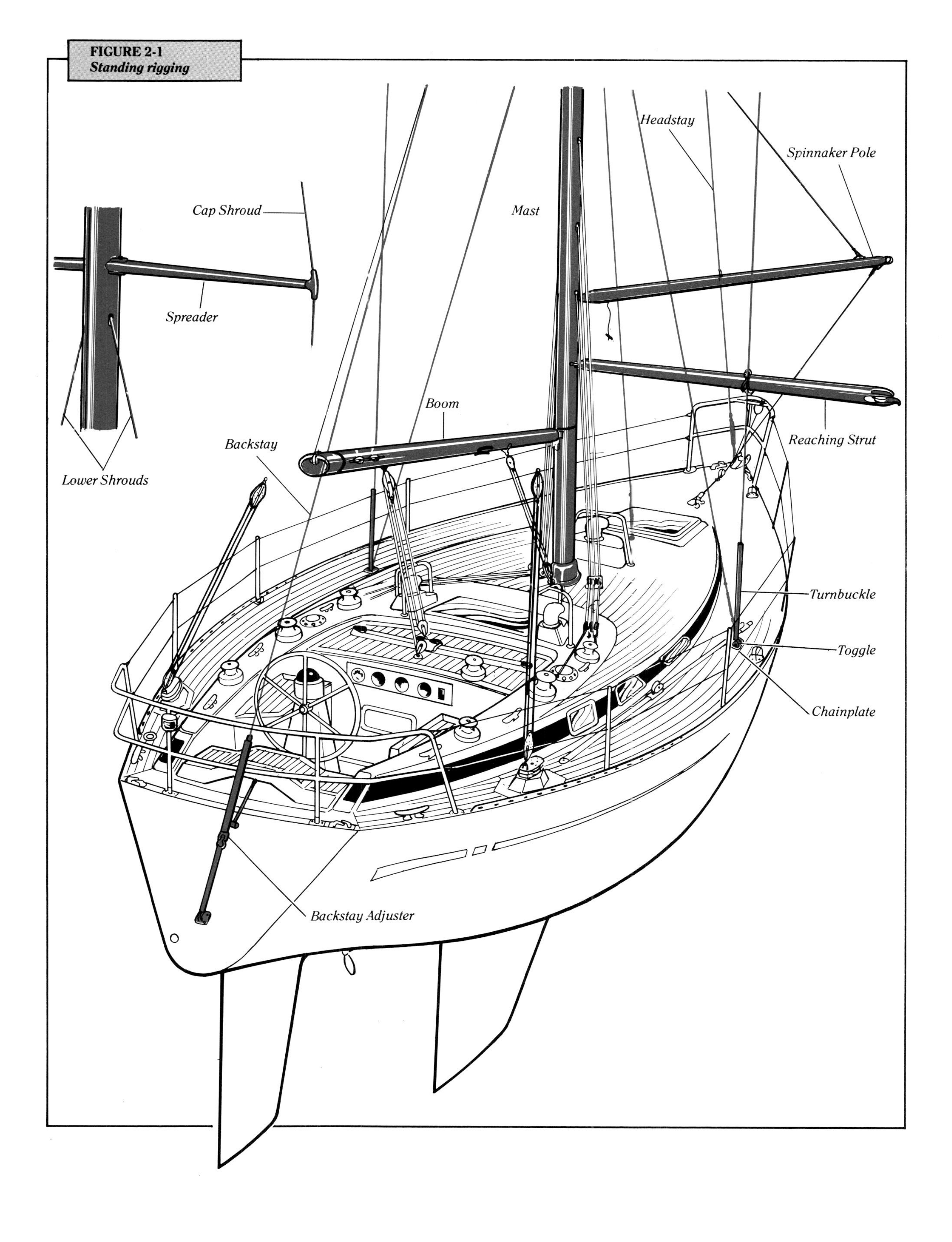

FIGURE 2-1
Standing rigging

Once the rig type and configuration have been chosen, the designer calculates what kinds of forces the masts will encounter under load in longitudinal and transverse directions. He can then look over catalogs of masts and choose a mast section strong enough to withstand the expected loads. Most mast manufacturers stock sections in the most popular sizes, and are usually willing to quote on any sail plan.

Once you and your designer have settled on a mast size and type, check the workmanship of different makers' sections. Look over a mast that is lying down, starting at the masthead and working downward. Here is what to look for:

The masthead should have a Windex wind indicator—even on a cruising boat—so that the helmsman can see where the wind is actually coming from without backwash from the sails. There should also be a light shining upwards on the Windex for night use. Also at the masthead, there should be suitable wiring for a tricolor masthead light. The wiring should be 12- or 14-gauge and double-insulated. Check to see that the spinnaker cranes are adequately strong and that the fitting for the forestay and backstay look substantial. They should survive a whack from a 16-ounce hammer! Also check the welding: poor welding can lead to problems fairly quickly. Good welds are evenly beaded, with no gaps or distortion. Ensure that the masthead sheave boxes are also welded properly, and get the correct sheaves—remember wire sheaves have a groove in

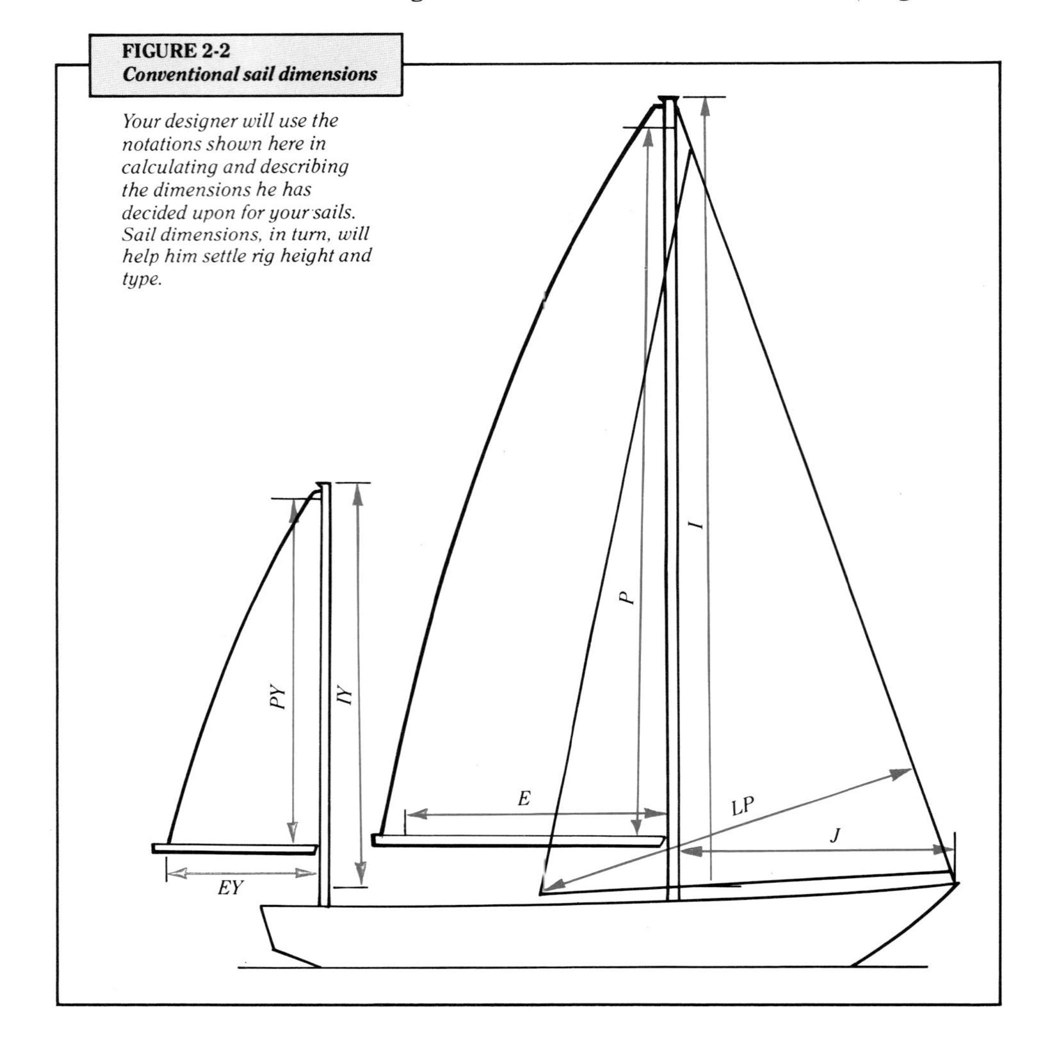

FIGURE 2-2
Conventional sail dimensions

Your designer will use the notations shown here in calculating and describing the dimensions he has decided upon for your sails. Sail dimensions, in turn, will help him settle rig height and type.

them, rope ones do not. A wire sheave should be 16 times the diameter of the wire halyards; a rope sheave should be eight times the diameter of the rope. The boxes should also be narrow enough so that the rope or wire cannot jump out of the sheave, jamming the sheave.

Under the masthead fittings on either side of the mast are the tangs for the upper, or cap, shrouds. Make sure the tang holes are of a reasonable size yet with plenty of solid metal around them. Also ensure that the shrouds—on interior tangs—fit properly and are not bent aft or forward by a poorly positioned hole. On the way down the mast look over the steaming light and staysail or topping lift sheave boxes. At the spreaders, make sure there are no sharp edges that need filing off, taping or removing. Look over the inboard ends. Check for good strong welding, snug fit for pins and bolts, no sharp edges and a clean aerodynamic shape. Inspect the lower shroud tangs, as well as the spinnaker pole or twin pole tracks. All tracks must run true and straight. If possible, fit the poles and try them for ease of movement—any binding at this stage can mean a freeze-up on the ocean. Look at the exit boxes and winches fitted on the spar, making sure that the leads from exit box to winch to cleat are fair, with no crossovers or chafing points. Also look for winch handle pockets near the base of the mast, and bails on which to clip spare halyards. See also that cleats are angled, and that all nonaluminum fittings are insulated from the mast with plastic or nylon gaskets, to prevent corrosion.

There are many makers of fine alloy masts. Among the best are Jack Holt, Hood, Kemp, Palmer-Johnson, John Powell (custom only), Proctor, Selden, Sparlight and Steam.

If you desire a wooden mast, have it designed by a competent naval architect (see Appendix B). The mast will probably be made of a number of pieces which are glued together. The exterior is then planed until it is nicely rounded and the spar is straight.

The ideal wood for such a mast is Sitka spruce, native to the northwestern United States. The trouble is that such wood is very

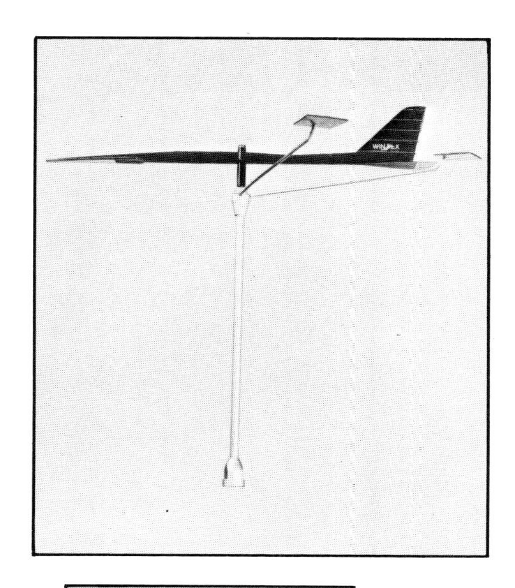

Windex wind indicator. The fixed arms precisely indicate the apparent wind angle.

FIGURE 2-3
Fairlead from an exit box

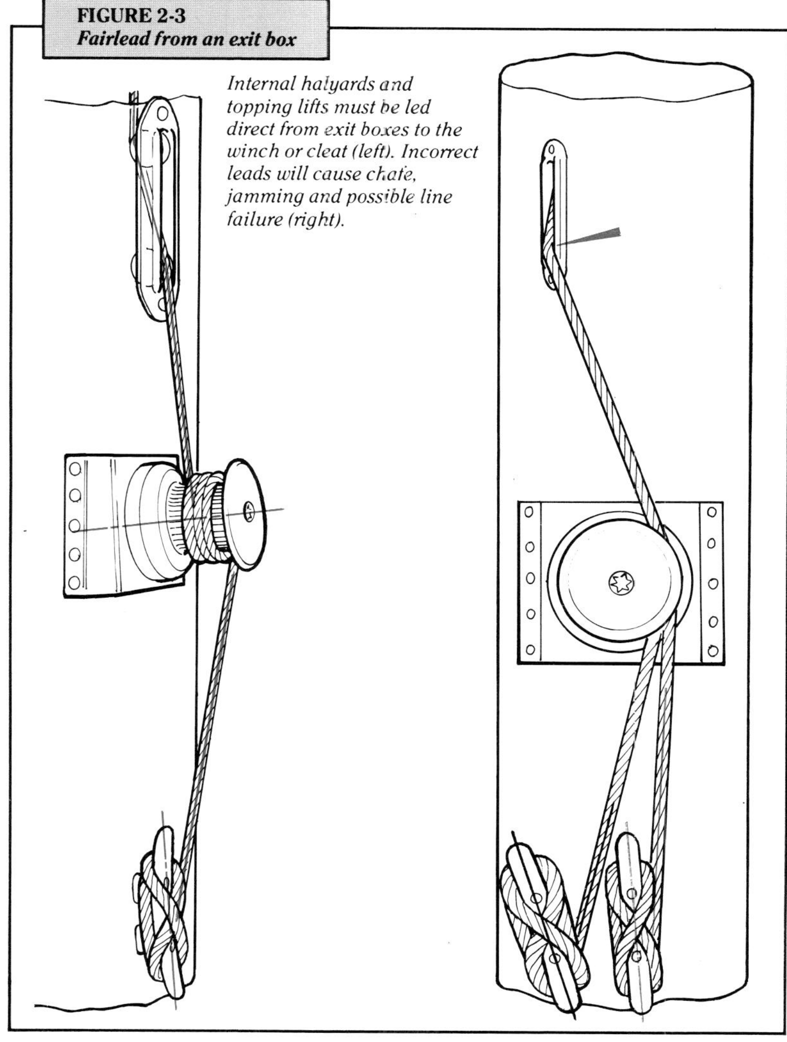

Internal halyards and topping lifts must be led direct from exit boxes to the winch or cleat (left). Incorrect leads will cause chafe, jamming and possible line failure (right).

difficult to find in big enough lengths. However, Barry Noble in the U.K. has recently patented a new method of laminating wood masts, which will enable the builder to utilize different woods for their varying properties. Furthermore, in lengths of 40 feet and over, the Noble mast is almost as light as aluminum!

The wall of a wooden mast is much thicker than that of its aluminum counterpart. The bolts and screws that hold the mast fittings in place must be able to carry the loads of the fittings without pulling loose. All screws must penetrate just short of the thickness of the mast wall, and be of a thickness at least one-seventh the length of the screw. Working down from the masthead, check all the items listed for an alloy mast; also look for areas where rot and deterioration could occur. The bottom of masthead sheave boxes, for example, should slope outwards to allow rainwater to run off, and the area should be carefully varnished.

Tangs

Tangs fasten the shrouds to the mast wall. Most are custom-made for the mast, constructed out of stainless steel. They can be either internal or external. Use the external tang on wooden masts or cruising boats, because it is easily maintained and accessible if anything breaks. For racing yachts, you should choose the internal tang, because it reduces windage. Most boats are supplied with external tangs and it is hideously expensive to replace them with the internal type.

Spreaders

Spreaders basically lessen the compression loads on the mast. The more spreaders a boat has, the more evenly those loads are distributed.

To withstand the forces generated under sail without support, a mast would have to be tremendously thick. Shrouds alone can lend sufficient stability to short masts—like those on old gaffers—but most masts need spreaders just to keep the rig in the boat. The average sailboat is long enough to support the mast in a fore-and-aft direction by means of stays alone, but it is not wide enough to support the section transversely without the help of spreaders. These ensure that the angles at which the shrouds strike the spar are large enough to stabilize it.

The simplest rig uses one set of spreaders. Almost all masthead rigs use this configuration, because it is the easiest to set up and tune, and uses the least number

FIGURE 2-4
Possible spreader rigs

Single spreader rigs are the simplest and most suitable for cruising boats up to 40 feet LOA. When mast height begins to tower, double spreaders will be necessary to spread the loads. Triple and quadruple spreader rigs are delicate pieces of machinery suitable for the front-line racer, demanding constant, critical adjustment.

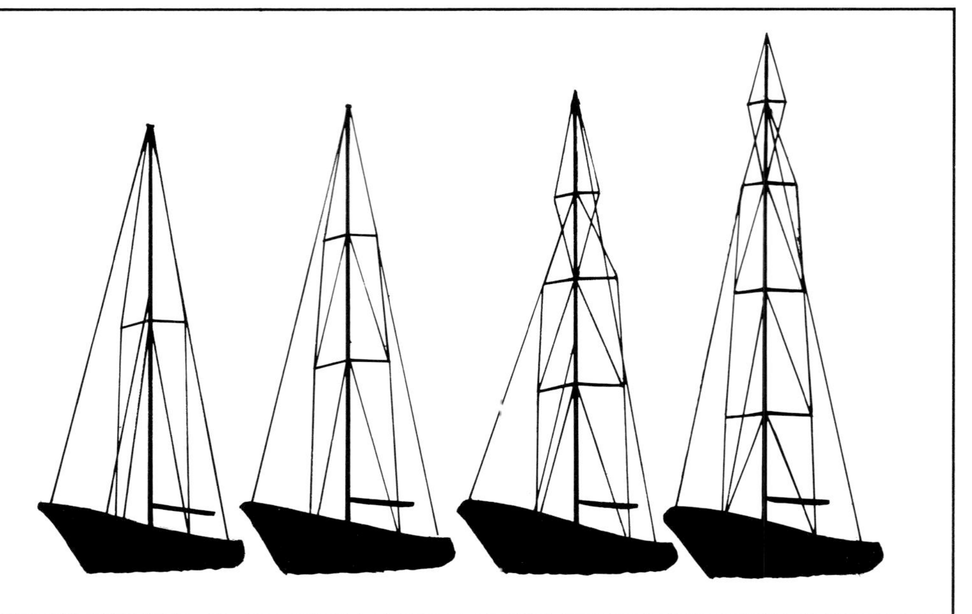

of controls. Double lower stays (two on each side) are most often used, though a single set of lower stays coupled with a babystay reduces windage. Runners and midstays are rarely used.

Big boats and fractional racing rigs may use a double-spreader configuration. More spreaders reduce distortion in a long mast and allow for closer sheeting angles. The double-spreader rig, however, uses a lighter mast section and in a lumpy sea often requires the use of midstay and runners to keep it from bouncing around. This rig is harder to tune than a single-spreader mast.

The ultimate in performance are the three- and four-spreader masts that use a very small mast section and a large number of controls to keep the rig in the boat, such as Tim Stearn's rigs. Such rigs are used only by Grand Prix racers. They are very adjustable, but require exquisite skill to operate.

No matter what configuration they may be arranged in, spreaders should be as aerodynamically streamlined as possible, peaking slightly outboard. Some captive device for the shroud itself is to be highly recommended.

Booms

The boom should be more than a mere support for the mainsail's foot. It should have all the fittings required to reef the mainsail, as well as an efficient sheeting system. It must be strong enough to resist bending loads exerted on it by the sail or the vang. In addition, outhauls and end fittings must be well thought out. Top mast makers also manufacture the finest booms (see page 31)

Reaching Struts

The reaching strut holds the guy off the shrouds and improves the angle between the guy and the spinnaker pole. Therefore, its length is usually about one and a half times the distance between the shroud and the mast. The pole end fittings should be easy to use. The outboard end should have a jaw with a sheave in it, while the inboard end may simply be a blunt spike which fits into a hole in the mast. There are other types of fittings—a ring on the mast over which the strut hooks or a spinnaker pole cup or spike onto which the strut is fitted—but all these suffer from being more costly and complicated than the spike-in-mast fitting. Forespar, Schaefer and Lewmar all make good struts.

Spinnaker Poles

The spinnaker pole length should be equal to the distance from the forestay to the forward face of the mast. Its diameter is calculated from compression loads only. The method of rigging it and the type of end fittings are left to the owner.

On smaller boats (under 25 feet) it is usual to put a bridle on the pole to hold the topping lift while a second bridle is connected to the foreguy. This arrangement facilitates end-for-end gybing, but it does mean that both end fittings must be exactly the same.

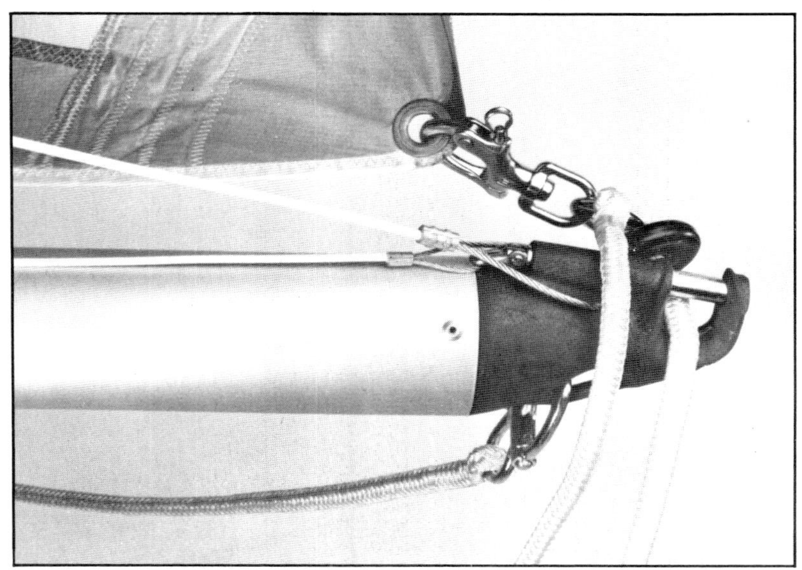

Spinnaker pole end fitting. Wire trip lines allow remote release of the sheets and the casting contains a fitting for the guy shackle.

Because larger boats use a different gybing technique, their spinnaker poles have more complicated fittings. The outboard end fitting should have eyes on which the foreguy and topping lift can be clipped; the inboard end fitting then can hook onto a ring, slide over a piston or fit into a cup.

All these fittings slide up and down the mast on a track whose height is equal to 25 percent of the "I" dimension on IOR boats. The height of the track also governs the height of the topping lift sheave in the mast. The topping lift should make an angle of not more than 45 degrees to the mast when the pole is horizontal and at the top of the mast track. Information on spinnaker poles is available from any major mast maker.

STANDING RIGGING

Almost all sailboats require some form of standing rigging. On racing boats this may be stainless steel lenticular section rod, while some types of cruising rigs make do with wire rope. The wire, of course, stretches more than rod rigging. Rod rigging can increase the efficiency of the sail as an airfoil, but if it breaks at sea, you're out of luck. It is therefore *not* recommended for blue water cruising.

On a typical production yacht, the rigging is 1 × 19 wire whose thickness is found by a calculation based upon the righting moment or stability of the yacht. This wire stretches about 3 percent, but for all practical purposes the stretch is hardly noticeable. When it is stainless steel, the wire does not need maintenance during the season, but some older boats have galvanized-wire standing rigging, which does need maintenance. Before Robin Knox-Johnson sailed around the world aboard *Suhali*, for example, he spent two days greasing all the shrouds, stays and splices with a mixture of tallow and white lead.

A racing yacht usually has all rod rigging, with the shrouds shaped for minimum wind resistance. Because the stretch on tight rod rigging is only about 1 percent, the rod will not absorb much shock without breaking. If the boat were to sail off a large ocean wave, a compression failure of the mast could result.

For an offshore racer intended for a

TABLE 2-1
Suggested Wire Rigging

• This chart shows the appropriate diameter (in inches) 1 x 19 wire rigging for representative boats.

STAY	BOAT TYPE											
	Soling	5.5 meter	Etchells 22	Dragon	1/4 tonner	Light 1/2 tonner	Heavy 1/2 tonner	Light 1 tonner	Heavy 1 tonner	Cole 43	2 tonner	Admirals Cupper
Forestay	5/32	5/32	3/16	3/16	3/16	7/32	9/32	9/32	5/16	3/8	3/8	7/16
Backstay	1/8	1/8	1/8	1/8	3/16	3/16	1/4	1/4	9/32	5/16	3/8	7/16
Main or Upper Caps	5/32	5/32	3/16	3/16	3/16	3/16	1/4	1/4	9/32	5/16	5/16	7/16
Lower Caps	—	—	—	—	7/32	7/32	9/32	9/32	5/16	3/8	3/8	1/2
Intermediates	—	—	—	—	5/32	5/32	7/32	7/32	9/32	5/16	5/16	3/8
Lowers	5/32	5/32	3/16	3/16	3/16	7/32	9/32	9/32	5/16	3/8	3/8	1/2
Runners	—	1/8	—	1/8	—	—	—	—	—	—	7/32	7/32
Inner Forestay	—	—	—	—	5/32	—	—	—	—	—	9/32	5/16
Main Halyard	1/8	1/8	1/8	1/8	1/8	5/32	5/32	3/16	3/16	3/16	7/32	1/4
Genoa Halyard	1/8	1/8	1/8	1/8	5/32	5/32	3/16	3/16	3/16	7/32	1/4	9/32

Source: Ronstan Marine.

round-the-world race, a combination of rod and wire is probably the best: rods for the headstay, backstay and upper shrouds with 1 × 19 wire for the diagonals. This setup steadies the mast, while allowing it to bend enough to absorb any shock loads.

MacWhyte rod rigging is well known, but Navtec makes even better cold-formed terminals and fittings. The special Navtec terminal unit reduces fatigue and has less corrosion, so the rigging can last longer. South Coast Rod Rigging in the U.K. produces a comparable product.

Toggles and Turnbuckles

Turnbuckles are known in the U.K. as rigging screws. Fitted with toggles, they allow effective adjustment of the standing rigging. Any shroud or stay that is subject to both fore-and-aft and sideways movement should have a toggle fitted to reduce fatigue. For all wire rigging, the toggle is fitted below the turnbuckle, but for the more sensitive and delicate rod rigging, Navtec integrates toggles with the rigging itself. This practice should be standard among all riggers, because it better protects the rods from athwartships stress.

A turnbuckle is used to tension the rigging and should always be an "open" type so you can see how much thread is in the screw. Turnbuckles should not be fitted with a large amount of "slop" simply because there is no toggle. On some types of rod rigging, the shroud itself is turned to tighten the turnbuckle. This reduces windage at deck level, but is really only practical for racing yachts.

Navtec's rod rigging with integral turnbuckle has rigid ends and adjustable center screw, just the reverse of the standard rigging screw.

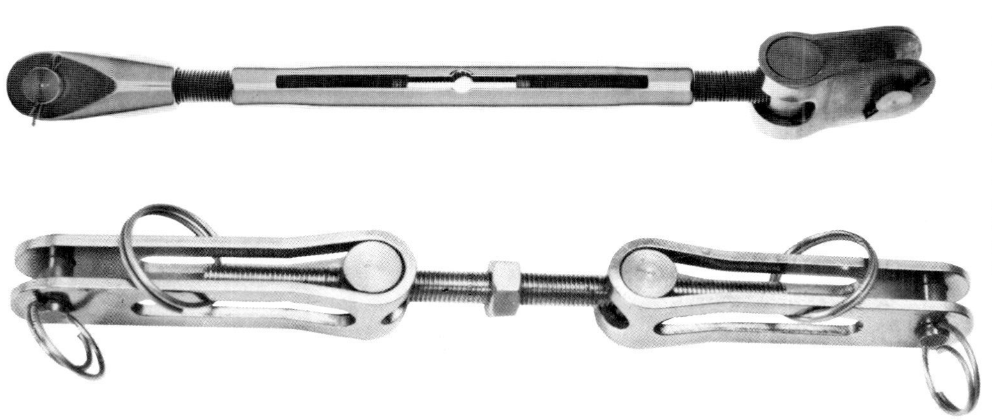

Top, the Gibb rigging screw with integral toggle and open body. Bottom, C. Sherman Johnson turnbuckle, a modification of the L. Francis Herreshoff design, obviates the need for separate toggles.

Chainplates
It is the designer who has the final say about the size and material for chainplates. All an owner can do is ensure they are solidly bolted to structural members. They should be stainless steel (or aluminum if the hull is aluminum) and should be electrically insulated from a metal hull.

Hydraulics
Three manufacturers—Stearn, Navtec and David Carne—make a variety of hydraulically operated fittings. If you want to, you can hydraulically operate your backstay, forestay, vang, babystay, spreaders, outhaul, centerboard and any other fitting where the load is high and the distance to be moved is short. With modern hydraulic technology all the above systems can be controlled by a single panel positioned anywhere in the vessel and driven by a single hand-operated pump located on or near the panel. Such systems are, however, quite expensive, and those which control the standing rigging often increase the speed but reduce the safety margin of the rig considerably.

Navtec hydraulic backstay adjuster allows sensitive adjustments to the rigging's tension.

RUNNING RIGGING

The standing rigging holds the mast up, and the running rigging holds the sails up. It does more than that though. All the sheets, guys, halyards, tackles, vangs and sundry lines are running rigging. They bring the sails into position, so that the airfoil meets the wind at the most efficient angle. They are therefore subject to the same stresses as the sails themselves.

A line with very little stretch should be used in any position where the load is high. On a 12-meter yacht or large offshore racer this would mean wire genoa sheets, but for the average cruiser or club racer prestretched Dacron is best. New England Ropes, Samson and Marlow are about the best manufacturers, with Marlow preferable because their lines come in easily identifiable colors. In an emergency a new crewman is more likely to grasp the right line if you say, "Let go the blue one!" than if you shout, "Let go the vang!" when the vang is just another white line.

Halyards and afterguys, however, are sometimes made of wire, even on smaller boats. Halyards are most often wire with a Dacron tail spliced in. This is simply to control stretch—a Dacron halyard may stretch, be winched up again, and later shrink, pulling the eyesplice into the masthead block. A halyard should be measured so that at least three turns of wire are on the winch drum when the sail is drawing, keeping the weaker splice away from the critical load area between the winch and mast. Increasingly, however, small cruisers are using prestretched Dacron halyards, because they're cheaper, longer lasting, easier to change and free from the dangerous "fishhooks" that can develop in wire.

Afterguys are another matter. Anyone who has tried to control a spinnaker pole with a rope guy will know how difficult it is. A wire afterguy is by far the better solution. It should be covered with a Dacron sheathing (similar to the sheathing on pure Dacron lines), which will provide a good grip for the operator and on the winch. Galvanized wire is best for halyards and guys, because it bends more easily than stainless steel.

Just making their appearance on the market now are Kevlar- and graphite-cored ropes. These are extremely low stretch, but they fatigue rather easily. Distance cruisers should avoid them, though the most dedicated racers—who care less for durability—prefer them. New types of weave are also making headway. Multi-ply weaves offer decreased stretch, while those with aligned filaments reduce abrasion.

Wire and rope halyards. Low stretch Dacron (Terylene) makes for a safer line. Racing boats, however, will need to fit wire halyards for more precise luff control. The wire halyard shown is beginning to show dangerous "fish-hooks," which can tear sails.

TABLE 2-2
Line and Wire Strength

This table shows the approximate strength (in pounds) of commonly used wire and synthetic lines.

Diameter		Stainless Steel Wire			Yachting Ropes					
mm	inches	1 x 19	7 x 7	7 x 19	16 Plait Matt Polyester Type III	8 Plait Matt Polyester	Double Braid Polyester	Prestretched 8 Plait Polyester	Multi-Plait Nylon	Multi-Filament Polypropylene
2	5/64	790	650	760						
2.5	3/32	1200	920	1050						
3	1/8	2100	1700	1760						
4	5/32	3300	2600	2400				650		505
5	3/16	4700	3700	3700		670		880		
5.5	7/32	6300	4800	5000						
6	1/4	8200	6100	6400		1035	2530	1245		880
7	9/32	10300	7600	7800				1695		
8	5/16	12500	9100	9000	2465	1230	3740	2235		1540
10	3/8	17500	12600	12000	4400	2235	4400	3500	4575	2200
11	7/16	22500	16500	16300						
12	1/2	30000	21300	22800	6600		5940		6600	
14	9/16	36200	26600	28500	7260				9020	
16	5/8	47000	32500	35000	8800				11660	
18	3/4	67500	45500	49600	11440				14740	
22	7/8	91400	60200	66500						

Source: Ronstan Marine.

Vangs

A vang is the most complicated form of running rigging. (In the U.K. it is called the kicking strap.) Today, the hydraulic vang has virtually replaced the mainsheet on racing boats as a device for tensioning the leech of the mainsail. It can precisely adjust higher than ordinary loads. On such boats the mainsheet is relegated to the role of positioning the mainsail at the correct angle of incidence to the wind. But for sailors who do not have a hydraulic vang, the mainsheet and rope vang must both do their part in controlling the sail. Various manufacturers make tackle systems that will suit both the mainsheet and vang. Lewmar makes a handybilly. Merriman Holbrook, Nicro/Fico and Schaefer make similar systems, all of which do the job equally well. The slow, hard-to-use rod vang is gradually disappearing from the scene.

If you are looking for hydraulic vangs with all their associated piping and plumbing, Stearn Sailing Systems, Navtec and David Carne make the best systems.

DECK GEAR

Once the mast and sails are securely supported, it remains to find equipment to adjust them. All the shackles, blocks, winches and cleats serve one of two functions. They either provide a mechanical advantage to the sailor trying to move the sails, or they secure the lines in their adjusted position. Mechanical efficiency and stability under load are thus the two parameters the buyer needs to consider. Other deck hardware—pulpits, stanchions, hatches and the like—keep the crew on board or provide access to the cabin.

This useful Gibb snap shackle has a fitting to allow direct attachment to a sheet.

Shackles

All sailors have used the "D" shackle at some time during their sailing life. The pin may be attached by a screw or by a key that fits through a slot in the shackle. Variations of this shackle are the twist shackle, bow shackle and long "D" type. Each of these units may be cast or stamped, the cast version being stronger for the same size. All reputable manufacturers produce the stronger, cast version.

The headboard shackle—the shackle at the top of the mainsail—should be very strong and need not be a snap type, because the mainsail and the halyard stay attached until the cruise or race is over. With this in mind, most manufacturers make special headboard shackles, wide enough to fit any headboard. Though they do come in single-threaded and key types, the double-screw type—threaded so as to prevent the pin from working loose—is the preferred choice. Wichard, Schaefer and Lewmar make the best.

On all lines that must be uncleated quickly there should be a snap shackle. All halyards except the main, for example, should have snap shackles. Again, you should look for the pin-type shackle with a short lanyard tied to the pin. Nicro/Fico probably has one of the largest selections of shackles and swivel shackles. Barient, Schaefer and Lewmar also make fine headsail variants. They are smaller, and have no awkward projections.

Snap shackles are available with bail attachments and mounts suitable for different applications. A simple "D" shackle is fine for a single line, but a flared "D" is preferable when two lines must be fitted. "D" shackles fitted with additional rings work well as spinnaker guy shackles because they will not hang up in the pole's jaws. Trunnions eliminate twisting loads.

FIGURE 2-5
Sail-handling gear

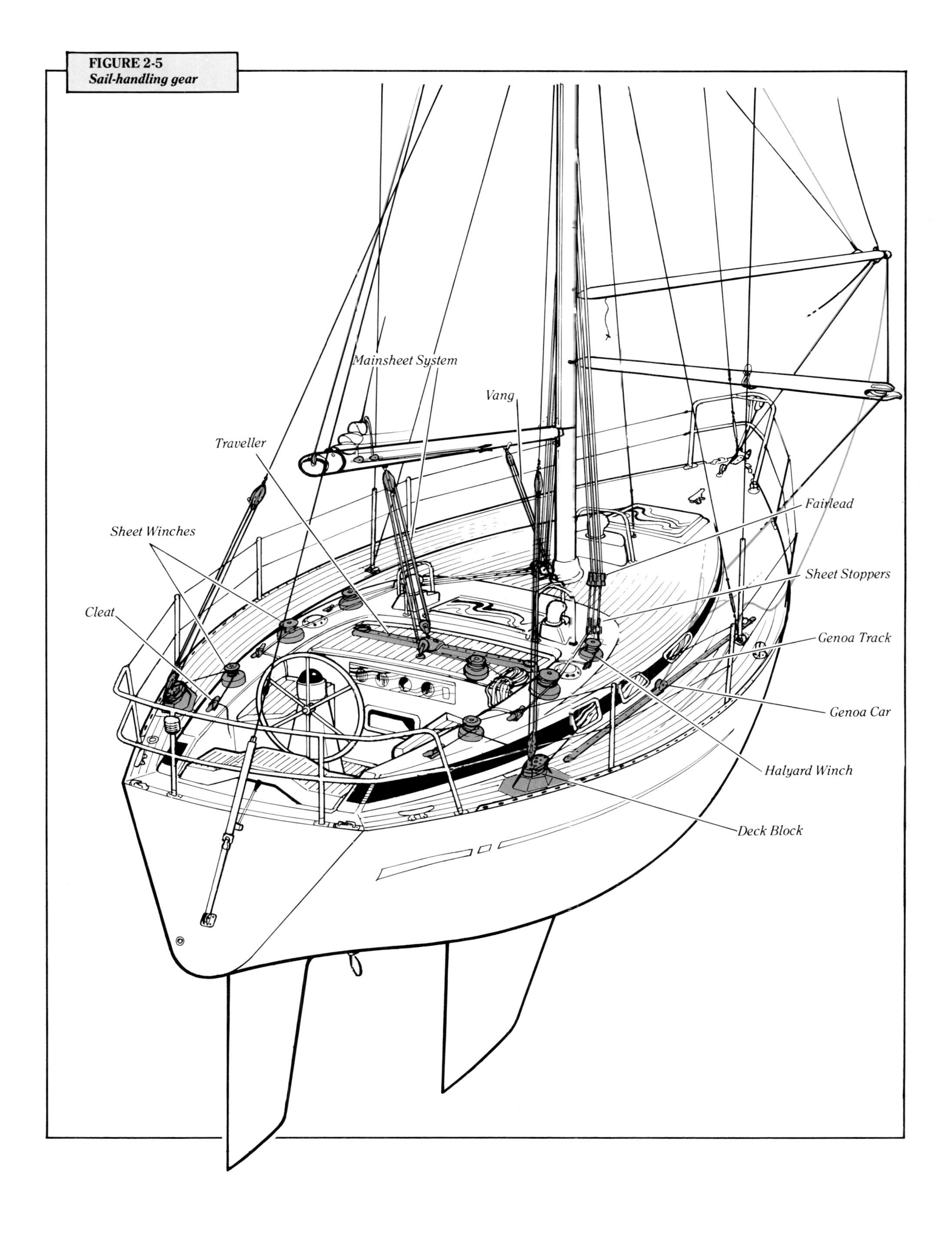

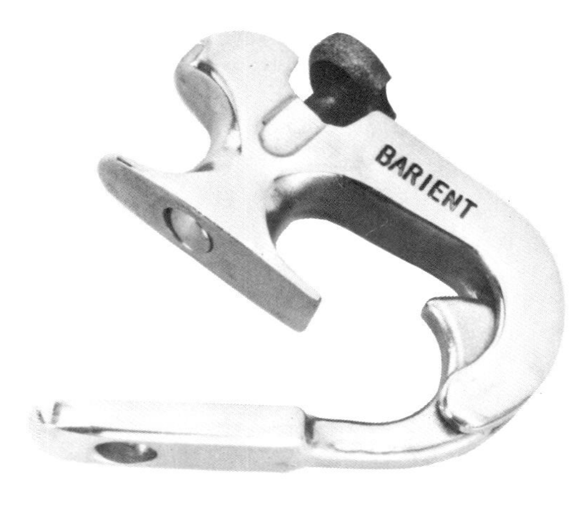

The Barient jibsheet shackle lets you release headsails even under heavy load.

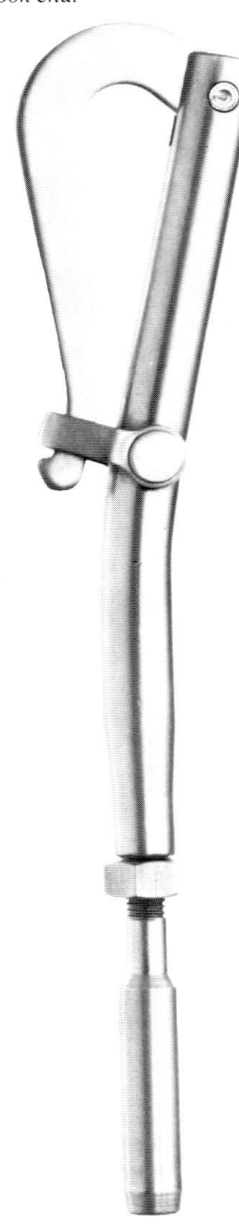

The pelican hook closes life-line gates, using an integral turnbuckle for tensioning and a clasp to secure the hook end.

Any discussion of shackles would be incomplete without mention of pelican hooks, which are used for holding life line gates closed. Though they don't control the sails, they help keep the sailor on board so he can control them. The pelican hook's "nose" should always be taped when the gate is closed to prevent it from opening, creating dangerous gaps in the life lines. Merriman Holbrook, Gibb and Nicro/Fico make good pelican hooks.

Blocks

The block has been around since ships first went to sea. Once, it was made of wood, with wooden cheeks, wooden pulleys and wooden pins held in place by smaller wooden pins. This block was entirely hand-made, secured in the rigging with a rope strop. Nowadays, blocks like these are rarely seen. Most modern blocks are made of steel, plastic or some form of aluminum alloy. On most quality blocks, sheaves are plastic, cheeks are aluminum and strops are stainless steel. Each type of block has its particular place and purpose.

When you open a manufacturer's catalog, pages and pages of blocks confront you. You may be amazed that anybody could make so many different blocks, or horrified, knowing that you have to decide among them. In choosing blocks for your boat, you must identify what size line you intend to use, and what you wish to use each block for. Making all sheets the same size reduces confusion and simplifies purchasing. You can save money by buying rope in large coils. Also, replacements for blocks and sheaves can be standardized

Most mainsheet systems use multi-part blocks shackled to the appropriate boom and deck fittings. On smaller boats a cam cleat mainsheet block is sufficient to secure the sheet. Larger boats will use winches coupled with traditional cleats. With mid-boom sheeting, a series of single blocks attached to boom bails led to a multi-part block on a deckhouse traveller will best spread the loading on the boom.

The real maze of blocks comes with headsail sheeting. The modern genoa car mounted on a "T" track is probably the most versatile and least obstructive block

FIGURE 2-6
Trunnion snatch block

While a snatch block allows sheets to be removed without running their entire length through the sheave, the trunnion shackle attachment permits the block to assume the correct fairlead position both athwartships and fore-and-aft.

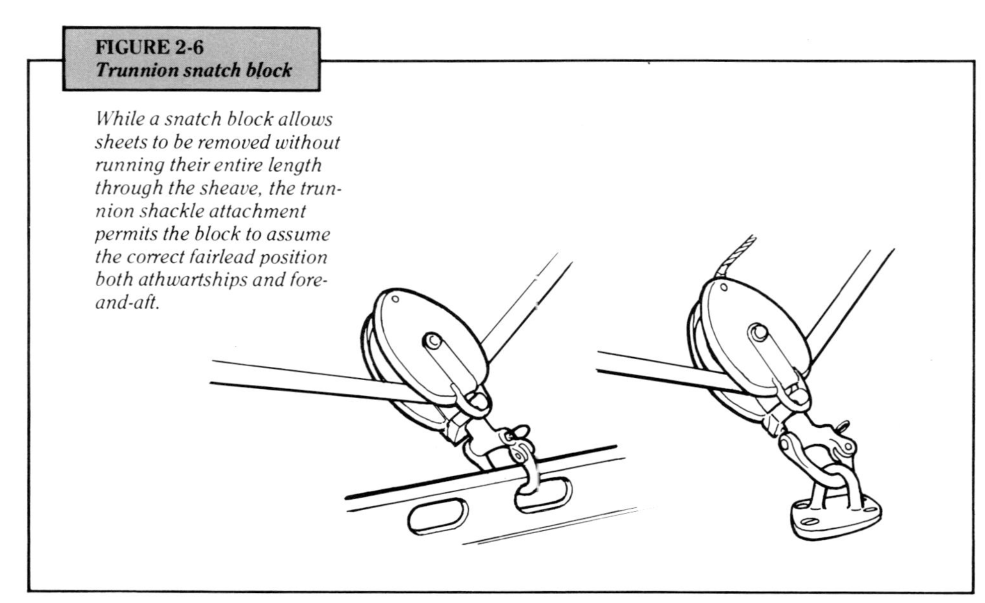

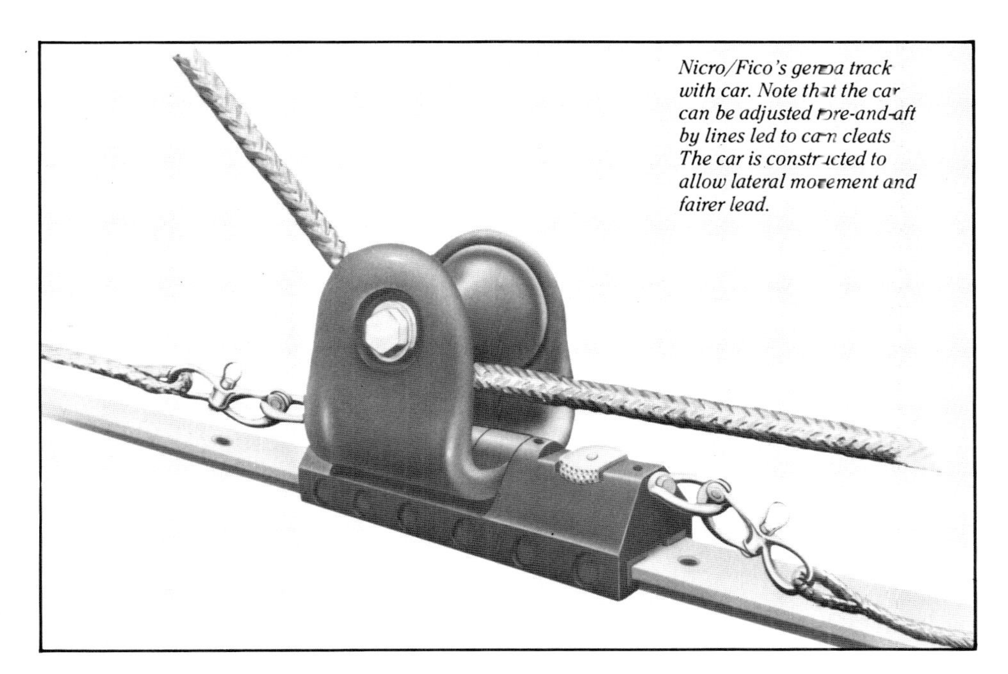

Nicro/Fico's genoa track with car. Note that the car can be adjusted fore-and-aft by lines led to cam cleats The car is constructed to allow lateral movement and fairer lead.

(see page 48). Snatch blocks attached to a perforated toerail allow for infinite adjustment, though they limit the sheeting angle. And for working jibs and storm jibs, fixed deck blocks or screw-in deck blocks obviate the need for a track on the foredeck and weather decks. For spinnaker sheets and drifter sheeting, turning blocks secured to the after coaming or as far aft on the deck as possible will keep things under control.

For ease of replacement, all blocks should be from the same maker. They should also be as versatile as possible. If you can afford the outlay, trunnion snap shackle snatch blocks probably can be used for more applications than any other type. However, reversible-shackle single blocks can be rigged for almost as many applications at far less cost. Your choice should be dictated by the sophistication of your sailing. For most cruising, a ship's block inventory can be appreciably smaller than aboard an ocean racer—in some cases a ratio of ten to one.

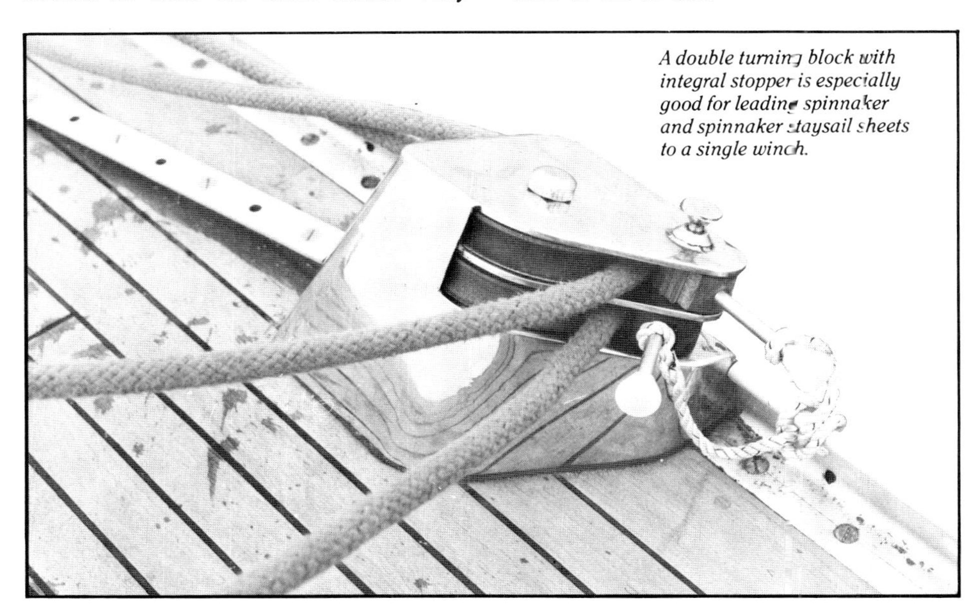

A double turning block with integral stopper is especially good for leading spinnaker and spinnaker staysail sheets to a single winch.

FIGURE 2-7
Mainsheet tackle

A four-part mainsheet tackle. The sheet is cleated with an integral clam cleat in the lower block. The system multiplies the force applied by the sheethandler 4 times.

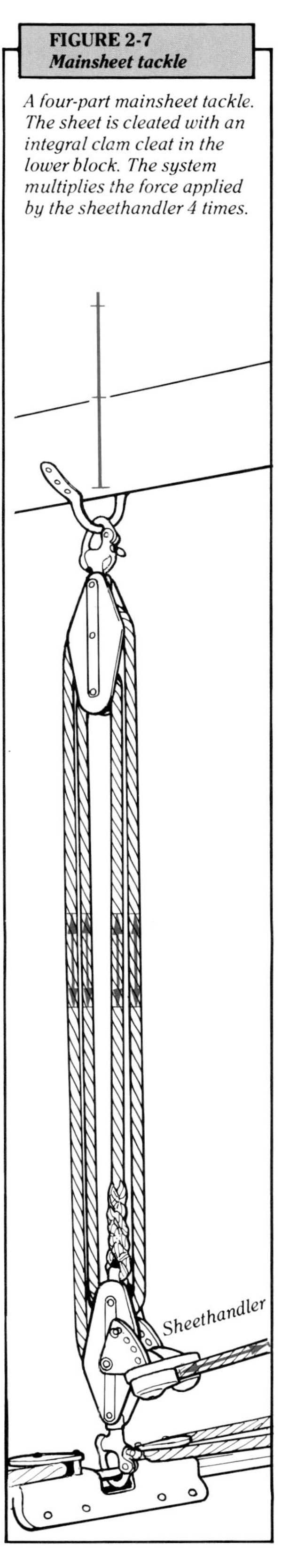

Which manufacturer's blocks you choose depends on the boat you use. For a small dinghy or yacht up to about 28 feet length overall (LOA), Nicro/Fico and Schaefer make the finest gear. The Lewmar blocks, which are low friction and extremely strong and attractive, are best for mid-size boats. For boats over 40 feet LOA, however, use Palmer-Johnson blocks. These blocks are made with a hole through the center pin. By running a wire through this hole, and fixing it to the mast base, you reduce the danger of hurting crew members if a block should explode under stress. This is a feature other manufacturers could copy to improve safety.

For boats with a lot of varnish, there are strong rubber-covered blocks made by Nicro/Fico and Merriman Holbrook. The rubber coating protects the varnished surfaces. If you have a wooden boat and want wooden blocks, Merriman Holbrook makes the strongest and longest lasting. My company is currently doing some design work on a 25-year-old boat which is still using the original M-H blocks!

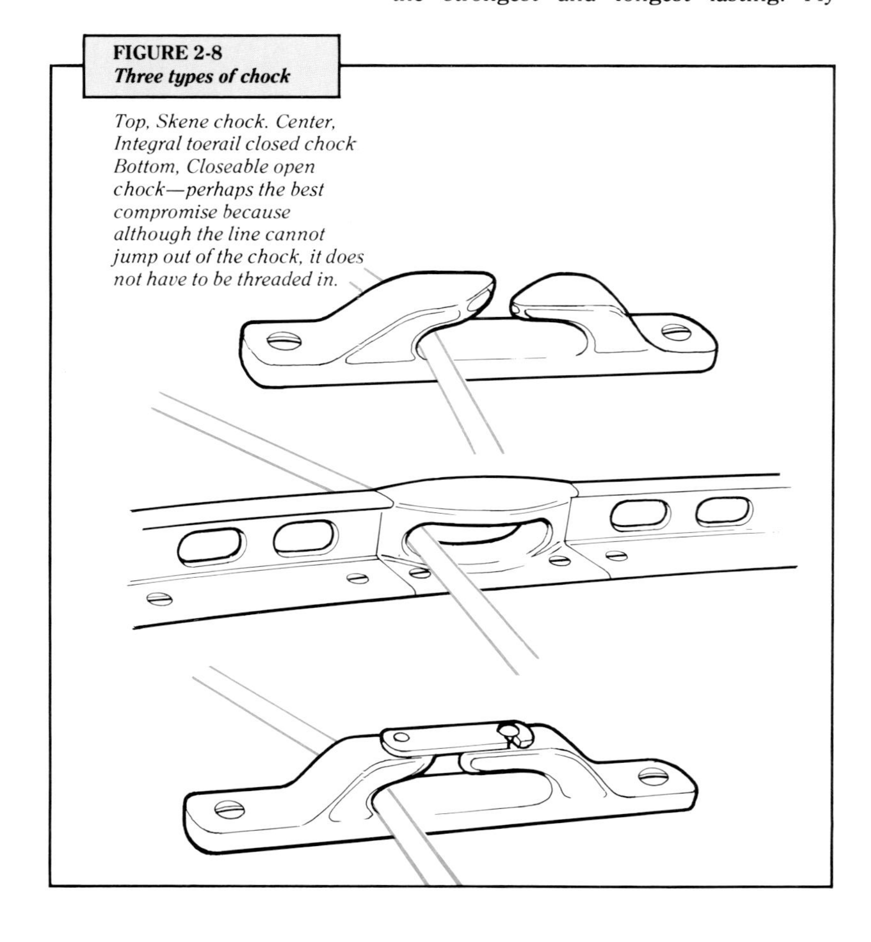
FIGURE 2-8
Three types of chock

Top, Skene chock. Center, Integral toerail closed chock Bottom, Closeable open chock—perhaps the best compromise because although the line cannot jump out of the chock, it does not have to be threaded in.

Chocks and Fairleads

At any point where a rope changes direction there should be a fairlead to prevent chafe of the rope. Fairleads can take the shape of the common chock (sometimes known as the skene chock), or they can be much more sophisticated, like an integral toerail chock or latching chock.

Often one of the problems with a skene chock is that it is set back slightly from the edge of the rail or sheerline. This is fine for mooring in a marina, but if an anchor is dropped using the fairlead, the line will lead over the sharp edge of the rail, causing chafing. A chock such as the Goiot or Gibb, which is an integral part of the toerail, has a distinct advantage.

Where a genoa sheet or halyard fall changes direction, the loads and friction in the system demand that some other form of lead be used. These usually incoporate some form of pulley wheel to reduce friction. The lead on the track can be adjusted fore and aft by pulling up the locating pin and moving it, but the turning block lead must be fair both into and out of the block.

There are various manufacturers of chocks and fairleads. Many are extremely good but some are poorly designed and built. The most attractive and most efficient are the Barbarossa models built in Italy, though they are rather bulky. Both Lewmar and Merriman Holbrook make less cumbersome, equally strong units.

Winches

In the days when the capstan was the sole winch on a boat it took over one hundred men to raise an anchor. Nowadays using modern materials and technology it is possible for one man to raise that same anchor. Mechanically efficient winches make the difference. Moreover, there are now varieties of winches for every purpose from raising the anchor to tensioning the outhaul on the main boom.

In certain situations aboard day sailers up to 22 feet, it is possible for a crewman to hold the jib sheet without a winch. This practice, however, makes for tired crewmen. Using a small handleless winch called a snubbing winch the crew can pull the sheet home and easily hold it.

The next step up from snubbing winches is the single-speed, top- or bottom-action winch. The top-action winch—in which the handle is put in a square hole at the top—is easier to use than the bottom-action variety, as the winch handle can make a full turn. Bottom-action winches usually let the handle protrude to one side of the winch base or through a coaming, so the line must be wound on by an awkward ratcheting motion. Bottom-action winches are very useful for single-handing, however, as the handle can't be lost, and turns can be thrown off without replacing the handle.

FIGURE 2-9
Genoa sheet fairleads

Top, direct lead from aft block is both inefficient and dangerous. Bottom, lead to turning block is safer and gives added purchase for greater sheeting efficiency.

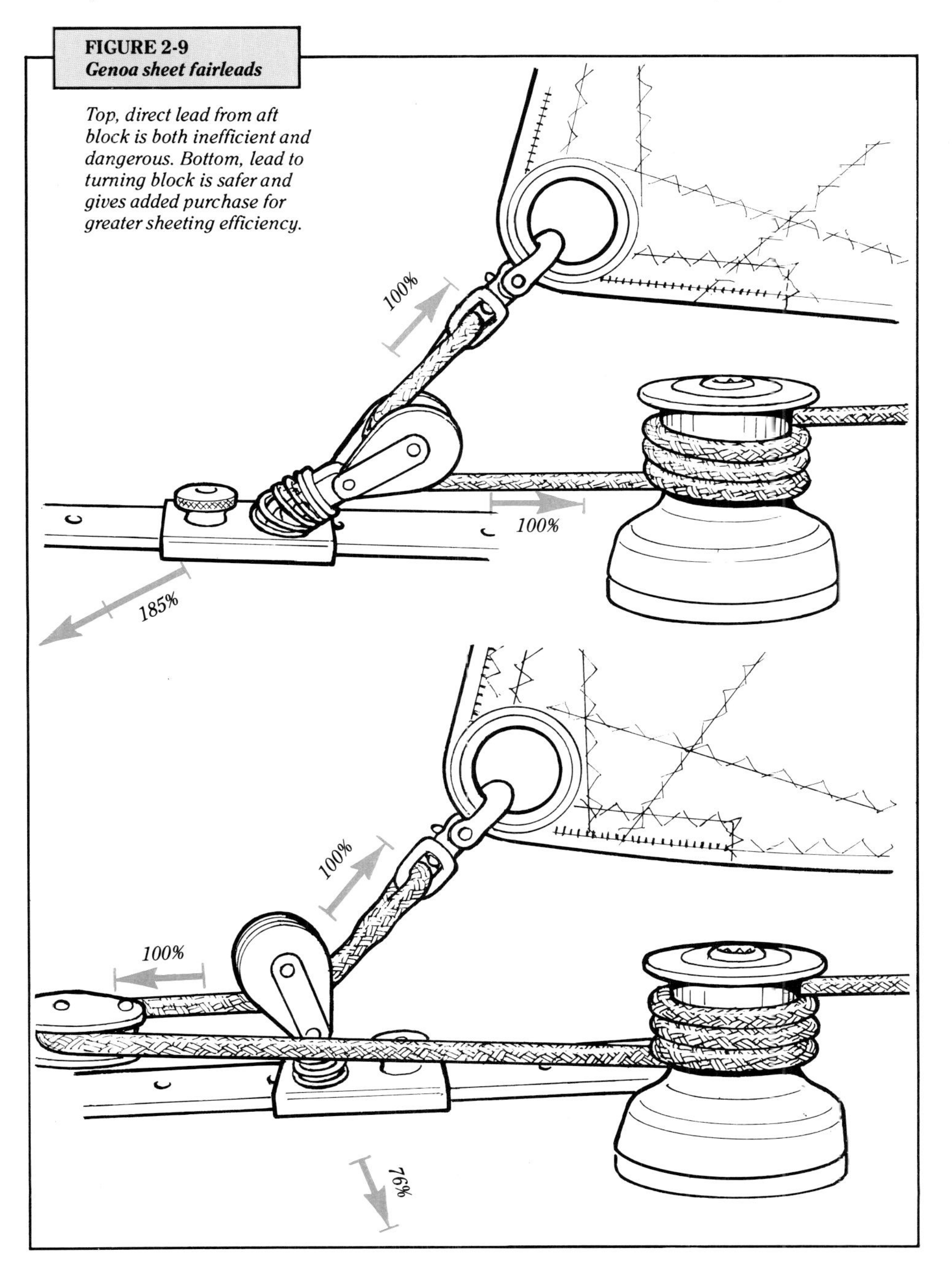

A modern racing boat will have a large number of winches surrounding the cockpit, arranged to separate crew functions and for maximum power on either tack. Sir Edward Heath at the wheel of Morning Cloud.

A selection of modern, multi-speed and self-tailing winches, showing the wide range available. Made by Arco USA.

All winch manufacturers have single-speed winches. Lewmar has the largest range as well as the most effective gear and power ratios. Of the major manufacturers, only M.S. Gibb has a large range of bottom-action winches.

Two-speed winches are the most commonly used winches on modern sailing boats. The crewman turns the handle one way (usually clockwise) for top speed, and the opposite way for second speed. Lewmar and Barient make the most dependable two-speed winches.

Most three-speed winches are very similar to the same size two-speed models, but are fully geared in the lowest speed. They are mainly used as sheet winches for racing boats. The Lewmar three-speed has a push button for changing into the third speed. Although both Barient and Barlow make excellent three-speed winches, Lewmar's push button makes it the most convenient.

There are no real four-speed winches, but Lewmar makes some winches with a backwind facility. This feature allows one to ease out the genoa sheet when it is under load, instead of having to slide the line around the drum. Only Grand Prix racers need such a complex and costly winch.

When sheet loads become very high it is difficult, sometimes impossible, to trim the sheet with a single winch, no matter how many speeds it may have. If this is likely to happen, the designer will specify either linked winches or a grinder.

Linked winches are useful in that two handles or a pedestal can be used to drive one drum. Essentially, linked winches consist of two winches with a gearbox between them. The majority of these systems are supplied by Lewmar or Barient, for use on racing boats. They are usually designed-in when the boat is built. Lewmar also builds a sophisticated cross link chain drive system. This is a lightweight unit which transmits more of the available power to the winch than the ordinary linked winch system.

The ultimate unit for large boats, the grinder drives a large diameter drum in an integral unit. Grinders are heavier and create more windage than linked winches, but they can handle greater loads. They are most useful in large cruising boats and ocean racers. The Barient MK XII and MK XVII and the Lewmar 95 are probably the finest integral grinder units ever made.

Self-tailing winches are most useful on cruising boats because they reduce line clutter without using up an extra crewman. The paint manufacturing firm of Woolsey was the first to make a self-tailing winch.

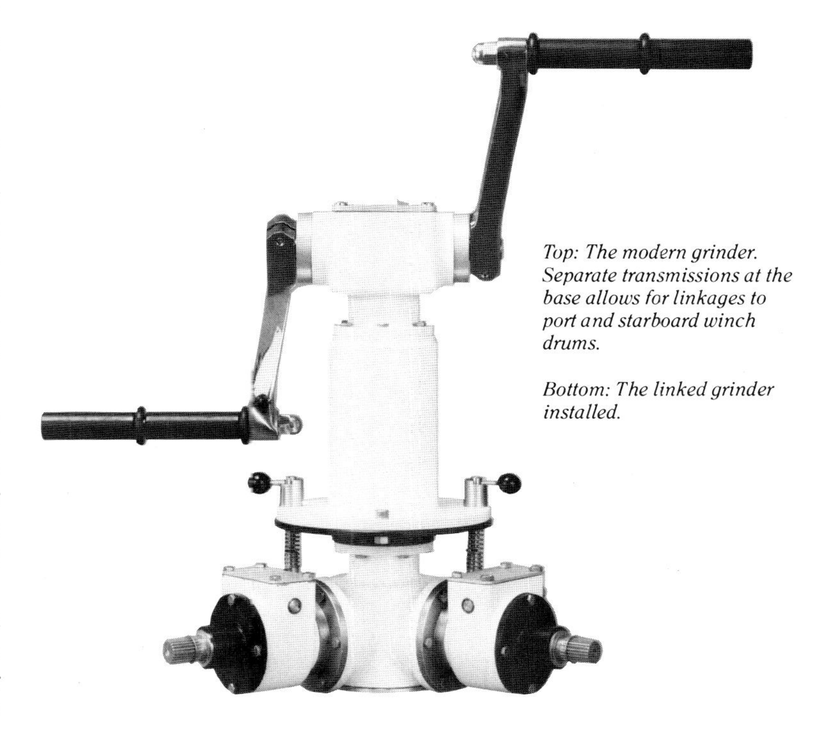

Top: The modern grinder. Separate transmissions at the base allows for linkages to port and starboard winch drums.

Bottom: The linked grinder installed.

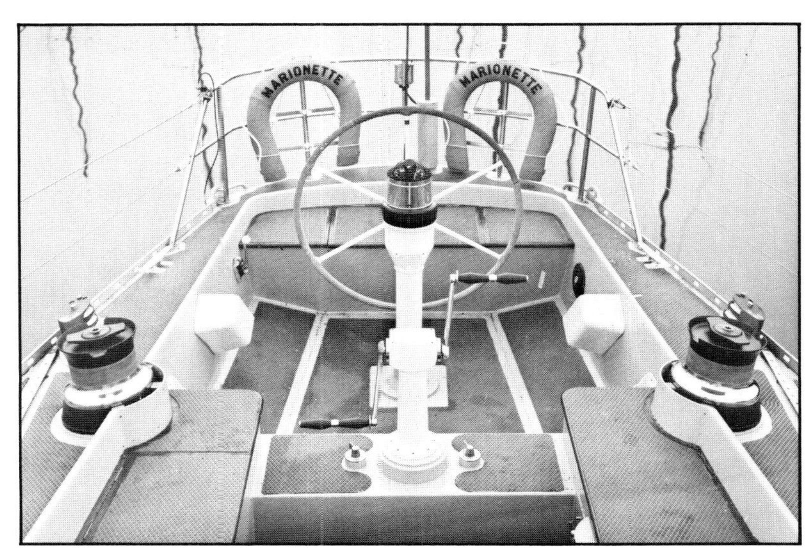

A Lewmar self-tailing winch. The arm and jaws on top serve both to cleat and strip the line. A backup cleat should also be installed.

Today, the Enkes, Lewmar and Barient systems are the best in the field, with very little to choose between them.

Among all the winches made today, there's only one type to avoid: the reel winch. Only the main halyard on a very large boat really needs to use one. Frankly, I wouldn't put the reel winches on any boat I designed. Faces, arms and wrists can be severely damaged by winch handles which reverse as the brake is let off. Furthermore, they are very slow. If you really need one, Goiot makes the safest in that the brake cannot be released until the handle has been removed.

For the sailor who doesn't want to wind winches at all, the electric winch is the ideal thing. Very large boats use them, especially when running short-handed. There are electric winches for almost any voltage—12, 24, 32 and 110 volts—but the breaker should be set at a fairly high amperage (above 80 amps), so that it will trip out if the winch stalls rather than burn the motor. Electric winches can also be used with a handle, provided a locking handle is used. Power consumption is very high, however, and ample battery capacity is a must.

Cleats

A cleat is the quickest and most convenient device for securing a line. A cleat should be sized to suit the line which it will hold, allowing an inch cleat per 1/16th inch of line size. For example, a 5/8th-inch line should be made up on a 10-inch cleat.

When shopping for cleats look for ones that have rounded edges and strong feet with plenty of room for large bolts. Cleats should be mounted with a solid backing plate and through-bolted using antivibration washers or Nyloc nuts.

There are many variations of the common cleat: cam cleats and jam cleats are the two main ones. Cam cleats will hold only as long as there is tension on the line. Tension holds the cams tightly against the rope creating an effective cleat, but moving parts can stick or break, a frequent problem with these cleats. The jam cleat, on the other hand, has no moving parts but holds the line securely. Its disadvantage is that a high load on the line can pull the rope through the plastic jaws, eventually burning off the teeth. Even with these limitations, carefully sized cam and jam cleats work well in situations where the load is moderate. Cam cleats are fine on multi-part mainsheets; jam cleats are best on foreguys. Nicro/Fico, Schaefer, Gibb and Main Marine all

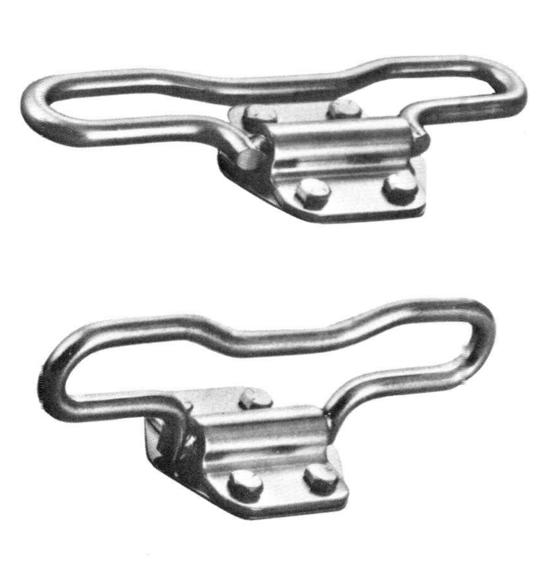

A folding cleat, by Johnson, keeps deck clutter low.

make serviceable cam cleats and horned jam cleats. The very best jam cleats are made by the English firm, Clamcleats.

Another type of cleat seen on many ocean racers is the sheet stopper, used when a number of lines have to be led to the same winch. One line can be tensioned and removed from the winch drum, after snapping the sheet stopper closed to hold the line in place. The major makers of cam cleats also make reputable sheet stoppers.

Bollards, Bits and Belays

Bollards and bits must be a special item, custom-made to suit the individual boat. Inquire at your local boatyard. There are certain guidelines, however, that must be observed if the installation is not to rip out as soon as any load is put on it. On a wooden boat a rowing bollard should go through the deck to the keel where it must be securely fastened. On fiberglass and metal boats, most bollards are fastened to a stout backing plate with some form of structure below it to carry the loads directly to the keel.

FIGURE 2-10
Clam and cam cleats

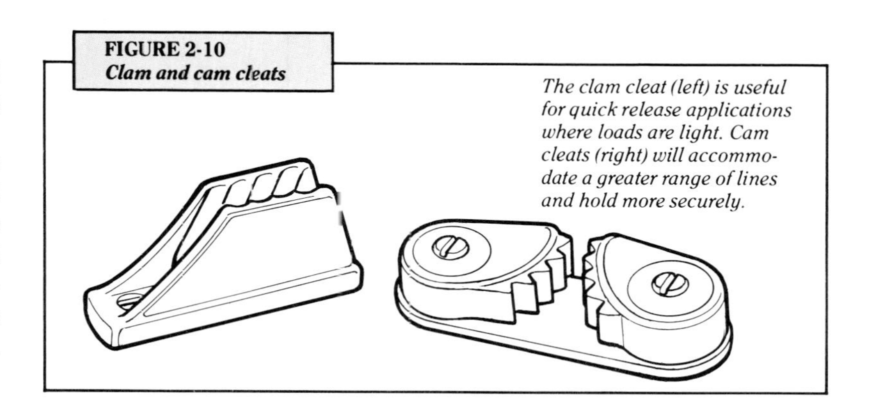

The clam cleat (left) is useful for quick release applications where loads are light. Cam cleats (right) will accommodate a greater range of lines and hold more securely.

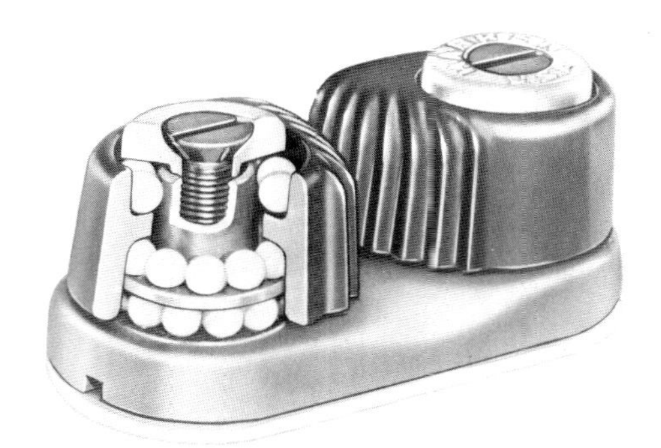

A ball-bearing cam cleat by Harken compensates for unequal pull and centers the line between the cams.

Sheet stoppers permit one winch to serve several lines. Mounted ahead of the winch, the stopper secures one line while you winch the other.

Mostly seen on older wooden craft, bits are custom-built around the mast to carry the belaying rails and pins, upon which to belay halyard falls. Like bollards, the bits should be secured to the boat in such a way that they will not buckle or rip up the deck.

Mainsheet Systems

As aspect ratios of the mainsail have increased in recent years, so the leech loading of the main has increased, necessitating stronger sheeting systems. This in turn has led to multi-part tackles, the fall of which is taken to a winch. The number of parts to the tackle depends on the amount of power required or the speed at which the sheet should be trimmed. For example, a single part mainsheet taken to a powerful winch is standard on a 12-meter, while a typical cruising boat might have a four- or six-part tackle and a small self-tailing winch.

The position of the mainsheet in the boat varies according to the vessel's layout. Ideally, the mainsheet should pull straight downward from the end of the boom, but since this may force the traveller to cut across the cockpit the traveller track is sometimes placed on the coachroof instead. This position pulls the center of the boom downward, requiring a much stronger spar to prevent its bending in the middle.

Dual tracks allow for more precise headsail sheeting angles.

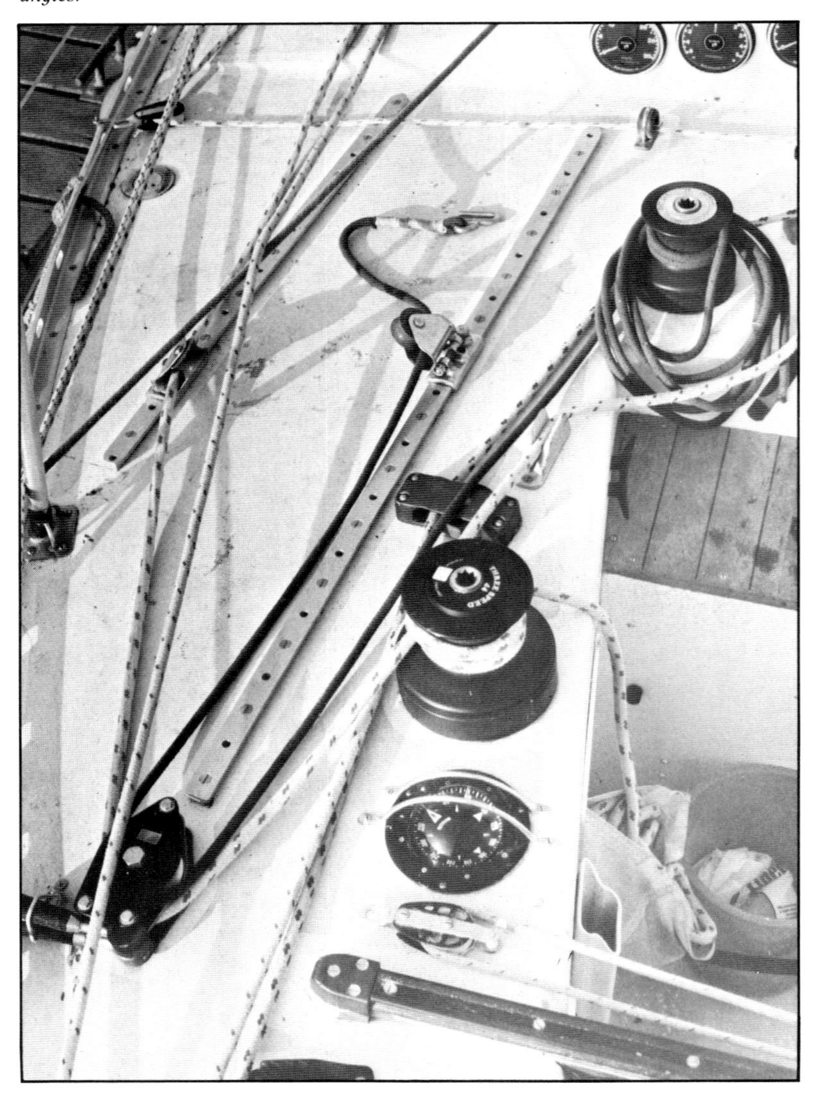

Tracks and Track Slides

Earlier, we looked at fairleads and blocks. The majority of those fittings were firmly fixed to the deck, but there are situations where the fairlead must be free to move. The most common case is the sheet lead, where the sheet has to carry the load of the sail from the clew to a winch and has to be adjusted for best trim.

Genoa tracks should be low-profile "T" tracks and their cars should be the most efficient possible. Use only cars specifically designed to fit the track. The Paul Luke cars are the best on big boats, although they should be modified slightly to prevent the jaws being pulled apart if the lead is slightly unfair. For medium-size vessels, Barbarossa, Lewmar, Merriman Holbrook, Gibb and Schaefer all make a good product. For smaller boats there are so many makers that a list would take up half a page, so pick from almost any manufacturer, but look for smooth movement along the track, rounded corners and ease of maintenance. The cars should be easily removable for oiling.

Mainsheet travellers use either "X" or "T" tracks. What you are looking for here is a large load-bearing surface, that is, the top of the "T" or "X" must be large and sturdy. Remember that the pull will usually be upward from the track, so the car will have to be able to move horizontally while under load. These tracks should be strongly bolted in place with either a strongback or solid plate underneath, to spread the loads and keep the deck from ripping out.

Most manufacturers make cars specifically to suit their track. Look for a car that has roller bearings for ease of movement, avoiding any car where two flat metal surfaces bear against each other. The latter will be hard to move when the track is new and almost impossible to adjust thereafter. Integral cleats, rather than cleats positioned elsewhere on the boat, are also recommended, because they reduce deck clutter. Nicro/Fico, Lewmar, Schaefer and IYE make good travellers and tracks.

Pulpits and Pushpits

Because of the large variety of bow and stern profiles, pulpits and pushpits are not usually stocked on marine suppliers' shelves. They are made to order, designed specifically for the boat on which they are fitted. Because they are locally made—often in a small machine shop near the builder—quality can vary considerably. Even so, there are many features that are common to every well-designed pulpit or pushpit.

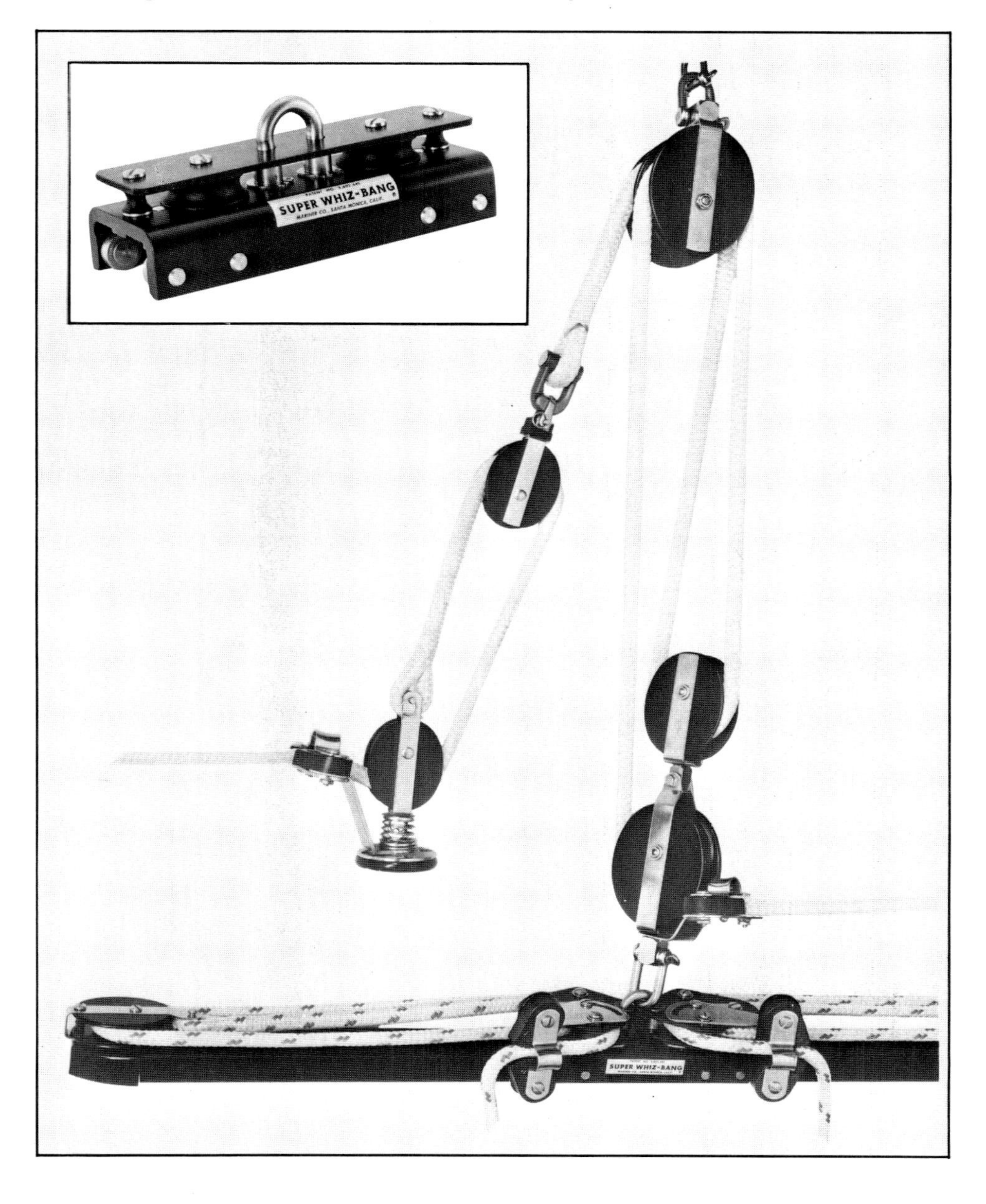

Mariner mainsheet system. Turning block and cam cleats permit infinite athwartships adjustment.
Inset: Traveller car, showing roller bearings.

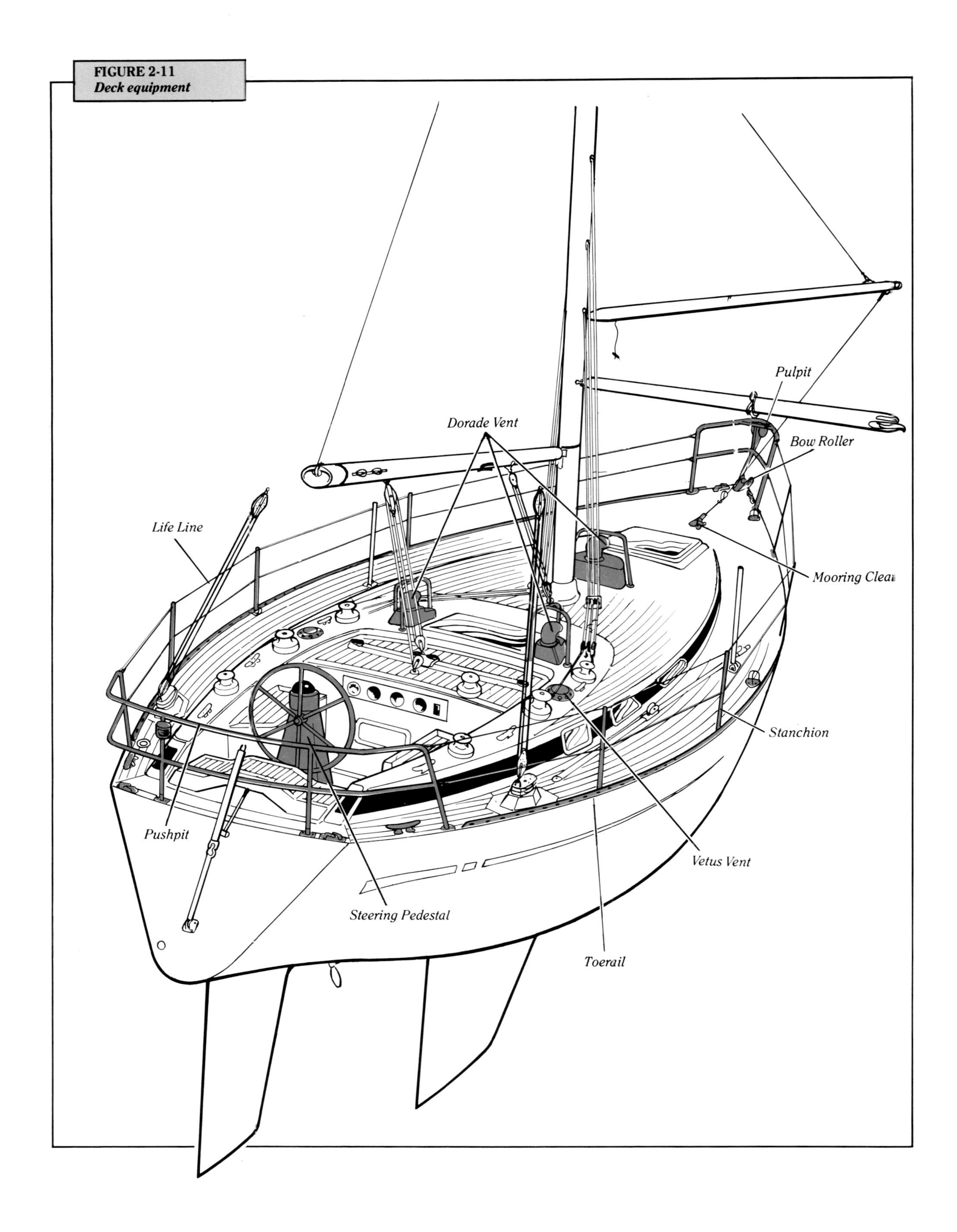

FIGURE 2-11
Deck equipment

It should be made of at least 1-inch diameter stainless steel, weldless tube. Avoid chromium-plated steel and aluminum tubing. The former blisters; the latter is too weak. Acceptable alternative materials are welded bronze and welded/galvanized mild steel. The feet should fit firmly into through-bolted bases and should be pinned firmly in place. For safety the pulpit/pushpit should have at least two rails, the top one 1 inch in diameter and the bottom one ½ or ¾ inch in diameter.

With careful design the basic pulpit can be made to fulfill many other functions. It should have $^{3}/_{16}$th-inch diameter wire loops welded to the top rail for clipping halyards. This will keep the halyards from slapping the mast while the boat is in harbor. The bend of the top rail can be used as a bow light mounting point, raising the bow lights so they can be seen more easily. The pushpit provides mounting space for the stern light, the ensign and a lifering or horseshoe.

Stanchions

Most stanchions are made to suit the Offshore Racing Council's (ORC) special regulations, which call for two wires, 12 inches apart on larger boats and one wire 18 inches high on craft under about 30 feet LOA. Stanchions should be fitted into through-bolted stanchion bases and pinned in place with a cotter pin or split pin, not held in place with a grub screw.

Many manufacturers make stanchions. The best pass all wires directly through the stainless steel post. Lewmar makes molded nylon eyes that hold the top rail. On boats that I have sailed, the top wire has sometimes cut through this nylon eye, leaving the life line dangling.

Life Lines and Guardrails

The trend in modern life lines appears to be to use a ⅛th-inch diameter stainless steel wire for the bottom line and a plastic-covered line for the top wire. Any corrosion that takes place on the bottom wire can be seen instantly; but on the plastic-covered top line, any cut or nick in the plastic can lead to hidden corrosion and failure of the wire. Although it does not look as nice, you should use ¼-inch stainless steel top wire

FIGURE 2-12
The well-made pulpit

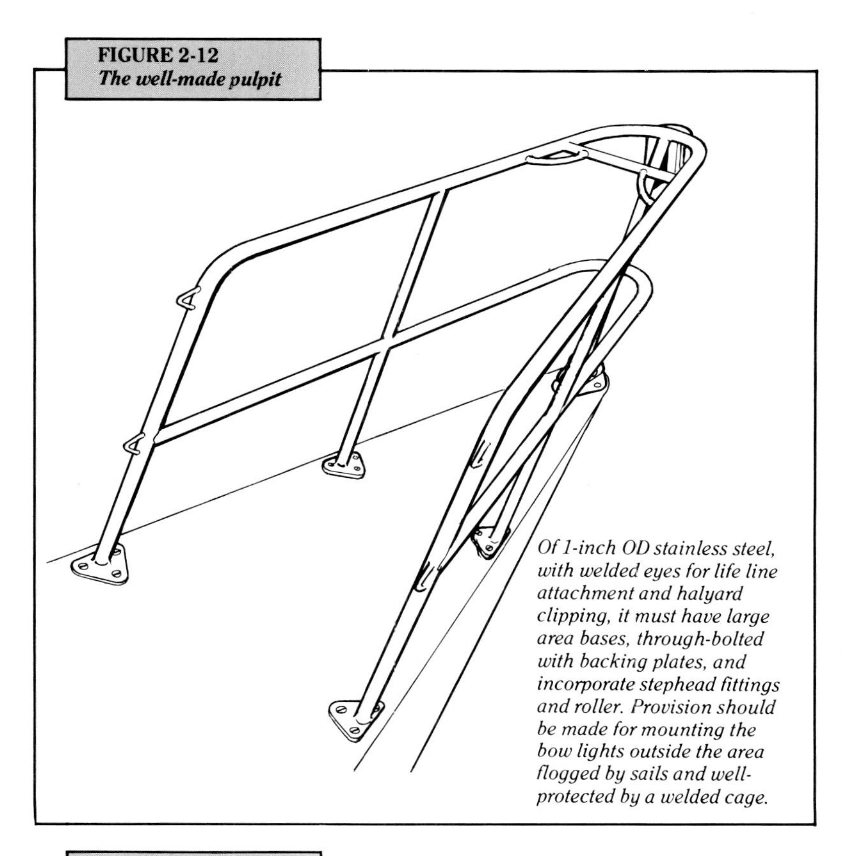

Of 1-inch OD stainless steel, with welded eyes for life line attachment and halyard clipping, it must have large area bases, through-bolted with backing plates, and incorporate stephead fittings and roller. Provision should be made for mounting the bow lights outside the area flogged by sails and well-protected by a welded cage.

FIGURE 2-13
Through-bolting

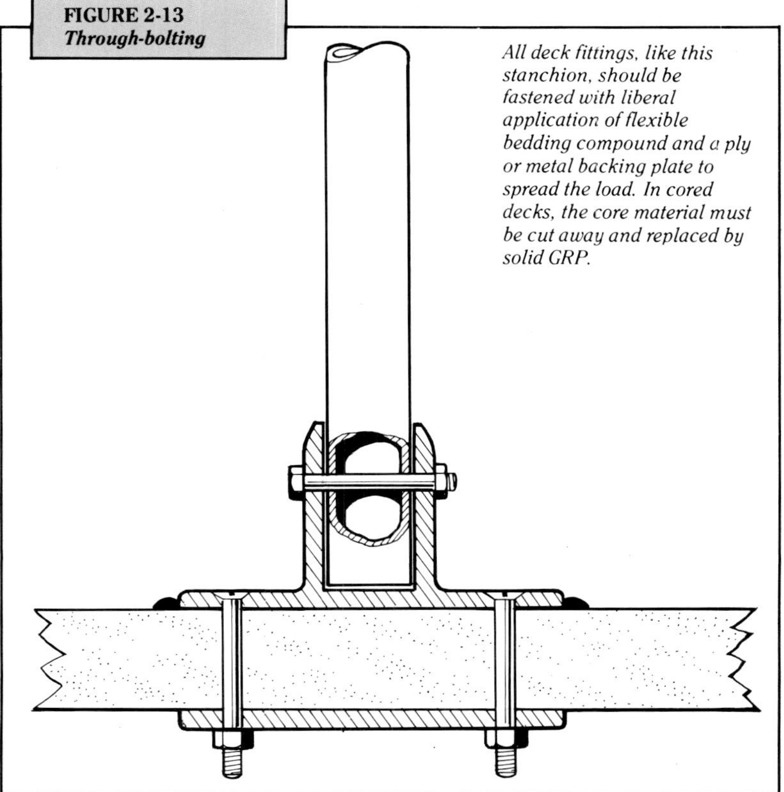

All deck fittings, like this stanchion, should be fastened with liberal application of flexible bedding compound and a ply or metal backing plate to spread the load. In cored decks, the core material must be cut away and replaced by solid GRP.

covered with clear plastic tube between the stanchions. The ends of the liferails should be secured to the pulpit and pushpit by means of an open turnbuckle or a nylon lashing. The lashing is better, insofar as it has some "give" in it when a shock load comes on the line.

Toerails

Although wooden toerails look the most attractive they are impractical for sheeting sails and require a lot of maintenance. The modern trend is to make them out of aluminum alloy with elongated holes.

This type of rail provides reinforcing for the hull-to-deck joint on a wooden or fiberglass boat, while on an alloy hull the toerail can be designed as part of the hull structure. There are various manufacturers of toerails. The Goiot rail, which has specially designed fairleads and stanchion bases made for the system, is probably the best. Unfortunately, the Goiot toerail looks rather clumsy and could do with a little streamlining. Gibb makes a similar system.

Most American-made toerails are very similar, but the Merriman Holbrook are the best, except in the largest size. Merriman's biggest models have such a large bead on the top of the rail that clipping shackles to the rail is difficult.

The points to look for when selecting any toerail are the following: rounded edges; easy to clip and unclip shackles; through-bolting; gaps in the bottom flange to allow water to drain away; and designed-in chocks and end fittings.

Hatches

Traditionally, the hatches on a yacht have been custom-made by the builder as an integral part of the boat, but today's builders frequently use stock alloy framed hatches on the foredeck and for opening ports or sail hatches. The best are made by Goiot, Atkins & Hoyle, Bomar, Canpa, Lewmar and Vetus. These are all well made and watertight.

Be wary of hatches that bend when they are dogged tightly. The largest sizes from some of the less expensive manufacturers are prone to bending.

A cruising boat that is going to sail in the ocean should have canvas hatch covers over all the hatches, allowing them to be left open when water and spray are coming on deck. The hatch covers should be fitted into a groove screwed to the deck. Wherever possible this groove should run about 6 inches past the hatch to stop water flowing around the hatch cover and down the hatch. Your sailmaker can make hatch covers to your special order.

The Bomar hatch. Its double dogs, braced hatch, adjustable support and wide flange make it strong and watertight.

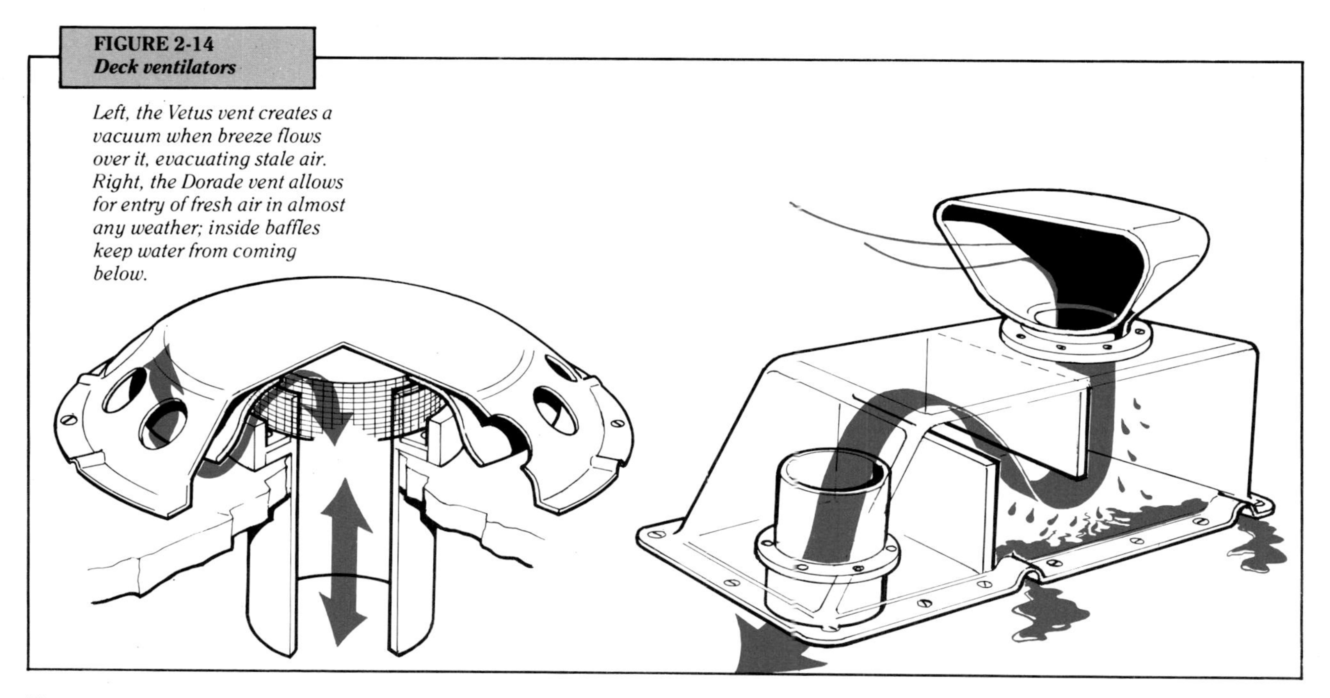

FIGURE 2-14
Deck ventilators

Left, the Vetus vent creates a vacuum when breeze flows over it, evacuating stale air. Right, the Dorade vent allows for entry of fresh air in almost any weather; inside baffles keep water from coming below.

Vents

Fine ventilators, both passive and blower-assisted, are made by Vetus and Simpson-Lawrence (Aeolian). Dorade boxes with cowls are excellent, though the cowls are best if brass or stainless steel. The plastic cowl can come adrift or crack, and it is usually too small and low to be effective.

Another fine vent is the "Sunshine box." Originally developed by the naval architect Gary Mull for the boat *Sunshine* (much as the Dorade box derives from Olin Stephens's *Dorade*), these are baffled, draining boxes built into the bow of the boat. Certainly the best method of ventilating the forepeak, they must be designed-in from the beginning to be most effective; otherwise, structural modifications will be necessary.

GROUND TACKLE

The secret in buying ground tackle is to buy the largest and strongest gear you can afford, because when everything else fails, it's your anchor that is going to save the boat, crew and skipper. Anybody seriously contemplating cruising for long distances should carry a variety of anchors. Best are the Danforth Hi-Test or CQR for sandy or muddy bottoms and a fisherman anchor for anchoring on rock or coral bottoms. The best modern fisherman models are based on Herreshoff or Nicholson designs.

The Danforth anchor is fairly easy to stow. In fact, many designers specify a hawsepipe in which to stow it. The CQR usually has some form of bow chuck, but with careful design of the fitting it too can be made to stow in a hawsepipe.

Stowing a fisherman anchor is another problem! The flukes and stock always seem to smash against the hull no matter how hard the anchor handlers try to hold them off. To handle this type of anchor properly some form of removable davit is a

Good for fair weather ventilation, the Vetus mushroom vent can be sealed when the going gets rough.

CQR (secure) anchor. One of the most popular anchors in the world, it was developed in the 1930s by a Cambridge professor. Not as efficient pound for pound as a Danforth, it is more versatile and will not break-out when the wind shifts.

Windlasses should be through-bolted with guys or beams under the deck to spread stresses. Chain pipe here allows for direct lead below.

must. Even so the prudent yachtsman should carry two anchors, preferably a CQR or Danforth and a fisherman type. The best fisherman anchors are made by Paul Luke and Simpson-Lawrence. All of the above anchors have their imitators, some of which are far inferior to the genuine article, so make sure you purchase the real item.

Most experienced American yachtsmen recommend using two or three fathoms of chain between the anchor and the rode to absorb some of the shock loads and help the hook dig in. Make sure your chain and shackles are all top quality. Quite often, high quality chain is used with a cheap steel shackle; as we all know, the weakest link—the shackle—will fail first. Note that if you use all chain, it should match the gypsy on your windlass. Don't arbitrarily buy new chain without making sure it will fit properly, or you will get slippage, damaging the chain and windlass.

A windlass should have a chain counter which can measure the number of feet or fathoms paid out. If the wildcat can be operated by a standard winch handle which stows in the base of the pedestal and the unit has its own built-in chain stopper, all the better. The handle should be able to wind up the chain in the event of electrical failure. The best are made by Ideal, Keefe, Lawrence (Francis) and Vetus.

The appropriate line for an anchor rode is invariably nylon. It can stretch and contract, absorbing the shock loads of a boat pitching in a heavy sea. The size of the nylon should be carefully matched to the size of the anchor line. Both should be able to absorb the same loads and the splices should be put in very carefully and tightly, preferably by a professional. When using nylon lines, take care to avoid chafe, as the nylon fibers will wear quickly on a fixed bow chock. Make a rubber, plastic or leather line guard to protect the rode while the boat is in harbor.

RUNNING LIGHTS

As of July 1981, all lights under the 1972 COLREGS must conform to Coast Guard and Department of Trade Regulations (see illustration, p. 55).

Navigation lights should ideally be mounted as high as possible. The most visible is an approved masthead-mounted tricolor light. The difference between 5 feet above the water and 40 or 50 feet, in terms of visibility, can be as much as a couple of miles in heavy weather. Port and starboard lights, bicolor lights and stern lights, mounted on pulpit and pushpit, are also acceptable, but mounting in the topsides or on the cabin sides is an invitation to disaster, since either high seas or foresails will obscure one of the lights.

Unfortunately, a masthead tricolor light alone may not conform to COLREGS, which specifies that the white light must ride *above* the bicolor when the yacht is motoring. Moreover, any boat you meet at close quarters may have trouble gauging your length, unless you have both bow- and stern-mounted lights. The best solution for a seagoing yacht is to carry a masthead tricolor, a pulpit-mounted bicolor *and* a single, white pushpit-mounted light.

The best approved navigation lights are made by Aqua-Signal and Marinaspec. Size should be in accordance with COLREGS, though the largest light you can fit is generally the best. After all, the whole point is to be *seen*. Elegant little biblelots just won't do.

FIGURE 2-15
Running lights

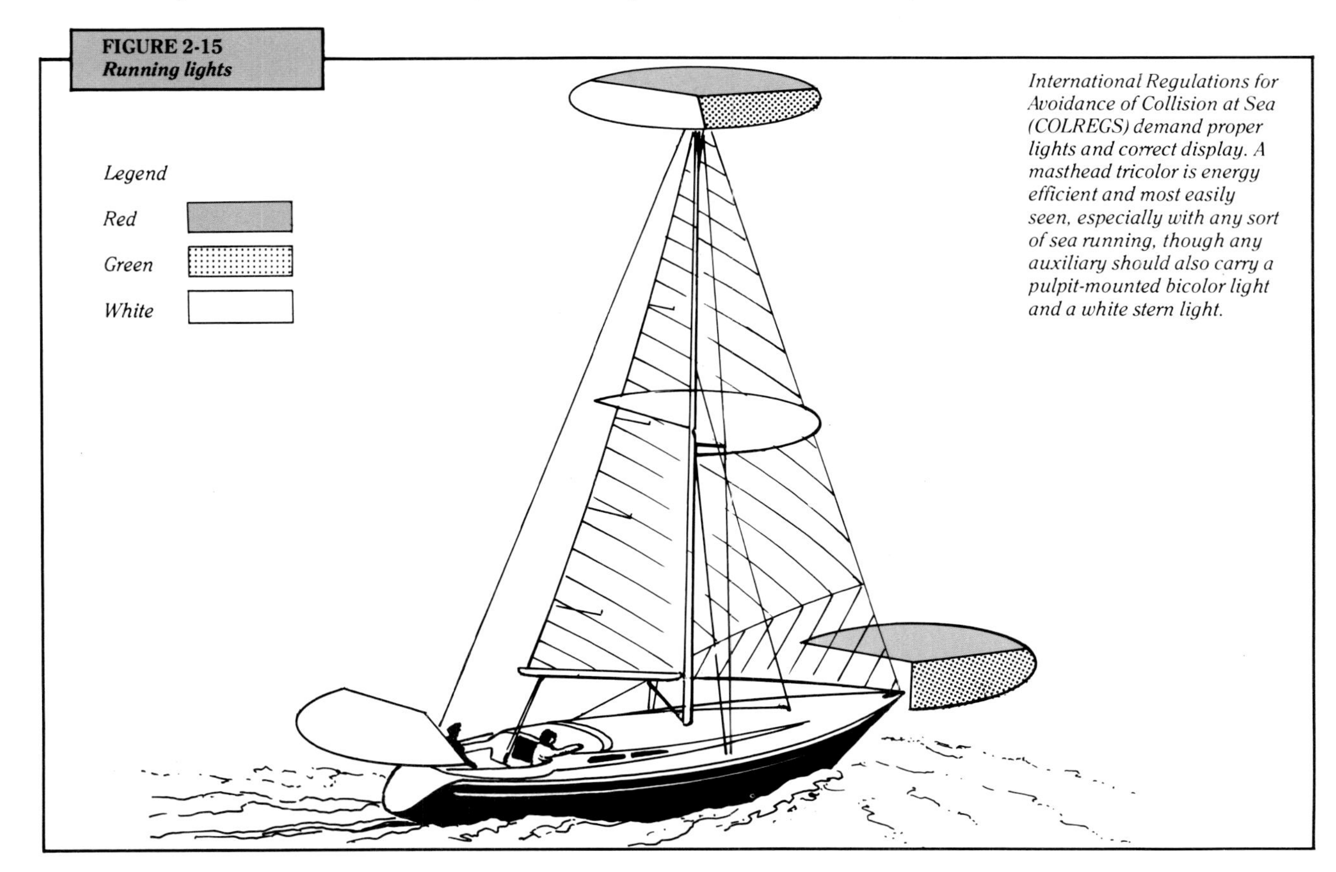

International Regulations for Avoidance of Collision at Sea (COLREGS) demand proper lights and correct display. A masthead tricolor is energy efficient and most easily seen, especially with any sort of sea running, though any auxiliary should also carry a pulpit-mounted bicolor light and a white stern light.

A good deck light is useful, especially for foredeck work. The traditional spreader lights are unaerodynamic and can foul sheets and halyards. Much better is the streamlined light, made by Simpson-Lawrence and Guest, which attaches to the foreside of the mast at about spreader level. Because it is connected directly to the mast, it causes no fouling and comparatively little turbulence.

The best lights are made with quartz elements and anodized aluminum reflectors. The quartz bulb uses less energy than other types, because it provides 25 percent more lumens per watt. Brightness is important, since the COLREGS specify that a masthead light be visible from a distance of 5 miles on yachts 65 feet and over, 3 miles on medium boats (40 to 65 feet), and 2 miles on yachts under 40 feet. Under COLREGS-specified conditions, lights visible at up to 2 miles will have a specified luminous intensity of 4.3 candelas; those visible at 3 miles, an intensity of 12 candelas; and those visible at 5 miles, an intensity of 52 candelas.

COLREGS requirements for lamp color combinations are complex and somewhat ambiguous. Sailboats under 40 feet may use a masthead tricolor light. Some companies offer such a light in combination with a separately activated emergency strobe light. While a strobe is not specifically permitted by COLREGS, many sailors feel that it is an effective rescue beacon. Regardless, yachts over 40 feet must carry bicolor sidelights and a white sternlight. When motoring, any yacht must carry a masthead light, sidelights and sternlight.

Masthead tricolor lights are more easily seen than deck lights and more energy efficient. The one at right contains an anchor light/strobe also. Strobe lights can be effective beacons in emergencies.

Chapter 3

PROPULSION SYSTEMS

Generations ago, when the winds failed, the master of a square-rigger ordered the crew into the boats. Oar power towed the ship through the doldrums. Nowadays the sailing skipper cranks up an engine and motors through a calm in serene comfort. Once when gales threatened to put a ship on the rocks, the captain dropped the anchor and hoped the chain would hold. Now the cruising sailor defies contrary winds with cast-iron power. Purists praise the traditional ways of doing things, but no one today denies that almost every sailboat needs auxiliary power—for docking in close quarters, for exiting a busy harbor, for running inlets against adverse winds or tides, and for hastily clawing off lee shore.

The crucial element of a boat propulsion system is the propeller. The shaft itself could be turned by hand; indeed, lifeboats often have seesaw crank handles so that survivors can provide their own power. The crucial elements of the propeller itself are its blades. The blades are carefully designed so that the length, the width, the area, the curvature of the faces and the shape all integrate to provide optimum performance. No propeller will do its job, however, if it is not correctly matched to the boat. A propeller mounted in the rudder aperture blanketed by the deadwood ahead of it will behave differently than one on a shaft offset beside the deadwood. Also, because the boat heels, pitches and yaws as it proceeds through a seaway, any propeller will encounter interferences that can't be anticipated purely by design theory. In consequence the propeller dictated by theory does not always work well in practice. Sailboat owners should be suspicious of dockside experts who make casual recommendations about switching propellers. If a propeller doesn't perform well, consult a qualified naval architect (see Appendix 3); the fee is worthwhile if it saves buying several haphazardly chosen propellers.

The propeller—or rather its blades—do their job much as a sail does. That is, a fluid (water) passes over the curved face of the blade and must be "stretched" in order to pass from the leading edge to the trailing edge. The water becomes less dense because its molecules get farther apart, and the curved face becomes a low-pressure

FIGURE 3-1
Commonly used propellers

Two-bladed prop (upper left) with a strut is most common on fin keelers, though a variant lets the shaft through a small skeg. Folding props (lower right) cut drag under sail, but may not be as efficient as a fixed prop, especially in reverse. Aperture-mounted props (lower left) can be locked behind the deadwood and thus cut down on drag. Three-bladed props (upper right) belong on motor sailers and power boats: The drag they cause can cut sailing speed by as much as a knot.

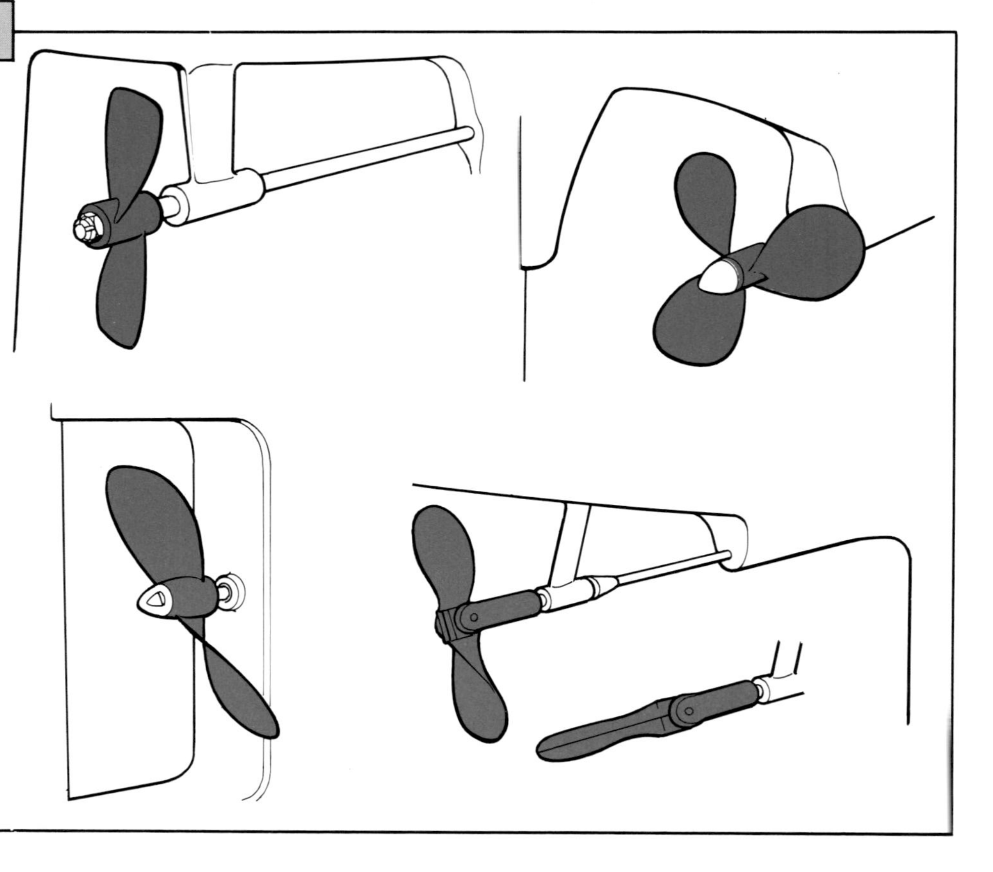

area. On the opposite face (the flat face) the pressure is normal—high in relation to the pressure on the curved face—and the water pushes the blade in the direction of the curved face.

The foregoing, called the *blade-element* theory because it looks at the form of the blade, works well for airplane wings and sails. It works less well for a propeller because the propeller blade moves in two directions at once: it rotates through a circle while advancing forward. As a result, the flow of water around the boat propeller blades actually resembles a vortex, and another theory, the *vortex theory*, is needed to explain this phenomenon.

No matter how the blades do it, propellers still develop thrust, by sucking in water at one velocity and discharging it astern *at a higher velocity*. The energy imparted to the water returns to the boat via the propeller and shaft, thus moving the boat. Note here that this *momentum theory* looks more at the physics of the weight and velocity of water than at the propeller as an object. What makes life uncomfortable for the naval architect is that all three of these theories influence the propeller he is trying to design.

When specifying the engine, reduction gear and propeller for a given boat, the naval architect must first determine the theoretical horsepower needed to move the boat, then establish the brake horsepower that will actually supply the power needed at the propeller, and finally choose the propeller that will transmit the needed horsepower to the water. The horsepower theoretically needed depends on the displacement and speed of the boat; most designers work toward the theoretical maximum economical speed, the so-called *hull speed*, of a given boat. First, the designer must correctly estimate how much resistance your boat's hull will create. Obviously, the friction of water flowing past the hull plus the water displaced by the moving hull resists the thrust from the propeller. As

FIGURE 3-2
Propeller pitch

Pitch is a function of the diameter of the blades and the angle at which they are pitched. An 18"×15" prop, for example, has a diameter of 18 inches tip to tip, and the forward travel of the prop is 15 inches through the water in one complete revolution. If the blades' angle of orientation were increased, however, a smaller diameter blade could make the same headway through the water. The "pitch" of the two props would be identical.

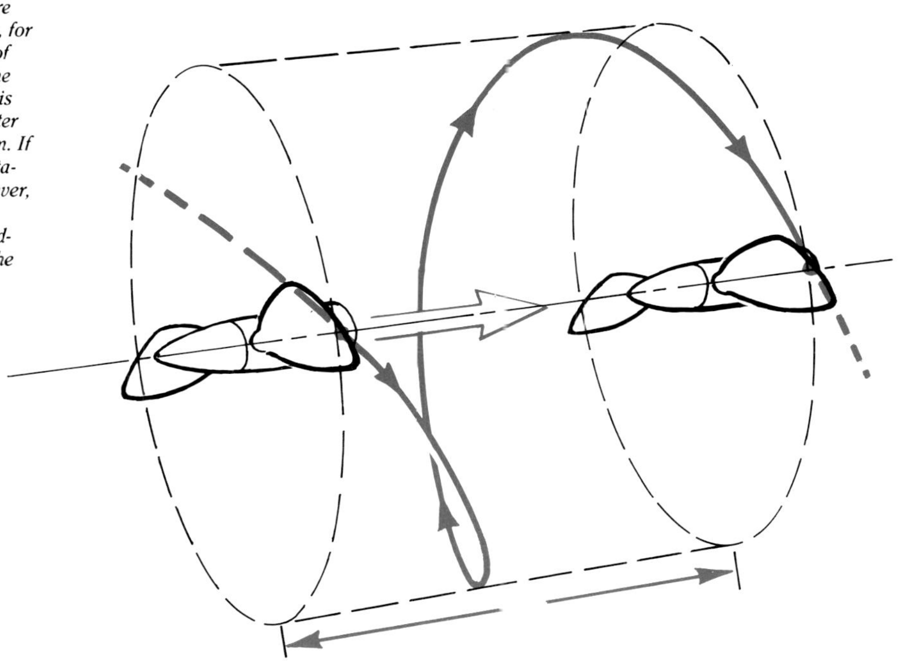

a general rule the resistance (R) of an average hull will be 40 pounds per short ton; for fat, beamy hulls, R is 45 pounds per short ton, and it is 35 pounds per short ton for fine hulls.

Once the resistance factor has been chosen, the maximum economical speed can be worked out: that is, the speed at which the bow and stern are each supported by wave crests that have a single trough between them. The boat can't exceed this velocity, because it would outrun its own sternwave. The stern would then fall into the trough, and the boat would spend its power trying to climb its own bow wave. The horror stories common among square-rigger crews—about ships that dove straight for the bottom when the crew couldn't reef sail fast enough in a sudden storm—have their factual foundation in this natural law.

The nineteenth-century hydrodynamicist David W. Taylor established that a wave system advances at a speed in knots of 1.34 times the square root of the distance between crests. The factor of 1.34 relates the speed of a wave system to its length and is called the *speed length* ratio (S/L). Since a boat creates a wave system that advances in relation to the speed and length of the boat, the theoretical maximum economical speed for a displacement hull is stated S/L × LWL = knots, where LWL is the boat's load waterline. Thus, the maximum economical speed for a boat with a 25-foot load waterline would be 6.7 knots; since knots plus 15 percent equals miles per hour, 7.7 mph is its maximum economical speed. This speed is commonly called the *hull speed* of the boat.

This formula works well enough for average boats—but the formula has been applied too dogmatically to all boats. In practice fat, heavy boats may have an S/L of 1.1 or 1.2, and fine hulls may have an S/L of 1.4 or 1.5. When specifying the propulsion system the designer must choose an S/L figure that makes sense for your particular boat. That choice is another of those intuitive elements that makes naval architecture as much an art as it is a science.

With resistance (R) and maximum economical velocity (V) established, the designer calculates what is called effective horsepower (EHP) by means of the following formula:

$$EHP = R \times V \times .003$$

Where R = the resistance factor × the number of tons and

$$V = S/L \times \sqrt{LWL}$$

For example, a certain average boat has a 30-foot waterline and weighs 16,000 pounds.

$$R = 40 \times 8 \text{ tons} = 320$$

$$V = 1.34 \times \sqrt{30}$$
$$= 7.3 \text{ knots } (8.4 \text{ mph})$$

$$320 \times 7.3 \times .003 = 7 \text{ EHP.}$$

Effective horsepower is the theoretical amount of energy, measured in horsepower, needed to move so much weight so fast against a certain resistance. Unfortunately, not all the power generated by the engine can be used to propel the boat. A propeller is not an efficient energy-transmitting device; only about one-third to one-half the energy put into the propeller is converted into thrust. The rest is lost to friction and wake formation. The shaft horsepower (SHP) delivered to the propeller must be roughly double the EHP, if the boat is actually to move. The boat in the example needs 14 SHP if the propeller is 50 percent efficient, and about 20 hp if the propeller is only 35 percent efficient. Even more power is wasted in getting from the engine to the propeller—the marine transmission and reduction gear consumes some power, as do the stuffing box and cutless bearing (and strut, if used). Therefore the required SHP must be increased yet more—by about 15 percent—to establish the brake horsepower (BHP) the engine must deliver to put a 7 EHP boat in motion. In the above example, BHP becomes 16.5 at 50 percent propeller efficiency, but since no one wants to run an engine at maximum output all the time, the BHP is increased by another 15 percent. That way, the engine can operate at about 85 percent of full power. In the end, then, the boat needs an engine of 19 BHP.

If you performed such a calculation on stock boats, you'd find that many are unnecessarily overpowered. Some latitude —up to about 20 percent—makes sense, for the oversize engine will compensate for a fouled bottom or for a barnacled prop, but the excess represented by a 40-hp diesel in a boat needing only 15 or 20 hp cannot be justified logically.

Besides wasting space and money, an oversize engine complicates the relationship of boat, engine and propeller. Suppose that the boat in the above example needs 19 BHP, and the owner wants gasoline power. The Universal Stevedore—rated at 20 hp—would seem right, but the margin of excess is so slight that the buyer chooses the 30-hp Universal Atomic Four instead. He proposes to run it at reduced speed, say around 2,500 rpm, at the point where it only develops 20 hp. The designer must choose a propeller that suits this reduced rpm and the engine must be kept down to that rpm. If a propeller intended for a maximum engine speed of 2,500 rpm (whatever the gear reduction ratio) is run faster, blade tip speed may go above the commonly accepted limit of 8,100 feet per minute and the pitch of the blades may begin to hinder overall performance. The propeller may suck in air from the surface (*ventilate*) or it may create low-pressure areas and vapor bubbles in the water flowing around the blades (*cavitate*). Ventilation leaves air bubbles and cavitation leaves bubbles of water vapor but the effect is the same: the propeller has insufficient water to work in and develops little thrust. Also, as the bubbles on the faces of the blades implode from the surrounding water pressure, the force of the implosion can knock a microscopic chunk of metal off the blade. Several hours of cavitation can destroy an aluminum propeller and so roughen a bronze one that its efficiency falls off drastically. The proper relationship between boat and propulsion system can be crucial.

Three-bladed propellers generally provide more thrust for a given diameter than two-bladed props, but also have higher drag when the boat is under sail.

PROPELLERS

Once the horsepower requirements are established the designer can begin to specify the appropriate propeller. Because a large column of water moving relatively slowly imparts more energy back to the boat than a small column moving relatively fast, the designer wants the largest diameter propeller that will fit the available space. Whether the propeller fits into an aperture in the rudder, is on a shaft offset beside the deadwood or mounts between a fin keel and a spade rudder, the tips should clear the hull or the aperture by at least 15 percent of the diameter; 20 percent is better. Also, the propeller should stand back from the deadwood by 30 percent of the diameter and clear the rudder aperture behind it by 15 percent of the diameter.

On many boats the angle of the propeller shaft limits propeller diameter. Ideally the shaft should be parallel to the water line and the propeller should be perpendicular to it. The realities of engine installation mean that the shaft ends up at an angle. Propeller thrust diminishes with the cosine of shaft angle, so 15 degrees is considered the maximum allowable deviation from the horizontal for the propeller shaft. Since the propeller on the end of the shaft must clear the hull/aperture by 15 percent of its diameter, shaft angle thus dictates propeller diameter.

As already noted, the propeller's blade tips generally should not rotate through their circle at a speed greater than 8,100 feet per minute. This means that the maximum allowable propeller diameter itself may influence the choice of engine, gear reduction ratio or both. Conversely, if the engine and reduction gear are already established they may dictate diameter because of tip speed considerations.

Once diameter is established, the designer must determine the *pitch* of the blades. Pitch takes into account the angle at which the blades mount relative to the shaft, but it is commonly defined in terms of screw-thread pitch, that is, the distance the propeller will advance in one full revolution if it advances as a wood screw does. A large diameter propeller with its blades slightly angled may travel through the same distance in one revolution as does a smaller propeller with more highly angled blades. Both would be said to have the same "pitch." Of course the propeller does not advance that way (except above about 60 mph, at which speeds the water becomes effectively solid). Rather, the water collapses under blade pressure and the propeller advances a distance less than its stated pitch. The difference between theoretical, or nominal, advance and actual advance is *slip*.

Slip relates to the momentum imparted to the column of water ejected by the propeller and thus to the thrust imparted to the boat. The propeller must slip to increase the velocity of the column of water and to create thrust. That is, slip is not a bad thing, though many people speak as if it were. Also, slip must not be confused with efficiency. Efficiency is measured as the difference between the energy delivered to the propeller and the energy imparted back to the boat. Slip is simply a matter of nominal and actual advance.

For example, suppose a certain boat makes 6 mph and the propeller turns 1,500 rpm. At 6 mph the boat advances 6,336 inches per minute; if the shaft turns 1,500 rpm the propeller must advance 4.22 inches each revolution. At 35-percent slip, the propeller must have a nominal pitch of 6.5 inches to achieve an actual advance of 4.22 inches. The difference of 2.28 inches is slip. In practice slip is not a matter of such simple arithmetic, for the boat drags an envelope of water with it; thus the water the propeller works in is not actually still water and the designer must enter a factor into the calculations to account for this *wake fraction*.

Sailboat propellers should slip about 35 to 50 percent, depending mainly on the shape and width of the blades. A propeller that does not slip enough (at sailboat speeds) will not transmit enough energy to the water; a propeller that slips too much imparts more energy to the water than the boat needs.

Propeller selection, then, involves complex relationships of hull type, boat speed, engine output, propeller speed, shaft angle and many more sophisticated elements of propeller design such as blade area, blade width and the curve of the blade faces. The relationships are too complex for a boat owner who has not studied the matter in depth. Accordingly, problems with propeller performance should be referred to a qualified naval architect, instead of to the first idler standing on the dock (see Appendix B).

Most propeller problems (other than those caused by damage) arise from a mismatch of engine/shaft speed and propeller. The engine may suit the boat, but the shaft angle or rudder aperture may not allow a large enough propeller; or in an attempt to overcome the deficiencies of an undersize propeller, the propeller may be overpitched for the shaft speed or the speed over the bottom. Faults of this sort often arise when the owner repowers but tries to use the original propeller, so that a fast gasoline engine is matched with a slow diesel propeller, or vice versa.

Even a propeller that performs well may be a source of annoying vibrations because of the peculiar fact that it does not develop uniform thrust over the whole circle through which it rotates. For example, a clockwise-turning prop, if viewed as a compass card, develops most of its thrust from 30 degrees to 150 degrees. Most authorities differ about why this phenomenon occurs. Some ascribe it to shaft angle and the fact that, with an angled shaft, the downward-moving blade takes a bigger bite than its nominal pitch while the upward-moving blade gets a lesser bite. Others believe that the offset thrust arises because the ascending blade suffers interference from the hull while the descending blade works in water that is more open. Either way the offset thrust tries to bend the shaft every time a propeller blade enters the high-thrust zone. Similarly the ascending blade pushes water against the hull and causes it to flex inward, while the descending blade pulls water away and causes the hull to flex outward. These pulsations can set up noticeable vibrations and people spend large amounts of time and money trying to stop the vibrations with new shaft bearings or engine mounts.

No propeller discussion would be complete without attention to the question of whether a propeller should be allowed to rotate—to "freewheel"—while the boat is under sail. The question is largely an argument about whether the propeller imposes more drag when rotating or when locked. Despite the many arguments about propeller science, everybody does agree that a propeller should be locked properly with a shaft lock when the engine is not in use. To lock the propeller by shifting into forward or reverse invites an accidental crank-up with the boat in gear, a possibility that underscores the wisdom of a neutral-start safety switch. The shaft should be marked so that a two-bladed propeller can be locked behind the deadwood.

Since some people insist on allowing the propeller to freewheel, sometimes to turn a generator, the issue is whether freewheeling damages the gearbox. Generally, all gearboxes except the Borg-Warners may rotate. Most of the Borg-Warners may rotate for short periods of time, and the new 1000 series Borg-Warners may rotate indefinitely. However, because the provisions of warranties vary from company to company, the question must properly be reserved for the individual manufacturers.

Folding propellers are generally conceded to have the least drag of all. However, opinions differ about their efficiency. The manufacturers feel that folding propellers designed for cruising boats are as efficient as fixed-blade propellers, but naval architects differ on the subject. Boat owners, however, generally report that folding propellers work well enough. Martec and Gori make the best.

One caveat must be entered here and it applies equally to fixed-blade or folding propellers: propellers designed to move a boat will do a decent job of it but propellers designed for and intended to suit racing rules probably will not. This is not to disparage the racing people, but simply to

Folding propellers reduce drag to only one-fifth that of a fixed propeller. The Gori folding propeller in varying positions.

note that minimum drag is more important to them than the most efficient propulsion under power.

ENGINES

However well the propeller performs, something must turn it and that means a liquid-fueled, internal combustion engine of some sort. Agreed, somebody somewhere may run a boat on external combustion steam power or on liquified petroleum gas (LPG) and agreed, battery-powered electric motors appear in small boats but most of the boating world motors along on gasoline or diesel power.

The proper distinction between gasoline and diesel engines is one of the most misunderstood and misrepresented elements of boating. The notion that diesels must be large and gasoline engines small is absurd, as the following consideration of engine power should show. The proper measure of engine output is torque, or twisting force, and the rate at which the torque can be applied. Horsepower figures derive from torque figures; in the metric system horsepower and torque ratings are combined in a rating in watts. Torque can be understood by analogy with a winch handle. A sheet handler can apply 25 pounds to a short winch handle while making rapid turns or can apply 50 pounds at a slower rate to a longer handle, but the amount of genoa sheet hauled in could be the same.

Volvo Penta MD5A. A compact and reliable diesel, it belies the notion that diesels must be large.

When testing any engine the manufacturer connects it to a loading device, usually a water brake, and gives it full throttle. When the engine has reached the rotating speed—the *revolutions per minute*, or rpm—that is the maximum permissible for the strength of the engine components the water brake is applied. The load imposed by the brake is increased gradually, which causes engine speed to decrease; the engine is kept loaded so that its speed falls to idle speed. Then rpm and load are plotted on a graph to produce the torque curve, torque being expressed in pound-feet, i.e., so many pounds continuously applied to a lever 1-foot long. The water brake acts like the load which resists a sheet handler's efforts to turn a winch. Most engines designed for ordinary service produce a rapid torque rise from idle to about the half-speed point, deliver steady torque on up to about two-thirds of maximum speed and fall off near the full speed point.

Once the torque figures are established horsepower numbers are derived via the following formula:

$$\text{hp} = \frac{\text{torque} \times \text{rpm}}{5252}$$

If horsepower has been specified by a horsepower curve, torque can be derived by simple substitution:

$$\text{torque} = \frac{\text{hp} \times 5252}{\text{rpm}}$$

In the United States the standards for engine ratings are established by the Society of Automotive Engineers (SAE). In Europe the standards of the Deutsche Industrie-Norm (DIN) are used. Generally DIN standards are conservative so that an engine rated 30 hp DIN will be comparable to an engine rated 35 hp SAE. Add 10 percent to a DIN standard to get the SAE rating for the same engine.

Although peak torque occurs in the middle of the rpm range, peak horsepower occurs near peak rpm because the lesser torque is applied at a more rapid rate. The fact remains though that horsepower is horsepower—a number derived from a formula—whether its source is gasoline or diesel. If different engines are run at the speeds where they develop equal horsepower they are equal at that point. Most of the nonsense about "big diesel horses" and "little gasoline ponies" arises because people compare a gasoline engine that peaks at 3,500 rpm with a diesel that peaks at 2,500 rpm when both are running at, say, 2,000 rpm. They fail to notice that at this point the diesel is three-fourths of the way up on its power curve while the gasoline engine is only halfway up on its curve.

So much for conventional nonsense about big and little gasoline and diesel horses. The proper distinctions between gasoline and diesel engines begin with the fuels. Gasoline has a heat value of about 20,000 BTU per pound and 120,000 BTU per gallon. Diesel fuel has about 19,300 BTU per pound but, at seven pounds per gallon, gives about 135,000 BTU per gallon. When used as engine fuels, gasoline and diesel fuel are mixed with air that has been compressed by a piston. The more an engine compresses its fuel/air mixture before the fuel ignites, the more heat and pressure will be released as the fuel burns. However, compressing an air-gasoline mixture too much causes the fuel to ignite prematurely from the heat generated by compression; the fire will start too soon relative to piston position. Accordingly, in a gasoline engine, compression is kept low and an electric spark is used to ignite the fuel at the optimum moment.

Rudolf Diesel, who developed the system that bears his name, had two motives: to increase efficiency by using high compression to obtain high pressure and to exploit a fuel oil that had more heat value than other hydrocarbon liquids. The fuel—modern diesel fuel—could have been atomized and mixed with air, just as gasoline is atomized in a carburetor, but to do so would have entailed an unduly complex system. Furthermore, diesel fuel would have suffered the same problem of preignition. Diesel's solution was to wait until the piston was in the optimum position in its compression stroke, force the fuel into the cylinder via mechanical action and allow heat from compression to ignite the fuel. That's how diesels got started and that's how they work 80 years later.

Perkins 4.108M, one of the most widely used and reliable medium-sized auxiliaries. Spare parts are available worldwide.

Thus the first difference between gasoline and diesel engines is that diesels compress the air they draw in much more than gasoline engines. This difference has consequences for the fuel each uses and for the method each uses to ignite the fuel. The second difference is that diesel components must be heavier and stronger than the comparable elements of a gasoline engine because diesels develop more heat and pressure during each combustion cycle. Furthermore, the weight and mass of diesel components, plus the diesel combustion process, reduce reciprocating/rotating speeds so diesels operate at lower rpm. All the other differences between gasoline and diesel engines will be seen to follow from these two differences.

Because they use spark ignition, gasoline engines must have a battery, ignition coil, distributor, spark plugs and interconnecting wiring, and all these components are susceptible to corrosion and to short-circuiting induced by water. The battery must be cared for since a dead battery means a dead engine. In addition, a gasoline engine must have a carburetor to mix air and fuel, and the innards of the carburetor are susceptible to corrosion from water

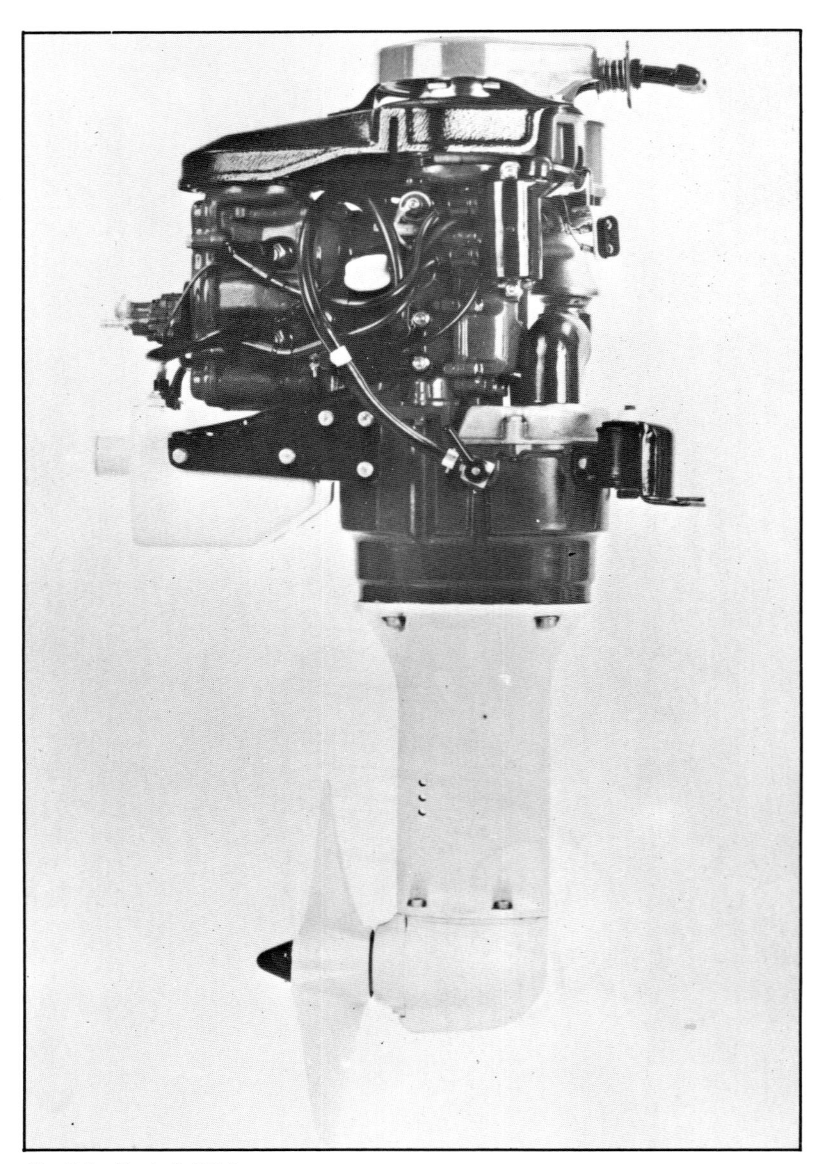

The Volvo Penta Sail Drive unit is easily installed in modern, shallow-hulled yachts: only one hole need be cut.

in the fuel and clogging from rust. Finally, gasoline vapors from poor fuel-system connections—and sometimes from fueling—can ignite explosively at the slightest spark; accordingly, all marine-quality electrical components have spark suppression and the carburetor has a flame arrester to prevent the ignition from backfiring.

Diesels need no electrical system except for cranking and for *glow-plug* starting assistance. If kept in good tune—which means proper fuel injection timing and minimal carbon deposits—diesels under 15 hp can be readily hand-cranked. In practice, the diesel's reputation for reliability means that it gets neglected even more than a gasoline engine, so boats with diesels of only 10 hp will often have battery capacity of up to 100 ampere-hours just for cranking. Most diesels above about 15 hp are electrically cranked and equipped with high-resistance wire elements, called glow plugs, that protrude into the combustion space. These devices get red hot when energized by the battery, helping ignite the fuel when the engine is cold. Glow plugs require more current than a dozen gasoline ignition systems, so in the end diesels enjoy no exemption from electrical problems. However, diesels will run when soaking wet and the fuel, while smelly, is not dangerously volatile or easily ignited.

Diesel fuel can, on the other hand, be contaminated by water, causing rust in the injection pump and injectors or mechanical damage due to water displacement of lubrication from the fuel. Diesel fuel can also harbor colonies of bacteria that form a slimy mess, clogging the whole system. Thus, neither a gasoline nor a diesel system enjoys an absolute advantage over the other. If properly maintained both systems will enjoy equal longevity.

Diesels are generally heavier, by 50 to 100 percent, for the same output, and cost roughly twice as much as comparable gasoline engines. However, because they get more out of their fuel, they travel about 25 percent farther on the same amount of fuel.

Gasoline or diesel, an engine requires maintenance, especially regular oil and filter changes. Combustion by-products get into the crankcase where they form acids that etch away metal from bearing surfaces while the engine sits idle. Most engine wear comes from this downtime corrosion. The only corrective for it is regular use of the engine and/or frequent oil changes. Though diesels form less acid, they have more trouble with fuel dilution of lubricating oil, and either condition is exacerbated if the engine runs cold. Make sure you use a proper thermostat and allow the engine to run long enough to reach operating temperature each time it is used, in order to burn off acid deposits.

The BMW D-50 is a highly sophisticated, lightweight diesel.

Both engines require periodic adjustment of valve-train clearances, for loss of clearance reduces combustion quality causing carbon deposits which lead to hard starting. Too little clearance also leads to burned valves which creates dead cylinders, increasing oil contamination from faulty combustion. Gasoline engines, of course, need tune-ups—periodic replacement of ignition system parts and ignition timing adjustment. Diesels also need tune-ups: Besides valve adjustment, the quantity of fuel delivered by the injection pump and the timing of fuel injection should be periodically checked and brought back to original specifications.

The importance of regular maintenance suggests the importance of finding replacement parts and qualified mechanics. Generally, the larger the organization or the longer it has been in business, the better the network of dealers. For example, Volvo Penta is a large organization with service centers all over the world; Universal Motors-Medalist (Atomic) is a small organization, but it has been serving sailors for over 40 years and its service network is also international. However, this does not mean that every engine must be backed by a global service system; if the engine is well served in the area where most cruising is done, that should be good enough. Bukh, Sabb, Farymann Diesel, Renault, Watermota and Sabre all have excellent service organizations.

The conventional inboard installation consisting of an engine, gearbox and shaft is a sensible one for most boats and a generation ago would have been virtually the only system. Nowadays, lighter boats, the growth of trailer boating and the popularity of fin-keel boats have enabled outboard motors and a relatively new system known as *saildrive* to provide alternatives to conventional inboard systems.

Outboards are two-cycle engines (except for the Honda gasoline outboards and the Carniti diesel outboards) and, to jump over a lot of semi-technical material about the difference between two- and four-cycle systems, the relevant distinction is that in two-cycle engines, the lubricating oil is mixed with the fuel. For optimum service a two-cycle oil approved by the Boating

Industry Association (BIA) or the newly formed National Marine Manufacturers Association (NMMA) must be used.

In modern outboards, the ratio of fuel to oil is 50 to 1, i.e., 1 pint of oil for 6 gallons of fuel. Years ago, before the maturity of outboard metallurgy and modern lubricants, the ratio was as low as 12:1, a proportion that caused outboards to foul their spark plugs or leave trails of blue smoke. To sailing folk who felt that any engine was beneath their notice the outboard was an object of special contempt.

All that has changed. Superior engineering, especially loop-charging, plus less oil in the fuel, solid-state ignition systems (pioneered by the outboard manufacturers) and surface-gap spark plugs have made the outboard about the most simple and reliable form of auxiliary power. Nowadays, the majority of trailerable sailboats use outboard power. The noise is beyond the transom and because the engines are superbly balanced, they produce little vibration. Their propellers work in relatively open water, so they are highly efficient. Because they typically run off portable 6-gallon tanks, they obviate the problems of onboard fuel tanks, allowing the tank to be taken ashore to a service station. Finally, because they can be steered directly, outboards give enhanced maneuverability.

Of course nothing is perfect and outboards do bring problems, the first of which is mounting. Ideally, the outboard mounts on a vertical transom. Canted or reverse transoms may require special brackets. Also, the outboard mounts low, so boats with high transoms may require remote controls (because the outboard control tiller has no room to swing). Since the outboard mounts well aft, its power head often gets dunked by a following sea, though a brief dunking won't put enough water under the cover to drown the engine. Also, the lower unit will often be hoisted clear of the water as the boat pitches and the engine will overrev noisily as it comes out of the water and transmit a jolt to the boat as it reenters. This amounts to saying no more than that outboards are not ideal for all conditions but, then, neither is

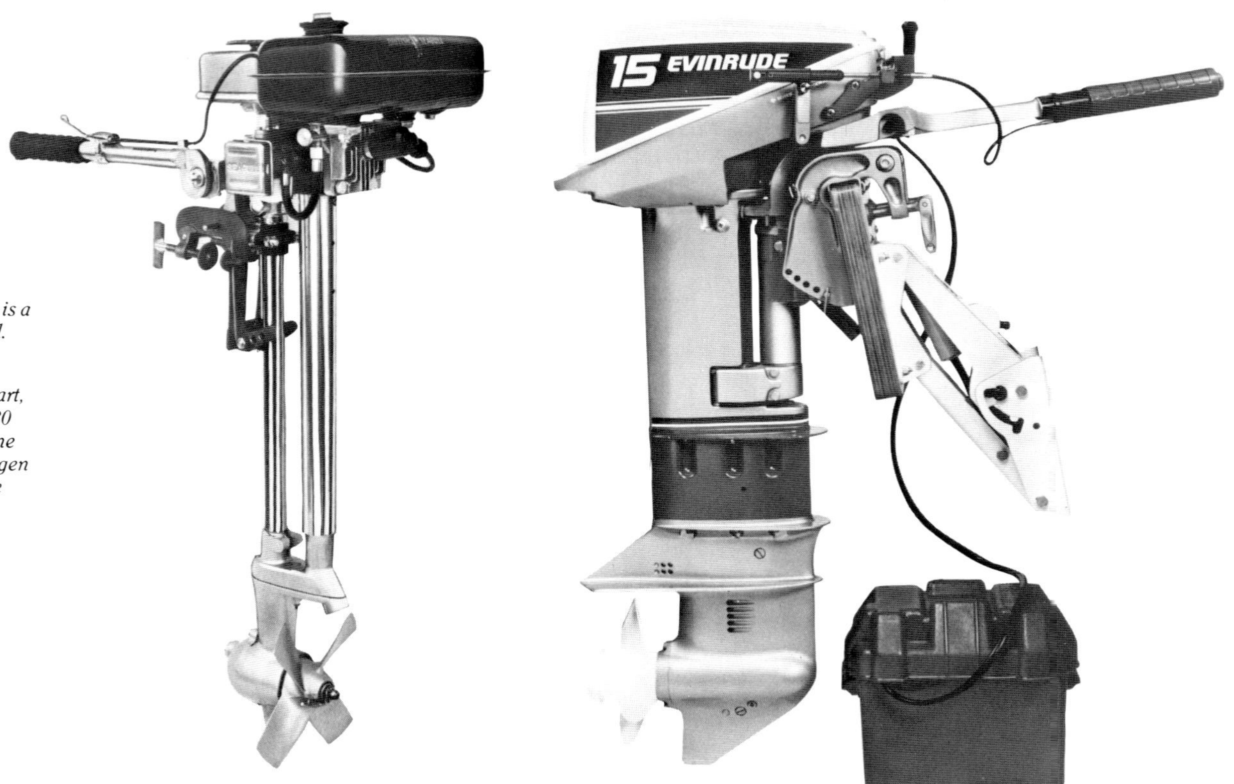

The old reliable Seagull is a simple, rugged outboard.

OMC/Evinrude 15-hp outboard with electric start, suitable for boats up to 30 feet. Note the OMC engine mount, featuring a nitrogen cylinder to help raise the engine.

anything else. Volvo Penta, Seagull, OMC, Suzuki and Honda make the finest ones.

A near ideal system—because of its simplicity, efficiency and low drag—is a saildrive unit, but only fin-keel, swing-keel or centerboard boats can use them. A saildrive consists of an engine inside the hull that drives through an outboard lower unit on the outside of the hull. Outboard Marine Corporation (OMC), which pioneered the system, uses a 15 hp outboard power head; Volvo Penta units use a 10-hp, four-cycle gasoline power head, or a series of diesels of up to 35 hp. Bukh, a Danish diesel firm well known in Europe, has just entered the American market with 12- and 43-hp diesel units. All three companies supply saildrives with a folding propeller that has very low drag. The actual cost can be considerably less than a traditional engine and shaft because of the ease of installation and the simplicity of mechanical hookups.

The limitation of the saildrive, unfortunately, is that it only fits boats that have unobstructed space between the keel and rudder. However, this type of hull continually grows in popularity, partly because the saildrive is available to power it.

Whatever the engine, it must be held firmly in place, cooled, controlled and monitored. Transom-mounted outboards present the fewest problems, although transom angle can demand ingenuity in the mounting. Assorted adjustable brackets are available, though, so scour the chandleries before resorting to some jury-rigged system of wedges to keep the outboard perpendicular to the water.

Saildrives use a kind of bedplate that bolts to the hull. The engine above and the drive below mount in this bedplate via some sort of resilient material that minimizes vibrations. Inboard engines should likewise have resilient mounts; first, to reduce vibration and second, to assure that the hull is able to work and flex without fighting the rigidity of the engine. Use of resilient mounts though, is not an excuse for sloppy alignment of engine and shaft.

For cooling, most outboards draw in seawater through ports in the lower unit

The OMC Saildrive system permits one-hole installation, and saves space in fin-keeled yachts.

housing and discharge it from under the engine or through the propeller hub. They are thus *raw water* cooled. Raw water cooling was the standard for years. However, in salt water, it led to corrosion of cast-iron engine blocks and in fresh water it led to accumulations of sand and silt in cooling systems. Although many boats still happily use raw water cooling, fresh water cooling is to be preferred. In a fresh-water-cooled system (abbreviated as FWC in advertisements), engine coolant circulates through a heat exchanger that is cooled by seawater; corrosion and deposits will occur only in the heat exchanger, which can be disassembled for periodic cleaning. Sen-Dure Products makes one of the best.

The cooling water enters the boat via a through-hull fitting—that has, of course, a proper seacock on it. Bronze is the standard material for through-hulls but in recent years it has become very expensive. As a result, various plastic through-hulls have come into use. The plastic through-hulls are acceptable, provided they are not located where they can be exposed to underwater hazards. A rock or piece of coral can cut the outer flange right off a plastic through-hull. This rule applies to all through-hulls for whatever purpose. They should be located behind keels, certainly away from the area just beneath the water line.

The engine exhaust pipe gets hot, presenting the hazard of a fire or a burn, so cooling water is usually dumped into the exhaust pipe to cool it. The water also muffles sound. It must not, however, run back toward the engine, nor must seawater run up the exhaust pipe to the engine. Accordingly, the exhaust system must have a *riser*—an element that takes the exhaust pipe to a level above the water line. An exhaust can also be run dry, that is, with shrouding or insulation around the exhaust pipe and no cooling provided. Dry exhausts were common in the old days but have no more place aboard a modern boat than manila halyards.

Vetus waterblocks prevent seawater from backing through the exhaust system.

The engine should have instruments to monitor what it is doing and raucous alarms to declare when something is wrong. The three most important instruments monitor oil pressure, coolant temperature and generator/alternator output. If the instruments are carefully monitored, the alarms need never go off, but they should be there in case the sublime sea captures the attention of the helm tender. These should be supplied with the engine. If not, Borg-Warner and Vetus make good ones.

To throttle up and down and to shift gears, the boat should have marine-quality housed cables. The choke can manage with a wire in a spiral-wound housing but the throttle and gearshift must work positively against some load and so must be of high quality. Don't use control cables meant for trucks or agricultural equipment unless they are approved for marine use, the marine cable being especially sealed against moisture. Even marine cables do wear out, so replace a binding cable at once. Generally, the cable begins to bind when the wire cable inside (which constitutes a long spiral) begins to wear away the lining through which it moves. The dust from the lining gets packed by the auger action of the spiral. Thus, once a cable begins to bind, it is on its way to freezing completely. So, replace it at the first sign of rough movement or incomplete engagement.

MARINE TRANSMISSIONS

The propeller drives the boat and the engine drives the propeller, but the marine transmission provides the necessary link between the two. The gearbox must allow the engine to run without turning the propeller, provide for forward and reverse propulsion, and reduce engine speed to a suitable propeller speed. To do these things, the gearbox uses two primary elements: a clutch and a gear system.

A clutch consists of one "driving" piece, connected to the engine, and a second piece, connected to the shaft, that is driven by the first piece. The two pieces are brought into contact by mechanical action or hydraulic (oil) pressure. In a *dog clutch,* the driving part has teeth that protrude to engage corresponding teeth in the driven part. Dogs are usually designed to lock tightly under load, so the system cannot be shifted from forward to reverse unless the engine is throttled down and it cannot be forced into engagement when the engine is running above fast idle. Dog clutches are used in outboards and saildrives; their virtues are simplicity, small size and low friction.

Cone clutches replicate the action of one paper cup stuck inside another. The tapered faces of the cones, plus the fact that they run in a bath of oil, means that engagement is smooth and can occur safely even at relatively high engine speeds. The deficiency of a cone system is that it must be fairly large to provide sufficient friction surface and heat dissipation. Cone systems are used with many of the Volvo Penta engines.

Multiple-disc clutches consist of one set of discs driven by the engine and a similar set that drives the propeller shaft. The discs are arranged in alternating order —engine-driven, shaft-driving, etc. Mechanical action or oil pressure forces the discs together. The large friction-surface area provided by several discs gives smooth engagement and allows the clutch to be "bumped" for slow, close-quarter maneuvering. Hurth gearboxes use multi-disc clutches that are mechanically engaged. Paragon gearboxes may be mechanically or hydraulically engaged. Borg-Warner gears are hydraulically engaged. The earlier Borg-Warners—the 71 and 72 series—depended on an oil pump turned by the engine for lubrication and, thus, could be damaged if allowed to freewheel for long periods of time. The new Borg-Warner 1000 series gearbox, designed for smaller engines, is not so limited and may be allowed to freewheel.

The gearbox also has gears for gear reduction and to reverse the rotation of the propeller shaft. Sometimes the arrangement of the gears allows the propeller shaft to be lower than the center of the engine crankshaft, which in turn allows the engine itself to mount higher and reduces the problem of finding room for the flywheel housing.

The gears themselves will be spur gears, bevel gears or planetary gears cut as spur gears. Spur gear teeth are cut parallel to the axis of rotation, though spiral teeth, which lie on a spiral path from one face of the gear to the other, are sometimes used to increase the amount of tooth contact.

Bevel gears have teeth cut at an angle to the axis of rotation, so they are used to "bend" power around a corner. For example, in an outboard, the engine's power goes straight down from the power head, then makes a right-angle turn onto the propeller shaft. On a "vee drive," too, power comes out of the engine in one direction and goes back to the propeller in the opposite direction and at a different angle. Bevel gears enable the power to make these turns in the most efficient way possible.

The Newage marine transmission can take left- or right-handed propellers. It includes a separate, oil-operated multi-disc clutch.

A planetary gear system is an efficient way of getting forward, reverse and neutral into a small fore-and-aft space. The system consists of a central sun gear that has several—usually three—smaller planetary gears on its perimeter, the planetary gears being mounted in a planet carrier and surrounded by the ring gear that also engages the planetary gears. Power can be applied to and taken off any one of these three elements. Generally, in forward, the whole system is locked together so that sun gear, planet carrier and ring gear rotate as a single unit, with engine power applied to the sun and shaft power taken from the planet carrier. For reverse, the ring gear is held stationary and the planet carrier is unlocked; power goes from the sun to the planetary gears and thence to the planet carrier, but with the planet carrier rotating in the opposite direction to the sun. If the planet carrier provides input to a reduction gear, two sets of planetaries may be used to keep rotation at the reduction gear, in forward, the same as engine rotation. The ring gear is typically locked by a band that surrounds it; a multi-disc clutch locks the whole unit together.

FIGURE 3-3
Three gear systems

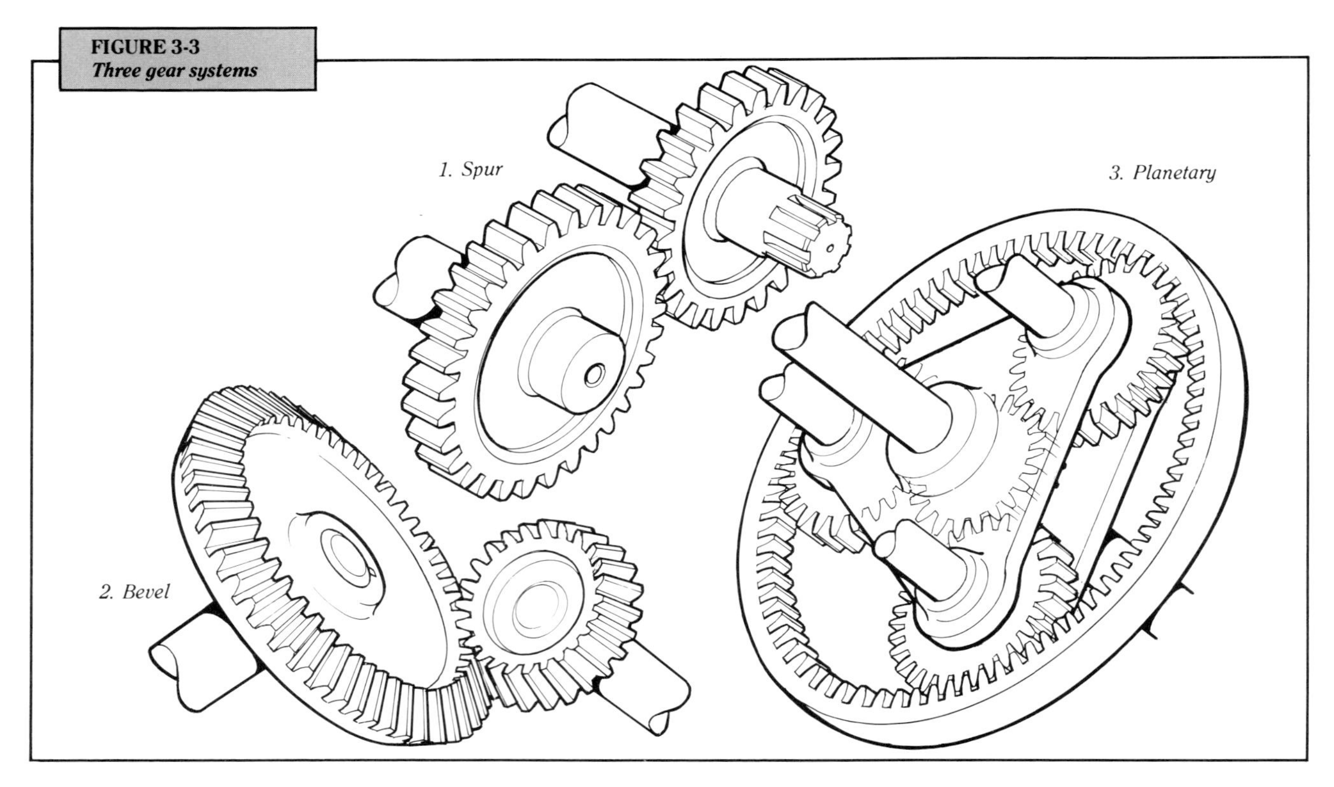

Gearboxes require lubrication and little else, though disc-clutch gearboxes may require oil cooling. Loss of lubrication will cause cones and discs to grind themselves to powder. Loss of cooling (where called for) will cause the friction surfaces of the discs to burn up.

The worst enemy of the gearbox is hasty shifting from forward to reverse at relatively high engine speeds, such as when docking against adverse currents or winds. The sudden reversals cause cones and discs to slip and wear their faces. The wear increases clearances so that more slippage occurs during normal shifting. Even a gearbox that is never abused should have the clearances between its cones or discs checked after several years of service.

SHAFTS

Power from the engine and gearbox gets to the propeller via an ordinary-looking shaft with a flange fitting on the engine end and a taper and thread on the propeller end. Three requirements affect the shaft: it must be big enough for the job, it must line up with the engine and it must pass through a hole in the hull.

The first of these is rarely a problem. However, if a shaft develops a bend in normal service, its size relative to the power it transmits should be evaluated and a different shaft should be chosen to replace it.

The second problem is more serious. The centerline of the shaft should act like an extension of the centerline of the driving shaft from the engine/gearbox. If the centers of the driving shaft and the propeller shaft do not coincide, the shaft will work in a constant bend that puts excessive strains on the shaft log (and strut, if used). If the centers meet but the propeller shaft is at an angle to the driving shaft, the propeller shaft will go through a bending cycle with every revolution. Either condition will fatigue a shaft, as well as ream out the stuffing box and cutless bearing. A fractured shaft or a leaky boat may result.

A boat fresh from the factory has assorted stresses in the hull that were formed by the manner in which the hull was supported during construction, storage and transportation. Once in the water and evenly supported all around, the hull will assume a final shape with its assorted stresses at peace with each other. As this happens, the water line, presumably straight, could become a curve with a chord of as much as—or more than—¼ inch. The curve would not be detectable by the eye but could upset shaft alignment enough to produce annoying vibrations or even to bend the shaft.

This means that a new boat or a boat coming out of storage should not have its engine and propeller shaft flanges bolted together until the boat has been afloat at least 24 hours; 48 hours would be better for a new boat or an old boat which has been laid up for a long time. Also, it means that when a boat comes out for winter storage, the flanges should be unbolted.

In practice, absolutely perfect alignment is difficult to achieve and small shafts that transmit low horsepower at relatively low rotation speeds can tolerate some misalignment. However, to minimize vibration, shaft fatigue and wear to stuffing box and bearing, flexible or resilient couplings can be installed between the two flanges. These couplings are worthwhile refinements, but they are not substitutes for correct alignment.

The shaft log guides the shaft through the hole in the hull and restores the watertight integrity of the hull. Accordingly, it must be properly caulked. The shaft log contains a cutless bearing (nobody seems to know why it is called "cutless"), which is a heavy-walled rubber bushing with spiral grooves that admit water for lubrication and cooling. In recent years, models made of plastic have appeared on commercial fishing boats; these plastic bearings, being of denser material, presumably wear longer and keep the shaft more exactly in line. However, they haven't yet become common in sailboats.

The stuffing box is at the inboard end of the shaft log where the shaft enters. It contains the seal that keeps water out. The traditional seal is a jute fiber impregnated with pitch, or oakum; the fiber is wound around the shaft and held (stuffed) into the sealing race by a threaded collar. When wound and stuffed in the perfect way, the stuffing box will admit one drop of water about every five seconds while the shaft is turning, and no water when the shaft is not turning. Few ever achieve this level of perfection. Most stuffing boxes drip all the time, even if slowly. This means you'll need a good bilge pump, applied as needed (see page 154).

The Vetus flexible coupling reduces vibration and permits slight errors in engine-shaft alignment.

The modern stuffing box seals with a rubber or neoprene O-ring that surrounds the shaft. It works no better than the traditional oakum and when it wears out, replacement requires that the shaft flange be uncoupled and removed; in this matter, the old way is probably still best. Buck-Algonquin and Simpson-Lawrence make the best modern stuffing boxes.

As noted earlier, the propeller can't always be allowed to freewheel, and the habit of locking the shaft by engaging the gearbox is not safe. So use a proper shaft lock. This means a disc bolted onto the shaft and locked by a caliper, much like an automotive disc brake. Local yards can usually rig one.

The Scatra universal coupling is one of the most sophisticated flexible couplings. It allows the engine and propeller shafts to mount at different angles.

ELECTRICALS

Some sailboats get by without electrical systems. They use hand-cranked diesels, kerosene running lights and the like. Others have elaborate 12-volt and 32-volt systems for engines and small appliances, plus 110-volt and 220-volt generators or dockside power systems. Electrical systems are straightforward set-ups that are commonly compared to water systems: one wire goes from a power source (battery, generator, dockside receptacle) to a load (engine starter, light bulb, etc.), passes through the load and returns to the source. On the way, the wires will be interrupted by switches, circuit breakers, terminal blocks, junction boxes and other devices. The complete path, from power source to load and back to source is a *circuit.* If electric power, or current, is thought of as water, the wires as pipes and the switches as valves, the analogy with water is clear enough.

Electricity, of course, differs significantly from water in two ways. First, high voltage—which usually means 110-volts but may mean less—can kill people. Electricity tolerates no foolishness. Second, defective electrical systems can cause corrosion that destroys metal fittings, such as through-hull mountings and shaft logs, or eats holes through steel and aluminum boats.

Because of the hazards of faulty systems, electrical systems have received much attention from the Coast Guard and from the American Boat and Yacht Council (ABYC). The Coast Guard, with official responsibility for boating safety, imposes a number of mandatory standards on electrical systems. The ABYC, a voluntary association of boat and equipment manufacturers, endorses the mandatory Coast Guard standards and, in addition, sets many more recommended standards of quality and performance. Whether a boat goes off a trailer once a week or spends months offshore, its electrical system should be no less than that specified by the CG and ABYC. A system that meets the standards, if maintained in that condition, will never sink a boat. The full standards are too long to be given here. They are available from the American Boat and Yacht Council, P.O. Box 806, Amityville, New York 11701. The cost for the electrical section of the complete standards will be about $10.00.

No other country has quite the same conjunction of official and quasi-official standards for safety, but most countries do have some sort of stipulations by which a pleasure boat can be evaluated. Perhaps the best known are the ratings issued by Lloyd's Register of Shipping, 17 Fenchurch St., London, EC3, U.K. Lloyd's ratings are made so that the insurance company can decide upon a premium for a certain vessel—or decline to insure it at all. While the Lloyd's standards are not mandatory, they do provide a measure of the quality of a boat and its gear. The rating may be applied during construction or by a survey, and the boat must be surveyed periodically by Lloyd's agents to retain its rating.

Without going into the complete set of standards, some basic caveats about electrical systems can be made. First, the primary enemy of electrical systems is that same, basic component so necessary to boating: water, and especially salt water. Water causes corrosion of the dozens of loop terminals on the ends of wires and the screw terminals to which they attach. Corrosion insinuates itself between the two contact surfaces, gradually insulating them from each other until no current can flow; the pipe gets clogged, so to speak. Faulty connections can be devilishly hard to find.

In the following example, the numbers are the progressive number of connections. Suppose current goes from the battery post (1) to a main switch (2), out of the switch (3) to a main circuit breaker (4), out of the circuit breaker (5) to a terminal block (6), then to one side of a fuse (7), out of the fuse (8) to a switch (9), out of the switch (10) to a light (11), out of the light (12) to a bus bar (13), and from the bus bar (14) back to the battery (15). If the light fails to work, the faulty connection could be at any one of these 15 connections plus the connection within the switch, the two connections inside the fuse holder, and the two within the bulb socket—20 possibilities to check on. In practice, all 20 will rarely be at fault

FIGURE 3-4
The electrical system

Schematic diagram showing electrical supply, circuits and accessories.

1. *Stern light* **2.** *Bow light* **3.** *Batteries* **4.** *Engine instrument panel* **5.** *Instrument panel* **6.** *Compass lights* **7.** *Pilot bunk, P & S* **8.** *Saloon P & S* **9.** *White 225° steaming light* **10.** *Tricolor* **11.** *Switches* **12.** *Chart table* **13.** *Log* **14.** *Depth sounder* **15.** *Radio* **16.** *Genoa deck lights*

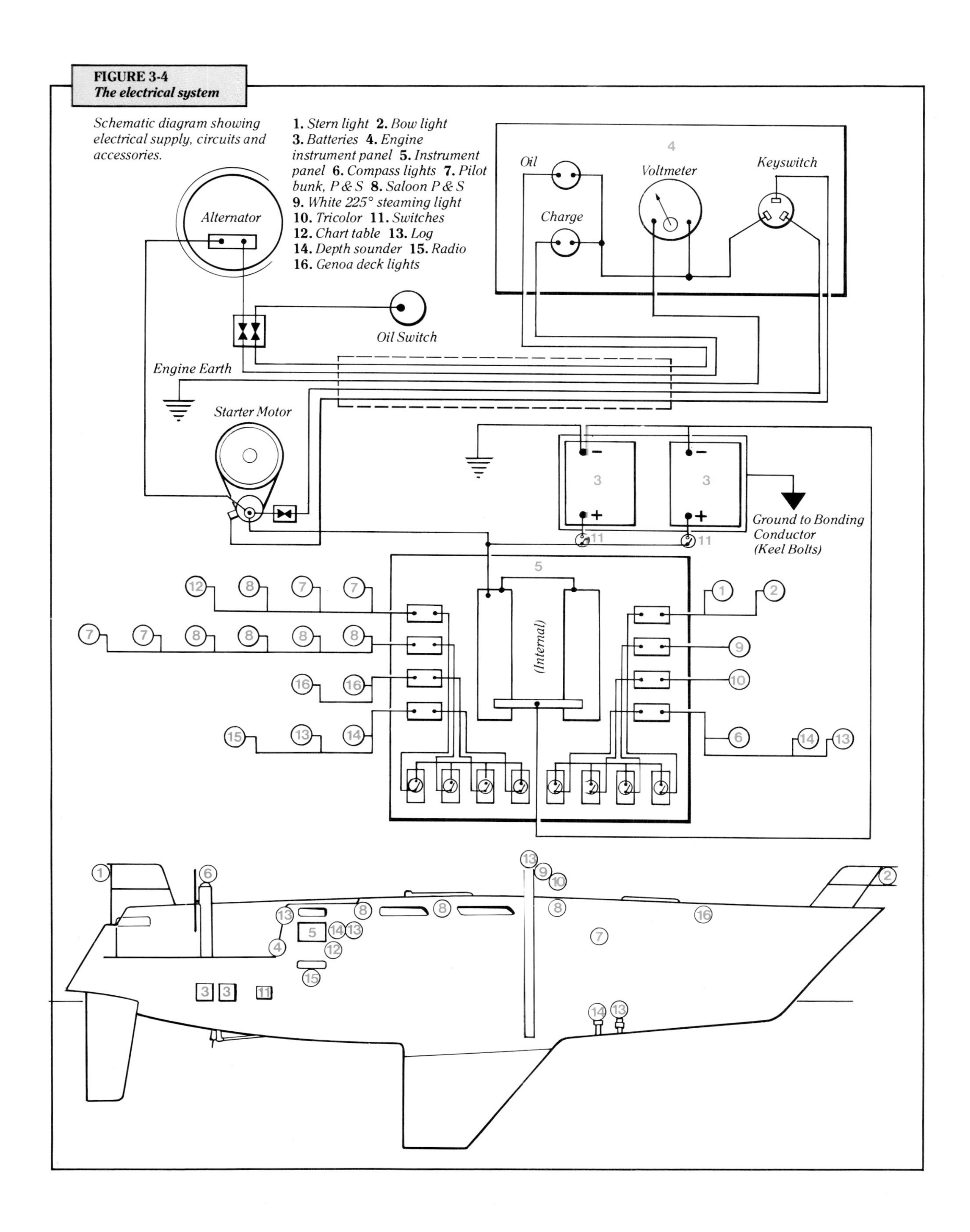

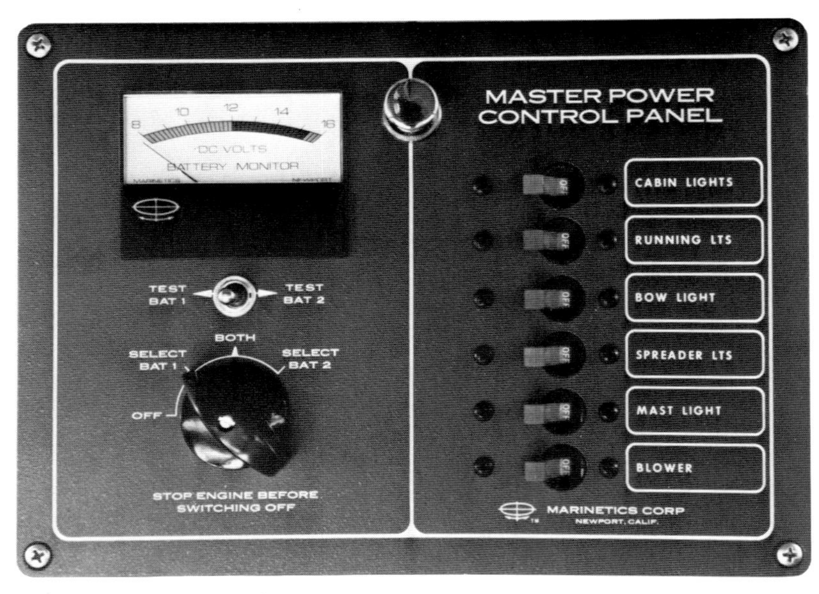

A Marinetics electrical panel with master battery switch and circuit breakers. The Marinetics line of panels is among the world's finest.

and the search can be narrowed down. For example, if one switch controls both port and starboard running lights and only the starboard light fails to go on, then everything up to the point at which the two circuits diverge is obviously working.

Still, electrical faults can be maddening and the best defense, as in warfare, is a good offense. Electrical systems deserve as much maintenance as the standing and running rigging. At least once a year, every one of those connections should be taken loose so the contact surfaces can be cleaned. If greenish or whitish deposits betray corrosion, clean things up at once. Spraying connections with water-displacing penetrating oil will protect them for a while, but such oils must be applied often, say about once per month. The silicone sprays do not, in the marine environment, seem any better than the penetrating oils and have fewer overall uses, so it's best to keep the latter aboard. Some people cover terminals with grease to seal out moisture; if following this expedient, be sure to use a noncorrosive grease like Vaseline, lithium grease or lanolin. The chandlery will have it. Although grease works well enough it may drip from horizontally or vertically mounted connections. However, it can easily be cleaned with common solvents. As an alternative, terminals can be covered with wax dripped from a candle; but the candle wax will be harder to clean off when you want to service the connection.

Batteries deserve—and demand—a lot more care than they get. Most replacement batteries are needed because the boat owner was lazy, not because the battery was deficient. Battery problems typically begin when the terminals corrode until they can't deliver enough power to crank the engine. Sometimes, too, the terminals and the top of the battery may be left damp, allowing current to drain via the circuit provided through the surface moisture. A third trouble spot is the terminals on the engine generator/alternator. If they are corroded, the battery will not get sufficient recharging. Whatever the cause, the boat owner finds the battery chronically unable to crank the engine and immediately resorts to jump-starting with a fully charged battery. The dead battery cannot accept the rapid charge from the charged battery and suffers heat distortion of its plates; eventually, after multiple discharge and rapid recharge cycles, the battery will be ruined.

The other response to a chronically dead battery is a cheap trickle charger. A trickle charger does not turn itself off after the battery is fully charged so it continues to charge until it boils the water out of the battery, causing the plates to swell and warp, which also ruins the battery. If battery maintenance proves a continual

Surrette marine batteries are much more heavily constructed (and expensive) than auto batteries.

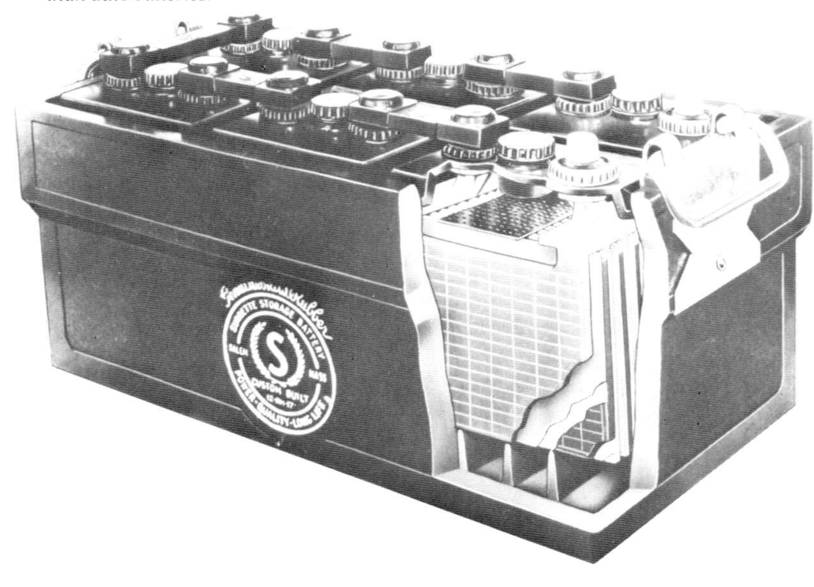

problem, the solution is a proper marine AC/DC converter that reduces the battery-charging rate as the battery approaches full charge and which can even maintain the proper charging rate despite voltage fluctuations in the shore power system. Simpson-Lawrence and Raritan make the best.

Boat batteries suffer considerably from vibration and pounding as well as from moisture. Hence, the marine battery typically has thicker plates and heavier grids to contain its lead elements. Batteries intended for automotive service will deliver power to a boat as readily as to a car, but the more use a boat gets, the more it needs durable, marine-quality batteries.

Auxiliary Generators

The larger the boat, the more electronic gear it will have. When electrical demands exceed what the batteries and engine alternator/generator can supply, an auxiliary generator may be needed. The first stage is to install an oversize 12-volt alternator on the engine—increasing the output, for example, from 35 amps to 60 amps. This approach means that a 40-hp engine may be running just to drive a 12-volt, 60-amp alternator; this would be 360 watts (volts × amps = watts) out of 40 hp and would be hideously inefficient. A separate, diesel-powered auxiliary generator might be more desirable. Such a unit costs a fair sum and needs its own starting batteries, and probably should have its own separate fuel supply. As another alternative, a portable, gasoline-powered generator could be used; the portable units can supply both 12- and 110-volt systems and can be run for short periods of time, for example to keep a refrigerator cold. Obviously such units bring with them all the hazards of gasoline as a fuel. Honda and G&M Power Plant make very compact and efficient units.

Onboard systems must be installed with proper attention to access for maintenance, cooling systems, exhaust systems and noise insulation. Finally, the 110- or 220-volt wiring for such a unit must be absolutely above reproach (no chafe, secured cable, no leakage, circuit breakers and moisture-proof seals). Any laxity in this area can mean potential loss of the boat because of fire or corrosion, not to mention loss of life due to shock.

Some boats use wind-driven or propeller-driven generators to maintain a full battery charge. The very wealthy and *moderne* use solar cell panels. None of these systems enjoys sufficiently widespread use for competent assessment of their worth—especially off soundings—to be made. A wind-driven generator on the masthead is vulnerable to salt and water and is difficult to repair at sea; a shaft-driven generator is reasonably reliable, though the drag from the freewheeling propeller makes it a questionable choice, given the small amount of power such a unit can deliver and the hassle of installing pulleys and belts for it. Solar panels are glamorous and, like most glamorous things, are vastly overrated and overpriced. In time, as the cost decreases, solar cells will offer much more. At the moment, they are useful mainly as counters in yacht club one-upmanship. If your primary concern is to keep a battery charged,

The Honda portable generator operates on AC and DC. It is handy aboard medium-size boats.

the portable generators are probably the cheapest and most efficient solution. If the primary concern is to operate numerous electrical appliances, the onboard generator is the better choice.

Bonding

Bonding is the tying together and grounding of all metal objects aboard the boat. For example, a copper strap or an American Wire Gauge (AWG) #4 cable runs from the engine to the stuffing box, then to the rudder stock and last to a copper ground plate outside the hull. Bonding grounds electrical leakage—stray current—so that it does not cause corrosion. While bonding is not a matter of electrical installation, it fits here better than elsewhere. The ABYC electrical standards cover the subject fully.

FUEL SYSTEMS

Obviously, the engine must be supplied with fuel, which means the fuel must be stored somewhere and conducted to the engine on demand. Hence, the fuel system has much more to it than most people appreciate. As with electrical systems, the Coast Guard sets a number of mandatory standards for fuel systems; the American Boat and Yacht Council (ABYC) endorses those standards and sets additional standards that reputable boat manufacturers observe. A properly built boat, though, does not always stay that way; things are added or changed by do-it-yourself owners and by boatyard mechanics. Even new boats suffer the effects of the Monday-morning hangovers or Friday-afternoon impatience of factory workers. Accordingly, the buyer of a new or used boat should give the fuel system a thorough looking over.

Start with the filler: above decks, the filler should ideally be mounted so that water will drain away from it. Since this ideal cannot always be served in practice, the removable filler cap must have a good gasket and must be screwed down firmly after fueling. The normal quality of human luck means that a spare filler cap and the wrench to remove it should be among the spares. Below decks, the filler will usually connect to the tank via a neoprene (*not* rubber) hose. This hose should have double clamps at both ends; a metal ground strap that makes contact with the hose clamps (usually by being under them) should connect the filler fitting with the tank itself to prevent corrosion.

Auxiliary generators are really only practical aboard large yachts. They permit the use of auxiliary electrical gear and appliances. (Cross Power, Inc.)

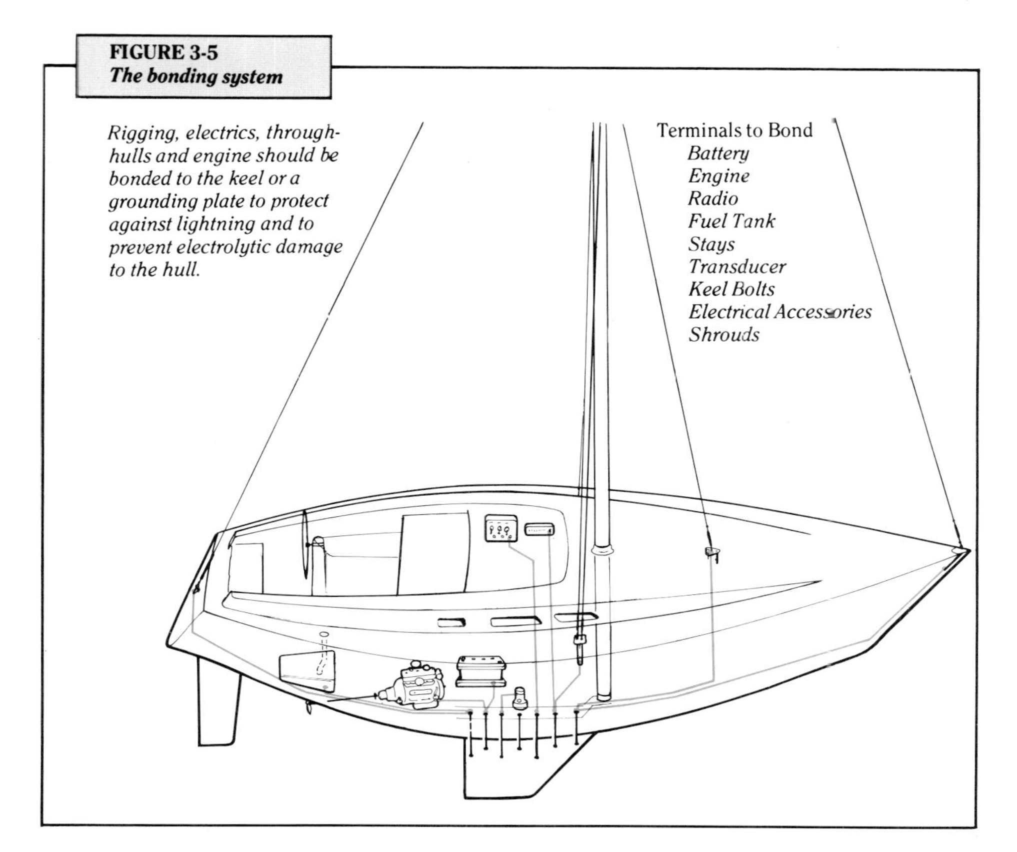

FIGURE 3-5
The bonding system

Rigging, electrics, through-hulls and engine should be bonded to the keel or a grounding plate to protect against lightning and to prevent electrolytic damage to the hull.

As the tank fills with fuel, it displaces air. To allow the air to come and go, the tank must be vented, taking care the vent does not conduct water into the tank or vapors towards any ignition sources. The vent consists of a round fitting, about 1 inch in diameter with a hole in the lower periphery that is mounted outside the hull. This fitting connects to the tank by metal tubing and hose connections; here again the hoses must be healthy and free of cracks and the connections must be well clamped.

The tanks themselves can be made of various materials—galvanized iron, black iron, steel or fiberglass—the crucial point being that the material must meet Coast Guard standards for strength and fire resistance; diesel fuel tanks, however, *must not* be galvanized, for the fuel will react with the zinc. Also, certain stainless steels must not be used because of their propensity for corrosion, so double check the tank to see what material has been used.

Where the fuel line leaves the tank, install an antisiphon valve to serve as a check valve, preventing fuel from passing unless the engine is operating and the fuel pump exerting suction on the line. The conventional wisdom—inadequate as usual—says antisiphon valves are not necessary unless the fuel tank is mounted higher than the engine. This attitude, of course, overlooks the manner in which the relationship of the fuel level to the engine can alter as the boat works through a vigorous seaway. Some people dislike antisiphon valves on the grounds that they hamper the flow of fuel; if a valve does so, it is simply too small. Antisiphon valves should be standard equipment and should be large enough for their job.

Standard fuel filters, which must be installed somewhere between tank and engine (usually between the fuel pump and the tank), provide an opportunity—too often taken—for misguided economies. In gasoline systems, the filter is often no more than a paper element, little bigger than a thumb. Diesel systems, with cartridge-element filters, are some improvement, but "some" is all. What the boat needs is an honest, serious filter and water-separater unit. Some units combine the two functions and some use separate canisters for each but, in any case, the reliability of the whole propulsion system depends on the capability of the filter/water-separater. Save money, if necessary, on the place mats, but not on keeping the fuel clean.

Fuel lines themselves, properly of seamless copper or copper-nickel alloy, should be supported every 16 inches, and should have flared fittings rather than compression, or ferrule, fittings. Flexible sections, of course, must meet Coast Guard standards. All connections must be tight and drip free; look for reddish discoloration on gasoline fittings and oiliness on diesel fittings. Faults in a gasoline system will put explosive vapors in the bilges and cannot be tolerated.

Fuel system care extends to the fuel itself. Moisture gets into tanks despite the best efforts and chemically reacts with fuel to cause corrosion. Gasoline evaporates and leaves varnish deposits. Bacteria, once introduced into diesel fuel tanks, can form colonies that show up as a sludgy slime clogging filters, injection pumps and injectors. Fuels long in storage at marinas may degrade. A number of fuel additives can be used to solve these problems and such additives should be part of the regular maintenance program. Consult your engine manufacturer for the additive best for your engine.

Chapter 4

NAVIGATION AND ELECTRONICS

When man first ventured upon the water, he didn't travel far. Not until the Renaissance did navigation become a science, allowing men to sail uncharted seas. With the introduction of the first primitive compasses a sailor could ascertain his heading with some accuracy. As time went on, the compass became more sophisticated and the rudiments of astral navigation began to develop. In the days of Bowditch and Cook in the eighteenth century, the triumvirate of instruments which allow the seagoing navigator to pinpoint his place on earth—the compass, the sextant and the chronometer—were finally perfected. Today, these basic instruments have been supplemented by an astounding array of electronic navigation and communication aids.

BASIC NAVIGATION TOOLS

The compass is without question the most important piece of navigational gear aboard any ship. If it is not adequate no amount of sophisticated electronics, ancillary equipment or horse sense will do you any good. The classic rule of thumb in selecting a compass is to decide on how much you can spend, then double it. Oddly enough, despite the advances in technology and construction, it is becoming more and more difficult to find a good compass.

An effective compass is robust and has perfect freedom of movement within the bowl. Sun, rain, sleet, salt air and bumps do not make for a peaceful atmosphere for what is a delicate instrument. Added to that, temperature variations, humidity and misplaced beer cans and batteries wreak their insidious havoc on bearings, housings, damping liquids, pivots, diaphragms and mountings.

A good compass must have a massive housing, preferably brass, totally impervious to the elements and as protective of the works as possible. A number of the newer compasses, made with composite plastic cases, are fine for coastal cruising or occasional daysailing, but sunlight and ultraviolet rays cause almost any plastic casing to discolor and eventually break down. Furthermore, even the strongest plastic has a tendency to flex, encouraging misalignment and incorrect bearings.

The best of the best—Ritchie, Sestrel, Danforth and Plath—are brass encased. Even these makers are now producing plastic-housed compasses, but if you want the best, don't settle for the plastic ones.

Other features make for better or worse performance. Gimbals can be either internal or external. The traditional sailor's compass is externally gimballed, which is fine if you keep the pivot points lightly oiled, the set screws tightened and the whole thing protected from bumps and bangs. Unfortunately, it is rather difficult to

Left: A through-bulkhead compass can be read from helm and cabin.
Right: The Sestrel "Moore" is a highly versatile instrument.

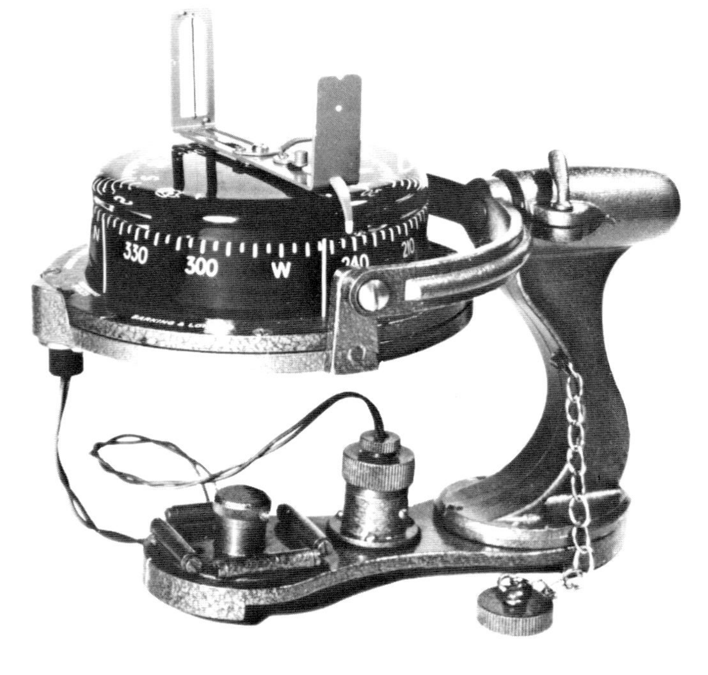

light an externally gimballed compass since any wires will probably interfere with free pitch and roll.

Internal gimbals solve most of these problems, though they only work with spherical compasses. Since the internally gimballed machine is mounted within a self-contained housing, a hood can be incorporated containing the appropriate lighting apparatus.

The spherical compass, as pioneered by Danforth-White, tends to have less error than a bowl unit, because modern techniques allow for the creation of an almost perfect sphere. The sphere is best made of glass, whose shape is less affected by the elements, but even if it is plastic it should contain a diaphragm to compensate for temperature and humidity changes. Cards can be flat, dished or raised, as long as friction is kept to a minimum and damping is effective. Direct-reading cards have a singular advantage: they can be seen from any place in the cockpit, and providing they have sufficient lubber lines, can be used when perched on the coamings.

Though Ritchie, Plath, Danforth and Sestrel make the best of the best, Plastimo and Silva produce sound instruments at reasonable prices if your needs are not of the highest order. After these, come the great mass of cheap compasses. Stay away from them.

Having bought a compass, you will still have to mount it. It should be readable at close to eye level, mounted away from any machinery or ironmongery, and totally protected from crew feet, sheets and the elements. A bridge deck is a good location, though the aft bulkhead of the cabin house is acceptable. Fore-and-aft alignment is of paramount importance. A binnacle is the best place, provided it is really solid. In any location, some form of shock damping, using gaskets, is a good idea. Once it is installed, leave it there. Unless you live in Greenland, there is no reason to remove it. Every time you do, you have to reswing it and recalibrate deviation.

Most of us will never use a sextant. There are even some offshore sailors who don't carry one. One sailor voyaged from Los Angeles to Hawaii with no ocean charts, no sextant, no navigation tables. When asked how he actually found the islands he replied, "I followed the jet trails." Few ocean passages are undertaken in such ideal conditions. Heading east or west, no doubt you will eventually reach land, but you might well expire in the process. A sextant is the key to accurate course plotting.

All a sextant does is measure angles very accurately. The angle most sought is that between the position of the sun and the horizon, at a particular time on a particular day of the year. That angle, when worked out with Almanac, tables and a few simple formulas, tells you where you are. All the mystery of celestial navigation is not to be taken too seriously. After all, if you are capable of basic arithmetic, you can reduce a sight.

Sextants come in many forms, shapes, sizes and prices. I know one very experienced offshore navigator who likes his as light as possible. Others swear by heavy brass models. Though light, plastic sextants are not as reliable as metal ones. Instability of the materials leaves some doubt as to the accuracy of readings taken with a plastic sextant. As a spare or backup instrument, however, the Davis and Ebbco plastic units are acceptable.

Sextants, being relatively complex and delicate instruments, are not made by many firms. Plath, Tamaya, Heath, Sestrel and Zeiss all make first-class instruments. Plath's Navistar is one of the best. It has a constant error, certified, so that you don't have to make corrections yourself for any in-use error.

Any sextant should be kept well protected, clean, oiled and ready for use. A lanyard should be required equipment, as the thought of losing a sextant overboard has been known to make even hardened salts cry.

To calculate your position offshore you must know the time relative to Greenwich mean time (GMT), and to do this accurately you need a chronometer. The history of man's search for a reliable, accurate timepiece is fascinating reading,

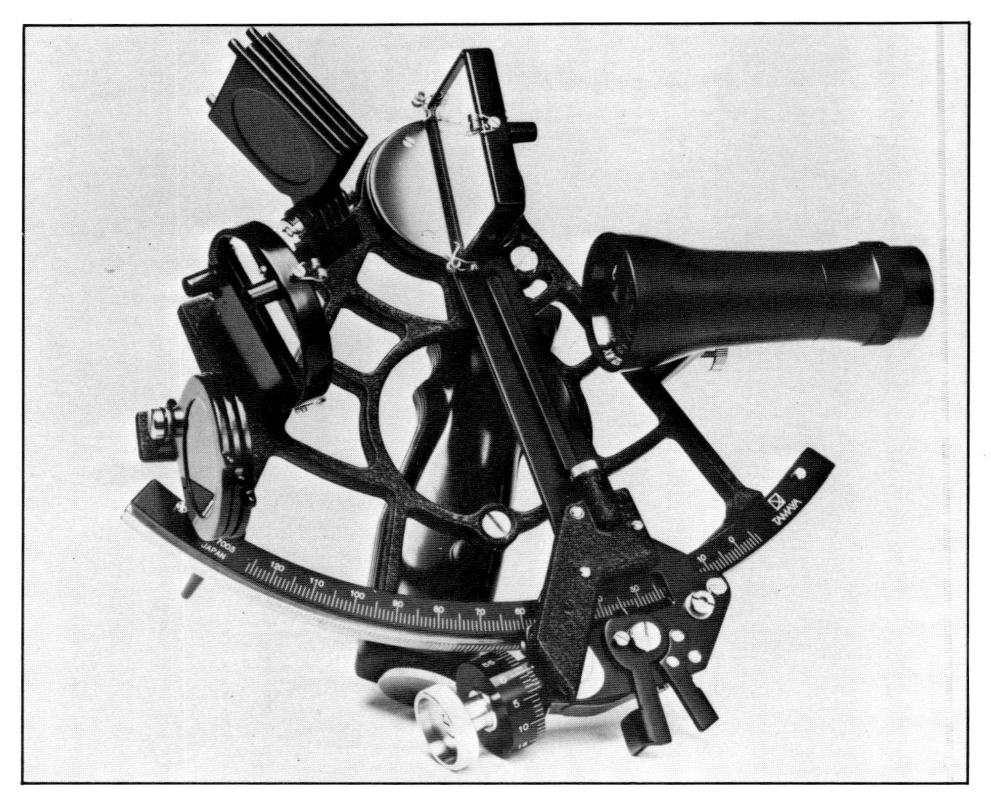

The Tamaya sextant is a fine full-size instrument.

The modern quartz chronometer is cheaper and more accurate than any mechanical model of the past.

but modern technology has all but eliminated hundreds of years of painstaking instrument making. We now have the quartz movement, which with a properly tuned crystal and proper safeguards against shock, humidity and temperature variations is extremely accurate and reliable. If you have doubts, radio time checks, receivable worldwide, allow for regular synchronization of any onboard timepiece.

A backup is needed, of course, and my own experience is that a decent digital quartz watch is reliable enough for most offshore work. Two are better. An additional advantage is that reliable watches can be had for a third of the cost of an average chronometer.

ELECTRONIC NAVIGATION

The best in marine electronics is remarkably better than it was just a few years ago. There are digital depth sounders, automatic Loran C's with coordinate converters, computer-clarified radar displays, digitally tuned direction finders and, everywhere the all-knowing, all-doing microprocessor.

If anything, we suffer these days from an excess of possibilities. Manufacturers introduce new, sophisticated equipment but keep existing, amortized models in production. After all, the more products you list, the better your chances of making the sale. Digital and analog meters continue side by side, as do synthesized and crystal-tuned radios, or digital and flasher-type depth sounders.

This chapter guides you toward the best for your boat, your pocket and your purpose, but asks that you never rely altogether on anything more complicated than a block-and-tackle. Be prepared with a backup—be it duplicate equipment, traditional devices or plain old-fashioned nautical skills.

The first investment the sailor makes for marine electronics should be in a depth sounder. Given some water under the keel, things can't be all that bad and a depth sounder can give you a precise idea of your position. Contour navigation, easier than many suppose, becomes possible with a depth sounder on board. Then, because knowing your position is essential to safe sailing, the next investments should be in a radio direction finder, Loran (or in certain cases, Omega and satellite navigators) and radar—in that order. Yes, radar is first and foremost a superb navigational tool.

Depth Sounders

Any sailboat too large to be pushed off the mud by its crew deserves a depth sounder, so manufacturers have spewed forth more depth sounders than any other kind of marine electronic product. As it happens, most models work reasonably well. The operating principle is so simple and has been implemented for so many years that the chances of buying a "lemon" are quite remote.

Simply, depth sounders work in this way: A short burst of ultrasonic radiation enters the water from a fist-sized, solid-state device (transducer) installed somewhere below the water line. The transducer then waits, counting the time until the ultrasound bounces off the bottom and returns to the boat. Because we know, more or less, how fast sound travels through water, the round-trip travel time of the ultrasound pulse can be transformed into useful information about depth.

The only fundamental difference among depth sounders is in how they deliver their information. Rotating flashers, digital displays, chart recorders and combinations thereof all have their dedicated adherents. The arguments in this matter are more than metaphysical, for the type of boat and how one uses it—aside from budget considerations—will often make a difference.

The rotating flasher generally costs least for a given level of performance, shows the presence of fish and may reveal something about the character of the bottom. This last virtue especially commends itself to the sailor. On the other hand, no one has ever succeeded in making the flasher truly visible in direct sunlight. Also, electrical interference causes confusing multiple flashes and most flashers are inconveniently large and water vulnerable.

The chart recorder is even less suitable for the average sailor. Such units best serve the serious fisherman. They're expensive and bulky, but reach very far down and offer a permanent record with extremely fine detail. Impressive, too, but inessential, are recorders with video displays, sometimes with color and zoom features.

Digital depth sounder. Analog units are not nearly as readable in heavy going.

When all is said and done, most sailors will do best with the newest versions of digital depth sounders. Liquid-crystal displays (LCDs) are clearly visible by day or night, and there is a certain comfort (though not greater accuracy) in seeing depth displayed in unequivocal numbers.

Instrument cases are small and well sealed for cockpit installation. Indeed, some digital depth displays now appear together with knotmeter and wind instruments in a single, compact unit. Signet's System 4000 and 1000 units and the Brookes & Gatehouse Hercules series are fine examples of this approach. For more information on these, see the Instrumentation section of this chapter.

Digital depth sounders also lend themselves to computerization, producing innovations like the following: infinitely adjustable depth alarms with simultaneous deep and shallow water settings; offsets for transducer depth to display either depth below the surface or below the keel (the former especially useful for contour navigation); conversion to metric depth; memory correlation to reject interference and anomalous signals; and low power drain. Some of the latest models use so little power they don't even include an on/off switch. Surprisingly, most of the traditional, large flasher manufacturers have not moved quickly into purely digital sounders. Leadership has gone, by default, to specialist firms, such as Datamarine, who produce only digital equipment. Two traditional instrument manufacturers Kenyon and Signet, however, also have pioneered in digital systems.

Best for most sailors is the digital sounder. Ultrasonic frequencies in the 150- to 200-KHz range allow conveniently small transducers and depth readings to 100 fathoms off a hard bottom. However, as depth sounders become increasingly integrated with other displays, their qualities may become less important to the serious sailor. He will choose a display system more for its wind-and-water performance features, trustingly settling for whatever depth sounder the manufacturer provides. The result may be increasing mediocrity in depth sounders in use, unless the buyer insists on going to a specialist depth sounder manufactuer.

Be that as it may, your depth sounder must have enough transmitting power to work well when the transducer is mounted inside the hull. In this position, its range will usually be cut in half, because the ultrasound must travel through the comparatively dense hull material.

Beam angle should be sufficiently narrow to permit convenient installation without reflections from the increasingly popular deep keels. Digital sounders, by their very nature, are especially vulnerable to keel reflections. Figure 4-1 shows the relation between beam half-angle and keel depth for two successful installations. The same geometry should be considered when installing the transducer ahead of the keel (remembering to account for the depth of a fully lowered centerboard).

Finally, consider sonar, the underwater equivalent of radar. It works by scanning the depth sounder beam in a full circle around the boat. The result is a "picture" of the bottom quite useful when navigating in confined waters. Semi-submerged obstacles are also revealed. Drawbacks include high cost, bulk and a rather large (though sometimes retractable) underwater transducer. Most boatmen who own sonars profess to be very pleased with their performance. Western Marine Electronics (Wesmar), the only consistent supplier of sonars to the pleasure-boat market, has several models of varying sophistication and price.

Radio Direction Finders

Long before the wonders of Loran and navigation satellites, sailors were getting from here to there by radio bearings taken on commercial-broadcast or specially designed beacon stations.

Because radio antennas can be made to receive signals only from certain directions relative to themselves, radio direction finders (RDFs) exploiting this feature can be made to work with reasonable accuracy. Even the most expensive RDFs are nothing more than sensitive radio receivers with directional antennas. When the antenna signal is weakest (null) the antenna is in line with the transmitter and a radio bearing then can be taken from a built-in compass or compass rose.

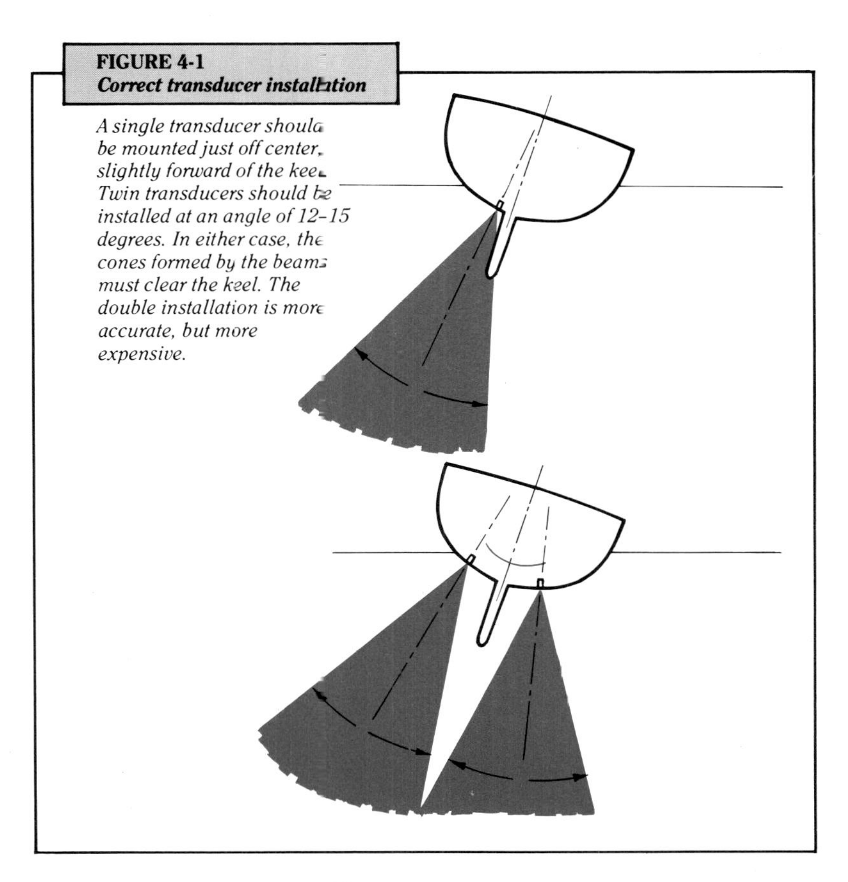

FIGURE 4-1
Correct transducer installation

A single transducer should be mounted just off center, slightly forward of the keel. Twin transducers should be installed at an angle of 12–15 degrees. In either case, the cones formed by the beams must clear the keel. The double installation is more accurate, but more expensive.

Two, or preferably three, such bearings from different stations and the sailor knows where he is, give or take a mile or two. Successive bearings on the same station (the so-called running fix) also can be used to establish position. The navigator can even use the RDF to home in on a specific beacon or to avoid it by staying outside its danger bearing.

Hundreds of radio beacons established in nearly all navigable waters are accessible to the sailor with even the simplest of direction finders. Every man's shoestring electronic navigation system, it is made even more useful by the few Consol stations still operating in European waters. (In the United States, the widespread acceptance of Loran has already caused abandonment of the Consolan system which never enjoyed the support of a manufacturer's lobby.)

Nevertheless, today's RDF market remains quite vigorous—especially as so many popularly priced RDFs simply graft a few direction-finding niceties onto a multiband receiver. That approach is typical of the many tabletop or flat-pack RDFs now on the market, whether manual or automatic. Such RDFs are better suited to vessels with inside steering and, in general, are not suitable for sailboats.

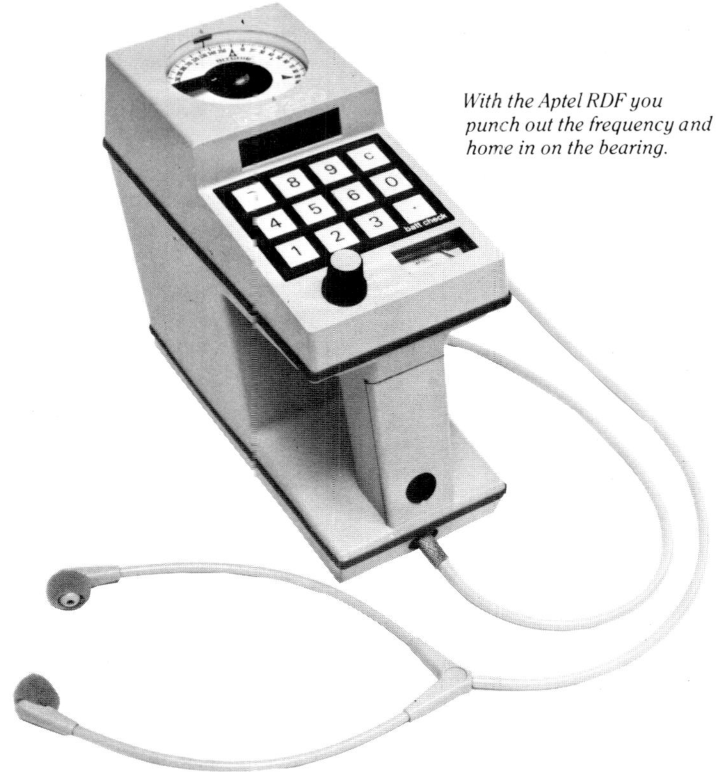

With the Aptel RDF you punch out the frequency and home in on the bearing.

There are several reasons why this is so. Consider the errors and inconvenience that accompany radio direction finding. There are vessel-induced errors from rigging, life lines, spars, sail tracks and metal window frames. Accurate direction finding requires that the antenna be well removed from such error sources or that the RDF be calibrated for those errors when used in a specific onboard location. That location, incidentally, should also be remote from the electrical "noise" caused by engines and generators.

For a bulky and not too weatherproof tabletop RDF, these requirements invariably mean a below-decks location not accessible to the helmsman in the cockpit.

And, because tabletop RDFs usually include only a compass rose, the helmsman must hold a known, accurate course while bearings are taken by a second member of the crew (if there is one). Clearly, the whole concept was thought out by someone in a warm, dry design office.

Best for the sailor is the handheld direction finder with built-in compass, which can be operated by the helmsman singlehandedly. The resultant magnetic bearings can be plotted directly on the chart. Their accuracy will be enhanced if you hold the RDF outside the rigging and away from engine noise.

Sense antennas to avoid 180-degree bearing errors generally are not fitted on handheld units, but any ambiguity will be obvious or can be revealed by a two-point running fix on the beacon. Signal-strength meters also tend to be absent from businesslike, handheld RDFs. The human ear does well enough in locating the direction-finding null.

The biggest obstacle to successful direction finding is the identification of a specific beacon. Most of the beacon stations are crowded into a small range of frequencies near 300 KHz. They are identified in Morse code and, in some areas, several beacons share, in turn, a single frequency, so that several bearings can be taken without returning. One could hardly design a system less conducive to accurate use by a tired, wet and perhaps frightened sailor.

Matters are improving, however, thanks again to the advent of digital design. Many of the newer tabletop RDFs feature digital readout of frequency. Other tabletops such as the well-rated Benmar 555A make provisions for one or more crystal-controlled frequencies.

A similar approach in handheld RDFs is the Vecta unit with separate plug-in tuning modules for specific beacon frequencies. Modules also are available for

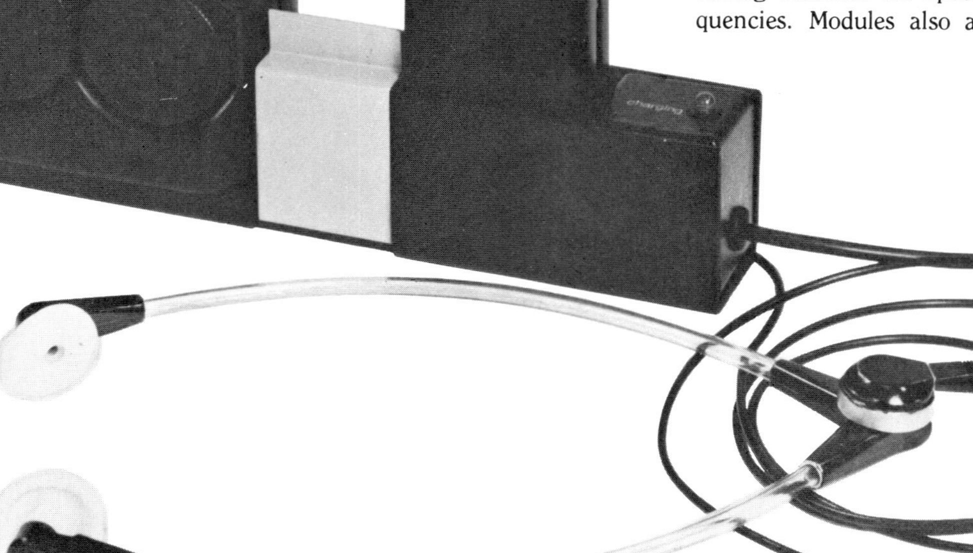

The Lo-Kata RDF is similar to Aptel's, but features an integral Sestrel compass.

weather and broadcast stations and to convert the entire unit into a loud hailer.

Smartest of all the new units is Aptel's handheld DDF-300. Push-button tuning permits unequivocal selection of any frequency. A built-in 6-minute digital clock helps to sort out sequenced beacons and a null meter is also provided. It's surprising that there is an undamped compass on this comparatively expensive unit, but other well-reputed RDFs also could do better in this respect.

First-rate handheld RDFs can be very expensive. Top of the line are the Brookes & Gatehouse Homer/Heron system and the Sailor 108/171 combination. Both feature a below-decks receiver connected to a handheld antenna-compass headphone unit. Moreover, B&G offers a digital tuning option. A newer, but similar, unit with built-in digital tuning is International Marine's Locator I. It is available either as a self-contained, handheld RDF or with a separate, below-decks receiver.

Be warned, however, that the cost of some handheld units can approach or exceed that of the newer Loran receivers. Not that Loran doesn't have its share of the problems, but beyond a certain price threshhold, opt for Loran combined with a cheap, backup RDF. In handhelds, a sensible compromise between price and performance would be the previously mentioned Vecta or the internationally available Seaspot unit. This latter model does not offer digital tuning yet.

Some relatively kind words may be said about commercial-grade automatic direction finders with permanently installed on-deck antennas. Raytheon, Furono and Si-Tex are among the internationally known makers in this product area. The equipment is first-class and usually includes digital or crystal-controlled tuning. Because the antenna is separated from the receiver, each can be mounted for best accuracy and convenience. But, here again, you will pay as much as you would for the more convenient Loran.

Finally, consider VHF direction finders such as the Regency Polaris and the Intech Mariner 360. Because there are no beacon stations in the VHF band yet, these RDFs are useful mainly in rendezvous with a VHF transmitter-equipped boat in rescue work. Coast Guard stations now so equipped can triangulate the location of a distress call from a vessel or emergency beacon.

Loran, Omega and SatNav

"Where on earth am I?" That is the question sooner or later asked by every sailor, be he Columbus groping for a landfall on Hispaniola or the modern yachtsman racing toward Bermuda. For the most accurate reading, what Columbus needed was one of today's classy Loran receivers.

Loran stands for Long Range Navigation. Something very much like it first was used on D-Day to guide Allied landing craft through lanes swept in the German minefields. The basic principles of Loran have not changed since then—though microprocessors and such have made Loran more accessible to the electronically unsophisticated.

Very simply, here is how Loran works. Two well-separated radio stations broadcast a simultaneous signal. At any point those signals will arrive at slightly different times. This time difference, which may be anywhere from zero to a few thousandths of a second, is measured and displayed by the Loran receiver.

Now realize that a given time difference can occur at many locations which, as it happens, lies on a specific hyperbolic curve. Other sets of locations, related to other time differences, lie on other hyperbolic curves. Thus, by consulting a special chart, the boatman can determine his position along one of a family of such curves generated by a given pair of Loran stations. A second pair of Loran stations generates a second family of curves—one of which again provides a line of position for the sailor. The intersection of these two Loran lines fixes the vessel's location.

Computer analysis of today's very complex Loran signals allows position-finding to within a few hundred yards and return to a given location to within a few dozen yards. Loran signals of sufficient strength blanket waters in most of the Northern hemisphere and Southwest Asia.

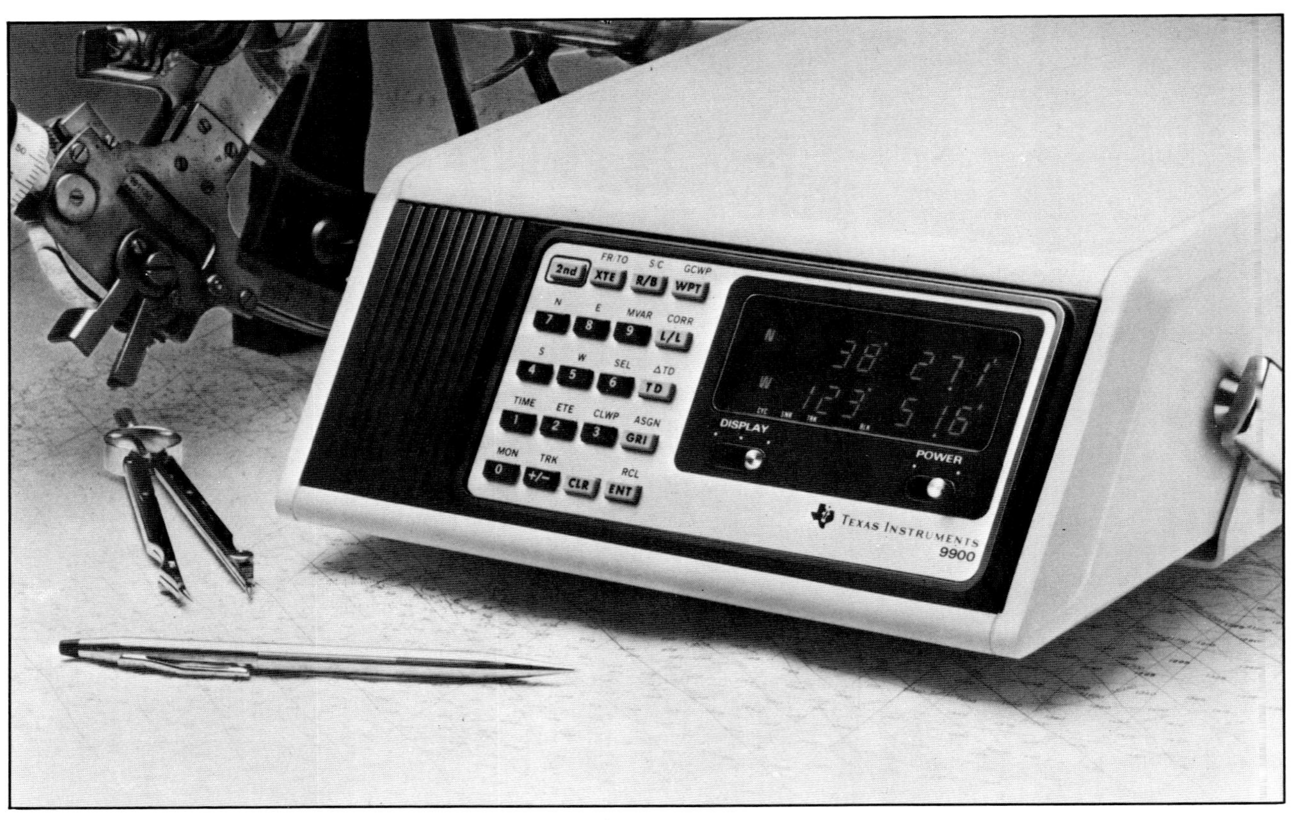

Texas Instruments Loran receiver. Not yet available in the U.K., Loran C is the simplest positioning system yet. The latest models even have voice synthesizers to tell you when you've gone wrong.

The basic Loran receiver is an excellent position-finding tool, but once microprocessors enter the picture, what can be done is limited only by your imagination and pocketbook. For example, the more elaborate, full-feature Loran receivers can automatically convert time differences to latitude and longitude readings, thereby avoiding the need for special charts. Navigation way points can be stored so that the receiver can compute course-to-steer, cross-track error, speed and course over the bottom, time of arrival, and the like. The new Northstar 7000 Loran even displays verbal instructions and data as well as numbers. Some Lorans can be coupled to the ship's automatic pilot which will then steer according to instructions from the Loran. Other receivers drive a chart plotter that traces the ship's course as, for example, in a search pattern for fish or in rescue operations.

The last few years, then, have revolutionized the design of Loran receivers for the boatman. Dozens of manufacturers are hotly competing for the Loran dollar and no one can predict which ones will survive. Choose equipment carefully, avoiding untested innovations. Use the following guidelines, which apply to bare-bones and sophisticated receivers alike.

Setting time of a minute or two is required for the receiver to lock in on the signals and produce an accurate Loran line. The shorter the specified setting time and the better the sensitivity rating, the more useful the receiver on a worldwide basis. Many Lorans will work perfectly well near the transmitter or in the dealer's showroom. Only those with the best sensitivity will operate accurately at the fringes of Loran-signal coverage.

A good receiver also should indicate whether it is operating on what it considers to be a marginal signal. Self-diagnostic alarms should be provided to note weak and noisy signals, loss of signals or reception of less accurate, "sky wave" signals.

Notch filters should be provided to cut interference at specific frequencies in the

Loran radio band. At least two, but preferably four, filters are required to assure good worldwide operation. These filters may be adjusted by the dealer or the user for best results. Some receivers will display, on a meter or otherwise, the optimum adjustment of the filters. Others, such as the Northstar 7000, are designed to tune the filters automatically.

The *number of secondaries tracked* refers to the signal pairs or lines of position (LOPs) that the receiver can handle. Most Loran-station chains permit four LOPs; a few offer five. Thus, a proper receiver should track simultaneously at least four pairs of signals within its specified level of sensitivity.

Don't settle for the lowest-cost, preprogramed units that can receive only one Loran chain. They are handy enough for home waters but must be reprogramed to do the job in another part of the world.

Power consumption of the new Loran receivers is reassuringly low. The typical 20 watts or less, at 12 volts, is very desirable, since a navigator may choose to operate the receiver continuously following a particular Loran line that coincides with the desired course or using the steering function of more elaborate receivers.

Multiple display panels are better than a single panel on which several Loran lines or other data are sequentially displayed. However, low price does inspire some corner cutting. Eliminating display panels at least has the virtue of affecting only user convenience rather than equipment performance.

At this writing it is too early to unequivocally recommend any of the newer products. Most haven't been on the market long enough to reveal any flaws. Believers in the tried-and-true may wish to look at the Simrad LC-123 or the Northstar/Raytheon 6000. Both are good, but comparatively large and expensive. Furthermore, they may become obsolete as their own manufacturers introduce the newer microprocessor-based receivers.

First of the new-generation microprocessor receivers was the Texas Instruments TI-9000A. It has been joined by that manufacturer's TI-9900 with full navigation features and a lat-long coordinate converter which translates raw data into latitude and longitude figures. Comparable value for money seems very attractive for both units. Also worth a look in terms of performance, small size and low power drain is the new Si-Tex/Koden 757 receiver, which incorporates automatic notch filters and a full panoply of navigation functions. There is also an optional lat-long converter for those who want one.

Converters are a good idea, but guard against blind faith in them. Due to propagation anomalies of the Loran signals in certain areas, the lat-long program can be wrong by as much as a half mile. In fact, designers cannot always agree on the computer programing to compensate for such errors; two different makes of Loran converters may show two altogether different positions aboard the same vessel. When in doubt, check your position by time differences on a new Loran chart. Such charts are continually updated as errors come to light, but it is much harder to reprogram a receiver's built-in computer.

In those parts of the world not served by Loran signals, you can use the Omega system. Omega resembles Loran in that it involves reception of synchronized radio signals and interpretation of time differences between them to establish lines of position. Because of the particular frequencies involved and the long ranges at which signals are received, however, errors are considerably larger than for Loran—1 or 2 miles is typical.

Moreover, position-finding can be ambiguous if the navigator cannot deduce his approximate position in advance. In addition, any lengthy power interruption to the Omega receiver can return the navigator to square one.

The newest Omega receivers can include lat-long converters similar to those in Loran systems. However, demand for Omega receivers is comparatively low and manufacturers are few, so the price is high and the rate of innovation in no way compares to that of Loran. Consider other systems first.

Almost overnight, on the other hand, satellite navigation receivers (SatNav) have become affordable—at least to the wealthy. What had been one manufacturer's monopoly, is now the province of at least seven competitors whose products sell at a fraction of the old cost. For this, we can thank microprocessors and competition.

As one might expect in modern economics, more SatNav for worldwide electronic navigation means less Omega. And interestingly, complex, fragile satellites 550 miles aloft may turn out to be more dependable than terrestrial broadcast stations subject to avalanches, earthquakes or terrorists.

For the pleasure boatmen, SatNav (like Omega) begins where Loran C stops. The Caribbean, South Pacific, South Atlantic and Indian oceans, and much of the East Atlantic and Mediterranean, are beyond the useful range of Loran. In some respects, SatNav also can supplement or back up Loran C navigation.

Loran C and Omega both use continuous signals broadcast by networks of terrestrial stations. Position, therefore, is available to the navigator at all times. With some oversimplification it can be said the two systems offer either range of coverage or accuracy. Thus, Loran C is accurate to a few hundred yards at ranges of some hundreds of miles, while Omega fixes positions within a mile or so anywhere in the world. Both systems can be upset by weather, sunspots, atmospheric noise, man-made interference and even time of day. Both systems also require "initialization" in one form or another. Omega demands knowledge of one's approximate position, but so does Loran. Comparatively speaking, Loran receivers are cheap while Omega equipment costs as much as, or more than, some satellite receivers.

In contrast, SatNav receivers fix position from signals broadcast by an orbiting satellite, doing so only when the satellite is in view. Accuracy is comparable to that of

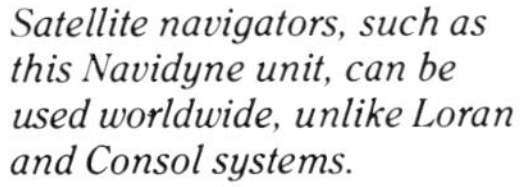

Satellite navigators, such as this Navidyne unit, can be used worldwide, unlike Loran and Consol systems.

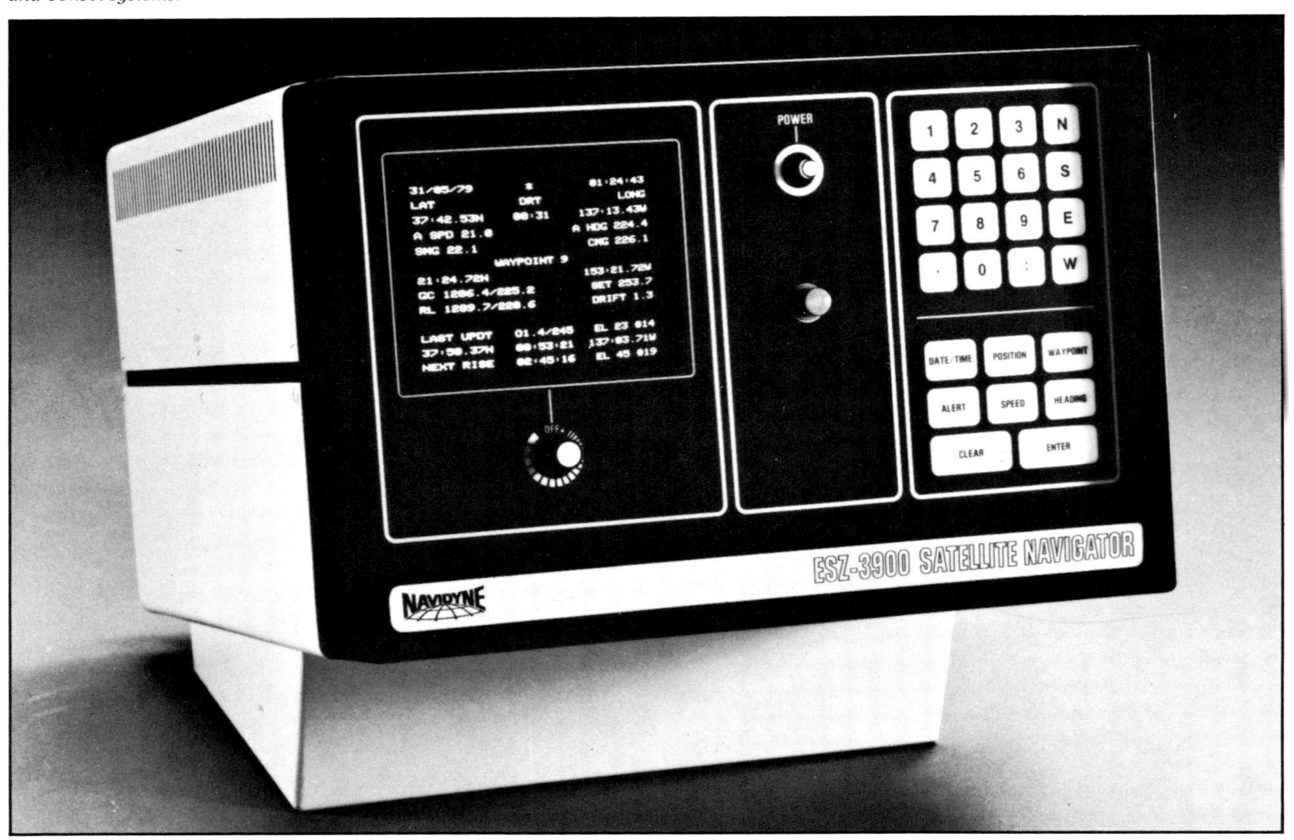

Loran, and the system is essentially immune to propagation and interference.

With five satellites on the air, and one standby, average time between fixes is about 90 minutes. Between passes, position can be established by dead reckoning, either automatically from compass and log inputs, or manually by the navigator. In this case, accuracy between fixes will depend on quality of dead-reckoning inputs. An "ultimate" system would employ the high accuracy of SatNav updated by continuous but less accurate Omega fixes.

SatNav receivers inform the navigator of position directly in latitude and longitude. If dead-reckoning inputs are provided, a variety of computer navigation functions also become available. Installation is almost do-it-yourself, especially if the dead-reckoning inputs are avoided. Antennas are small and simple. Power drain is 2 amps or less, at 12 volts.

Shopping for a SatNav receiver today does have some pitfalls. Advertised prices often omit the additional cost of interface circuits for the compass and log (if desired). Standby batteries to keep the computer alive in the event of power failures and special compasses also are options (if available at all).

Magnavox has been building SatNav receivers longer than others, but Decca and Wesmar make equally good gear. Then, too, Tracor produces reputable Omega equipment as well as SatNav receivers. Finally, consider Rauff and Sorensen—by-appointment purveyors of electronics to the Royal Danish Navy.

Radar

Think of radar more as a navigational tool than as a collision-avoidance machine. With radar on board, your vessel appears at the center of the radar screen surrounded by an accurate chart of nearby waters. Bearings and distances can be measured directly on the screen regardless of weather and visibility. The radar-equipped boat can undertake passages safely in conditions that would keep other vessels on their moorings. Most sailors will opt for the lower end of the radar price and performance scale, because of power and space restrictions. Weight aloft also becomes troublesome when the larger radars are considered. A 10-kilowatt radar, ideal for the large power yacht, will draw 10 to 15 amps at 12 volts and carry a 4-foot, 100-pound antenna. Its 48-mile advertised range makes little sense if one realizes that collisions usually occur at extremely short range. Moreover, range also depends on such factors as target material, target size and antenna height.

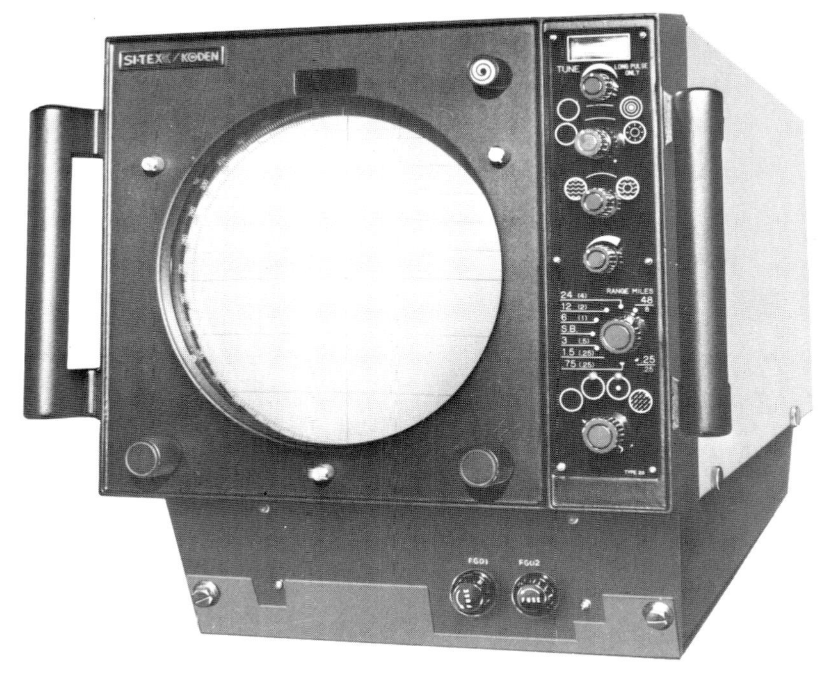

The Koden radar receiver is a very high quality unit often used aboard commercial vessels but suitable for larger yachts.

Advertised peak power is somewhat misleading as a measure of overall radar performance. What really counts is the average power developed by the transmitter —usually just 1 or 2 watts. The radar transmitter generates thousands of very short high-power pulses each second. But what the radar "sees" depends on the length and the number of those pulses. Look at it this way: peak power is equivalent only to the speed of a bullet; average power also tells us something about how many bullets are fired each second and their weight. All other things being equal, the higher the average power, the better the overall radar performance will be.

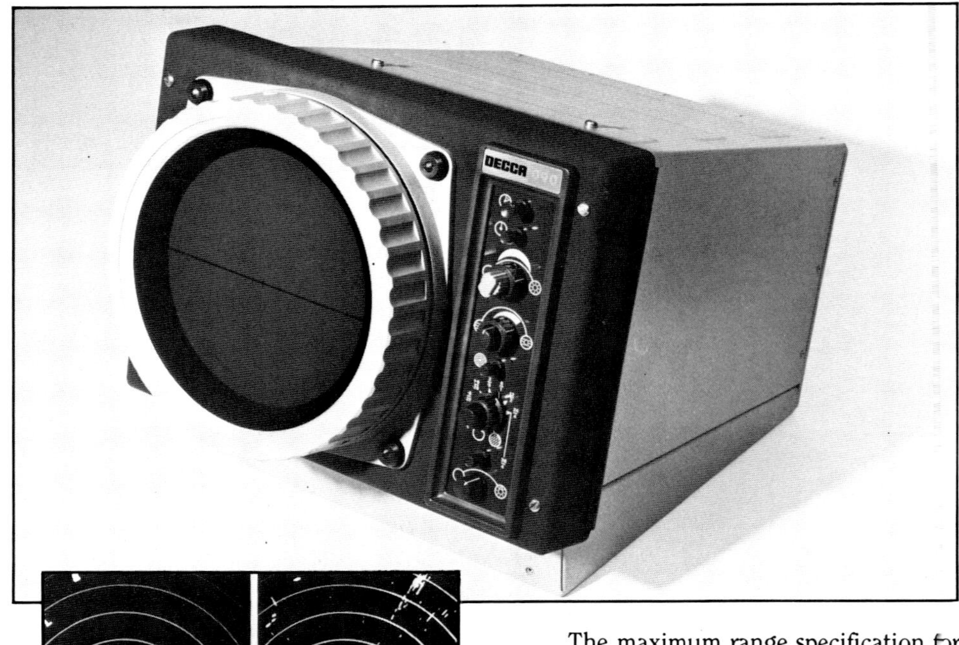

Decca 050 radar. Best for pleasure use are units specifically designed for yachts: the scanner is smaller and lighter than that on commercial units. The video processor (inset), now available for small-boat radars, clears clutter and makes true targets brighter. Unprocessed scanner is at right; processed is at left.

If the sales literature doesn't mention average power, you can calculate it using the following formula: Average power is equal to peak power (in watts), times pulse length (in microseconds) divided by 1,000,000, times the number of pulses per second. The values for those features should always be advertised as part of the product specifications.

Most radars have long- and short-pulse duty cycles. Use the values given for the longer pulses, at which average power is more meaningful.

Don't confuse range with power. Although more power tends to allow greater range, antenna height, antenna design and receiver sensitivity also influence maximum range. The designer may have several objectives in mind. He cannot simply build a radar for maximum range without incurring some penalty, be it a larger, heavier antenna, greater cost or more vulnerability to interference.

The maximum range specification for most small boat radars is somewhere between 20 and 36 miles, but most radar targets of interest lie at much shorter ranges. Maximum range is more of a talking point than a practical matter. Good minimum-range capability and display clarity are more important to the fog-bound navigator. Maximum range is of greatest interest to someone making a landfall, but even so, the nature of the coastline affects the range at which it will appear on the radar screen. A low-lying Bahamian cay is a much poorer target than a steeply rising Maine headland.

Just as a large television screen is easier to watch than a small one, so a larger radar screen is easier to read. Therefore choose the largest possible screen (all other things being equal), but avoid magnifiers as they tend to distort the image, giving off annoying reflections.

The color of the display is relatively unimportant. Yellow-green or orange display colors may be used. The orange screen is somewhat more persistent and kinder to night vision, while the green phosphor is more durable and will not be damaged if the radar is left on inadvertently when in port.

Size, shape and color of the display cannot express the total quality of a radar display the user sees. Specifications aside

TABLE 4-1
Radar Range

Antenna or Target Height (in feet)															
10	15	20	25	30	35	40	50	75	100	150	200	250	300	400	500
3.5	4.4	5.0	5.6	6.3	6.8	7.2	8.0	9.8	11.5	14.0	16.1	18.2	20.0	22.9	25.5
Visibility (in nautical miles)															

Note: Remember to add antenna height and target height to calculate visibility. If your antenna is 25 feet high and the target is 50 feet high, for instance, visibility is 9.8 miles.

the picture that looks best to the user is the one that will be most useful. We do suggest, however, that you make your decision under realistic operating conditions rather than in a store or at a boat show. Rain clutter and sea clutter, for example, just are not a factor at the New York Coliseum or Earl's Court.

Beyond the obvious external features that distinguish one radar from another, you must check detailed specifications. Here are the important ones.

Vertical beam width. The radar beam formed by the antenna resembles a piece of pie stood on edge. The up-and-down (or vertical) angle of this wedge is fairly wide so as to illuminate the target even though the vessel may roll and pitch. Too wide a beam wastes power; too narrow a beam may lose the target, restricting minimum range. Most radars use a 30-degree vertical beam width—a good compromise.

Horizontal beam width. The narrower this beam dimension, the better the separation of closely spaced targets. A small fishing boat anchored beside a buoy would challenge this capability. Overall detail also improves with narrower beams. In pleasure-boat radars, the beam may be anywhere from 2 to 4 degrees wide. As a rule, the wider the antenna, the narrower the beam. For example, a typical 36-inch antenna forms only a 3.5-degree beam, while a 48-inch antenna has a more useful 2-degree beam. Most radar users do well enough, it seems, with the wider beam of the smaller, more practical units. Horizontal beam width also equals the radar's specified bearing resolution, which may be stated in the specifications instead.

Side lobes. To a greater or lesser extent, all radar antennas suffer from side lobes, or radiation outside the main beam patterns. Excessive side lobes may produce false targets on the display. Side lobes can plague the designer who strives for extremely narrow beam width from a relatively small antenna. It may be better to accept a somewhat broader main beam and achieve good side-lobe suppression.

Side-lobe information isn't always given in sales brochures. You may want to discuss this important specification with a knowledgeable dealer. Side lobes are measured in decibels, the more negative the side-lobe number the better; a figure like —26 db, for example, is typical and is better than —24 db.

Antenna rotation. The rate at which the antenna scans the horizon must be fast enough to "paint" the display tube before the echo from the previous scan has faded. It's also good to have a rapid update of the situation when maneuvering in close quarters. For antennas and motors of reasonable size, and for the decay times of most tube phosphors, about 30 revolutions per minute is satisfactory.

Pulse length. The duration of each pulse emitted by the radar influences minimum range, maximum range and range resolution. A long pulse embodies more power than a short one, thus increasing the range. On the other hand, if two objects at nearly the same range are illuminated simultaneously by the same long pulse, they will register as a single target. As for nearby objects, the radar is blind to anything inside the distance for which the round-trip travel time of the radar signal equals the pulse length. For example, a 0.5-microsecond pulse, suitable for long-range performance, excludes all targets closer than 250 feet. Thus, most radars are designed to provide two pulse lengths, one short and one long, which change automatically with range selection. Some radars offer up to six choices.

Pulse repetition frequency. The number of radar pulses generated each second is the pulse repetition frequency (or PRF). At longer ranges, the PRF is automatically decreased from its value for short-range operation. False targets could be displayed if a pulse were emitted before a previous pulse returned from a target beyond the selected maximum range. The average power for long PRFs is maintained at a useful value by increasing the pulse length. PRFs of 1,500 per second (long pulse) and 3,000 per second (short pulse) are fairly typical.

Range resolution. This term describes the minimum distance between two objects that can be distinguished on the display screen. As previously noted, the resolution is mainly determined by the pulse length and therefore varies with range. It is usually specified for short-pulse, short-range operation. A typical value of 25 yards is sufficient for most purposes and should allow one to pass an obstacle or buoy with room to spare.

Whether it is better to use a radome or open antenna is a never-ending debate. Size for size, open and radome-housed antennas are equivalent in performance. Open antennas can be seen to rotate, but most sailors opt for the better nonfouling characteristics of the radome.

It's difficult to nominate one best radar from among those on the market, but one noteworthy unit from the sailor's point of view is the Epsco-Brocks Model EB. Its 55-pound weight aloft is comfortable enough and its 16-mile range should be at least adequate for the coastwise navigator, though the blue water cruiser needs more.

An important new development is computerized video processing to improve picture clarity beyond what signal conditions would normally provide. Rain and sea clutter nearly vanish, as do other forms of false echoes and interference. Never mind how it's done technically, the result is sensational. At this time video processing is available only with some of ITT-Decca's large pleasure-boat radars. Competition being what it is, however, it seems likely that this feature will appear on some smaller radars soon enough. When it's available, insist on it.

Small-boat sailors should learn of the Whistler portable radar. This peculiar device is simply pointed in the direction of interest and signals the operator audibly if there's anything out there. Amazingly to some, the Whistler radar works well enough to spot buoys and what-have-you a mile or so distant. Its price is no bargain except perhaps in comparison with a standard radar, but consider the advantages of its bread-box size and negligible power drain.

ELECTRONIC COMMUNICATIONS AND INSTRUMENTATION

Electronic navigation has done much to make the sailor feel at home on the sea, but if he is so unfortunate or inconsiderate as to be in distress, he will find that electronics also provides the most efficient way to summon help: from nearby, on VHF radio, or from afar, via single side band. Communications also enable one to keep in touch with ones subordinates, stockbroker and other loved ones.

Once these essentials are satisfied, most sailors will want to look at wind and water instruments, which in their own way contribute to navigation and safety. But before we all succumb to the prevalent "instrumania," let it be said that every sailor should be able to judge boat speed within ½ knot and wind speed within 5 knots simply on the evidence of his eyes and ears. The nonelectronic, utterly reliable piece of string displays wind direction to within ±5 degrees. The Windex wind indicator is even better, since it will accurately point into the slightest breeze.

VHF Radio

Except for the depth sounder, the VHF radio is the single most important item of marine electronics. No sailboat should be without one—and that includes any day sailer venturing outside a sheltered harbor. A handheld portable VHF radio (perhaps stored in a waterproof bag) is reasonable and ample, even for the very smallest boats. Handheld radios offer only a few crystal-tuned channels. But that's adequate for emergencies and for receiving weather broadcasts.

On larger vessels, we suggest the all-channel synthesizer-tuned radios. The air waves are increasingly crowded, and sailors cruise into waters where other radio channels are in established use. For a little extra, you can get an all-channel radio, which can operate worldwide.

With this by way of background, let's examine the specifications and features of today's VHF radios. Maximum power for VHF radios is limited by law to 25 watts. All radios, except portables, operate at this power level. More power won't help because the earth's curvature limits range to line-of-sight distances (usually about 30 miles). Only by increasing the height of transmitting or receiving antennas can you achieve a substantial increase in VHF range. For in-harbor use and other short-range communications, there's also a 1-watt power setting.

Power ratings assume fully-charged storage batteries. Weak batteries can reduce power output drastically, but what actually happens also depends on the design of the radio and on the particular components it contains. Ask the dealer to check output power of your radio at various voltages before accepting delivery. If it's less than 25 watts at 13.6 volts or 15 watts at 11 volts, try another sample or another brand. Most mail-order houses don't even uncrate equipment before shipping to the customer, much less perform such tests—a good reason to buy communications equipment in person from a reputable stocking and servicing dealer.

Handheld radios generally develop only 1 or 2 watts of power, but that's enough to be heard at considerable distances by rescue services Coast Guard antennas, for example, usually are located on high ground and feed into sensitive, communications-grade receivers.

With transmitter power regulated by law, what are some aspects of transmitter performance? We've already noted the need for low-voltage performance. A quality transmitter also generates fewer spurious

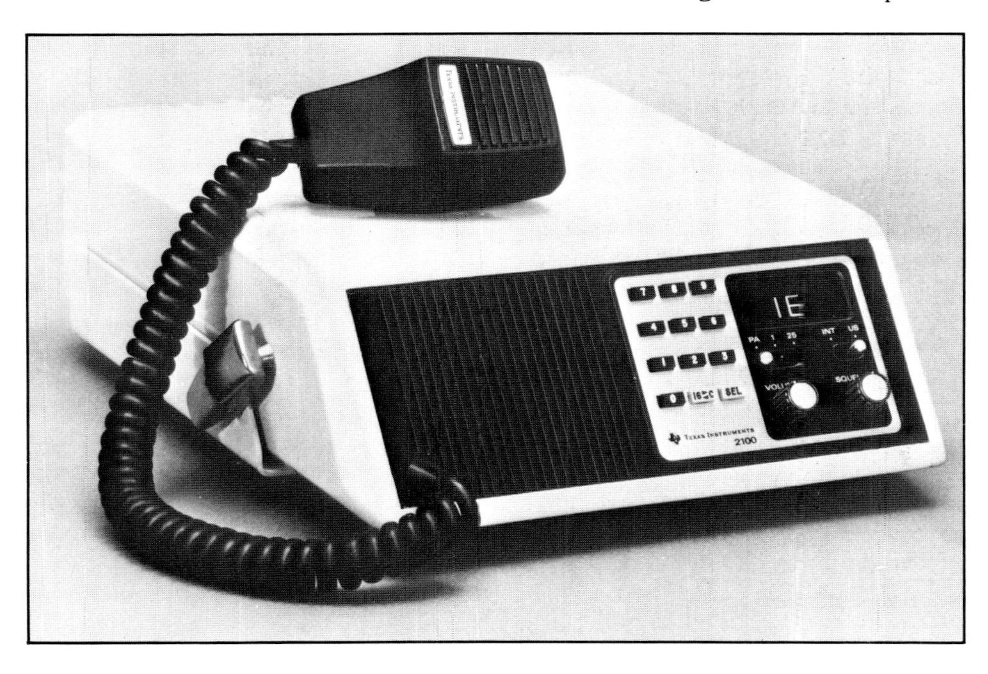

Texas Instruments' VHF radio. The Fastnet disaster showed how necessary a VHF radio can be. Two-way communication makes rescue more likely.

and harmonic signals that may interfere with other users. Thus, a better transmitter will be a better neighbor.

At any price level, insist on a radio with output transistor protection. This feature preserves the transmitter if the antenna is accidentally damaged or disconnected from the radio while the radio is in use. Such protection is not always mentioned in advertising or sales brochures. Again, check with a knowledgeable dealer.

Receiver performance is an area where you can definitely get more for your money. Better receivers are more sensitive and let the user listen, if not talk, at longer ranges. The critical specification is *microvolts per 20 db of quieting.* It should be half a microvolt or less. The smaller this number, the more sensitive the receiver will prove.

Rejection of adjacent-channel signals and other spurious transmissions is also the mark of a good receiver. These specifications are noted in decibel values. Minus 70 db is adequate; −80 db, much better; and −90 db, excellent.

TABLE 4-2
VHF Radio Range (in miles)

Assuming base station antenna 50 feet high:

Mean height of antenna over water (in feet)	Antenna type (in feet)		
	5	9	20
5	15		
10	18	22	
20	24	28	30
40	30	34	38
60	34	38	42

Assuming base station antenna 100 feet high:

Mean height of antenna over water (in feet)	Antenna type (in feet)		
	5	9	20
5	18		
10	24	28	
20	30	34	38
40	38	42	44
60	42	46	48

· *Note: A 25-watt radio is assumed in calculating range.*
Source: Telesonic Marine.

Increasing price brings certain features which may or may not be important to you. Some radios offer dual receivers for continuous monitoring of the emergency channel (16) or the very useful bridge-to-bridge channel (13). Remote control stations may be useful for the largest vessels or motor sailers. Priority selection can give instant access to channel 16 or other preselected channels at the push of a button. Signal strength meters, on the other hand, look impressive but are largely irrelevant. Transmitters fail catastrophically rather than gradually. If your signal can't be heard you'll know soon enough, with or without a meter.

Separate weather channel positions allow full use of the radio's built-in channel capacity for communications, so the more weather channels the better. This is especially the case with crystal-tuned radios of limited channel capacity.

As with depth sounders, manufacturers of VHF radios tend to come and go. Brands that have stood the test of time and that are available from reliable dealers merit first consideration, whether crystal-tuned or synthesized. Brand names that have been with us over the years and that tend to be distributed by servicing dealers include Raytheon/Apelco, Standard, ITT/Decca, Sailor and Motorola/Modar. All these manufacturers offer radios in a variety of price and performance categories.

Single Side Band Radio

If the modern sailor accepts the need for radio communications, the blue water sailor will welcome today's high-performance single side band (SSB) radiotelephones. Compared to VHF equipment, SSB radios are not cheap, nor are they easily installed. Battery drain also is rather more than most sailors would prefer. Nevertheless, the facility for truly worldwide communications, whether for emergency, convenience or pleasure, compensates for much aggravation and expense.

Without getting bogged down in technical details, suffice it to say that the single side band method of transmission uses broadcast power much more efficiently than does VHF-FM or the now obsolete AM marine radio system. Radio waves at the frequencies used in SSB also have the happy faculty of bouncing off certain electrically charged layers of the atmosphere, thus further extending the range of communications. So when all is said and done, 100 watts of SSB power at the right frequency (and transmitted through an efficient antenna system) is effective at ranges of several thousand miles. With SSB shore stations on every atoll that boasts United Nations membership, the state of the stock market or of Aunt Martha's health is available from wherever at sea her nephew may inquire.

SSB transmission is assigned to seven possible frequency bands between 2 and 22 MHz. The lower frequency bands tend to be more useful, especially the 2-MHz coastal band. Though its range is only a few hundred miles, it includes the universal 2182-KHz distress frequency. Every SSB radio should include this band. Longer ranges come with the higher frequency bands. The 4- and 8-MHz band adds somewhat more versatility.

This multiplicity of bands is necessary because the reflectivity of the atmosphere varies according to frequency, time of day, season of the year, location of transmitter and even the state of the sunspot cycle. Within reason, and with some understanding of the constraints posed by multi-band antennas, the more bands that are available for communication, the better.

Several channel positions should be available within each band. Synthesizer-tuned radios now reaching the SSB market greatly ease matters in this respect.

Thus, the two most important factors in the performance of a single side band radio are its power and frequency coverage. In principle, the more power, the better. Sailors should opt for the most powerful radio relative to price, size, weight, power drain and desirable auxiliary features. However, range does not improve directly with power. For example, doubling power from, say, 50 to 100 watts will not double the range. For substantial range increases, one must look to radios in the 500- to 1,000-watt bracket. Alas, the 1,000-watt single side band radio would be hard to live with on sailboats under 50 feet, and the electrical requirements also would be formidable. Reasonably speaking, most sailors will opt for radios delivering about 100-watts or less for reliable offshore communications and reasonably adequate worldwide service.

Channel capacity of a single side band radio should be specified as *half duplex,* which means alternate transmission and reception on different frequencies. *Duplex* means simultaneous transmission and reception on different frequencies as, for example, in ship-to-shore conversations which use both halves of a duplex channel. In contrast, ship-to-shore calls generally use the *simplex* mode which is alternate transmission and reception on the same frequency. In most SSB radios a duplex channel can be used for two simplex channels. This allows more ship-to-ship channels to be installed, though at the expense of ship-to-shore channels.

The best SSB radio is worthless without a correctly installed antenna system. The first thing that needs to be understood is that the antenna length depends on broadcast frequency. In the high-frequency

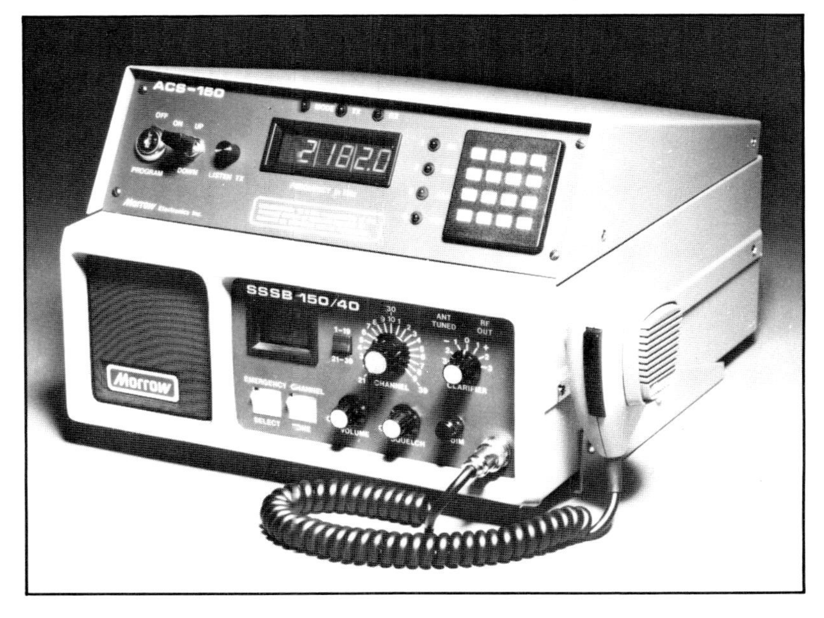

Single side band (SSB) radio is necessary for long-range communications because its range is not limited by the curvature of the earth.

bands where SSB operates, this optimum length for a vertical antenna varies from about 120 feet at 2 MHz to 11 feet at 20 MHz. Admittedly that's a bit much for most sailors.

However, we can electrically shorten the antenna at some sacrifice in efficiency. Practically speaking, reasonably good SSB antennas will be somewhere between 20 and 40 feet long. That's still not as short as some sailors would like, but tolerable. Tuning the antenna to each frequency band is a delicate process and must be exactly correct. The tuning circuits required for each band are housed in a device called the coupler, usually located at the base of the antenna. The typical 100-watt coupler is about the size of a large telephone book and weighs about 10 pounds. Sometimes the coupler can be located within the radio itself. Such an arrangement can save money but may not be suitable for all installations.

At lower frequencies, all other things being equal, the longer the antenna, the better it will work. At higher frequencies, performance of a longer antenna may well depend on its location or band or how it is tuned. Sailboats, with their long backstays or triatic stays are ideal for SSB installations, but the emergency of a dismasting automatically takes with it the antenna through which help is to be summoned. Consequently, you should keep on board a partially assembled whip antenna tuned to a distress frequency, reserving one channel for the radio and one position in the coupler to match the emergency antenna at that frequency.

Such gloomy prospects aside, a properly tuned backstay, or other stay terminated at each end with a high tensile strength insulator provides a superb SSB antenna.

For best antenna efficiency, one should demand no more than a 2- to 12-MHz capability from a single antenna. If more bands are desired two antennas should be specified: one for 2- to 4-MHz service, the second for higher frequency bands.

Whatever the antenna finally accepted, it will work better at all frequencies if properly grounded to the water. For various reasons, a simple length of wire immersed in the water will not do at all A considerable mass of metal must be brought into play. On some boats, the undersides of deck houses, decks, cockpits, lazarettes, sail lockers, etc., are lined with copper mesh and interconnected to form the ground. Other convenient metal masses, such as engine blocks, water tanks, keels, life lines and so on are bonded to the mesh as well. Finally, the assembly is connected to seawater via propeller, through-hull fittings or an external keel. A metal-hulled vessel, particularly of aluminum, is in itself an ideal SSB ground.

Against this background, the chances of buying a good SSB radio are rather easier than those of buying a good depth sounder. The major market for SSB equipment is among commercial vessels and fishermen. Because these are more demanding customers than the average yachtsman, shoddy products quickly fall by the wayside. The generally higher standards of SSB construction also are reflected in the price. One can buy three or four acceptable VHF radios for the price of a single SSB unit.

Noteworthy among the current population of SSB radios are such synthesized units as the CAI model CA35MS with 40 frequency slots and the Morrow 39-channel ACS-150. Among crystal-tuned sets, the SGC Europa One offers 36 channels.

Other household words in SSB radios include Raytheon, Motorola and Furono. More oriented to commercial-grade equipment are such companies as Marconi, Northern Radio and R.L. Drake.

One final buying tip: Because SSB radios so closely resemble amateur radio equipment, a friendly "ham" would be an invaluable resource in helping you to choose a marine SSB radio.

Instrumentation

Progress, for better or worse, has caught up with cockpit instrumentation. Long ago perhaps even before fiberglass, the name Kenyon was synonomous with knotmeters that worked most of the time, and that's all there was to know.

Then came engineers who sailed for pleasure. The result was new companies, new products and cockpit clutter. Knotmeters, anemometers, and apparent-wind meters—there were so many meters that special consoles to accommodate them all became necessary. Some new names also won merit as household words—Signet and Brookes & Gatehouse come to mind. Digital displays also gained vogue—most recently the sunlight-readable liquid crystal (LCD) types.

Now the trend has moved to computer-assisted, multi-function instruments that present many types of information on one or more digital panels. The computer also derives certain induced measurements by manipulating the conventional inputs. True wind, VMG, boat acceleration, speed trend and variable damping of the displayed quantities all are available, using the ubiquitous microprocessor.

All this ability, all this agility, does not come cheap. All of it is complex and, keep in mind, not user-repairable. Nevertheless, when it works (as it does most of the time) it works very well indeed.

Whether you opt for the fanciest equipment or merely individual cockpit instruments, the transducers that drive this equipment are the same in either case. A close look at the transducer can tell a great deal about the rest of the system.

Consider, for example, water-speed sensors. Some very subtle and devious methods have been invoked to measure boat speed. Ultrasonics, electromagnetics and strain-gauge wands have all had their moments of glory in the pleasure-boat market. Some of these have the merit of great sensitivity and are nonfouling, but the paddle-wheel impellor or propeller has generally proved superior, or at any rate, the most practical.

The impellor should be retractable into the boat for cleaning or repair: guards and gadgets notwithstanding, all impellors will foul. Moreover, the impellor should be user-repairable. At the very least, the paddle wheel and axle should be replaceable on the spot.

Wind transducers work hard and keep on doing so during the 99 percent of the time the boat is at its mooring. There's absolutely no room for compromise here. If a product appears flimsy or dubious in any way, pass it by. The arrangement for mounting and adjusting the transducers at the masthead should be convenient and connectors unequivocally rugged and sealed. It's better to pay more for the mystique and implied quality of a famous brand than endure unscheduled trips aloft.

Most wind-direction indicators offer a full, 360-degree display; a few impose a 60-degree dead zone forward. It's cheaper that way, perhaps, but it's also annoying and confusing.

The Stowe Log is an extremely accurate electronic trailing log.

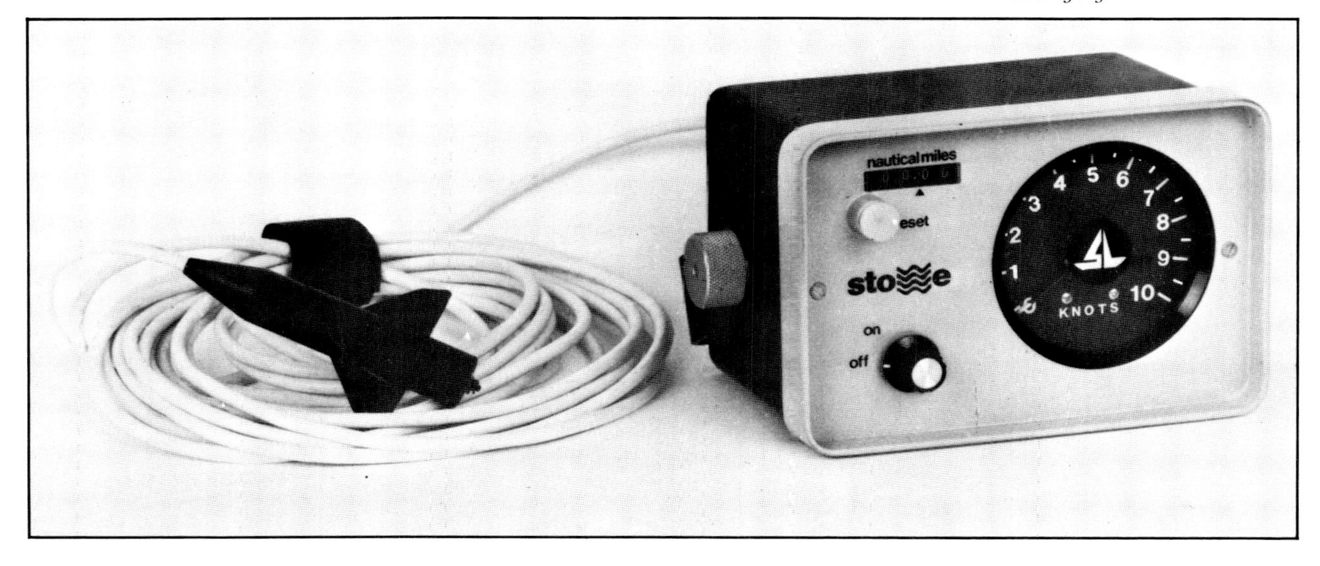

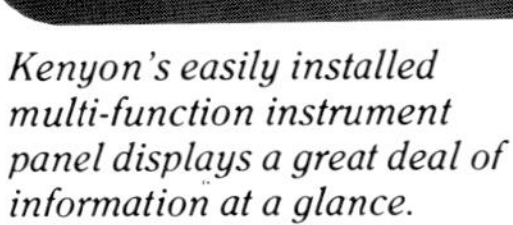

Kenyon's easily installed multi-function instrument panel displays a great deal of information at a glance.

In choosing any instrument, avoid exotic transducer schemes. There are as many ways to measure wind and water data as there are brilliant engineers to conceive them, but most brilliant new ideas don't seem to survive. Avoid them until someone else has proven them out for you.

As to dials versus digits, only the perfectionist racing sailor would care to know that his speed is exactly 5.9 knots and the apparent wind exactly 29 degrees. For other sailors dials are preferable. They are especially appropriate for apparent wind and give one a sense of speed trend or acceleration without recourse to complex electronics.

Digital displays, of course, become mandatory in multi-function instruments. Such equipment represents the leading edge of technology and is ideal for the racing sailor when affordable.

Most ambitious is the Hercules 190 from Brookes & Gatehouse. Up to 32 types of data can be developed and displayed on digital panels. Unfortunately, each panel allows only four selections of data, so several panels may be necessary for a reasonably complete information center. Analog dials also can be driven by the system's central computer so that the sailor can have the best of both worlds.

Similar, though less complicated, is the Signet System 4000/5000. This unit has the advantage of a built-in analog dial for apparent wind. Signet also offers its new System 1000 with water speed and depth readings and a companion System 2000 for wind information. These units are new on the market, but from a well-reputed manufacturer. They are noteworthy for their comparatively low prices.

Another relative newcomer, but already proven in America's Cup use is the Rochester Sailing Computer. This device shows true wind speed and direction as well as the more conventional apparent-wind data. Knotmeter, log and efficiency data also are presented on its four digital panels.

Chapter 5

STEERING SYSTEMS

A good steering setup transfers the feel and action of the boat to the helmsman. A boat with poor steering will either feel sluggish or skittish, depending on whether the system is too powerful or too delicate. The distance cruiser will want a system powerful enough to steer the boat without constant adjustment, while the racer will sacrifice convenience for precise pointing. The kind of action your boat has depends both on the rudder you use and on the system that moves the rudder.

RUDDERS

Different types of rudders are appropriate for different hull forms. Spade rudders, transom-hung rudders, skeg-hung rudders, spade rudders with a skeg, barn-door models, keel-hung rudders and balanced rudders are the types most prevalent aboard sailboats today. Hull configuration dictates rudder type to some degree, but the owner and designer must still make an informed choice.

Many features comprise a good rudder. Knowing these, a person interested in buying or replacing a rudder will be able to ascertain what is a good product and what is not. The following are characteristics of a good rudder:

At the top of the rudder shaft, there must be a hex or pair of flats machined on to facilitate attachment of an emergency tiller (or the normal tiller, if the boat is so equipped). A hole drilled and taped into the top end of the shaft is most helpful. An eyebolt can easily be threaded into it to

FIGURE 5-1
Rudder and keel configurations

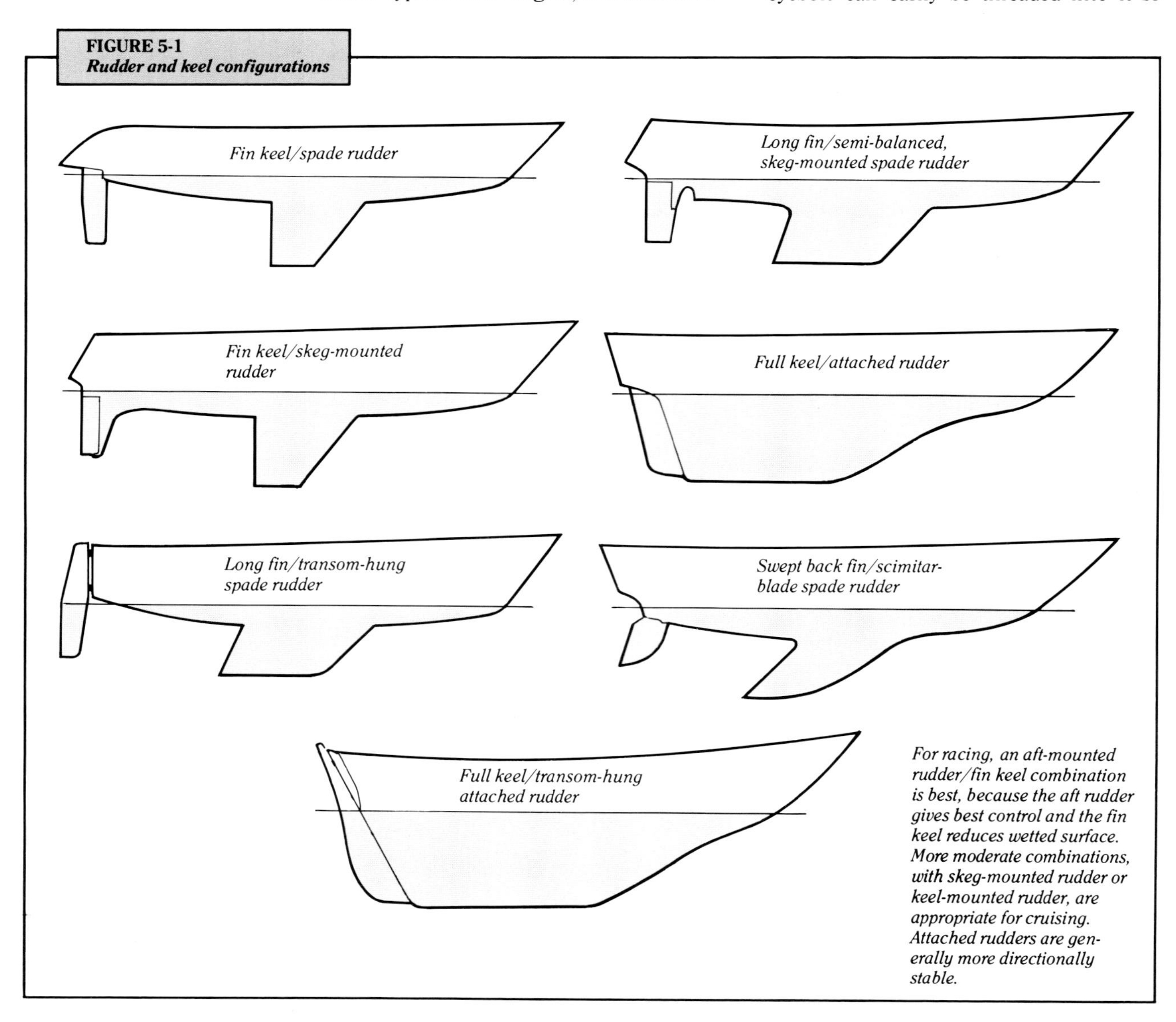

For racing, an aft-mounted rudder/fin keel combination is best, because the aft rudder gives best control and the fin keel reduces wetted surface. More moderate combinations, with skeg-mounted rudder or keel-mounted rudder, are appropriate for cruising. Attached rudders are generally more directionally stable.

attach a line or wire, allowing you to pull the rudder up through the packing gland and hold it in position until all necessary permanent attachments have been made.

The rudder shaft, whether it is solid or tubular, stainless steel, aluminum, carbon fiber, titanium or composite must be strong enough to sustain severe shock loads and twisting moments. The twisting force exerted on a rudder, particularly a spade rudder, when the blade is turned hard over against the stops can even bend the shaft, if design calculations are incorrect. A tapered rudder shaft saves weight but must be reduced carefully, leaving sufficient strength to handle the heaviest loads. The shaft is attached to the quadrant, worm gear, rack or tiller by means of a machined flat, with set screws, a keyway or even through-bolting. The edges of the machined flats and keyway should bend smoothly over the full shaft diameter instead of abruptly terminating in a sharp corner. Sharp bends can be a source of future cracks and resulting failure. One large bearing is all that is needed on smaller boats or boats with a large trim tab and small rudder (12-meter boats, for example). On most installations, however, two bearings are preferable, a bottom and a top one. Also, to reduce the influx of unwanted water at this crucial through-hull point, a good packing gland is a must. Annual renewal of the packing and periodic checking for more than an occasional drip will keep the operation smooth and as friction-free as possible.

The leading edge of the rudder itself should be rounded, not sharp. A rounded nose at the bottom corner reduces premature stalling, while a sharp, tapered trailing edge helps prevent rudder hum, particularly on racing boats. High-speed surfing and surging create severe harmonics if the trailing edge is left too blunt. The surface of the whole rudder should be smooth, with the leading and trailing edges free of nicks and imperfections. The rudder skin may be of any material, as long as the inner structure contains ample framing (webs). When building a rudder, it is often a good idea to make several internal waterline-shaped false bottoms so that a smaller rudder than originally fitted may be tried, and area reduced by 3- or 6-inch cut-offs.

Correct rudder size is very important, particularly in marginal downwind or reaching conditions. Designers always insist upon minimal rudder size for reduced wetted surface and the smallest possible frontal area. Skippers, on the other hand, prefer a large rudder because it makes the boat easier to control. Ted Turner, for one, almost always adds to the rudder size of the boats which he sails, usually on the bottom edge. On board George Coumantaros's *Boomerang*, we sailed one and a half years with a rudder attached to a skeg and had continual reaching and heavy air running steering difficulties. When the boat was later altered and a more powerful stern fitted, rudder-size calculations revealed that the original rudder had been a full 25 percent too small. It was no wonder the boat was uncontrollable in skiddy downwind conditions.

Good hull fit is equally important. The rudder must fit about the hull as closely as possible without touching it, thus minimizing turbulence due to cross flow. Furthermore, a close fit helps the hull act as an end plate, preventing water from spinning inefficiently off the end.

The lighter and more buoyant a rudder, the more sensitive and light to the touch it will feel. Heavy rudders often fall to leeward in blustery conditions, creating a rather mushy helm. International Offshore Rule (IOR) boats have long favored bow downtrim. A buoyant rudder helps to achieve this.

TILLERS

Tiller steering is unmatched for pure sensitivity, simplicity and low cost. The time-honored pintle and gudgeon approach is still the only way to steer sailing dinghies and larger one-design and custom boats up to 35 feet LOA. Although there are proponents of tiller steering who would advocate its use aboard boats up to 60 feet, the trade-off actually begins to occur with wheel steering as length approaches 35 feet. An effective tiller on boats longer than 35 feet would dominate the cockpit, since it would require more space to achieve the same leverage as a steering wheel. Furthermore, as boats become wider and wider, it becomes increasingly difficult for the helmsman to move far enough outboard to keep his vision clear.

A boat with tiller steering should have through-bolted pintles and gudgeons, supplied with adequate backing plates to offer a solid, nonflexing attachment to the rudder and the hull. The pintle/gudgeon fit should be snug. A good fitting pair of pintles and gudgeons coupled with securely fastened through-bolts avoids metal fatigue and hole elongation. The same parameters govern a rudder attached to a skeg (or the keel). A large upper through-hull bearing replaces the upper pintle and gudgeon, and a lower cup bearing replaces the lower gudgeon.

Complete tiller steering systems are available from boat manufacturers only. Steering companies do not offer tiller systems. Therefore, faced with the prospect of building or installing a tiller steering system, all you yourself can do is to be sure that only the finest hardware is used for components. Schaefer, Ronstan, Nicro/Fico, Gibb and Lewmar are all good companies offering excellent components. If you follow the recommendations discussed in this review, your tiller steering will be a sensitive, positive source of control.

Tiller extensions—used to allow the helmsman to sit far enough outboard to see—come in two distinct forms. They are either fixed length or of the adjustable telescopic variety. Each has its own distinct advantages and disadvantages.

Fixed-length tiller extensions, aside from oftentimes being lighter and simpler than their telescopic counterparts, offer the most positive control available. There can be no slippage of the kind which often develops in a worn telescopic unit. Fixed-length tiller extensions range in type from the yoke/handle models found on one-tonners to the small dinghy models available in lengths from 18 inches up. All consist of a single piece of wood or tubing and most have swivel bases to allow ease of control when tacking and gybing.

Telescopic tiller extensions are infinitely adjustable within the size range of each particular model, requiring only a twist, a push or a pull, and another twist to relock the new length into position. Continual adjustment is a favorite pastime of the nervous helmsman. Each manufacturer offers different sizes. The helmsman steers holding the end of the unit (the ball or "T"), or he may clutch it part way down as he would for a fixed unit. The telescopic models can be adjusted to suit changing situations from very light to extremely heavy air without any loss of comfort. They are more adaptable to the different conditions encountered, but they may become "sloppy" or actually slip, after extended use. They are also slightly more expensive than their fixed-length counterparts.

WHEEL SYSTEMS

Wheel steering systems offer power equal to any tiller's, though they consume only about half the space. There are eight basic types of wheel steering systems for sailing yachts. Each type has its own distinct advantages and disadvantages, so each—whether it be rack and pinion, worm gear, pull-pull, push-pull, hydraulic, mechanical, radial (disc) drive or conventional cable-and-sheave—will be better suited to certain yachts, installations and intended uses than to others.

Cable and Sheave

Of the eight varieties of steering systems, cable-and-sheave, or quadrant, steering is unmatched for sensitivity and power. It incorporates a quadrant in all instances, and just as the quadrant will appear in multiple configurations to suit different layouts, so the sheave layout and wheel placement may differ. Cable-and-sheave wheel steering enables the owner to incorporate an autopilot in the system with relative ease and at minimal cost.

Cockpit size and configuration dictate the wheel size and whether a pedestal, bulkhead or other type of wheel installation will be selected. A brake is a particularly good idea to include for installation on the bulkhead or pedestal since it affords the helmsman a chance to help out with other jobs after locking the wheel in the desired position. Furthermore, a brake keeps the entire steering system from shifting while the boat lies at dockside or on a mooring, thus reducing unnecessary wear and tear.

Proper sprocket and tooth size are key to arriving at the ratio desired to quickly turn the boat while still maintaining adequate power to control her in the most demanding heavy weather conditions. As a cable material, stainless steel, nonmagnetic roller chain offers the proper strength and corrosion resistance while avoiding any influence over the compass. Otherwise, 7 × 19 stainless steel wire rope affords an excellent steering cable material, since it too is nonmagnetic, corrosion resistant, supple and durable. Some wire ropes—notably types 302 and 304 stainless steel—can be slightly magnetic, although the fact is of such minor consequence that only Edson specifies Type 305 nonmagnetic wire rope for steering systems.

Sheave configuration, material and diameter are particularly important to minimize cable wear. Bronze or aluminum are the best materials; plastics like nylon and Delrin should be avoided. The standard rule for sheave diameter is that the root must be 16 to 19 times the diameter of the wire utilized. Proper sheave alignment is important in avoiding unnecessary sheave and cable wear. If improper sheave alignment occurs, as a result of either the initial installation or extended use, both the steering cable and the sheave will wear, and perhaps fail. Worn spots in the cables and metallic dust or shavings from the sheave cheeks are telltale signs of misalignment. They require immediate attention.

Pedestal, wheel, sheave and quadrant layout are dictated by the spaces which they occupy. The pedestal and wheel are confined by available cockpit space, while the sheave locations and the type of quadrant are controlled by the attitude of the rudder shaft and the space between the shaft and the wheel.

Easier for the designer to control are the mountings which hold the system in place. Sheaves should be mounted on large pads, so as to distribute the load over a greater area and avoid pulling the fastenings through the hull. A compression tube will maintain sheave separation, keeping the loaded block from tearing off the hull. Fairleads for the steering cables and the fewest possible sheaves keep unwanted friction in the system to a minimum. Rudder stops are also important, because they prevent damage to the rudder, hull, quadrant and sprocket. Two kinds of stops are most common for conventional cable-and-sheave steering: cables sized so as to restrict the quadrant's movement beyond a certain point and fixed padded blocks. The latter system is better, since it positively prevents the rudder from turning any further, even if the cable should break.

A steering system experiences loads every bit as heavy as those on the running rigging. Therefore, all steering fittings should be securely fastened. Dynamic loading is fine for well-fastened fittings, but wood screws and lag bolts will only work free and rip out over a long period of time. Through-bolting, welding or multi-layered

FIGURE 5-2
Cable-and-sheave (quadrant) steering

The most widely used system, it demands careful sheave alignment and proper cable tension to function effectively and reliably.

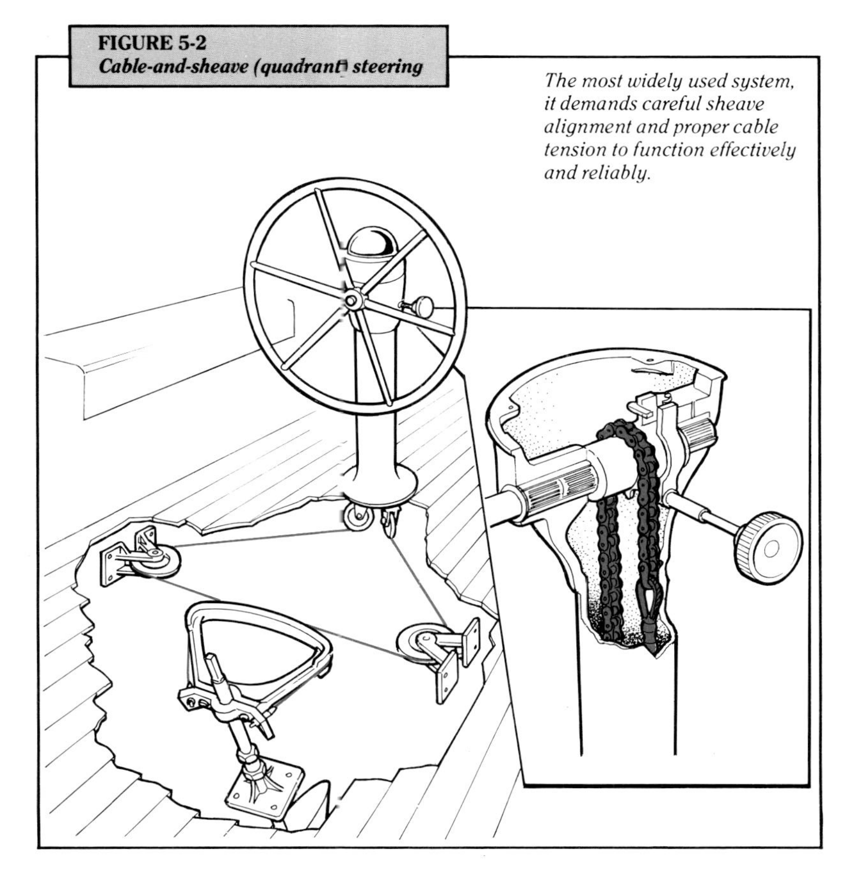

fiberglass reinforcement is critical to ensure a troublefree steering system.

Numerous manufacturers throughout the world produce quadrant steering systems, and many of them offer an excellent product. Although Simpson-Lawrence, Goiot, Whitlock and Foreman all make excellent gear, Edson and Yacht Specialties make the very best. These two offer not only complete lines of steering systems to suit any yacht, but also an array of components for every conceivable partner and type of installation.

Radial (Disc) Drives

Radial-drive steering systems, also called "disc drives," are modified versions of pull-pull, push-pull or cable-and-sheave systems. The difference is that the quadrants are circular. Extra sheaves are thus eliminated from the system. Radial drives are finding their way aboard an increasing number of boats today, especially in the 40-foot range. The system is ideal in installations where the cables can be led from the pedestal idler sheaves directly to the circular quadrant. Such a system eliminates an extra set of sheaves, extra wire length, reinforcements in the installation and compression tubes, all of which would otherwise add to the expense, the weight and the friction of the system. It is simple, economical and offers feel and performance as good as that of other systems.

The disadvantage of this system is that it can only be installed on certain boats. The disc must be fixed on the rudder shaft so that the steering cables lead *directly* to the grooves in the drive. The more nearly perpendicular the rudder shaft is, the better the system will work. Forward- or aft-raked rudder shafts cannot utilize a radial-drive system. A second constraint on the system is that the pedestal must be a minimum of 10 inches and a maximum of 72 inches from the rudder shaft.

Both Edson and Yacht Specialties offer excellent radial-drive steering systems. Edson calls their system "radial drive" and the quadrant is completely circular. Yacht Specialties, on the other hand, calls theirs a "disc drive," and it is not a complete circle, since there is a wedge-shaped notch taken out of the back.

Hydraulic

Hydraulic steering was first used around fifty years ago aboard commercial ocean-going vessels. It is highly efficient because its parts are less subject to fatigue. It has few bearings, no sheaves, no wire and built-in rudder stops. Moreover, it is very sensitive because it uses incompressible fluid instead of stretchy wire. Annual oil-level checks, inspection for loose connections or fractures and resulting leakage of oil, and tightening of nuts and bolts are the only maintenance procedures required. Rudder feel is present at all stations, even in a multiple-wheel setup aboard a single large boat. Wheels not in use do not turn.

Heavy gear reductions and loss of wheel sensitivity are unnecessary with hydraulic steering. The steering wheel operates a manual hydraulic system. Turning the wheel operates a precision hydraulic pump supplying (through steel or copper lines) a cylinder which drives a short arm on

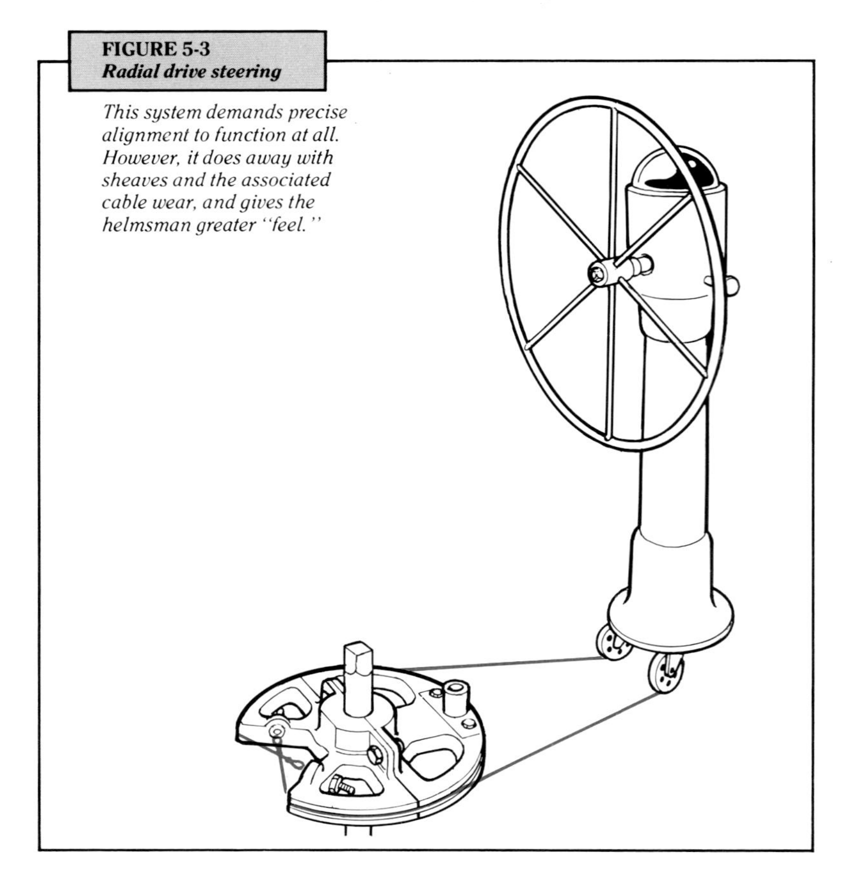

FIGURE 5-3
Radial drive steering

This system demands precise alignment to function at all. However, it does away with sheaves and the associated cable wear, and gives the helmsman greater "feel."

the rudder post. Since the oil used is nearly incompressible, all steering wheel movements create an immediate and positive source of rudder action. The system is quite sensitive, since increased loading on the rudder makes the wheel harder to turn.

It's important, however, to get the right size. If too large a system is used, there will be ample power but insufficient feel, but a steering system with too much feel will lack sufficient power to cope with the most demanding situations.

Hydraulic steering is quite adaptable. A lock valve, which has proven itself in many different hydraulic steering systems, can serve as a positive brake having three positions: reversible (full feel), nonreversible and bypass. Autopilots are easily connected and fitted to hydraulic steering via direct connection to the steering cylinder.

The best hydraulic steering systems manufactured for sailboats are the eight models created by Wagner Engineering of British Columbia. The eight models offer sensitivity options from 1.61 turns to 5.4 turns lock-to-lock. Wagner Engineering also manufactures hydraulic steering systems for the most demanding clients—tugboats, icebreakers and supertankers.

FIGURE 5-4
Hydraulic steering

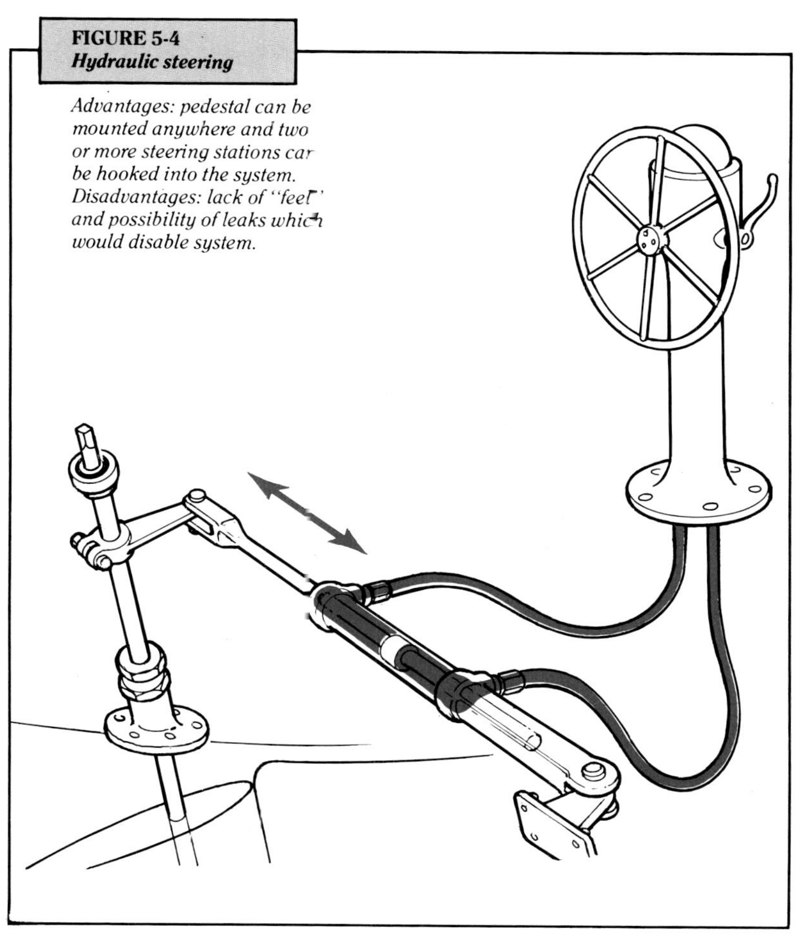

Advantages: pedestal can be mounted anywhere and two or more steering stations can be hooked into the system. Disadvantages: lack of "feel" and possibility of leaks which would disable system.

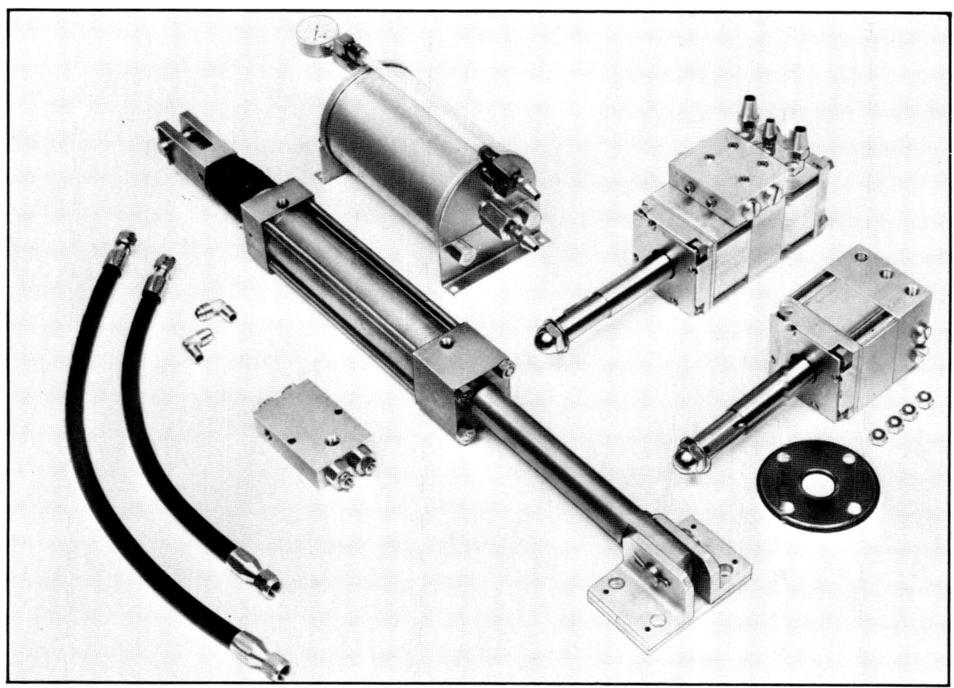

The Hynautic hydraulic steering system features a relief valve to prevent system overload and is available with or without rudder feedback.

Mechanical

Mechanical steering for sailboats enjoys widespread popularity in England. The system offers a very positive coupling of the wheel to the rudder ensuring excellent feel and precise helm control. Some of the well-known Admiral's Cuppers using mechanical steering are Arthur Slater's *Prospect of Whitby*; Chris Dunning's *Marionette; Coriolan II* sailed by the master himself, Paul Elvstrom; *Gunfleet of Hamble;* and many other stock boats from C&C, Bowman, Campers & Nicholsons, Moody, Rodgers, Ohlson and Swan.

Mechanical steering consists of a steering gearbox and torque tubes, connected by sliding universal joints on one end and a fixed universal on the other. The sliding end moves in and out on the splined torque tube, acting like a shock absorber to damp possible compression of the hull. Torque tubes are available from several manufacturers in 6-inch increments up to 10 feet in length, but it is not advisable to have any single tube longer than 8 feet. The tubes tend to twist under load and may even deflect when over 8 feet long. In an installation requiring longer torque tubes, special arrangements must be made to include tube supports, extra shaft bearings and idlers, all of which increase the friction and decrease the feel normally associated with a mechanical steering system.

Bevel boxes allow for all the "turns" in the system and can be geared to give the system sufficient power. A three-way bevel box should be incorporated aboard boats where a second steering station is desired. The aft-end reduction box is available in several different ratios to achieve the desired gear/power ratio. Another torque tube connects the aft-end box to the tiller arm and rudder post.

Mechanical steering adapts well to attachments. Dual steering station locations, wind-vane steering and an autopilot can easily be installed. It is therefore recommended for the yacht which includes such convenience extras. The system operates on boats up to 71 feet in length. Since all the items in the system are available from stock, it is easy to install.

Maintenance of mechanical steering is light. The owner should periodically grease universal bearings and ball joints with a grease gun, checking all the nuts and bolts to assure that they are snug. The gearboxes are sealed and lifetime lubricated.

The best mechanical steering systems and components are sold by K. Foreman Marine of Romsy, England which in 1976 began selling all steering gear manufactured by Camper & Nicholsons Marine Equipment under its own name. The K. Foreman catalog, which depicts a number of possible approaches to mechanical steering, is a useful tool for anyone contemplating such a system.

Pull-Pull

Pull-pull steering consists of a pair of flexible 7 × 19 stainless steel cables (wire rope) running through a pair of polyethylene conduits. The system is particularly suited to center-cockpit model boats, because the cables can be led aft around obstructions. The wheel may be pedestal or

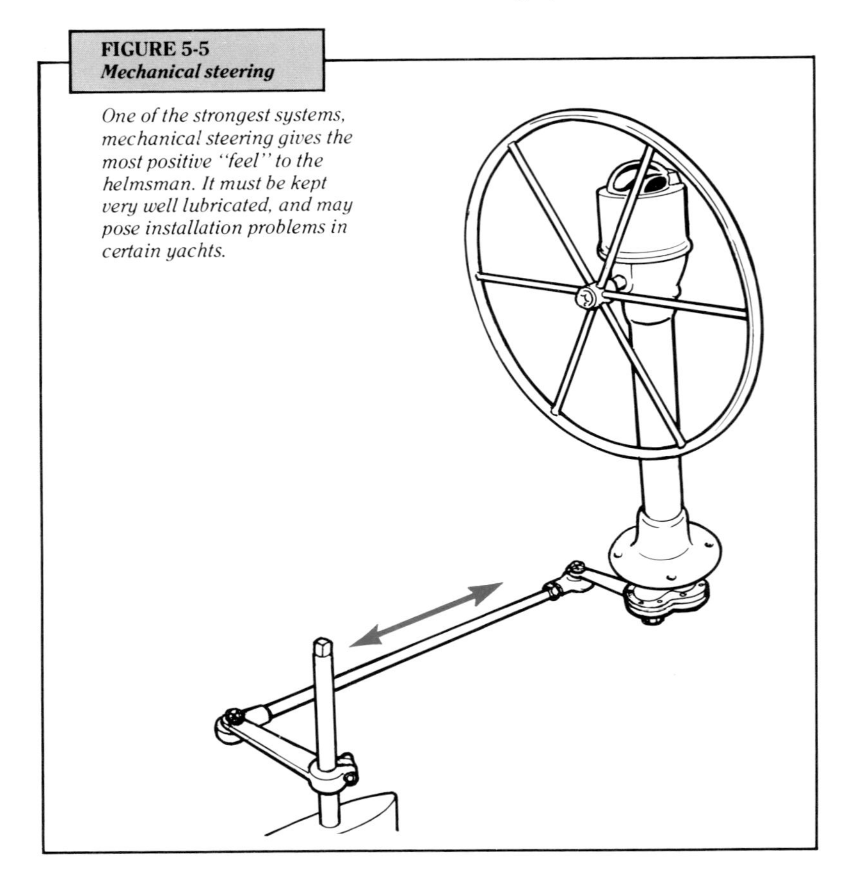

FIGURE 5-5
Mechanical steering

One of the strongest systems, mechanical steering gives the most positive "feel" to the helmsman. It must be kept very well lubricated, and may pose installation problems in certain yachts.

bulkhead mounted, and it can use a quadrant or disc attached to the rudder.

A pull-pull system is a cheap, "dirty" and simple way to put a wheel steering system in boats up to 30 feet LOA. The conduit is bent, twisted and snaked around obstructions, with a minimum radius of 6 to 12 inches depending upon the size of the cable and matching conduit utilized. The larger the cable and conduit, the larger the radius required, because the thicker material results in greater stiffness.

Of the eight different steering systems discussed here, pull-pull steering is one of the least desirable. It's available in two sizes, one for boats up to 28 feet and the other for boats 29 to 38 feet LOA, but in all instances the smaller the boat the greater the chance of success for the system. Its chief problems are high friction and sloppy response. The conduits, especially when they snake around many obstructions, put considerable drag on the cable, and the cable itself must be left fairly loose, making its response slow.

Both Yacht Specialties and the Edson Corporation offer good pull-pull steering systems, but you should usually avoid this type of steering. There are much better ways to steer a boat.

Push-Pull

Push-pull steering is a recent idea, developed from outboard-motor steering utilized with the larger motors. The system is light at roughly 30 pounds total. It requires around 3 hours of installation using only a saber saw, a drill, a socket set, an adjustable wrench and a screwdriver. The system is ideal for small (20- to 30-foot) trailerable boats with outboard rudders, though it doesn't have enough power for use on larger boats. The biggest constraint on the installation of such a system is that it needs a transom wide enough for attachment.

Teleflex, the parent company to Yacht Specialties, developed the original system for outboards, so it is no coincidence that Yacht Specialties is the premier manufacturer of push-pull steering systems.

Worm Gear

Worm-gear steering is ideal for long-keeled cruising yachts where little or no feel and a

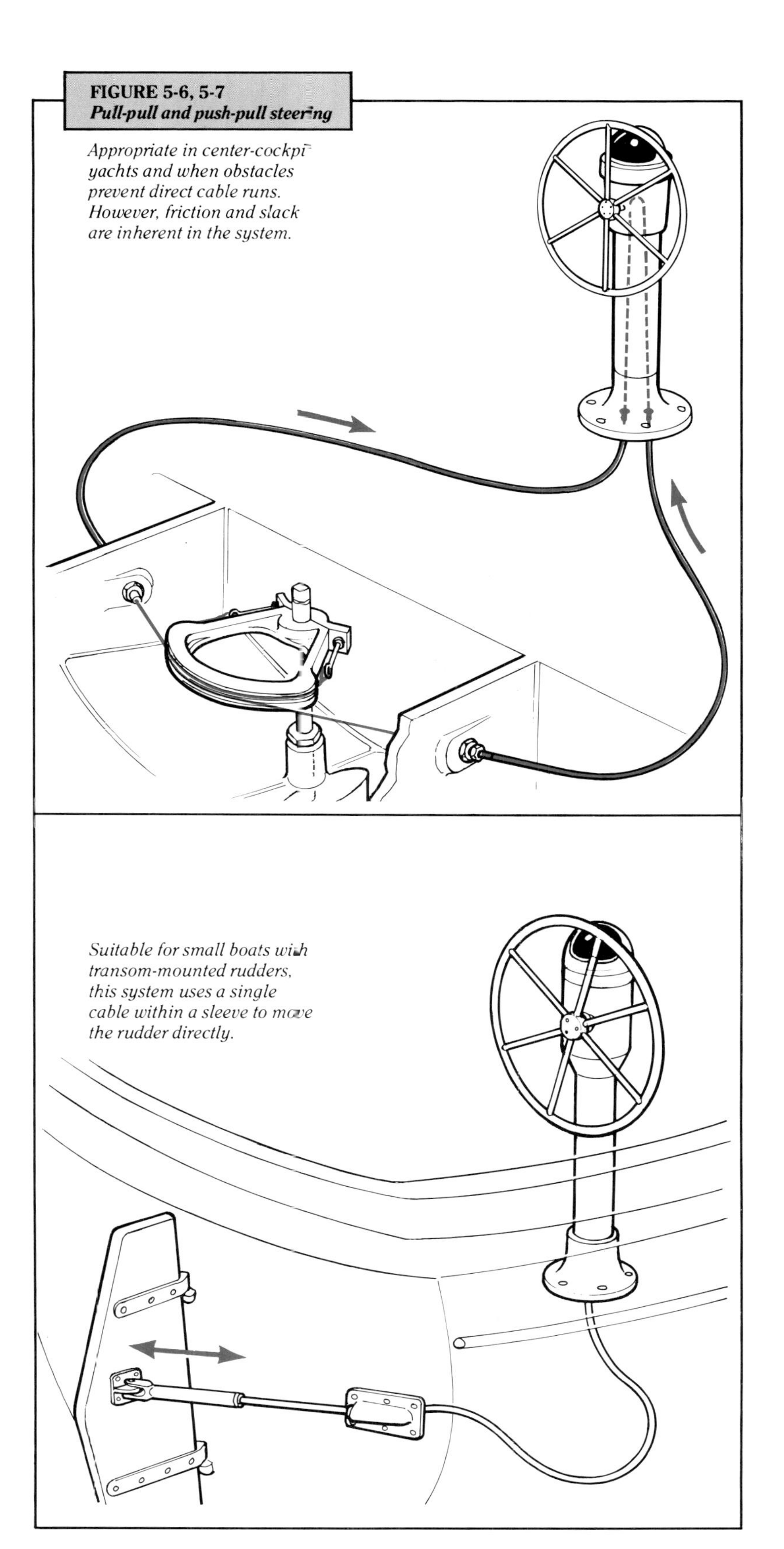

FIGURE 5-6, 5-7
Pull-pull and push-pull steering

Appropriate in center-cockpit yachts and when obstacles prevent direct cable runs. However, friction and slack are inherent in the system.

Suitable for small boats with transom-mounted rudders, this system uses a single cable within a sleeve to move the rudder directly.

large number of turns lock-to-lock are not a problem. Since long-keeled boats are in general less responsive than fin-keel boats, the loss of "feel" associated with worm gear is not crucial. Worm-gear steering is non-reversible since feedback from the rudder will rarely turn the steering wheel. Only if the boat is pitched by a wave, experiences excessive weather helm or rounds up in a sudden gust will the rudder cause the wheel to turn. It is not a good system for short-keel, tall-rigged racing yachts. In 25 to 35 years of hard use, however, worm-gear steerers have performed troublefree in many installations.

The systems are heavy: 33 pounds for the smallest to 120 pounds for the largest. These heavy weights are unavoidable since the gears themselves must absorb all of the forces put on the system by the rudder. The gears constitute the mechanical advantage in the system.

Traditional boats with heavily aft-raked inboard rudder posts are particularly suited to worm-gear steering. The worm gear eliminates the need for a quadrant, which cannot fit within the space beneath the cockpit floor. The system attaches directly to the rudder post at right angles. Many installations call for a universal joint and an extra bearing to place the steering wheel at the maximum comfortable angle off the shaft for the helmsman, but a universal joint should be avoided if at all possible, since it decreases the efficiency of the steering system. If it is asked to perform at an angle greater than 12 degrees, it will lose power and possibly cause clunking in the steering wheel.

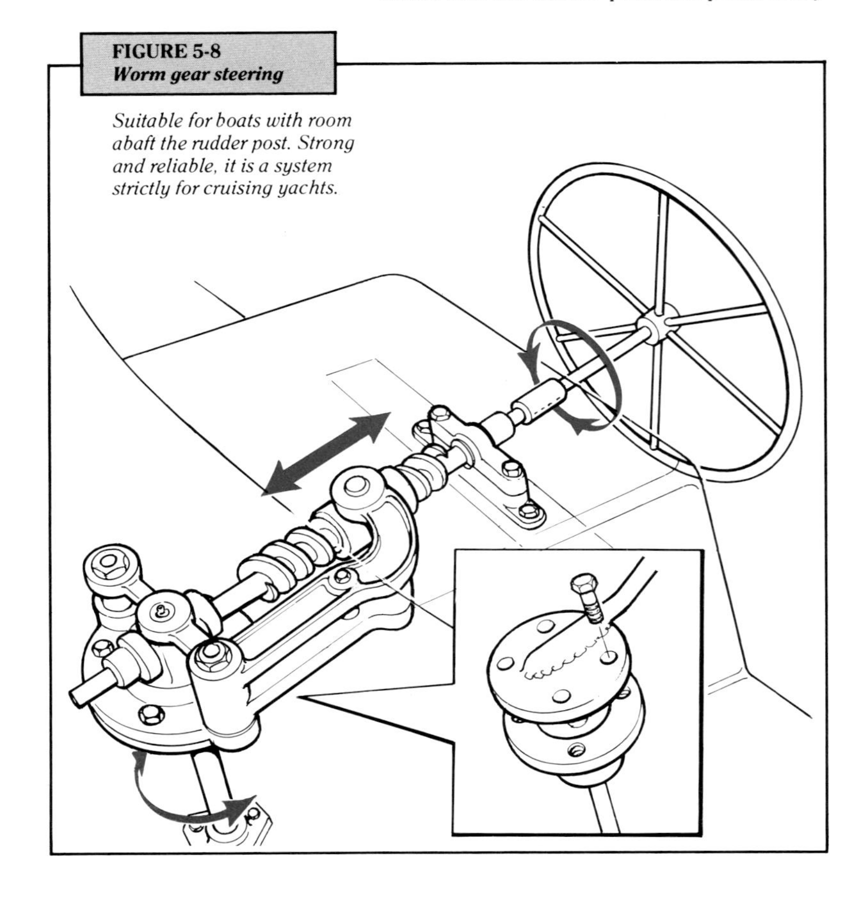

FIGURE 5-8
Worm gear steering

Suitable for boats with room abaft the rudder post. Strong and reliable, it is a system strictly for cruising yachts.

Brakes are available for worm-gear systems. A friction shaft brake holds the wheel in a positive position while the yacht is secured to her mooring or while the helmsman trims sail in short-handed situations. The system will also easily accept autopilot attachment. For yachts with waterlines of less than 20 feet, the 33-pound unit with 3.25 turns lock-to-lock is the answer. For yachts over 50 feet LOA, the 120-pound model with 4.5 turns lock-to-lock is the best.

With brass wheel struts, steel worms, bronze bearings and transversing replaceable babbitt threads, the systems are certainly durable. Also, routine maintenance is simple. Checking for snug nuts and bolts, and lubricating with waterproof grease (such as lithium or water pump grease) will ensure continued troublefree operation.

Edson offers three models—the Simplex, Robinson and Meteor—that mount either forward or aft of the pudder post. Whether a system is selected to fit forward or aft will depend upon the space available, the operation desired and the size of the unit.

Rack and Pinion

Geared rack-and-pinion steering is fine for sports cars, but it has made little headway aboard yachts. Although it offers without a doubt the most positive control available, it gives no shock absorption whatsoever. In heavy weather—survival conditions when a boat is caught offshore during a major storm—every force on the rudder is communicated directly to the helmsman. The stretch that absorbs shock loads in a cable-and-sheave system is absent here. A second disadvantage of the system is that the gears mesh on the same few teeth 90 percent of the time. The teeth wear down, eventually creating "slop" in the system. Nothing can rectify the problem, unless you replace the gears themselves, a very costly solution. This could very well be why of the last decade's well-known ocean racers only *Running Tide* has incorporated such a steering system aboard.

Rack-and-pinion steering is best suited for yachts in the 25-to-60-foot range, provided the boat is a long-keel model. The system is a particularly good selection where space beneath the cockpit floor is limited and where ease and simplicity of installation are important. Modern fin-keel boats can do better with other systems.

The premium rack-and-pinion steering components manufactured in the world are the seven models offered by Edson.

PEDESTAL AND BULKHEAD MOUNTING

Bulkhead steerers are suited for all types of sailboats. They may be installed in special pedestals or consoles, between divided cockpits or on the bulkheads themselves. On some models, the roller chain may exit at up to a 50-degree angle, thereby eliminating two sheaves and the associated weight, expense and friction. If the shaft of a bulkhead steerer is extended at the end opposite the side to which the wheel is attached, autopilot installation is simple and unusually troublefree.

Yacht Specialties and Edson make the best. Yacht Specialties has one model for boats up to 40 feet LOA, with a shaft extension and a brake optional. Besides this lighter duty model, the company makes a standard steerer with an autopilot shaft extension and brake included as standard equipment. The six Edson models include a needle-bearing system, offering unsurpassed sensitivity. The Cruiser series offers two models with autopilot shaft extension and an optional brake. Three extra-heavy-duty models provide dependable steering under the most severe conditions.

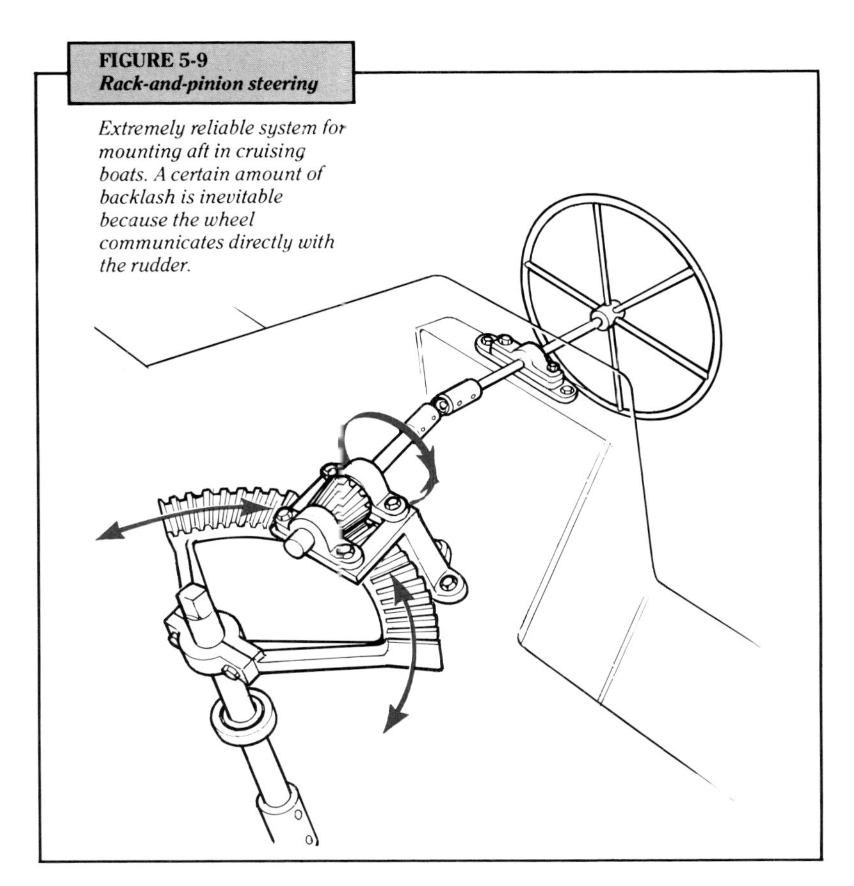

FIGURE 5-9
Rack-and-pinion steering

Extremely reliable system for mounting aft in cruising boats. A certain amount of backlash is inevitable because the wheel communicates directly with the rudder.

Pedestals are merely structurally sound housings which contain the sprocket, the stainless steel nonmagnetic roller chain or wire rope and the sheaves. The size of the steering wheel, the rudder quadrant and the sprocket all combine to determine the final steering ratio.

Pedestals appear with or without a binnacle. A "shortie" is specified when the pedestal is a bridge deck model or when a large radius wheel is installed to permit the driver to move far enough outboard to see the sails or the waves while still maintaining a comfortable steering position. A short pedestal lowers the center of the wheel hub so that the top of the wheel is not out of reach while the helmsman stands directly behind it.

Pedestals are manufactured from bronze, brass, aluminum, stainless steel and fiberglass. Aluminum and stainless steel are the best materials, since they produce the smallest magnetic effect on the binnacle or steering compass. They also have the best strength-to-weight ratio.

A steering pedestal should include a combination binnacle guard/hand rail both to protect the compass and to furnish a ready grab hold for anyone moving through the cockpit in inclement weather. A good grab rail will strengthen the pedestal and prevent it from wobbling around the cockpit. Ted Turner's 49-foot *Tenacious* had a pedestal which "cruised the cockpit" until a brace was installed to stiffen the installation.

A stiff steering pedestal adequately braced with a strengthening grab rail helps ensure a positive steering system. A pedestal which flexes and moves around cannot relay every action of the rudder to the wheel (and vice versa) since some energy is wasted by the moving pedestal. Furthermore, the pedestal or cockpit sole will eventually crack under the stresses.

Engine controls can be placed around the helm according to the preference of the designer, owner or builder. Unless the owner is on the scene when engine controls are installed, the builder or designer will probably mount the controls with an eye towards his own, rather than the boat's, convenience.

Controls mounted on the steering pedestal have two distinct drawbacks. First, the controls are difficult to manipulate when turning the wheel, especially if the wheel is too large to reach over or around. Second, particular care must be exercised in the installation of the control cables to ensure that in lumpy seas they do not swing around in the pedestal causing chafe and possibly jamming the steering. For peace of mind, the control cables must be secured at frequent intervals through the pedestal and all the way down to their attachment points on the engine. Whether single lever controls or dual controls with a separate throttle and gear shift are chosen, the right-hand side is the usual mounting location. Separate throttle gear and levers should be placed on opposite sides. Some installations feature removeable control levers which are put away when not in use to minimize the chance of fouling and reduce cockpit clutter. The disadvantage of such a setup is the danger of losing the handles or not being able to install them quickly during an emergency.

A brake on any wheel steering installation is an absolute must. Not only does a brake minimize wear when the yacht lies idle bouncing at a mooring or tied to a dock, it also frees the helmsman to temporarily lock the wheel and lend assistance to the crew. I have sailed on several boats without a steering brake, whose owners imagined that by leaving a brake out of the system they could reduce steering friction even further. *Boomerang* and *La Forza Del Destino* both had no brakes, and extreme effort was required to secure their systems.

When installing a pedestal, remember that wiring for the compass light must lead up through the pedestal (if the compass is mounted atop the pedestal). Compass light wires must be well secured to the pedestal side or run through the pedestal in a small aluminum tube or PVC conduit. Chafe in the wires and an eventual short circuit must be avoided. Furthermore, the wires must be kept clear of the sprocket and the roller chain. It's better to secure the wires at frequent intervals down the side of the pedestal housing, thus avoiding the complication, weight and expense of a conduit.

A terminal block situated near the top of the pedestal is another good feature to include, since it offers a test point to locate possible shorts in the system and to see if power is coming aft. It also makes annual removal and reinstallation of the compass easy since only a few screws must be loosened. The block must be kept well lubricated and dry to avoid short circuits. A good dab of silicone grease will normally be enough.

Among the options now offered for steering pedestals are integral instrument housings. Avoid these, since they place the electronic meters too close to the compass. Tables, seats, umbrella holders, glass holders, winch-handle holders, binocular holders and utility brackets are also offered nowadays as pedestal options.

The A-frame pedestal is a comparatively new type of steering pedestal. The most significant benefit it offers is that the wire may be led directly from the sheaves at the base of the pedestal to the quadrant, eliminating the weight, expense and friction associated with two more sheaves in the steering system. The system offers a two-footed pedestal, spreading the load of the steering system more than the popular single-stalk pedestal. The A-frame is far stiffer and stronger; however, it does consume more cockpit space than may be desirable aboard many boats.

The finest conventional pedestals are made by Edson and Yacht Specialties. The best A-frame models are made by the British firm, K. Foreman.

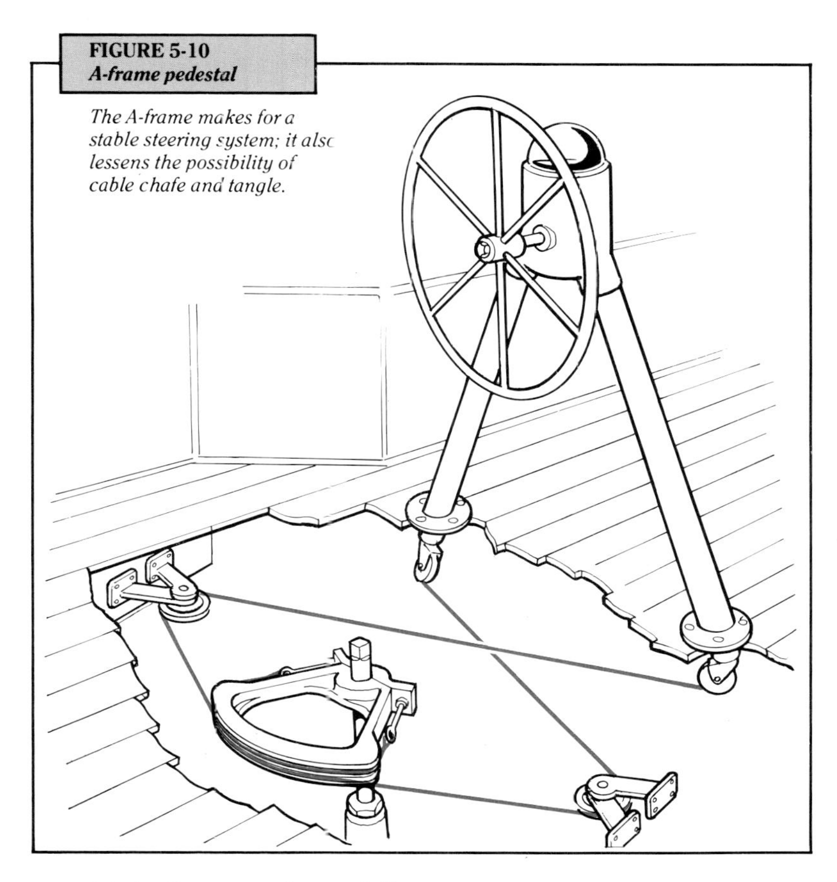

FIGURE 5-10
A-frame pedestal

The A-frame makes for a stable steering system; it also lessens the possibility of cable chafe and tangle.

EMERGENCY STEERING GEAR

It is best to try contingency plans for steering failure before the real thing occurs. Do not wait for the primary steering system to fail before ascertaining whether the emergency system fits and how it works. Instead, with your crew present, practice installing and operating the emergency setup at least once a year. Devise a set of logical steps to install the spare tiller, and decide whether a block-and-tackle or winch system is required to operate the unit. Oftentimes, the emergency tiller is so short and heavy that it lacks sufficient leverage to adequately steer the boat; in such cases, a small block-and-tackle system or two nearby winches can supply the power needed to control the boat.

If it is necessary to remove the steering wheel to install and operate the tiller, be sure to practice this transition with your crew. I was aboard *Tenacious* in the 1975 Miami-Nassau Race when the steering unexpectedly failed, offering a graphic illustration of the procedures to employ. When the steering went, Ted complained of the erratic feel of the boat. Quick attention to the sails helped us ease *Tenacious* back off to near course as the emergency tiller was passed up from its storage location below decks. The tiller was dropped onto the hex atop the rudder shaft immediately above the upper bearing. Ted fought to maintain control with the help of the mainsail trim, while the steering wheel was removed to permit installation of a tiller long enough to control the boat. Once this step was completed, three members of the crew worked to remove the damaged steering cables, free the system, install new cables and return to normal steering. All the while Ted merrily sawed away on the helm. The work was tricky but relatively quick, and soon the cables were snug enough to remove the second part of the two-piece tiller, replace the steering wheel, remove the short piece of tiller, mark the new center of the steering wheel and finish tightening the steering cables, as Ted swerved to slacken first one side and then the other. After several hours *Tenacious* safely reached Nassau. A good crew, adequate spares and a prior drill all facilitated a timely repair job with little loss in boat-handling capabilities. The key to the matter was knowing ahead of time how the emergency system was installed.

Though emergency systems are not sold as units, there are several guidelines to follow when you make them. Emergency tillers should not be constructed of ferrous metal. Otherwise, they may adversely affect

TABLE 5-1
Spares Checklist for Cable Steering

· *The following are the spare parts any offshore cruiser should carry for emergency repair of cable steering.*

RART	QUANTITY	REMARKS
Steering Cables	2 (or 1 complete)	Swadged or Nico pressed including all fittings.
Master Links for Stainless Steel Roller Chain	3	To splice broken chain or damaged links.
Cable Clamps	6	To splice broken cable or attach eye in end.
Grease	1 pint	Waterproof Lithium or Teflon.
Oil	1 can	Three-in-one.

the compass. Second, a two-part emergency tiller is preferable, because it's easier to stow, easier to install and can offer better leverage. There are no stock sources of emergency steering gear. Consult your local boatyard or machine shop if your yacht is not so equipped.

WIND VANES

Wind-vane steering gear serves as an automatic steering system, keeping a boat at a constant angle to the apparent wind while underway. Wind-vane steering is particularly well-suited to offshore passages where a sudden wind shift will not abruptly aim the boat for the dangers of shore. A good wind-vane steering system must overcome the friction inherent in the ordinary system without oversteering the boat (which increases the probability of broaching or yawing), and it must steer comfortably with little "slop," responding fast enough to changing conditions to minimize course fluctuations.

A wind-vane steering system must, in addition, be constructed as ruggedly as possible. It must perform the intended task with little or no attention on the part of the crew for long periods of time, under the roughest of conditions. One good way to choose a system is to find out where it has been used. If it has survived the rigors of the Observer Single-handed Transatlantic Race (OSTAR), then in all likelihood the unit will take any abuse.

Wind-vane steering first appeared in the early nineteen hundreds. In 1939 it accomplished its first documented transatlantic crossing aboard the motor yacht *Arielle*. In 1955 a wind vane steered a sailing yacht across the Atlantic for the first time. In the 1960s H. G. Hasler began to refine his designs for wind-vane steering. The system in these early stages was best suited to windward work, and the refinements necessary to steer a yacht in reaching and running conditions were yet to come. Today, it is a steering system which is readily adaptable to almost all monohulled boats. However, wind-vane steering systems are not well suited to multihulls. Multihulls have too much vibration, too much acceleration and deceleration and their speeds often exceed the wind speed causing the unit to steer all over the place.

An excellent system should steer only 5 degrees to either side of the selected course when sailing on the wind. When reaching or running this same system will not deviate by more than 10 degrees.

Because they incorporate many fragile components, wind-vane steering systems are particularly vulnerable to damage. Certain features incorporated in a system can help avoid damage or minimize its effect. An easily replaceable pendulum and vane is a must. A spring-catch release for the blade is a good idea to avoid breakage on sudden contact with flotsam. Sheer bolts on auxiliary rudders and a spare set of bolts will often aid in averting damage after striking an unseen object. Tiller lines with fairleads and free-running sheaves will ensure troublefree operation. Also, the larger the gear the more prone the system is to breakage in a storm since it presents more surface area to the wind. Smaller systems may thus prove more durable.

How does a wind-vane steering system work? The wind vane, through a linkage, turns the rudder steering the boat. When a boat alters course to the wind the vane turns, moving the rudder to bring the boat back on course. Often, the force required by the rudder for the vane to move it is far too great, and in these instances one relies upon the linkage to increase the power. The cheapest and simplest vane gears act directly upon the rudder. They are particularly suited to small boats which are especially light on the helm and well balanced. These units simply do not have sufficient power to effectively control larger vessels. Direct vane/rudder equipment was made popular by Eric Taberly, the noted French sailor and single-hander, when he used such gear aboard *Pen Duick I, II* and *IV.*

The second type of wind-vane steering is that which activates an auxiliary rudder one quarter the size of the main rudder. Hung aft of the main rudder, it achieves a greater turning moment with less pressure. In this type, a limited swing of the tiller ensures that course corrections are gentle. The linkage usually features a differential gear, providing the system with less abrupt corrections and more power to control the boat under even the most demanding conditions. In most auxiliary rudder wind-vane steering systems the main rudder is locked, increasing the boat's stability and tracking capabilities and correcting for excessive weather helm.

The third type of wind-vane steering is the trim-tab type. A trim tab is activated by the wind vane thereby turning the rudder. This particular system is more powerful than the previous two since the force is magnified in transmission to the rudder, actually moved by the water flow generated by the trim tab. Such a system is particularly suited to boats with aft-hung rudders since the installation and linkage is relatively simple. The further a trim tab is from the rudder pivot, the greater the effect the trim tab will have upon the rudder. On other yachts with different rudder locations, the linkage becomes far too complicated to be practical.

The fourth type of wind-vane steering is the pendulum variety. The vane activates a trim tab which is an independent component sticking down into the water, turning like a paddle on both a vertical and a horizontal axis simultaneously. The pendulum acts as a "messenger rudder" transferring the course change to the boat's

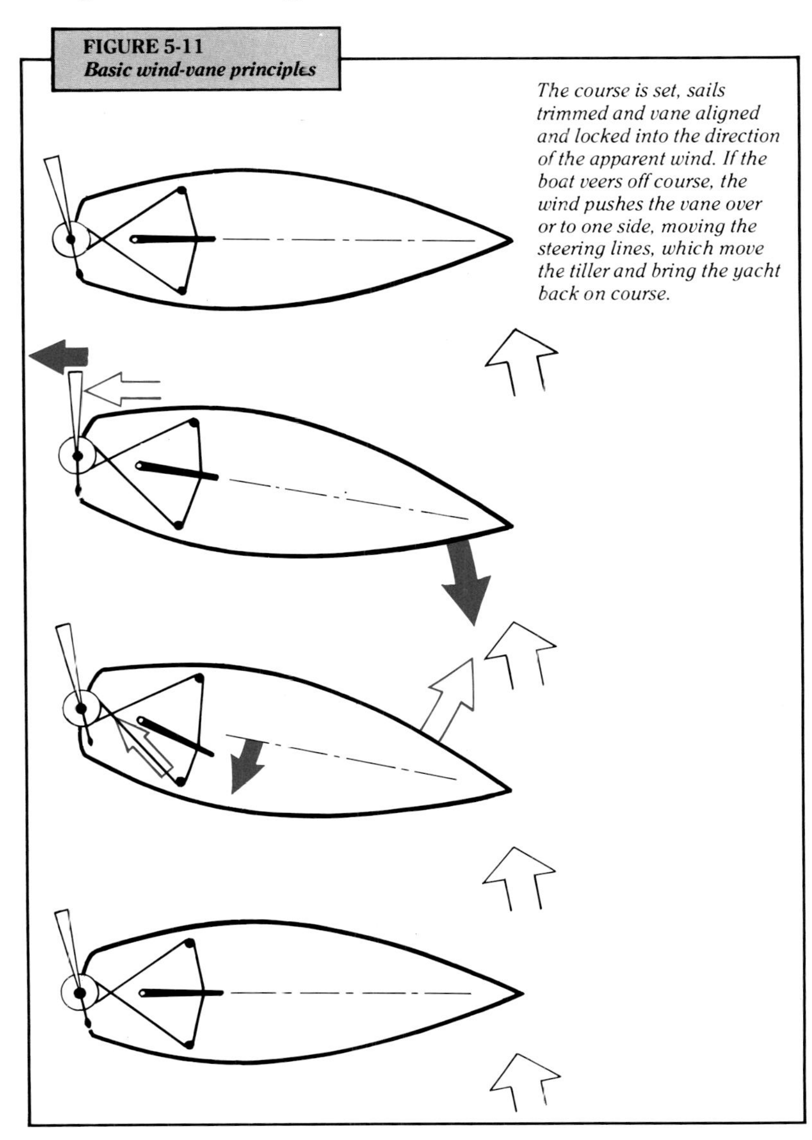

FIGURE 5-11
Basic wind-vane principles

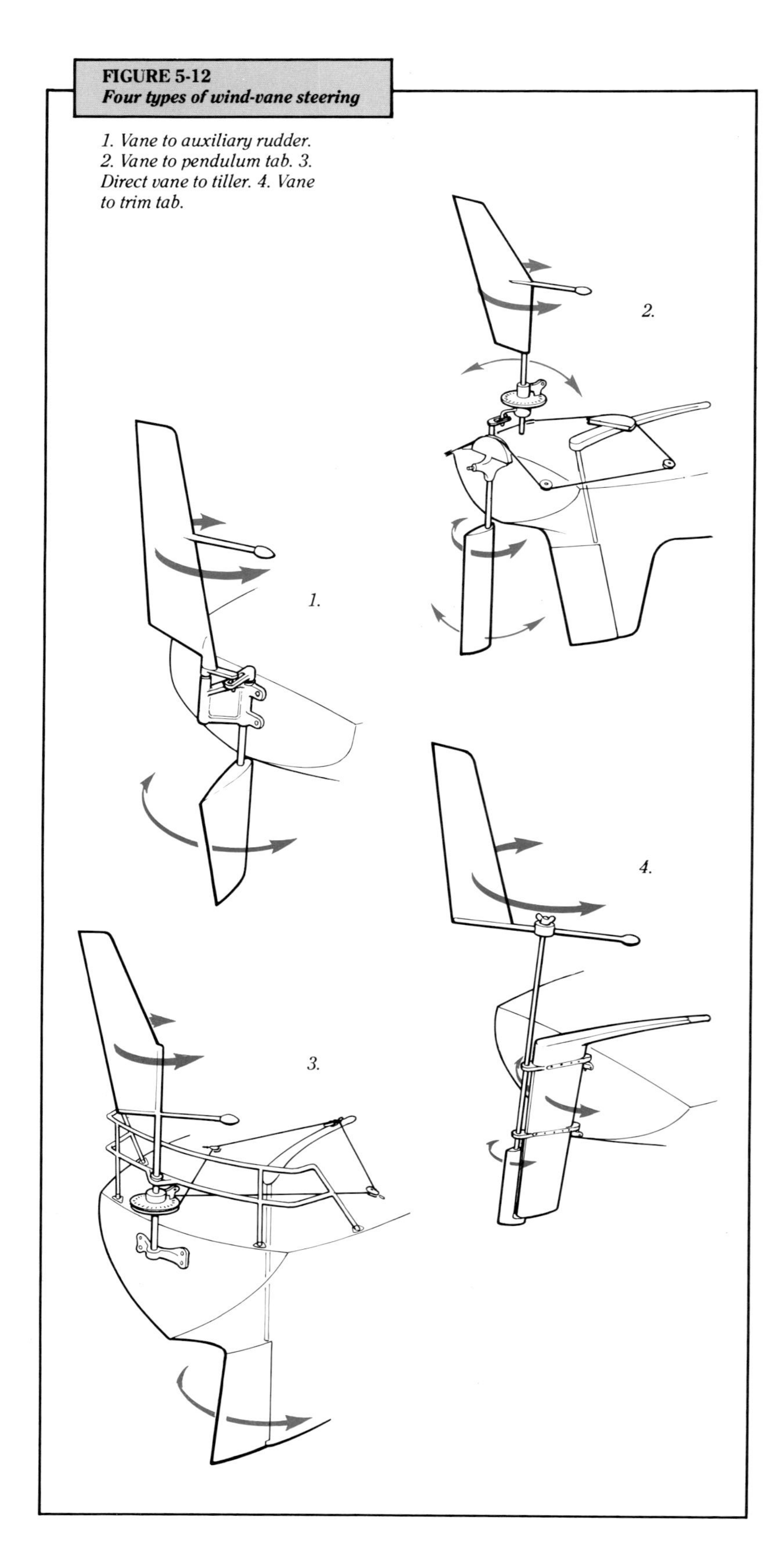

FIGURE 5-12
Four types of wind-vane steering

1. Vane to auxiliary rudder. 2. Vane to pendulum tab. 3. Direct vane to tiller. 4. Vane to trim tab.

rudder through a powerful linkage. The power is very great and the pivoting action corrects for yawing and overpowering.

Vertical axis vanes lose the apparent wind during course corrections making the corrective action occasionally unpredictable. Horizontal axis vanes push like a windward sail, holding the apparent wind as they move and adding more power to the system. When a horizontal vane is utilized, however, limited rudder action is very necessary in order to avoid oversteering. A smaller horizontal vane can adequately handle a boat which would require a far larger vertical model. In the horizontal vane the greater power that is generated requires a lighter vane and corresponding counterweight.

All vanes may be either flat or shaped. Shaped vanes are superior since they are streamlined and thus stall later than flat models. Choosing the correct vane size is a delicate matter, since a large vane is necessary for adequate power while reaching and running, but a smaller vane is fine when sailing to windward and is less easily damaged. Vanes today have incorporated spoilers on the trailing edge to increase sensitivity. As a general rule, the area of a vane and the distance between the vane and its axis determine the power which is generated.

Not only are there four types of vanes there are three types of wind-vane linkage. Each has its own distinct advantages. Direct linkage is such that a deflection of the trim tab or pendulum causes uncontrolled rudder deflection and negative feedback on the system. Yaw is not corrected. The second linkage is differential, where trim-tab deflection causes both an appropriate rudder deflection and positive feedback from the rudder. The third linkage is the fixed variety: adjustable trim-tab deflection causes proper rudder movement but does not counter yaw. The trim tab operates independently of the rudder. Differential linkages are better since the pivot is designed so that tab deflection lessens as the rudder moves one way or the other, thus preventing oversteering. Easy-to-design direct linkages are extremely popular with

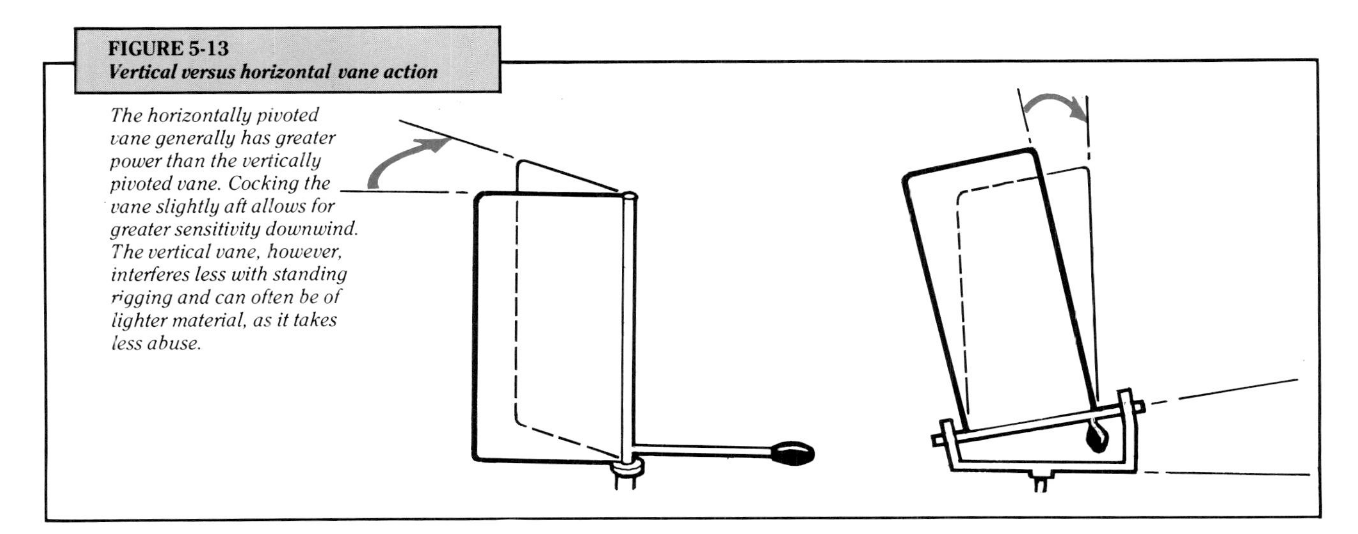

FIGURE 5-13
Vertical versus horizontal vane action

The horizontally pivoted vane generally has greater power than the vertically pivoted vane. Cocking the vane slightly aft allows for greater sensitivity downwind. The vertical vane, however, interferes less with standing rigging and can often be of lighter material, as it takes less abuse.

amateur builders, though they foster chronic oversteering. The degree of course alteration (vane deflection) is not proportional to the degree of course correction applied (rudder deflection).

Different wind-vane steerers, like different wheel steering systems, are best suited to particular boats. Compare features such as sensitivity, course setting, linkage and multiplication of power and steering before settling on a particular model for your yacht. The equipment selected must also fit the conditions under which it will be required to perform. Generally the cheapest gear available suits aft-hung rudders, while the more expensive types are necessary for inboard rudders. The boats that best utilize vane steering are easily balanced, generate slight weather helm and are not too slow in responding. They have a long waterline, moderate beam and short keel. Directional stability and reaction to rudder action are important factors to consider. Neither a squirmy boat which reacts too quickly for a vane to correct nor an old boat which is too slow reacting to the corrective measures of a vane is particularly suitable for efficient wind-vane steering.

A wind vane must be powerful enough to prevent undesired rudder movement caused by lateral water pressure when the stern of the boat swings. Only the more sophisticated vanes are powerful enough to work under all conditions. Lower quality vanes are for coastal passages only, serving as an aid to steering. A high quality vane will steer a yacht whether it is performing in force 2 or force 8 conditions. The vane will be large enough to react to the light air of force 2 and strong enough to handle the abuse dealt by a force 8 blow. In either case the vane must be powerful enough to return the boat to the preselected course. A steering system with a high degree of inherent friction will not react to a small vane system, even if power is multiplied in the tab/rudder system in an attempt to offer sufficient mechanical advantage.

Course-setting mechanisms are also very important. It is far better to have an infinitely adjustable system (as in the line or worm-gear methods) than to be limited to a gear wheel with only 36 teeth offering only 10-degree increments of adjustment. Assume you set a course of 50 degrees, for example, and the closest wind angle setting is 60 degrees apparent or 110 degrees magnetic. If the boat is on a reach, the best accuracy the unit can achieve is ±10 degrees. Then 20-degree course error may well ensue. With an infinitely adjustable system, 10-degree error is the very worst possibility.

What follows is a brief survey of manufacturers, divided according to type. Remember the general advantages of each type. Wind-vane steering gear is in its most basic, cheap and simple form in the units which activate direct wind-vane/rudder control. Trim-tab vane gears are the next step up and are still popular for home construction. They are also simple and cheap, and they work quite well, if a differential linkage is incorporated between the wind vane and the trim tab. Trim-tab gear is prone to yaw; this is perhaps its greatest weakness. The third step up the ladder is vane gear with an auxiliary rudder. A fixed main rudder in this approach offers increased directional stability for every boat so fitted. Additionally if the main rudder is damaged beyond repair, the auxiliary rudder can steer the boat. The fourth and final wind-vane steering gears are the popular pendulum gears. In this approach, course correction is proportional to the degree of deviation. Pendulum gears are easy to install and they are easily maintained, obviating the need for continual repairs.

Direct Rudder Units

Quantock Marine Enterprises makes a strong unit which is both simple and inexpensive. It can readily be linked to wheel or tiller steering, dismantles quickly (less than one minute) and stows easily. Standard Holt Allen parts can be used to fit it to pushpit or deck. The system is suitable for boats up to 30 feet LOA.

The German firm Windpilot sells thousands of its vanes throughout Europe. Suitable for yachts up to 12 tons, the independent units, once fitted, require no maintenance or adjustment. They are easily engaged or disengaged.

Trim-Tab Units

Hasler manufactures an adaptation of its gear, marketed by Gibb. The trim tab connects to the vane via a differential linkage. It is excellent for yachts with transom-hung rudders. Simple and inexpensive, it provides reasonable directional stability. The trim tab, however, when fitted directly to a conventional rudder, is unable to steady yaw since its lift forces oppose those of the rudder itself.

Quartermaster produces a low-priced unit, especially suited for small boats with aft-hung rudders. The tab is suspended independent of the rudder for better interaction. The vane is rudder-mounted for simplest operation. No differential linkage is available, because of the rudder mounting. The main rudder is served by a trim tab. The greater the distance between tab and rudder, the better the tab will work. Balanced, the tab will offer even more steering power. The system is best for boats with a great deal of inherent directional stability.

Auxiliary Rudder Units

MNOP, a French manufacturer, makes a unit designed by the pioneer in the field, engineer Marcel Gianoli. The first units were made for Eric Taberly for OSTAR in 1964. They have been proven under demanding conditions. They are available for boats up to 40 feet LOA. Differential linkage allows improved power. The system is free-turning when not in use.

The Italian company Mustafa produces a unit which has been used in the 1976 OSTAR. It works particularly well under spinnaker in both light and heavy going. An inclined-axis vane with overbalanced auxiliary rudder and trim tab, it is extremely sensitive even in light winds. The high-lift rudder has great corrective power, allowing it to react quickly to course deviations. A differential linkage is used. Three sizes for boats up to 60 feet LOA are available. The unit's main drawback is that it is very expensive. The system is locked amidships when not in use.

The Sailomat unit, made in Sweden, is well finished and soundly built. It uses a pendulum in place of trim tabs. The rudder is partially balanced at rest, but as it becomes more immersed, it becomes fully balanced. Roller bearings, pendulum and rudder connect transversely, rendering a usually vulnerable component very rigid. Comparatively lightweight, different sizes are available. Some allow conversion to autopilot. All are made with low-drag, high-lift profiles. Faultless under sail, the units may vibrate under power.

Riebandt Vane Gear features a vertically pivoting vane which activates the rudder blade through a trim tab. Since the rudder is hung aft of the skeg, the unit is strong. The RVG unit is robust, has few components and features a simple linkage. Though it is cheap and offers reasonable performance, it cannot counter yawing. Both vane and tab are shaped for increased efficiency, and the system allows for worm-gear adjustments. RVG vanes are good for boats as large as 60 feet LOA or as small as 25 feet LOA. Mounting brackets can be customized for each boat.

Hydrovane offers a horizontally pivoted vane with partially balanced rudder. The unit can steer well if the size of vane and rudder are well matched, but it has a tendency to oversteer since the vane flops over immediately when the boat deviates from course. The system is strong, well made and good looking.

Windpilot makes a vertically pivoting vane which drives a balanced auxiliary rudder though meshing gear wheels. The system is light, large, simple and available in different sizes.

Pendulum Units

Aires vanes are similar to Hasler gear (see below), but the Aires units employ heavy castings instead of the tubing, lines and light rods of the Hasler units. The inclined-axis vane is small but well constructed. Reliability is the system's most important asset, and it is widely used. A pawl and gear wheel limits the variety of courses you can select. The servo rudder flips up out of the water to stow when not in use, and a spare plywood vane is supplied with each unit. Replacement vanes, easily made from thin plywood, should be carried.

The Atoms unit is the most popular brand of French gear. The small vane develops great power and reacts quickly. Most French single-handed racers utilize this gear, on boats from 25 to 60 feet LOA. Spare parts are easy to stow and carry since they are very small, and the system itself is easily dismantled. Worm gear allows precise course selection, and an electric motor can set the course from remote positions aboard a yacht. Fine course selection is a real advantage in the system. Differential linkage is utilized between the axis, vane and pendulum. The "kick-up" pendulum is durable, since it rises when it hits floating objects; an alarm is included to warn the operator when the pendulum has broken away. Of 13 French yachts entered in the 1972 OSTAR, 11 utilized this gear.

Hasler vanes are widely used. They are now manufactured and distributed by Gibb. They are OSTAR veterans, and have been used by such yachtsmen as Sir Francis Chichester. Three sizes are available for boats of different displacements. They can be linked to a trim tab instead of a pendulum, but the former option is not as good. The vane-activated pendulum most accurately controls the rudder steering the boat. The system's fine workmanship means low friction, light weight, simple construction and simple operation, including sensitive worm-gear adjustment. The system is vulnerable, however, since a large vertical vane is utilized to achieve sufficient power. There is no differential linkage, so high loads are put on the supporting structure in stormy conditions.

Ratcliffe vanes are virtually custom-made, at reasonable prices, with tremendous attention to detail. The fiberglass vane weighs only 40 pounds total. The horizontal-axis vane attaches to the vertical axis of a fin, connected by a push-rod link. Ratcliffe also manufactures other types of wind-vane steering, but this is his best.

The French Navik system uses a small paddle activated by a trim tab, requiring a very small vane to drive it. It is not a very rugged piece of equipment, but it has some convenience features. An electric motor autopilot can steer by compass, replacing the vane when so desired. The vane/tab linkage is differential. The vane is very small and has easily replaceable component parts. The paddle lifts out of the water when not in use.

The German Schwing-Pilot vane moves along a horizontal shaft to suit force delivered by the vane to the boat. It features a counterweight and sensitive worm-gear course selection. The pendulum pivots on two vertical axes instead of the usual one vertical and one horizontal. The differential linkage is simplified by having the pendulum operate on two vertical axes. The pendulum swings sideways in reaction to the vane's movement, thereby ensuring that it will not come out of the water. It is very expensive compared to conventional pendulum gear with an inclined-axis vane, but it's the most sophisticated and adjustable unit marketed in the world today.

AUTOPILOTS

Autopilots steer a yacht by compass although one of the models we shall examine can readily sail a boat to a preselected apparent wind angle. They can't help you avoid hitting another boat or running aground, but with the rapid development of the microcomputer fields, it should be no small wonder to see in a few years a system which can scan radar and react accordingly, altering course to avoid both collisions and running the yacht aground. In the meantime, the sole purpose of installing an autopilot is to have a mechanical device relieve the helmsman.

An autopilot must, of course, be tough and dependable, but when used aboard a sailboat, it must also have low power drain, so as not to overtax the limited generating capacity. "Nonhunting" models are therefore preferred over "hunting" models. Hunting models continually turn the rudder, oscillating from one side to another constantly since the units have no null or neutral and only feature an on/off switch. The nonhunting type has a neutral or null, so the rudder moves only when a course correction is necessary. The rest of the time, this type of unit does not turn. Nonhunting types are best for yachts since they have a lower power drain.

Encron Energy Control Corporation offers two models of autopilots which precisely steer a boat in all sea conditions, at any speed, with a fully gimballed superstable compass. The larger model (77A) is well suited for heavier vessels, particularly ocean cruising sailboats 40 feet LOA and over. For boats under 40 feet, Encron offers a slightly smaller unit with less power consumption, for the same purchase price. The 77C is available for either mechanical or hydraulic steering. (It has been readily adapted to Wagner hydraulic steering.) The 77C is one of the best autopilots available because in addition to the design, engineering, top materials and precision production, the unit features automatic rudder trim to adjust for variable weather helm. Moreover, it has very low current drain.

Sharp and Company offers four models of autopilots which are well suited to sailing yachts. The Seapilot is available for hydraulic or mechanical steering in a solid-state, nonhunting autopilot designed to operate on boats up to 45 feet LOA. These models are easy to install, consisting of several units: the binnacle unit, the control unit, the steering unit, the optional rudder feedback unit and the optional (but most useful) remote control unit. The Oceanpilot is another model offered by Sharp, featuring a solid-state compass very similar to an aircraft compass with an integrated circuit which computes the rudder action required to keep accurate courses. Yaw control and automatic trim control can sense and adjust for vagaries encountered at sea. Sharp's least expensive and simplest unit is the Mate B-40 Autopilot, most suitable for small boats with cost-conscious owners. The Mate B-40 has only two controls to adjust, since a separate yaw control has been left out. The automated system applies corrective rudder as the vessel swings off course; the greater the movement off course, the faster the motor speed. Aside from the course selector dial a rudder control dial is included to let the unit adapt to changing sea conditions and different boats. The rudder control varies the ratio between the compass movement and the amount of rudder applied. Automatic trim is included with each unit to cope with changing helm condition and apply the necessary bias helm.

Metal Marine Pilot Incorporated manufactures Wood Freeman Automatic Pilots in four different models. Wood Freemans are the supreme autopilots manufactured in the world. The 500 series is unsurpassed for design, engineering, construction and sophistication. Nonhunting and hunting models are available.

All Wood Freeman automatic pilots utilize a magnetic compass to monitor the yacht's progress in relation to her preselected course. The type for mechanical steering gear has only three principal parts: the compass unit, the relay unit and the motor unit. The models intended for hydraulic steering are four-unit models: a compass unit and orienting assembly, a compass follow-up system, a relay unit to amplify and transmit all signals and a power-pack pump unit. The quality and the ruggedness of Wood Freeman products is indicated in the weights of the four models: the Model Eleven weighs 85 pounds; the Model Fifteen 105 pounds; the Model 420 120 pounds; and the Five Hundred Series, 145 pounds. The units are certainly not light, and for this reason they are best suited for larger (40 feet and up) yachts.

Autohelm manufactures autopilot units, of which the new 3000 Series offers a new adaptation for wheel steering. Autohelm is a British company, and the recent success of their units in the 1980 Observer Single-handed Transatlantic Race (OSTAR) aboard Phil Weld's Pen Duick class winner *Moxie* and Walter Greene's *Chaussettes Olympia* surely puts the company in the forefront in autopilots especially suited to fast sailing yachts. Both Weld and Greene were sailing trimarans. Phil Weld utilized the new Autohelm 3000 for wheel steering installations with great success. He carried three spare units with him in the 2,800 mile solo classic across the Atlantic and never had to use them since the original carried him all the way. Jerry Cartwright aboard *Le First* of the Jester Class also carried an Autohelm autopilot. Unlike Weld and Greene, however, Cartwright was sailing a stock Beneteau 30. All three of these boats proved that Autohelm produces reliable autopilots. The units performed under the most demanding conditions including two lows with winds ranging to force 10. From Phil Weld's 17-day 23-hour crossing to Jerry Cartwright's 26-day 22-hour crossing, Autohelm stood up.

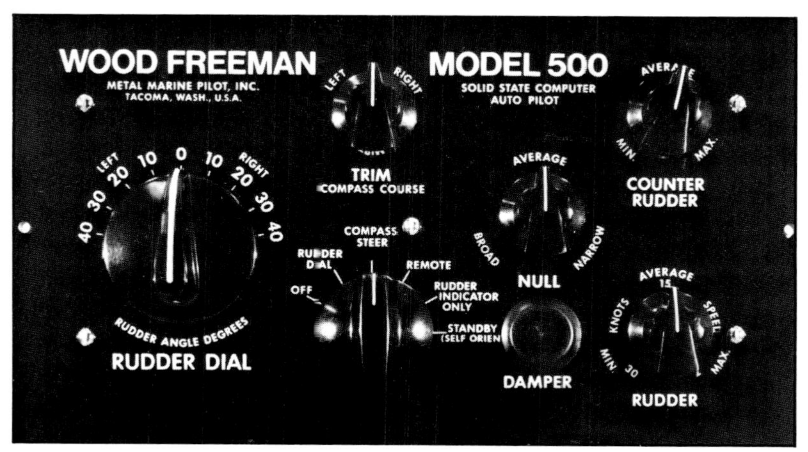

The Wood Freeman 500 is a sophisticated, highly adjustable autopilot.

Safe Flight Instrument Corporation manufactures an autopilot unit that will steer from a compass to a preselected course, or, if the operator desires, the unit may be directed to steer the yacht to any apparent wind angle. Although the first part of the unit is similar in function to the other autopilots we have examined, the second function usually is only achieved by a cumbersome wind-vane setup. The Safe Flight system is compact. The main unit operates hidden from view (housed in a lazarette, cockpit locker or pedestal) and does not interfere with other actions of the boat when not in use. Safe Flight is first and foremost a manufacturer of fine aviation

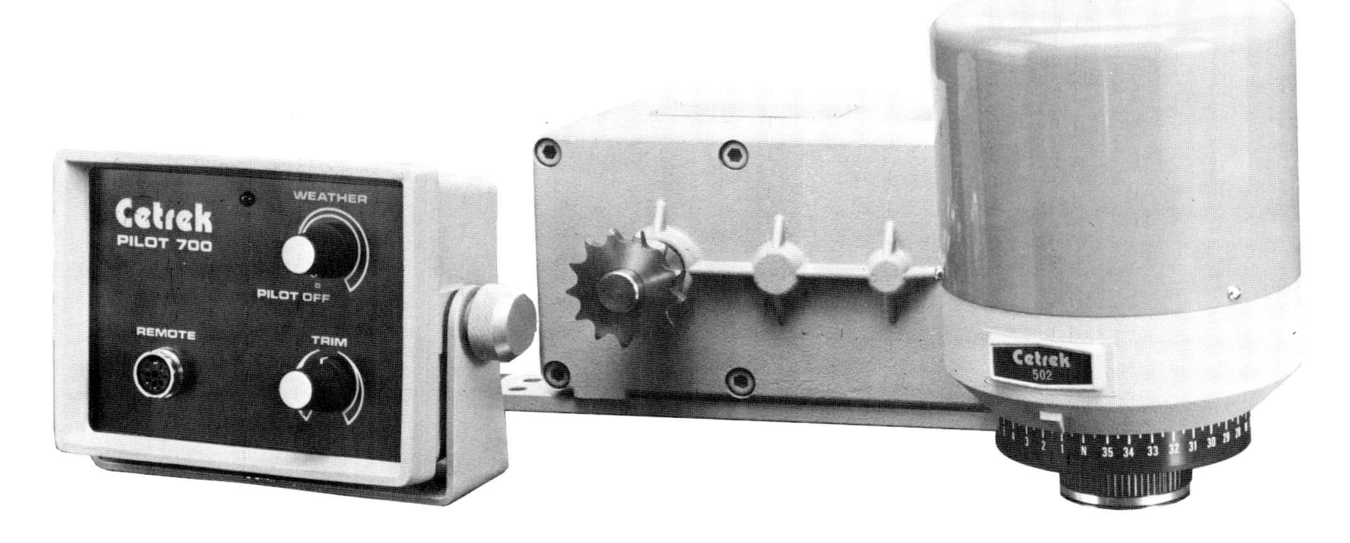

Cetrek autopilot. Control unit, motor drive and sensing compass make a small, dependable package.

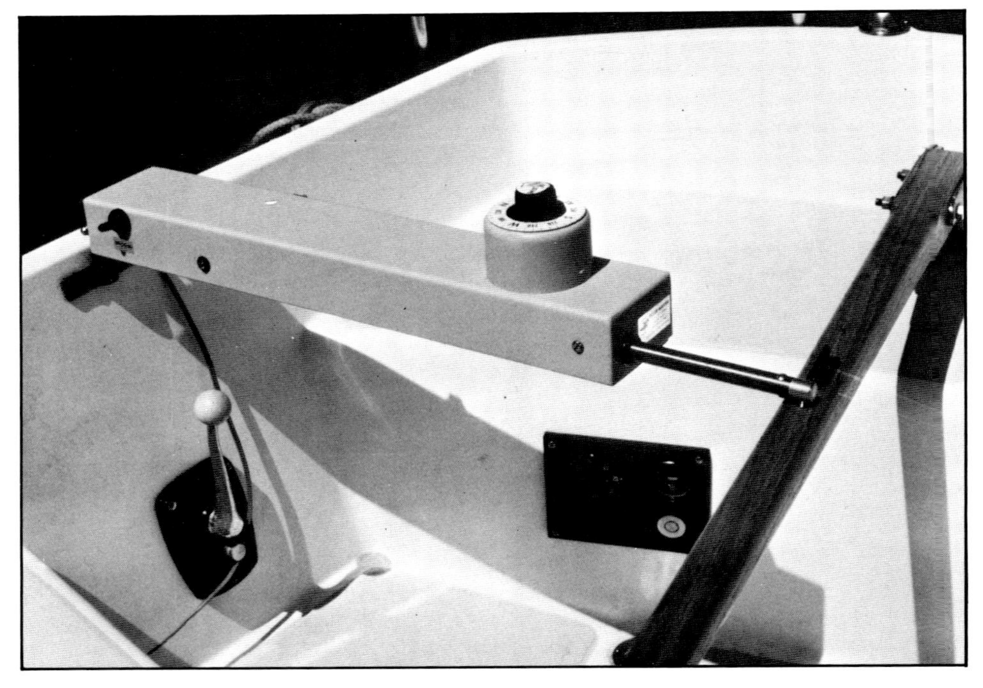

Tiller Master makes one of the simpler autopilots, suitable for smaller yachts. it can be adapted for use with tiller (as shown) or steering wheel.

equipment. The company's founder, Len Greene, has been an avid sailor for years. He has sought to develop a line of marine gear with the same precision and sophistication as aviation equipment. The hermetically-sealed Safe Flight Marine autopilot coupling offers a promising combination. The wind-vane attachment overcomes one disadvantage of autopilots: their failure to keep sails at the most efficient angle to the wind as it shifts.

Tillermaster manufactures an autopilot for tiller-steered boats. Tiller Master is a side-mounted autopilot containing its own magnetic compass. The units are compact, weighing only six pounds and fitting in a case the size of a man's arm. The system is nonhunting, so the tiller is turned only when corrective action is necessary for a course change. Tiller Master offers 100 pounds of push and pull for steering control. It is easily serviced since it has an easily removed plug-in electronic package. The system has evolved over a 20-year period, and now offers sophisticated features, including a mechanical feedback to prevent oversteering and resulting "S" bends in the wake. Phillip Steggall utilized two Tiller Masters aboard his 1980 OSTAR trimaran, *Jeans Foster*, to win impressively and finish close behind Phil Weld's much larger boat, *Moxie*. *Jeans Foster* had a 15-to-1 ratio Tiller Master for running and reaching to give the helm a quicker reaction period and a greatly stepped down 25-to-1 model which he used for windward sailing. The two units performed flawlessly and Steggall required only a few small inexpensive spares in case either unit needed a repair or overhaul. They did not.

Chapter 6

BELOW DECKS

The cabin area of any yacht serves as shelter, kitchen, bedroom, diningroom, storeroom and navigatorium. It takes careful planning to include all the above comfortably and safely. Bigger yachts have fewer problems fitting everything in, but perfection is seldom achieved.

In the latter half of the twentieth century, when high cost has made the custom yacht little more than an occasional glimmer in a builder's eye, the production boat is the norm. Some are very fine indeed, but most builders cannot afford to include too much specialized hardware or too many convenience features. Thus it becomes incumbent upon the owner to modify and embellish where the builder has not, making the boat truly habitable.

PLANNING CABIN SPACE

Since the cabin is the place where you spend most of your time after sailing, it deserves the best you can give it, in terms of design and fittings, especially as regards the equipment which makes life aboard more comfortable and safe.

Berths

The number of berths any yacht contains is determined, of course, by the builder, sometimes not very realistically. There are far too many 26-foot boats with six berths. They can sleep six, yes, but not comfortably. For extended cruising, four bodies on a 35-footer is about the comfortable maximum you can carry.

Berths, to be of any use at sea, must be parallel to the centerline head and foot, at least 78 inches long and not more than 24 inches wide. Any such berth must be fitted with stout leecloths or boards. Double berths are sensuous in harbor but can be rib-cracking underway unless a removable leeboard is fitted.

Quarter berths must be properly ventilated with an acrylic or plastic rain shield at the outboard end. Mattresses, if two-ply foam, can be as little as 3 inches thick, though 4 or 5 inches makes for more comfortable sleeping. V-berths are useless at sea in a pitching boat and conducive to the spread of athlete's foot in harbor. The forepeak is best if it is left for stowage and a chain locker.

Galley

Sustenance aboard is the key to crew contentment and efficiency. No one enjoys eating out of cans all the time. The galley area probably demands more detailed planning than any other installation on the boat, because it must accommodate facilities for stowage, heating, cooling, washing, cutting and serving, all in a remarkably compact space.

How to best use the space depends, of course, on the basic layout of the galley. The three most common types are in-line, L-shaped and U-shaped. In-line galleys, except in passageways on very large boats, have little to recommend them. They are impractical underway, take up space more appropriate for berths and stowage and ensure that the sink will not drain as long as the galley is to leeward.

On small boats the L-shaped arrangement is probably the only kind that will fit. With handholds and a good restraining belt it can work efficiently, provided that the sink is near the centerline and there is a small area where the cook can stand out of the flow of traffic.

U-shaped galleys can be as convenient as home kitchens, on larger boats, but there are two types of U's. The most common is

Interior plan of a Swan 391. Space is efficiently used, with pilot berths port and starboard, a galley removed from traffic flow and sufficiently large chart table. The pipe cots in the forepeak are strictly for harbor use. The starboard berth in the aft cabin lets you sleep while on port tack.

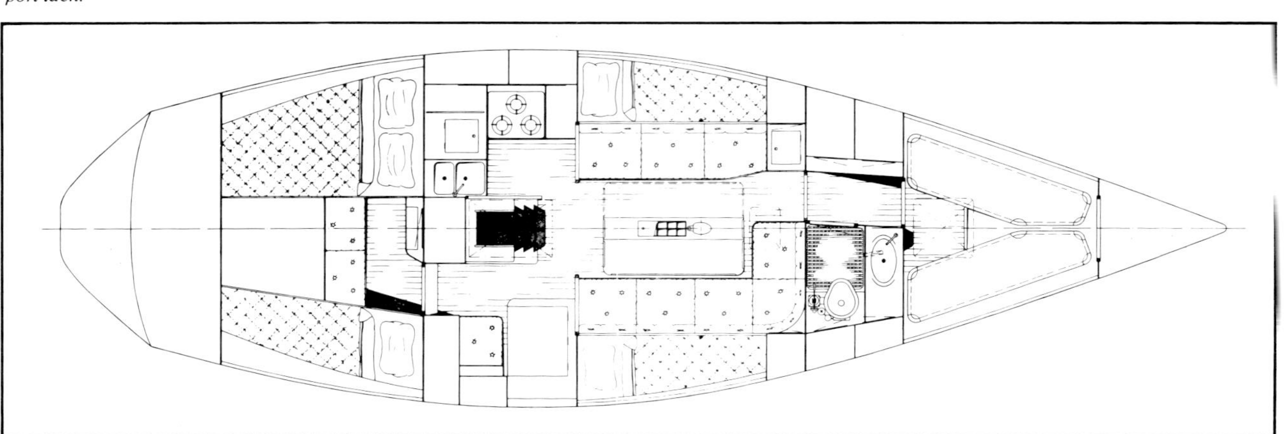

open on its inboard side, meaning that a belt is still necessary. Better, though rarely seen, is a U with one arm running parallel to the centerline, thus automatically restraining the cook no matter what tack the yacht is on. U-shaped galleys usually include a sink and counter space on one arm, an icebox or refrigerator/freezer on the other and a stove at the base of the U.

One problem with all galley arrangements is that the area outboard of the stove is usually devoted to stowage, either on shelves or in bin lockers. The danger of stowing anything often needed in such space should be obvious. Only little-used items—outsize pots and emergency rations—should be placed there. Reaching across a hot stove in a lurching boat invites injury.

Even the most complete galley can be upgraded by arranging more efficient stowage, adding racks and installing proper fiddles. These last should be at least 2 inches high—3 inches for offshore use. Drawers and locker doors should be so arranged that boxes and bottles will not fall and break over your head. Lips on shelves are a good idea, and racks, fitted to *your* dishes and crockery, are worth their time and expense in breakage avoided. Transparent plexiglas is a good material since it lets you see what's behind it.

A U-shaped galley aboard the C & C 46. Double sinks, plenty of storage space, adequate illumination and convenience to the companionway make it a fine galley. Crash bar across cooker is a vital safety item; the grabrail overhead is also worthwhile.

Pumps, through-hulls and all plumbing must be accessible and tough. Lurching against some of the galley pumps sold today will leave you with an empty glass and a hand full of bent and broken pump. Durable pumps are discussed later in the chapter (see page 134).

FIGURE 6-1
Pressure water system

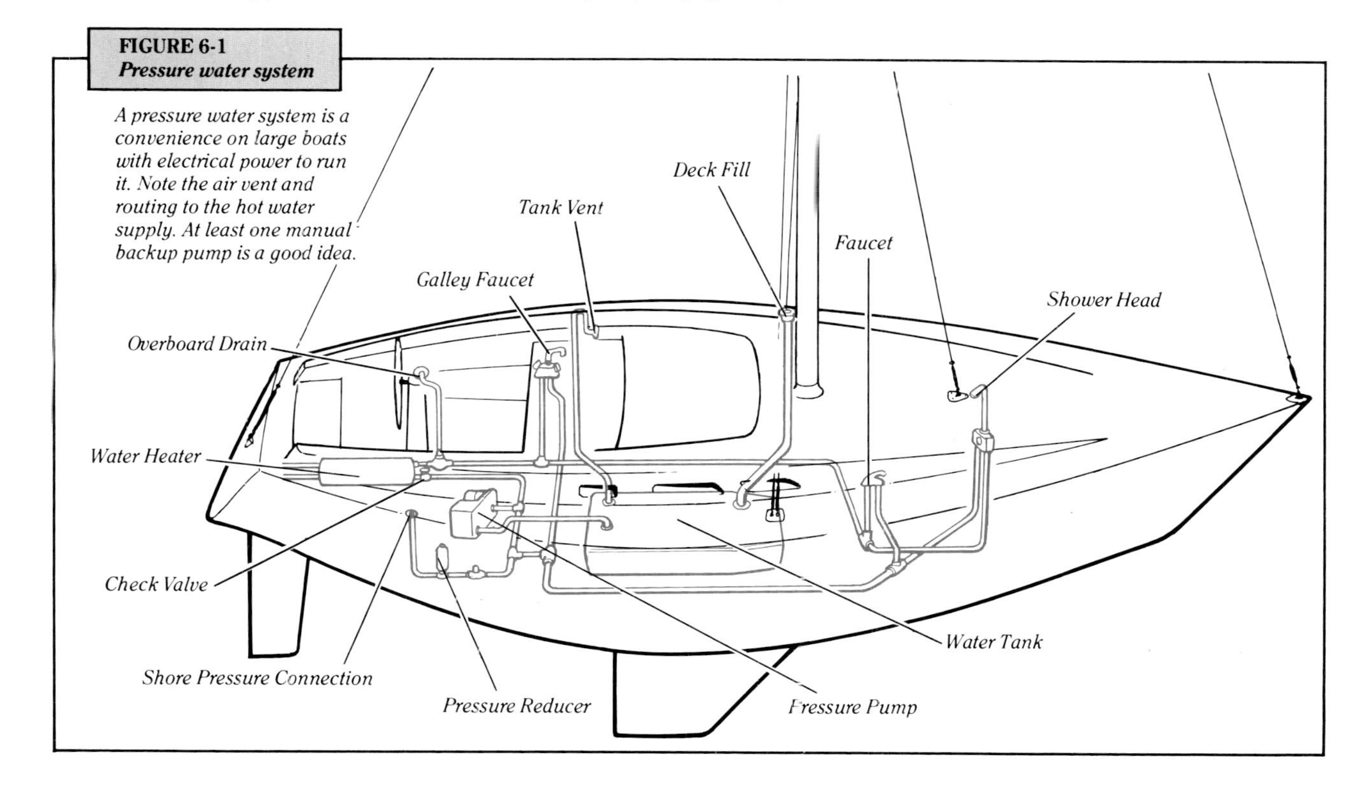

A pressure water system is a convenience on large boats with electrical power to run it. Note the air vent and routing to the hot water supply. At least one manual backup pump is a good idea.

Interior moldings make for an easy-to-clean head. *Note these efficient features: the teak grate on sole; the hinged panel under* head *for ready access to seacocks; a grab bar behind* head; *the fiddled shelf; the well-placed light fixture; and flush-mounted sink.*

Countertops should be scuff-resistant, easy to clean and impervious to alcohol and heat. Formica is the best material. Provision for a chopping block or cutting board with stowage is a good idea, but sink and stove covers only get in the way. Portable chopping blocks are best. Besides, a good deep sink is the best place of all—in a seaway—for hot or greasy mixtures.

Head

That other plumber's nightmare, the *head* compartment, deserves careful attention. On most boats under 35 feet long, the *head* will be located between the saloon and the forecabin; occasionally, you will see the forepeak entirely devoted to it. Though this is a good way to use the nasty little area in the bows, you may find yourself in intimate and violent contact with toilet seat or deckhead if you use such a *head* while pounding to windward. Nonetheless, center installation does have advantages when the boat is heeled. The midships compartment, though it has heavier traffic, is probably the best location. The *head* need not be more than 2½ feet square. (More, in fact, will lead to banging about.)

Little details are most helpful: a latch for fastening the lid, so it doesn't slam down; fitments for toilet paper and towels; a Dorade vent for fresh air; sound insulation (if you tend toward modesty); a sill for foot bracing; strategically placed handholds; and out-of-the-way lighting.

The vanity or sink can fold down or slide out. Both kinds not only save space, but allow the sink to drain into the head, saving you an extra through-hull mounting. Such a sink should have a positive locking device to keep it from slamming into the back of your head while you are enthroned. Simpson-Lawrence makes fine sinks of both types.

Sink and toilet installation is vitally important to the survival of the ship. Hoses must be looped way above the waterline, double-clamped and vented. The top of the toilet proper should be several inches above the waterline. Seacocks must be easily and instantly accessible—with no odds and ends stuffed in front of them.

Navigation Table

The last of the major working areas below decks is the chart table. Here is the control center, the nerves of the yacht where sits the person in charge of getting you to your destination. Surrounded by instruments, radios, charts and electronic gadgets, he is a *rara avis,* preoccupied, diligent, superior in his knowledge that he commands the destinies of men.

His needs are simple: a large, flat surface, a few shelves and some stowage space. The best chart table ought to be able to hold an unfolded chart, which depending on where you sail, could mean something on the order of a 3-by-4-foot sheet, not exactly the space available on most yachts. More realistic is a 2-by-3-foot surface, as it will hold once-folded U.S. and Admiralty charts. The chart surface must be flat, preferably with any hinges concealed.

Whether it will be athwartships or fore-and-aft in configuration is a matter of personal taste. You can sit down at an athwartships table, though fore-and-aft tables can be more convenient for quick work. The fore-and-aft setup provides for increased stowage space underneath the table, as well as extra lockers and instrument space outboard. Whichever alignment you decide upon be sure to cover the table's surface with green nylon felt or linoleum. White, glossy surfaces cause glare and chart slippage. The inboard edge of the table benefits from a removable fiddle and a padded end.

Chart stowage is a matter of priorities. If you plan to circle the globe, you need enough accessible space—in a bin under a hinged table lid, in drawers or in racks on the deckhead above the table surface for a 3-inch high stack of charts. Rolled charts are

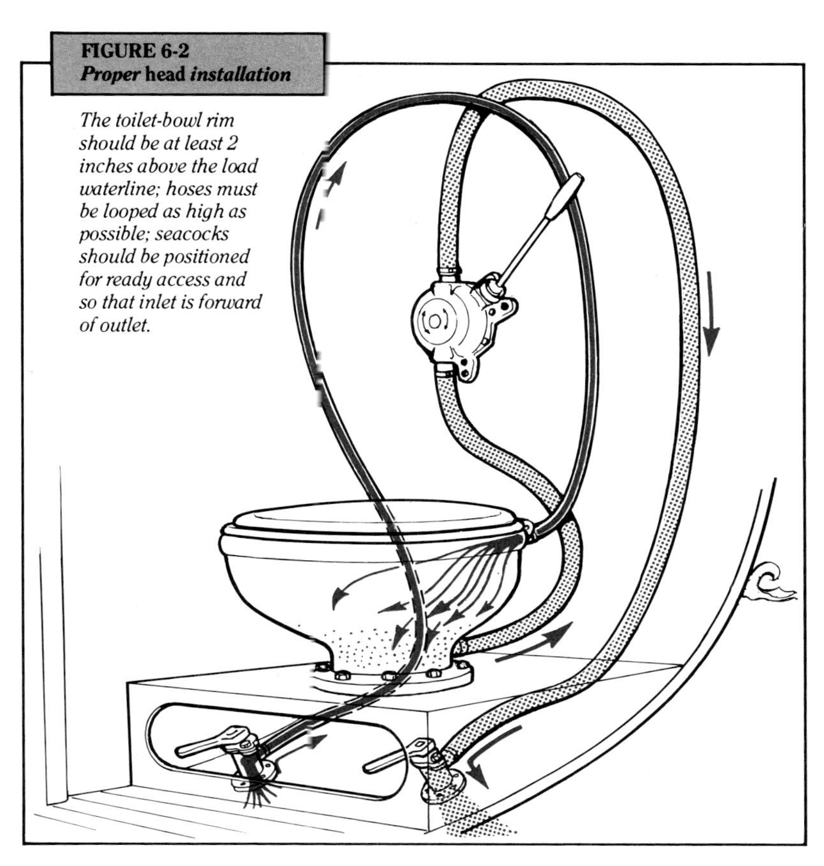

FIGURE 6-2
Proper* head *installation

The toilet-bowl rim should be at least 2 inches above the load waterline; hoses must be looped as high as possible; seacocks should be positioned for ready access and so that inlet is forward of outlet.

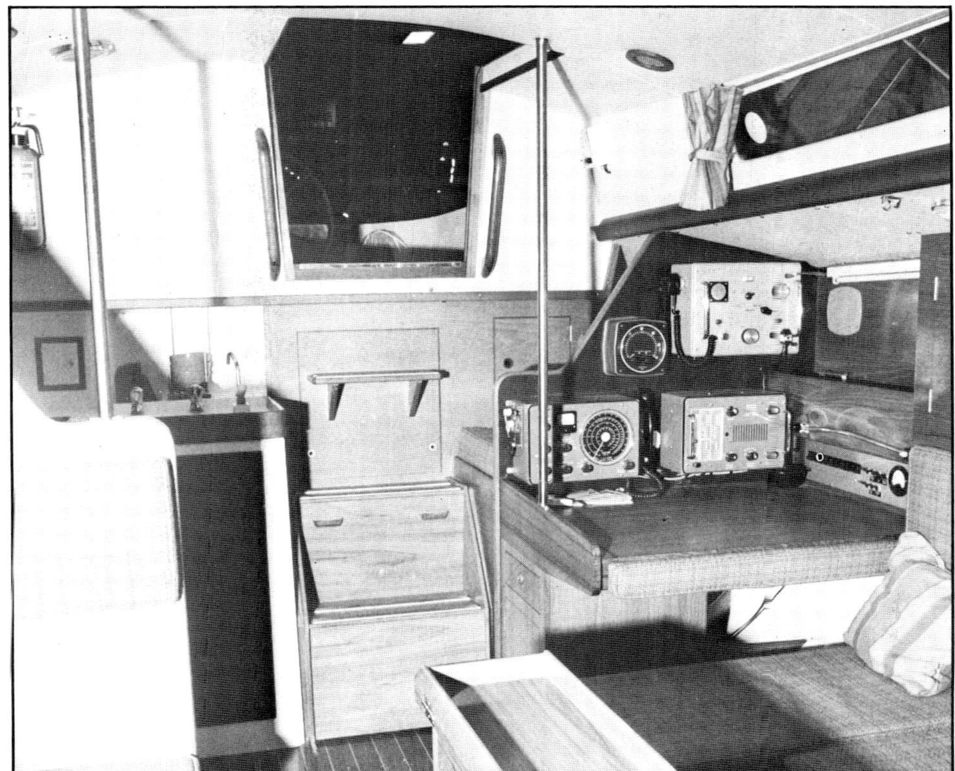

Chart table on the Nicholson 35. Though aft-facing, it has all the requisites and saves space at that. The padded edge is a good safety fixture. Bulkhead space for electronics is ample and convenient; and there are bins for books and charts.

a nuisance because—they often pop closed with all your dividers and rules and pencils trapped inside them.

Next to the working surface should be a rack for navigation tools. Mount electronics and other instruments on a bulkhead. A compass is a useful adjunct, but make sure it is isolated from any possible magnetic field. Pilot books, atlases, tide tables and light lists need a shelf big enough to hold them, or else a reasonably deep bin. Here, too, sextant and chronometer stowage can be permanently arranged.

Saloon Table

The current practice is to make the saloon table fold against the forward bulkhead for convenient stowage. Unfortunately, you can eat on such a table only in smooth water or at a mooring. It is a sorry sight when the table collapses at sea, spreading a muddle of hot stew, paper napkins and sharp knives across the sole. Why not build a proper table in the first place?

A proper table is permanently mounted with massive, bolted-down legs and supports. The surface should be impervious to stains, burns and nicks. If located on the centerline, or slightly offset, it may have fold-down leaves, hinged along their entire length. Suitable means must be found to secure the leaves when raised *and* lowered. Let the center section contain covered bin lockers for wine, silverware, decks of cards and poker chips, and let it be fiddled to help keep pots of food on the table. All corners and edges should be smooth.

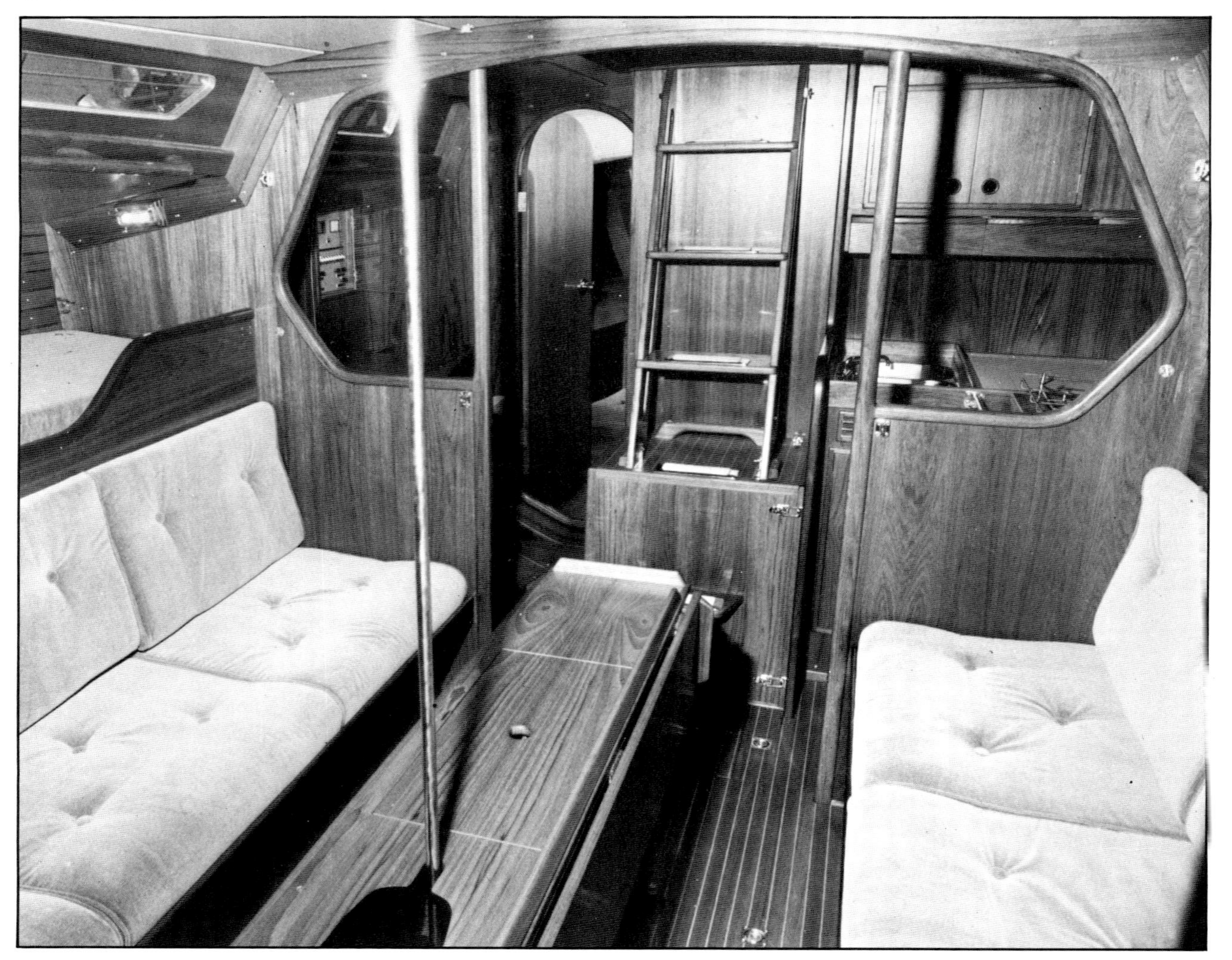

A really strong table must be permanently mounted. This Swan table fits around the mast and the tie rod makes for a handy support rail. Central bin storage and proper fiddle are useful.

Dinette tables can, of course, dispense with the passage-clutter problems, but they must be a solid slab. On larger boats, gimballed tables can be of use for holding foodstuffs in a seaway, though they are not really meant to be eaten on. As the boat tacks you may have the food at your knee level or the table at your mouth. Since you will not often eat at a table when underway —huddling in some well-padded corner instead—the gimballed table will at least give you a place to put the porridge while you sip your tea.

Storage Bins

To keep such items as clothes and tools dry, you need dry lockers, sealed from the bilges either by special construction or with plastic bins. Closets for hanging need not be large. Unlike sailors of Uffa Fox's day, few of us go to sea with dinner jackets and starched shirts. For two people, a 12- to 18-inch wide closet is enough. Foul weather gear, though, deserves a separate locker—the nearer the companionway the handier it will be—with drainage to the bilges.

Drawers and all lockers must be carefully secured. Use no spring catches, no magnetic niceties and no finger-hole access. The most effective way of making certain a hinged door of any kind stays closed is a good old-fashioned button catch or a sliding-bolt latch. Both are cheap, easy to install and will do no damage to your fingers or the lockers.

Sliding doors are also a good means of sealing things in, providing they are really substantial. Too often, they are thin ply. The best are made of sturdy plywood, at least ½-inch thick.

Finally, all locker space ought be divided to be useful: vertical partitions in upper-berth lockers; fiddles on all shelf space; and securing bars on book shelves. With care and ingenuity you can create a useful and comfortable environment.

GALLEY EQUIPMENT

The galley is the source of the sailor's greatest comforts, but it can also be the source of his greatest pains. Badly designed stoves and sinks slop food all over you. An undetected fuel leak can do worse.

A proper oily locker beside the companionway. Teak grate allows drainage to the bilges and engine heat keeps gear dry.

Stoves

The centerpiece of any galley is the stove. From heating the morning coffee to the midnight cocoa, the stove does yeoman's service in keeping the crew happy.

Marine stoves come in a variety of shapes, sizes and types. The four basic fuel types are solid, gaseous, liquid and electric. The advantages and disadvantages of each are summarized below.

Solid Fuel stoves are suitable for colder climates. Providing a constant source of even heat, they are good for drying and heating as well as cooking.

However, wood, coal or charcoal can be dangerous in heavy weather, as they give off sparks which can fly up the chimney and may ignite sails or deck fittings. There is no way to gimbal such stoves, and they are heavy and must be vented outside. The fuels themselves are dirty, awkward to store and burn fast. Solid fuel stoves are suitable only for larger, traditional vessels on coastal passages.

Liquid Fuel stoves burn diesel fuel, kerosene or alcohol. Each type has its own set of pros and cons.

Diesel is cheap and readily available. It can be fed from the same tank as the engine. Quick and hot for cooking, it can also be used for cabin heating. Diesel stoves, however, have some drawbacks. They cannot be gimballed, need very high stacks and may not vent properly at appreciable angles of heel. They may also create too much cabin heat, unless installed in a separate "stove room."

Kerosene (paraffin) fuel is easily available, cheap, hot and highly efficient, though stoves using it need to be primed with methylated spirits (alcohol). The flames can be hard to adjust and burners need frequent cleaning, but with care and maintenance kerosene stoves are the best choice for distance cruising.

The Shipmate stove can be fitted for alcohol, kerosene (paraffin) or LPG.

Alcohol is a very safe fuel in that water will extinguish the flames, but it's not readily available in many parts of the world. It is the least efficient and most expensive of all fuels. Stoves are available either with pressure burners, gravity feed or wicks. The wicks are preferable, because the burner types clog easily.

Gaseous Fuel stoves use propane, butane or compressed natural gas (CNG). Marketed under such names as Camping Gaz and LP Gas, propane and butane are heavier than air; compressed natural gas, on the other hand, is lighter than air. Leaking propane or butane can sink into the bilges, creating a danger of explosion. However, with careful installation on deck, flexible couplings and shutoff valves at both tank and stove, they provide the hottest, cleanest and most adjustable fuels for cooking onboard. CNG is slightly cheaper and safer, but it's widely available only in the U.S. and its fuel tanks will not hold as much.

For the international cruiser, however, all gaseous fuels pose two problems. First, fuel dispensers in many countries may not be located near the water. You may have to lug your tanks around by taxi looking for the right shop. Once you find the right place, you may still have problems fitting your tank to the dispenser as the couplings vary from country to country. Furthermore, cylinders are susceptible to corrosion, and you must take great care in their installation and maintenance; an alarm to detect leakage is essential. Vetus and Super Sniffa make the finest.

Electric cooking is not practicable except on very large motor sailers, because it uses too much power. You must either hook up to shore power or run a generator.

An electric stove supplies safe, steady heat. Unlike all combustible fuels, it releases no moisture into the cabin, so it will not deplete available oxygen. The stoves, however, cannot be gimballed and they take a long time to heat up and cool down. Moreover, if you are going abroad, you will need voltage regulators, assorted dockside plugs and transformers to handle foreign shore power sources.

Stove bodies should be made of marine-grade aluminum, stainless steel or brass. Cooking surfaces can be enamel-coated iron or stainless. Top panels should detach easily for cleaning, but burner rings should be well secured. Pot clamps and sea rails are a must. If the stove has an oven, make sure there is a positive bolt catch to secure the oven while underway. A method of securing the gimbal mechanism when cooking in port keeps a pot of hot water from slopping over.

Quality solid-fuel stoves are made in Scandinavia and the U.S. Shipmate in America makes a large variety, while Jotul closed-combustion stoves are splendid, if rather bulky.

Dickenson makes a superb line of diesel stoves, though they are not cheap, demand a steady power supply and cannot be gimballed. Hal Roth has cruised thousands of miles in *Whisper* with one and swears by it. Taylor in the U.K. produces a line for both pleasure and commercial vessels. Built to a very high standard in brass or stainless steel, they can be ordered with accessories such as heaters and hot water boilers.

Most kerosene (paraffin) stoves use Primus burners. Parts and fuel are available worldwide, making kerosene a prime choice for world cruisers. The best of these stoves is the self-lighting Optimus or any of the Shipmate models. All are built from heavy-gauge stainless steel, the Optimus having an oven as an option. The Shipmate stoves come in two- and three-burner models with or without oven. Both are gimballed, with pot clamps and searails. Taylor in England makes a line of superb kerosene stoves with or without ovens, made of stainless steel or brass. Sporting vitreous enamel hot plates, they are glorious just to look at. Some models come with integral tanks, but the larger ones use separate large-capacity tanks, making refilling a once or twice per season pastime.

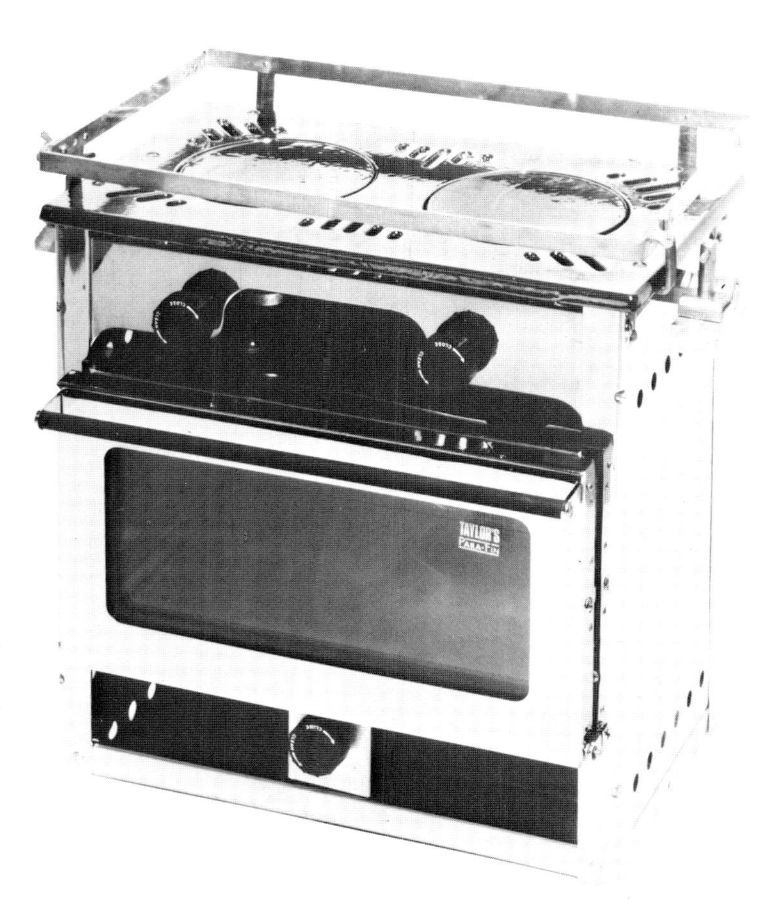

Taylor makes the king of paraffin ranges, made of brass and stainless steel. Only highly anticorrosive materials are suitable for marine stoves.

Alcohol stoves come from a number of top-flight producers. Paul Luke, New England boat builder extraordinaire, produces the Heritage stoves, works of kitchen art which are as well made a stove as money can buy. Homestrand, the old reliable, is serviceable though corrosion problems do exist in the grates and oven.

Shipmate alcohol stoves—identical to their kerosene models except for the burners—are to be highly recommended. One especially nice little cooking stove is the Swedish Origo, because it uses a wick instead of pressure burners, eliminating preheating and pumping. Though very reliable, it sells only as a two-burner unit.

Gas stoves (butane, propane, camping gas, etc.) are the most popular in Europe, despite their potential hazards. Everyone makes them—Homestrand, Maxol, Hillerange, Shipmate, Luke and others—but the Shipmate and Luke stoves are in a class by themselves for quality.

Double sinks mounted near centerline. Sinks are best made of stainless steel and should be a minimum of 6 inches deep. In this installation a fiddle is needed to keep water from running into the icebox. Note excellent crockery storage. The wash bar runs completely around galley counter.

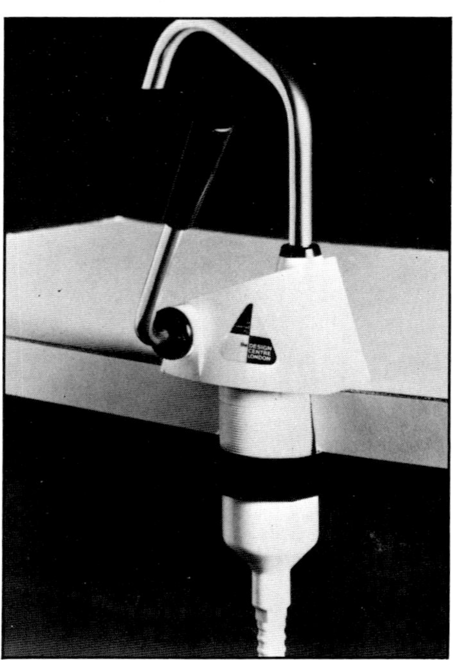

The Whale Flipper MK 111 is a versatile hand pump and faucet assembly for galley and head *use.*

Sinks and Pumps

The preferred material for sinks is stainless steel. Fiberglass sinks can delaminate after hard use, leading to leakage. The most useful sinks have either double drains (allowing for emptying on either tack) or a centered drain with sloping bottom. Most commercially available sinks are too shallow and too small. A good one should be at least 6 inches deep and be able to contain the largest pot or plate on board. If it is too shallow, you'll be washing up on the floor. A round sink does not use the available space advantageously. A good idea (not seen enough) is the double sink, one part narrower than the other, providing secure dumping grounds for dirty dishes and/or a draining space.

Ideally, the galley sink should be custom-built by a dependable sheet metal shop, and include a stainless steel surround flush with the countertop. Any measure to prevent the dirt buildup or the development of leaks should be undertaken, but draining boards are highly overrated, especially when integral to the sink surround. They can only be used in harbor and take up space better used for other chores. A splendid alternative is an open-bottomed rack *above* the sink, made of raw wood or coated steel, on which the dishes can be drained and stored.

The sink's plumbing should be as safe as that for *head* and engine-cooling apparatus. Reinforced, double-clamped hoses should be used. Make sure that seacocks are easily accessible. If the sink is as deep as it should be, it may not drain on one tack, so you may need to buy a foot pump. Whale makes the best.

There are two alternative means of transporting water to the sink: manual and power (electrical). A standard criticism in favor of manual pumps is that power pumps fail, use more water and need backups. True, all electrical appliances are susceptible to corrosion and failure at sea, but modern wiring practices and construction are reasonably robust. And power pumps do not, in fact, use more water, unless the user is heavy-handed. In short, there is no reason not to install a power pump.

Spring-loaded faucets are a very good way to save water. Even better is a spring-loaded power foot pump such as the one made by Whale. With a foot pump, you can wash both hands using the same small stream of water.

All pumps, no matter what type, must be of the most robust construction. The days of solid brass pumps are numbered, though Whale and Davey still supply them, as does Perko. They could be troublesome and clumsy, but rarely did they break. If you can find one and fit it in your boat, by all means do so.

The majority of modern hand pumps are constructed of light alloy, nylon or plastic. They are corrosion proof, self-priming and smooth working, but they may disintegrate if you lurch against them in a violent roll. Whale makes the best models, in different configurations for right- or left-hand action and for different mounting positions. Whale pumps have the advantage of being available in virtually every civilized country in the world.

Quality power pumps are made by Jabsco, Whale, Aqualite, Simpson-Lawrence and Perkins. The Aqualite and Perkins systems meet commercial standards and can reliably handle all the loads placed upon them. All power pumps must be carefully wired and regularly maintained, keeping the wiring out of the bilges. Separate circuit breakers or fuses for each pumping system should be installed. Regularly clean the contacts, coating them with Vaseline or some waterproof gel.

Hoses can be either vinyl or neoprene. The latter, specially reinforced, is preferable. Connections must be double-clamped with stainless steel clamps.

Refrigerators/Freezers

Depending on where you cruise, keeping foods cold will be more or less of a problem. An icebox suitable for the North Sea may be less than ideal for the Caribbean. For a transoceanic sailor, no cold box is probably the best bet. After all, you can't get ice west of the Azores!

If you do want an icebox, insulate it adequately. Invariably, the icebox will be installed flush against the hull. Usually abutting the stove. Most builders are satisfied with 2 inches of foam insulation, often forgetting the lid, but 4 inches all around is preferable. It *does* take up a lot of space, but if you are going to sacrifice space for fresh milk, you might as well have it stay cold longer on less ice. Carry the insulation on all faces of the box, maintaining vapor barriers both inside and outside the foam. Use asbestos sheathing to protect the cooler from engine heat. The box itself can be either molded fiberglass or stainless steel, the latter being more durable and less liable to absorb food odors. A drain with stopcock can be situated at the bottom. The box will be too deep to drain overboard, but it should not be allowed to drain into the bilges. A small foot pump is the answer, draining through a swivel-way faucet into the galley sink.

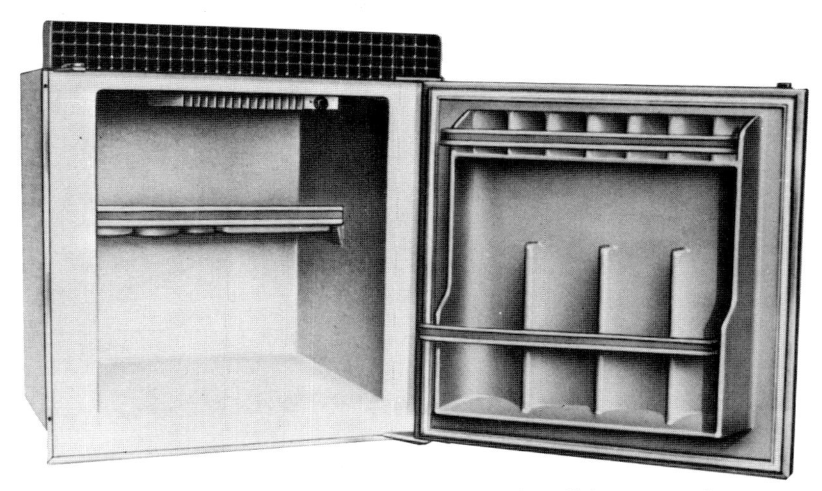

A small, heat-pump refrigeration unit for under the counter mounting, by Koolatron. Ideally, it should be in an athwartships installation and contain fiddled shelves.

The lid must be both insulated and secured. In a large icebox, it may be an advantage to hinge it in the middle or have two separate lids, one for the ice compartment and one for the food area. Recessed lift rings are the best solution for getting the lid(s) off, but make additional permanent closures, using button catches. Several hundred pounds of ice and bottles flung to the deckhead and across the saloon can do serious damage to boat and body.

A well-designed refrigerator can also provide counter and shelf space. Fiddles around the edges of the lids at least 3 or 4 inches high give you useful additional counter space. Within the confines of the box proper, make some sort of removable racks and shelves. Though teak is popular for these, rubber-coated steel or plastic is far easier to clean. If you use plastic, drill lots of good-sized holes in the shelves for drainage. Also attach lips or fiddles to all shelves unless you wish to have ready-mixed foods.

Of course, the problem of getting ice is not to be minimized. You can opt for mechanical or electrical refrigeration instead, though unless you own a boat with an onboard generator, forget about most electrical ones. They demand too much power to justify their use on any other boat. Mechanical systems usually work well, though a breakdown can produce disastrous results.

If you choose electrical or mechanical refrigeration, several options are available: compressor, solid-state, and absorption types, though each has its advantages and disadvantages.

The most common system is the engine-driven mechanical compressor with holding plates, which can be installed in existing iceboxes and customized for any boat. The good ones are expensive but well engineered, and can be set up to allow for redundancy. Mivis, Engel, Adler-Barbour and Grunert make excellent and durable compressor units.

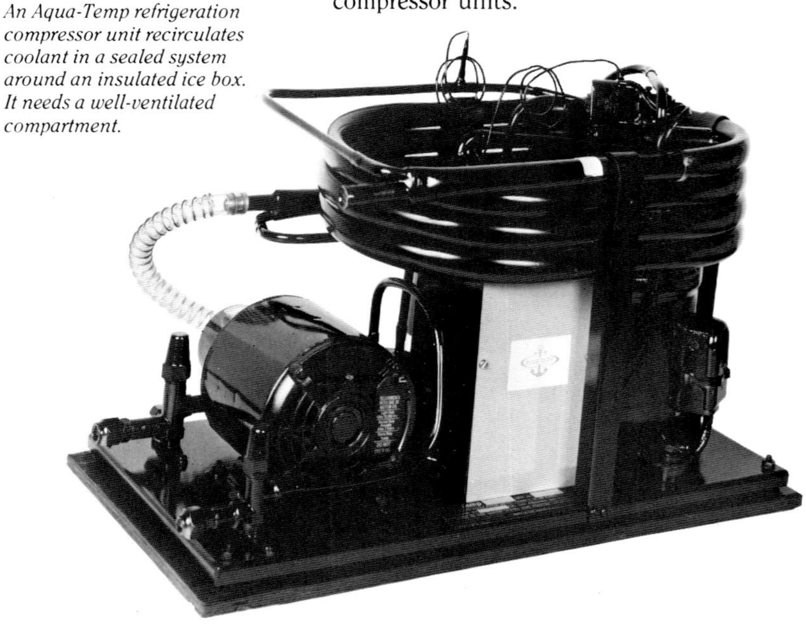

An Aqua-Temp refrigeration compressor unit recirculates coolant in a sealed system around an insulated ice box. It needs a well-ventilated compartment.

Solid-state units work on the Peltier principle. Though they are electrical, they use so little power they can be hooked directly to your battery. Using 12- or 24-volt mains, they cool the box when voltage is applied across the juncture of two dissimilar metals. Heat is removed from one and transferred to the other, thereby cooling the area closest to the first metal plate. Unlike other systems, they need only a small fan to dissipate heat. Otherwise, there are no moving parts. Unfortunately, limited power means that they will not drop ambient temperatures enough for ice making and can cool only small boxes. Koolatron makes some of the best units.

Absorption types, like the refrigerator in your home, use cooled Freon to refrigerate the box. Electricity or propane provides efficient cooling power, but the electrical systems need a generator to run effectively. Though they can be gimballed, they need lots of space for movement and ventilation.

Perhaps the best solution—since refrigerated items will not last more than a few weeks anyway—is a freezer system. Providing nothing defrosts, you have the advantage of a long-term supply of ice with less need to restock. If your yacht can handle the heavy power requirements, a freezer makes the most sense for the long-distance voyager. The makers of the best refrigeration systems can supply freezing apparatus to order. One further note: freezers demand even greater insulation than refrigerators—5 to 6 inches all around—so plan space accordingly.

Other Appliances

A host of convenience appliances exists for installation in the galley. Perhaps the most useful is the microwave oven. With its comparatively low power drain and almost heatless cooking, it is ideal for boats in the tropics or when previously prepared, frozen meals need quick preparation—say, during a round-the-world race. Generating equipment is often necessary, but on large yachts microwave cookery is a definite plus.

Almost everything else that might be installed in the galley will require 120 or 220 volt AC. To use such appliances except at dockside will require a transformer or

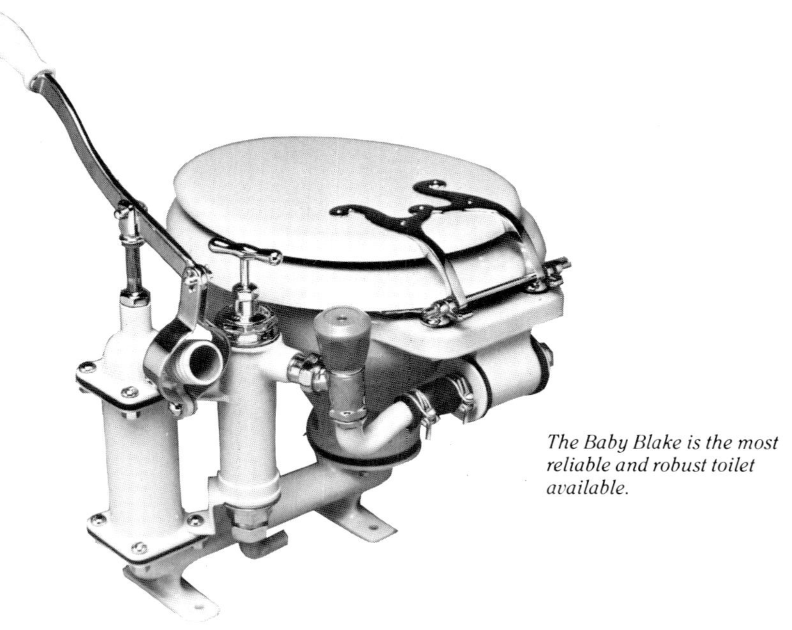

The Baby Blake is the most reliable and robust toilet available.

alternating current generator. Most cannot be used at any angle of heel, but some—blenders, mixers and food processors—can be great fun at anchor.

HEADS

Many manufacturers make adequate toilets, but be sure to keep a supply of the maker's spare gaskets, diaphragms and hardware on board. The best I know of is the sturdy and extremely reliable Baby Blake. For more cramped installations, the Lavac is highly recommended, because the detachable pump handle can be mounted where handy. Simpson-Lawrence, Raritan, Groco and Wilcox-Crittenden all supply reliable WC's. Electric *heads,* though convenient, are not recommended, especially if they are without a manual backup system. Too often you'll be reduced to the cedar bucket, which though effective, is not usually in keeping with the spirit of the modern luxury yacht.

No matter what, all toilet installations must be accessible in every way: seacocks, piping and vents must all be easy to reach. The discharge seacock must be aft of the inlet, with all piping looped above the water-line. I have been on one custom yacht where the water taken aboard in a matter of minutes might well have sunk the ship had not the inlet seacock (none too easy to find behind a decorative panel door) been closed with dispatch.

FIGURE 6-3
The sewage system

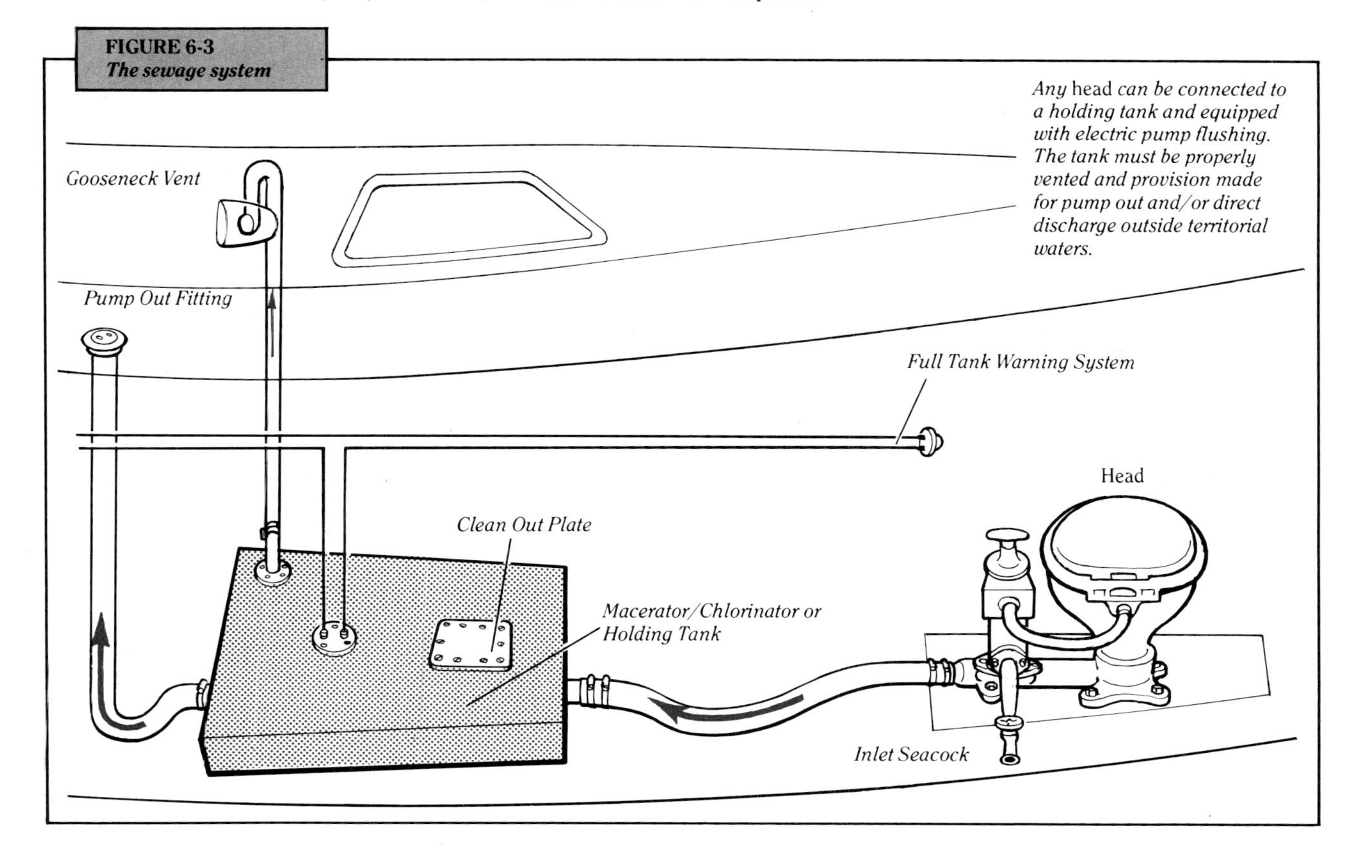

Any head *can be connected to a holding tank and equipped with electric pump flushing. The tank must be properly vented and provision made for pump out and/or direct discharge outside territorial waters.*

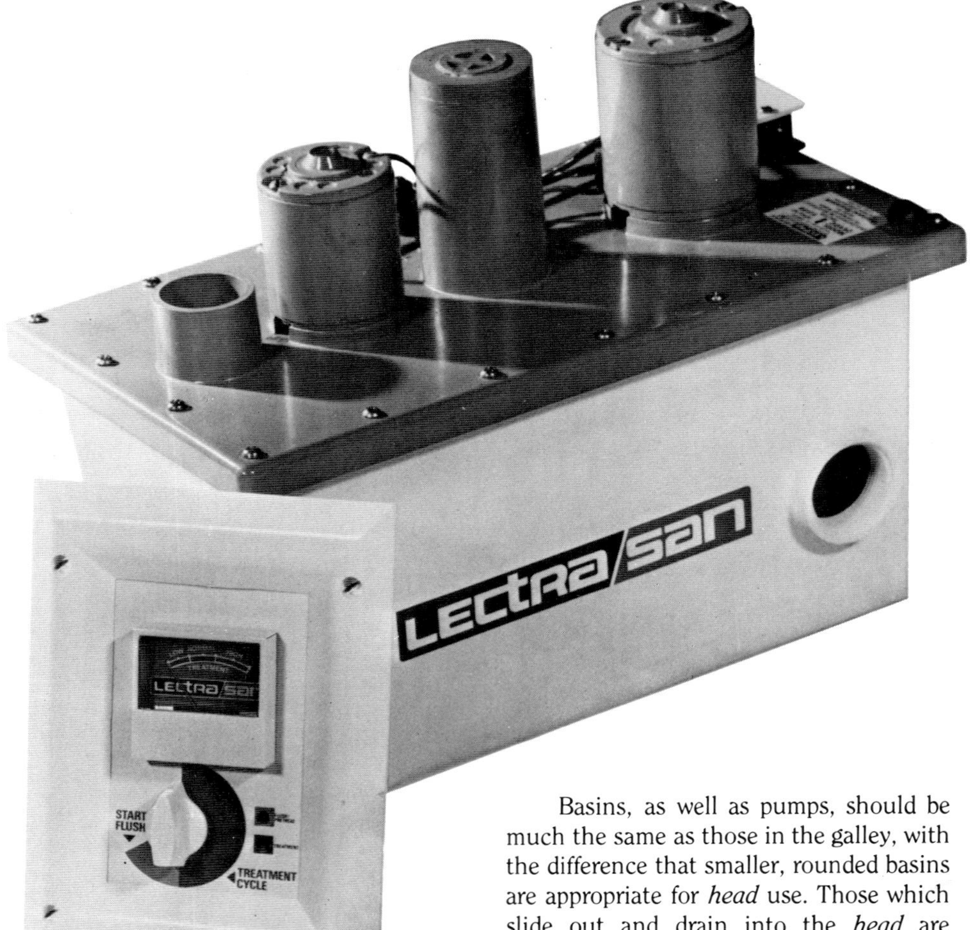

A macerator/chlorinator system. Though it uses much power, such an installation is preferable to a holding tank.

Sanitation regulations are most stringent in the United States, but Britain and others may soon follow suit. Holding tanks or macerator/chlorinator systems are mandated by law for American waters. Holding tanks are a nuisance, though they can supply a bit of additional ballast. In my area of the world, there are only two pumpout stations for about 50,000 boats! Both demand a stiff fee for the privilege of emptying your tank into theirs, from which it is invariably dumped into the municipal sewage system and thence back into the ocean.

If you plan or need such systems, the waste-cleansing macerator/chlorinator is far the better choice. It is, however, heavy, expensive and needs electricity. Reliable systems are made by Danforth, Mansfield, Microphor and Thetford.

Basins, as well as pumps, should be much the same as those in the galley, with the difference that smaller, rounded basins are appropriate for *head* use. Those which slide out and drain into the *head* are excellent for smaller boats and eliminate a through-hull as well. Showers are a mixed blessing. On a large yacht a separate stall is best. For smaller boats, a telephone shower is more compact.

Head compartment lockers should be fiddled and secure. Fitments for paper, towels and soap should be of Lexan or brass. Hardware meant for the home will not stand up to a salt environment.

LIGHTING

Since, other than sailing, most activities aboard are carried on below decks, within the confines of various cabins, some form of illumination is necessary to allow these diversions to be safely accomplished. Light, whether natural or artificial is easily obtained, but unfortunately it is not always used economically or to best effect.

Most production yachts built today are encumbered with lavish swathings of teak. We have been led to believe that the sumptuous atmosphere thus created will give the owner a feeling of pride and luxury. More likely it will remind you of being in a womb with splinters, somber ones at that, lurking around every fold and crevice. One of the best ways to provide light below is to eschew all the teak for flat white paint. Let the wood be used for trim.

Whatever paint you use, the cabin will still naturally be dark. Suitably protected holes—portholes, prisms and hatches—are therefore a necessity. The modern tendency toward plastics is not a good idea for frames, which should be of bronze, aluminum alloy or stainless steel. Plastic frames can leak, crack or break at the most inopportune moments. The window area itself can be made of glass (tempered or laminated) or plastics, though my own experience has shown that virtually indestructible Lexan is the best material for any port or hatch cover. It is certainly not cheap, but can easily be cut and fitted to existing installations. Dozens of manufacturers make hatches and ports. Vetus ports made by W.H. Denouden in Holland are excellent. Canpa, Bomar and Goiot all produce splendid hatches which do *not* leak. The best prisms, made by Simpson-Lawrence, can be installed in any deck for vastly increased illumination below.

Artificial lighting is usually a matter of electrical lights. Brass, plastic and aluminum are all suitable housings. Fluorescent lights for galley and *head* are a good idea, in that they drain much less power than their incandescent brothers. Bass, Simpson-Lawrence, Vetus and Perko are all good makers.

Kerosene lamps are quite picturesque, but they are almost impossible to read by. Have them for atmosphere, by all means, but make sure they are gimballed, and install heat shields above the chimney.

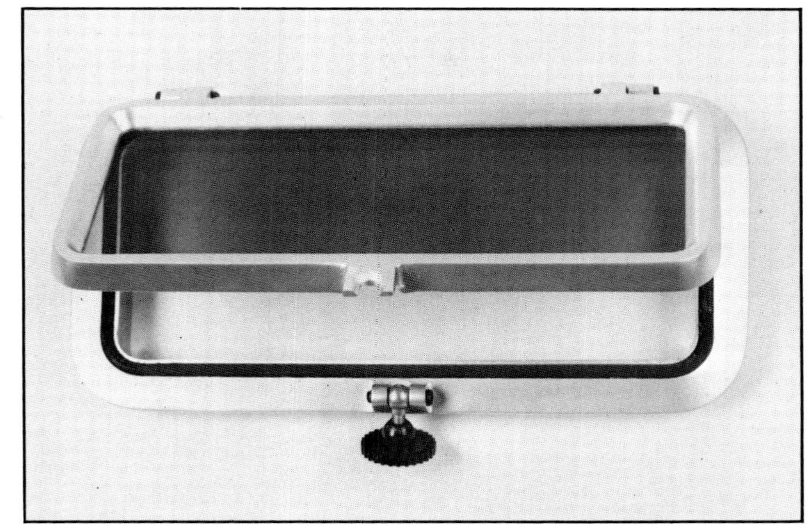

A Goiot Aluminum-framed portlight. Provision should be made for screens and storm shutters.

Goiot invented the modern alloy and plastic hatch. The sliding model is especially handy on larger yachts.

The reliable Tilley Stormlight will stay lit even in a gale.

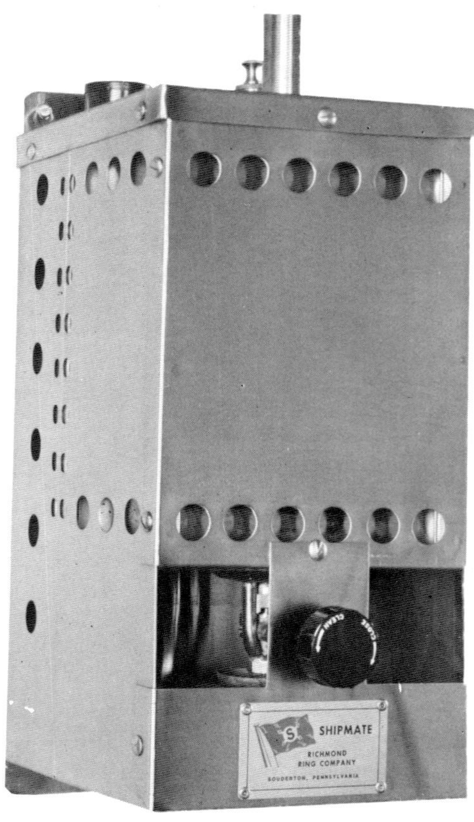

The paraffin cabin heater by Shipmate is compact, easy to repair and uses comparatively inexpensive fuel.

Pressure or mantle kerosene lamps are more practical for emergency lighting. The Tilley lantern is the only windproof lamp that works in a gale. Optimus and Aladdin products are good as long as they are kept below decks. All three supply the equivalent of a 100-watt bulb.

HEATING/VENTILATION

To keep a yacht warm in cool climates and cool in warm ones is a more difficult task than might at first be imagined. The demands of the human body are invariably at odds with those of the cabin of a boat. A warm cabin tends to have stale air, but fresh air can mean cold air. Special solutions are needed to reach a workable compromise.

The basis of comfort below is a well-insulated hull. In the days of wooden yachts such a hull was easier to find, because of both the natural insulating qualities of wood and the added protection afforded by the air space between the ceiling and the hull proper. Fiberglass and metal, on the other hand, have a tendency to sweat or build up condensation. Furthermore, these materials allow for the rapid interaction of inside and outside ambient temperatures, which means in practice that the ship is either too warm or too cold. Airex and balsa cores can improve the situation as can foaming a metal hull, but few stock boats use such expedients. One solution is to install cork or foam-packed vinyl over every available hull surface; another is to carry sweaters and swimsuits.

No matter what solution you pursue, adequate ventilation is a necessity. Hatches, ventilators, fans, opening ports can all be used, so long as they do not imperil the watertight integrity of the hull under sail.

You can heat a yacht in any number of ways. The simplest is a wood or charcoal burning stove or fireplace. For small boats, the Ratelco, the Shipmate and the Tiny Tot heaters are best. Using peacoal is a good idea, even better if it is prepacked in small paper sacks. Packaging prevents coal dust from spreading over the cabin. These stoves are usually bolted to the bulkhead with insulating panels behind and below. A flue and pipe stack run through the deckhead, topped by a "Charlie Noble." Some experimentation may be necessary to avoid downdrafts and care must be taken to install the stack so as not to foul lines or obstruct vital deck areas. Though not as useful at sea, the open fireplaces made by Paul Luke and Simpson-Lawrence are pieces of metalworking art suitable for the finest yacht.

Kerosene heaters must be installed in much the same manner. Most work on a Primus burner. Those made by Taylor and Shipmate are the best looking and best engineered. Available with either integral or remote tanks, they are the obvious choice if you also use kerosene for the stove, as both can be arranged to draw from the same tank. Being pressurized, they demand preheating and occasional pumping, but they can run almost forever, as long as the burners are kept clean and the draw is constant. Under severe angles of heel, they may experience drawing problems, but on most modern boats this will not be too frequent an occurrence.

Propane heaters, more popular in Europe than the U.S., are another possibility, as are alcohol and catalytic models. However, for long voyaging they are not to be recommended since they use so much expensive fuel.

Diesel heat may be the best solution for even distribution, especially for large yachts. Wallas, Eberspacher, Perkins and Dickenson make first-class units, which work on the same principle as a diesel stove. They require electric current to run the blower which ducts heat throughout the boat, but electrical requirements are small. Using the same supply as your engine, you can run the heater for long periods of time. Exhaust outlets are of extreme importance for diesel heaters, as the fume backup can cause dizziness and nausea.

The Eberspacher diesel hot air heater can pipe heat to outlets throughout the boat.

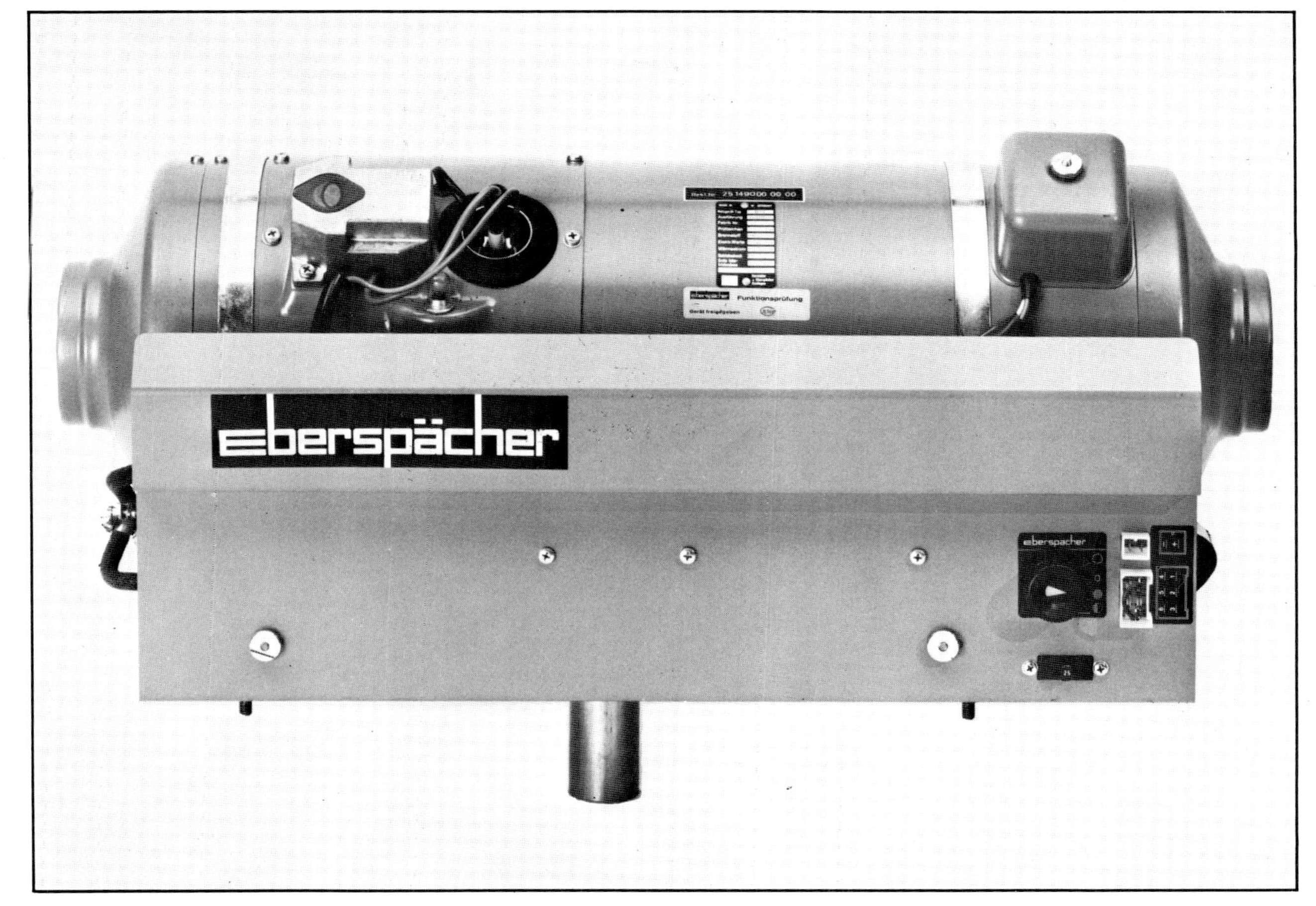

The Aqua-Temp heater/ cooler provides all-weather comfort for boats which can handle its 115-volt power requirement.

With any heating system, assuring an adequate supply of oxygen is vital. All use up air, and oxygen depletion within the confines of the cabin can be uncomfortable and even dangerous. Crack open a hatch or a port and make sure the ventilators are working before firing up any heater.

Unless you are equipped with a generator, it's best to forget air conditioning. The electrical consumption is vast, they take up a lot of space and installation is expensive. Air-Temp and Cruiseair, however, make reliable units, but these must be used with transformers and/or step-down units. If you have a diesel heating system with ducting, the air conditioning can use the existing ducts, but the sound of a generator may be more annoying than the heat!

Chapter 7

SAFETY GEAR AND CLOTHING

Safety at sea is first and foremost a matter of a sound vessel and good seamanship. No amount of special equipment will help if you don't know what to do with it or if the ship is not suited to the passage. Experience and judgment are not easily come by, but they make all the difference to safe sailing. The 1979 Fastnet disaster showed that bad judgment can cause more damage and fatalities than boat or equipment design. Rigs, rudders and ancillary gear were the most common failures, and few yachts actually foundered. Most of the deaths could have been prevented by more forethought on the part of the sailors who participated.

Good seamanship is important, but so are good equipment, construction and layout. Of the safety gear necessary to prevent injury, discomfort and loss of life aboard, some is installed at construction stage, some in the basic fitting out and the rest in the form of add-on devices. Proper clothing, too, enhances safety.

Hatchboard holddowns. The Fastnet disaster showed the need for such simple and obvious devices. In case of a knockdown they keep the saloon from flooding.

Of prime importance is the sound design and construction of both hull and rig. Lately there have been a number of cases of yachts not built to specification. Production economies, inexperienced workmen and substandard materials all can be cited as reasons for this. Nevertheless, a proper survey of any craft, new or used, is essential to guard against any deficiencies. The various survey classifications—Lloyd's Bureau Veritas, American Bureau of Shipping, etc.—are generally good guidelines. However, they do vary in certain areas, particularly in the installation of ancillary systems, and some are better than others. Lloyd's scantlings make for a heavy hull, while ABS standards make for the most efficient and reliable engine installations and electronics. The choice is a matter for the insurance agents, as long as your surveyor is satisfied that all is "to yacht standard." A surveyor is best recommended by a good naval architect, in the U.S.; in England they are separately licensed.

Rig safety is a more controversial topic, especially with the advent of high-technology, bendy, lightweight, hydraulic-controlled spars. Most production boats are fitted with masts and rigging whose safety margin is 2 ½ times the breaking strength of the rig. This should suffice for almost anything but a round-the-world voyage, providing it is properly tuned.

The high-tech rigs like Stearn's, however, allow for a safety factor of as little as 1½ times. Tha'ts no margin for your Sunday sailor as such rigs are very easy to overload. It must be remembered that every link in the rigging—tangs, turnbuckles, wire and chainplates—must be compatible in strength and position on the galvanic scale. For use of the wrong cotter pin, an entire rig may be lost.

The hull, deck and rig of your boat will probably be complete when you buy it, but there's still much to be added to make it safer. With very few exceptions, none of the following equipment is ever included as "standard" aboard any vessel. Nevertheless, any sailor venturing for more than a day's sail should have most of it aboard, and every ocean-going yachtsman must be able to

Rails to either side of the companionway provide an extra margin of safety

assure himself that the equipment necessary for survival is at hand in the event that his vessel is lost.

Safety equipment is no place for skimping: it must be of absolutely the best quality, regularly checked and tested. Your life depends upon the proper functioning of materials which are susceptible to deterioration over time. Safety gear deserves greater attention than anything else aboard, other than basic hull, rig and through-hull installations. At all times, and in all conditions, it must be able to function with little or no notice.

Every member of the crew must be well versed in the operation of all emergency and safety gear aboard. The time spent might just be worth the effort some stormy night offshore. Furthermore, all safety gear must be accessible, not at the bottom of some corner locker, not tied down with complex knots and not subject to constant immersion or exposure.

LIFERAFTS

Going any distance offshore demands provisioning the boat for that most appalling of eventualities—foundering. For this, an approved, regularly serviced liferaft is a necessity. Witness the Baileys's 118 days afloat in an Avon raft, after their 28-foot yacht was stove by whales and foundered northeast of the Galapagos islands. The 1979 Fastnet experience, however, has caused much rethinking of the design and structure of liferafts. In the freak seas experienced during that race, too many rafts were overturned, blown away or failed to open.

To be effective, a liferaft must be instantly inflatable, stable and capable of retaining buoyancy. It must also offer some protection from both sun and sea. In theory this may seem a simple task, but in practice it is not so easy to accomplish. Most rafts are from reliable makers: Avon, Beaufort, Surviva, Zodiac, Givens, Dunlop. All these companies conform to standards set up by the body which governs racing, the International Yacht Racing Union.

Less demands are placed on liferafts used by racing yachts: The positions of the yachts are known to the race committee, so in the event of trouble damaged boats can be reached relatively quickly. The long distance voyager, on the other hand, is often off the beaten track, or following routes no longer frequented by commercial shipping. For these sailors, and for anyone concerned with having the best and most reliable raft, only one standard should be accepted: the Safety of Life at Sea (SOLAS) Convention. This has been devised by the merchant and military shipping authorities to provide absolutely reliable lifesaving potential at sea. A SOLAS raft can cost twice as much as a yacht standard raft, but it's worth it if you value your life and those of your crew. Among the important features peculiar to a SOLAS raft are the following: It must be capable of being dropped from a height of 60 feet into water without sustaining damage. It must be easily righted even if accidentally inflated upside down. If one part of the raft is punctured, the remaining parts must continue to float. The raft's floor must be insulated against cold, and it must be able to withstand at least 30 days afloat. It must also have fittings which allow it to be towed.

As can be seen, SOLAS rafts are made to a much higher standard than off-the-shelf yachtsman's rafts. How much you are willing to spend for the ultimate insurance policy depends on how much you value your life. SOLAS regulations cover not only raft construction but also the raft. A standard SOLAS equipment package appears in Table 7-1.

It is wise, nonetheless, to carry extra emergency rations, medications, tools, fishing tackle and clothing. All must be carefully waterproofed and guarded against deterioration. In addition, as great a water supply as is feasible should be stored in jerry jugs and lashed to a rail near the companion way. Since dehydration is the major cause of death when adrift, the amount

TABLE 7-1
SOLAS-Mandated Liferaft Equipment

The normal equipment of every liferaft shall consist of:—

- One buoyant rescue quoit, attached to at least 100 feet of buoyant line.
- For liferafts which are permitted to accommodate not more than twelve persons: one knife and one baler; for liferafts which are permitted to accommodate thirteen persons or more: two knives and two balers.
- Two sponges.
- Two sea-anchors, one permanently attached to the liferaft and one spare.
- Two paddles.
- One repair outfit capable of repairing punctures in buoyancy compartments.
- One topping-up pump or bellows.
- Three tin-openers.
- One first-aid outfit in a waterproof case.
- One rustproof graduated drinking vessel.
- One waterproof electric torch suitable for signalling in the Morse Code, together with one spare set of batteries and one spare bulb in a waterproof container.
- One daylight signalling mirror and one signalling whistle.
- Two parachute distress signals of an approved type, capable of giving a bright red light at a high altitude.
- Six hand flares of an approved type, capable of giving a bright red light.
- One set of fishing tackle.
- A food ration, determined by the Administration, for each person the liferaft is permitted to accommodate.
- Watertight receptacles containing 3 pints of fresh water for each person the liferaft is permitted to accommodate, of which 1 pint per person may be replaced by a suitable desalting apparatus capable of producing an equal amount of fresh water.
- Six anti-sickness tablets for each person the liferaft is deemed fit to accommodate.
- Instructions on how to survive in the liferaft.
- One copy of the illustrated table of life saving signals.

must be proportionate to the size of the crew—5 gallons per person is best, if space permits.

Assuming you go out to buy a liferaft, certain considerations must be borne in mind. First, is it constructed to approved standards? A SOLAS raft is, but other rafts may not be, and it is up to you to decide which is best for your use. If you intend to make only occasional ocean passages a standard, off-the-shelf Avon or Zodiac is probably adequate. But buy one packed in a hard, fiberglass case. Valise packs are prone to ripping, deterioration from exposure and accidental damage to the tripping mechanism and release valves.

Second, is it stable? The Fastnet disaster showed that the stability of most traditional rafts is not much more than minimal in extreme conditions. If a raft flips over and cannot be righted, there's little chance you'll survive.

Some rafts can be fitted with sea anchors, stabilizing "fins" and such, but the only proven noncapsizeable raft is the Givens. Developed by Jim Givens in California, this raft has a large water chamber beneath the double floor which acts by capillary action to literally "glue" the raft to the water surface. In recent founderings in hurricane conditions, the Givens raft stayed upright in 30-foot seas and even survived being deluged by breaking seas and complete submersion.

Third, will it inflate when it's supposed to? An inflation valve is a relatively delicate piece of equipment. it is subject to damage and corrosion. Regular servicing by a Coast

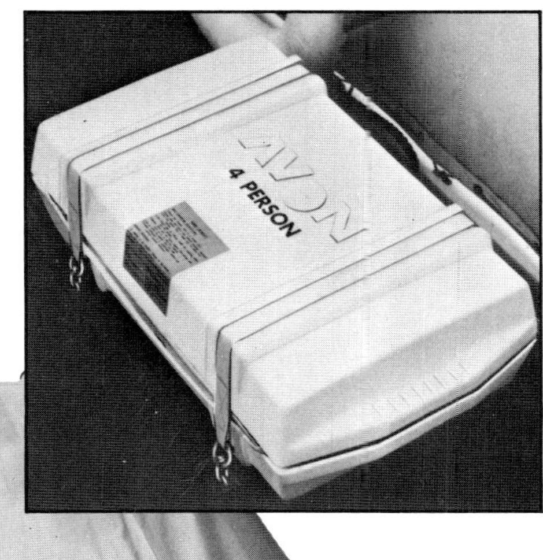

Liferafts should be encased in a fiberglass cannister for protection. Soft valises allow spray and salt air to enter, possibly corroding the inflation mechanism.

Inflated Avon liferaft. Note its double bouyancy chamber, entry ladder and canopy.

The Lirakis Harness is well balanced, centering the pull high on the chest.

Guard or Department of Trade approved service center is necessary for safety.

Fourth, will it remain buoyant if punctured? At least two flotation chambers are necessary to preserve buoyancy, and the raft should be equipped with materials for repair and pumps for reinflation.

Finally, does it really protect the crew from heat, cold, sun, rain and the sea? Double floors, a rigid canopy and a large sponge (for keeping the inner floor dry) are necessary. Accept less and you may well be in for discomfort or worse.

Many cruising sailors have recently become disenchanted with inflatable rafts, and with some reason. They are expensive to purchase, expensive to service and there's always the chance that they might not work. The alternative is to adapt a rigid dinghy to lifesaving requirements. Doing so has two advantages: you don't need to buy and stow a special raft, and perhaps more importantly, you can sail toward some land mass.

Adapting a dinghy requires a great deal of thought and planning, not to mention expertise in execution. Positive flotation, watertight stowage, a secure canopy and assorted fastening points for lashings and drogues are necessary. Assuming you have a first-class sailing dinghy to start with, some of the basic modifications are the following: strengthen the centerboard case and bottom with extra layers of fiberglass; build a tubular folding frame for a canopy; and build box section thwarts for buoyancy and stowage.

Since wood or fiberglass hulls are stronger than Hypalon-coated nylon, the chances of survival (or at least the maintenance of a floating platform) are appreciably greater. Chafe, puncture and decomposition through salt and the elements are no longer concerns. Also, with a watch and Dougal Robertson's *Sea Survival*, you could probably navigate with some assurance to the nearest downwind landfall.

It all depends on where you are going and what you sail. If stowing a rigid dinghy aboard is impossible, you will have no choice but to opt for an inflatable liferaft. However, probably the best solution for offshore cruisers and blue water sailors is to carry both. There's no cheap way out.

JACKLINES AND HARNESSES

In the never ending quest to stay aboard, despite all efforts of ship and sea to tip you off the weather deck, the safety harness may be the single most important and useful piece of personal gear.

In the days of commercial sail the watch would invariably be lashed to the wheel or binnacle in heavy going. In principle, the safety harness accomplishes the same thing with vastly greater comfort and the promise of mobility. Of course, depending on where you clip on, that can be mobility overboard.

A harness is valuable only if it is worn—an obvious statement, yet the number of sailors who neglect to wear a harness or don't slip it on until on deck is legion. In heavy air, when alone at the helm, when single-handing or at night, not wearing a harness is about as intelligent as letting a blind man drive you to the office.

Buckle up in the cabin and clip onto a padeye or jackline on deck before leaving the relative safety of the companionway. If you can't reach a strongpoint, install one!

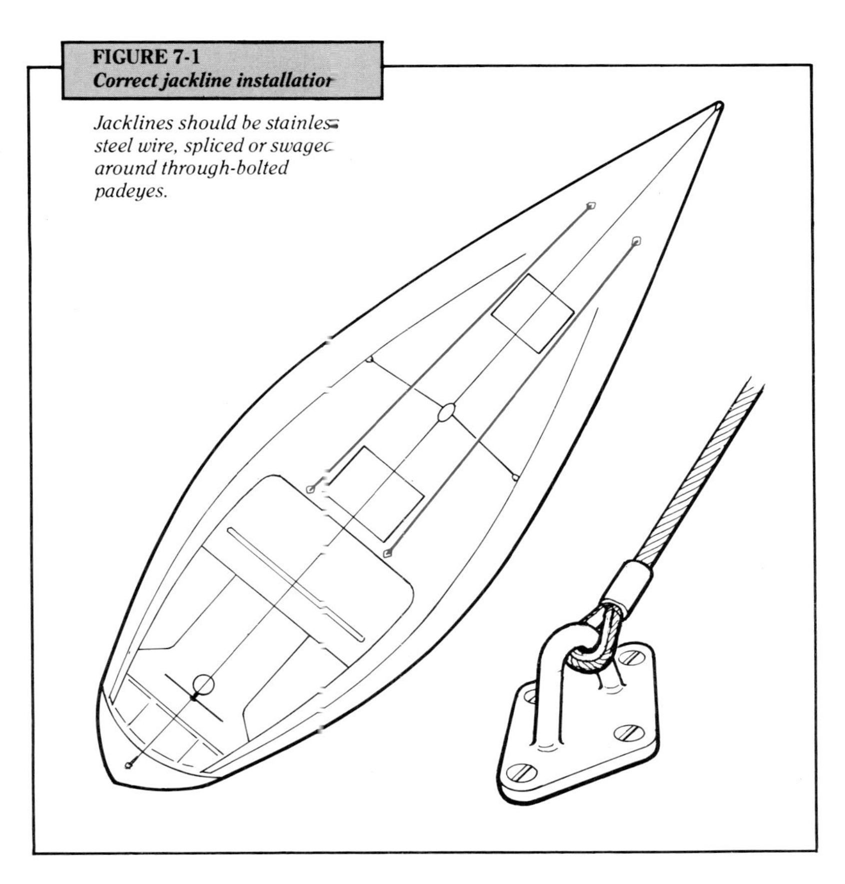

FIGURE 7-1
Correct jackline installation

Jacklines should be stainless steel wire, spliced or swaged around through-bolted padeyes.

Ideally, two very stout jacklines should run from the companionway to the fore end of the cabin trunk, as close as possible to the centerline, on either side of the mast. Made of at least ¼-inch stainless steel wire rope, they must be attached to through-bolted padeyes fore and aft, preferably with spliced loops around thimbles.

Other possibilities are sliders on tracks, though these not only clutter the deck, but are subject to jamming and distortion under load. Otherwise, one might install a series of padeyes on the centerline.

Clipping on to the stanchion's life lines is not to be recommended. The chances of being flipped overboard are greater and the strains, particularly against the upper line, are not healthy for the deck. Stanchions rip too easily. No matter which setup is adopted, strength is the goal. The forces exerted by a human body suddenly thrown are measured in thousands of pounds.

A first-class harness must be easy to enter, comfortable to wear and capable of failsafe operation. In the U.K., the Kitemark guarantees that a harness meets British Standard. Elsewhere, you must trust to reputation. The best harnesses I know of are made by Peter Haward, Crewsaver and Simpson-Lawrence in the U.K. and Lirakis in the U.S. Not to be overlooked are the oilskin/harness combinations, especially those from Henri-Lloyd and Atlantis. You put on both jacket and harness in one easy motion, and much greater freedom of movement is allowed.

Webbing on a harness should be 2-inch nylon, triple-stitched and strength-tested. Though it's an unlikely problem, make sure that the thread used is not a natural fiber. Only synthetic thread can withstand mildew and rot. All hardware must be tested and should be stainless steel. Periodic inspection for fatigue and stress cracks is also warranted.

Finally, make sure the harness fits. Many are adjustable, but some are not. Allow for underclothing, sweater and oilies, and make sure it fits high enough, i.e., firmly under the arms and around the chest. Another consideration is whether to have one line or two. I prefer two, each with its own snap hook. One line with two spaced hooks may seem neater and more convenient, but it makes it difficult to move from point to point easily.

Harness safety hooks have received a lot of attention lately, because they have been known to open under load or fail in some other way. Sailors who are also mountaineers suggest the use of carabiners. Unfortunately, these are often made of corrosive materials. Unless you are prepared to regularly dry such equipment and protect it with silicone, you should avoid it. M.S. Gibb has a better idea. Their patented safety hook is extremely strong, and it meets British Standard 4224, the only adequate standard for safety hooks.

The Gibb Safety Hook is designed to prevent accidental tripping while in use.

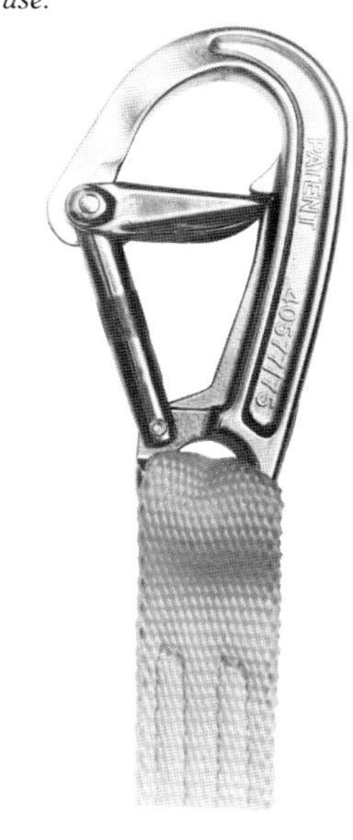

LIGHTS

In any emergency at night (and a few in daylight, too), a few lights of the right types can be a godsend. To pinpoint a man overboard, illumine a sail, supply emergency lighting, signal distress or find a buoy, lights are as necessary in our crowded waters as good ground tackle.

The first priority aboard any boat is a waterproof, high-powered torch. "High-powered" means at least 100,000 candle-power! It may be battery operated or work off the mains. If it floats, all the better. If it is battery operated, spare batteries must be carried. Guest, ACR, Q-Beam, Francis and Perko make the best searchlights.

Other lights serve other functions. Despite what is often written by assorted experts, masthead strobe lights may be one of the most effective distress signals available. Their brightness is unequalled, and masthead mounting gives them a range greater than anything other than parachute flares. Of course, a tanker or cargo ship could be drawn by the strobe flashes. Such activity could prove dangerous, especially in heavy weather when the mountainous topsides of a freighter could well crush a yacht, but in an emergency, the risk may well be worth it.

Another decent measure to take is to equip every member of the crew with small personal lights permanently clipped on to their foul weather jackets. These can be water activated if you wish, though accidental green water on deck can turn your crew into a covey of fireflies. Personally, I think the extra expense for strobe lights for this purpose is justified. Trying to see anything at night, in heavy seas, is very difficult. The extra brilliance of the strobe is worth the cost.

Provision should also be made to illuminate the compass from an external source, in case regular lighting should fail. Flashlights are not advisable; their casings and batteries are sure to cause deviation. One of the cheapest and most effective emergency lights for the binnacle is the chemical light sold in most chandlers for emergencies. It need only be bent to make it give out a low level of greenish light which will last by the compass card for at least six hours.

Boarding ladder. The stern-mounted ladder is handy, but may not be effective at sea where pitching will lessen its utility.

The criteria for all lights are reliability, waterproofness and handiness. A number of local manufacturers may supply what you need. Of the internationally available brands, Francis, Guest, ACR, Marinaspec, Aqua-Signal and Peters & Bey are all excellent choices.

LADDERS

Getting aboard is one of the more frightening tasks for the man overboard. If he is far gone, hoisting with sails or tackle will be necessary, but otherwise, some form of ladder will be the basic means of *leverage*. The italics are purposeful, because a ladder, to be effective, must allow for use as a lever. The traditional rope ladder cannot be recommended for emergency use.

However, builders and manufacturers have finally awakened to the idea that if something is there it may be used. Thus, we have seen an increasing number of yachts equipped with permanently mounted, swingdown stern ladders. They fill the gap in the pushpit and work well if they are sized properly and if the lower two rungs hang below the water line. Two rungs deep is necessary because if the ladder is stern-mounted, a certain amount of pitching must be allowed for. Also, if the ladder is stainless steel or aluminum, some sort of nonskid material might well be applied to the rungs. Chemically etching the metal and applying a "liquid carpet" of the type sold for deck coating is probably the most effective method.

One of the more clever arrangements for ladders is seen on the *Flying Dutchman,* designed by Eva Hollman and William Eickholt. In place of boarding gates, port and starboard, are hinged rigid ladders. When raised, they fill in the gates with solid protection, killing two birds with one ladder, so to speak.

Finally, come the portables. The Mastep ladder is the best known of these, but all work on the same principle. Made of nylon, plastic or structural foam, they fold up. They also twist and occasionally collapse. They're fine for boarding use and as swim ladders, but not recommended for emergency uses.

Mounted fore-and-aft, The Flying Dutchman's boarding ladder is reachable even when the boat is pitching.

MAN OVERBOARD

No call causes a more tumultuous response aboard a yacht than the cry, "man overboard!" Whether crossing an ocean or in a favorite bay, this is cause for the most immediate action, but adequate emergency equipment and clear thinking are equally important. Loss, hypothermia and drowning can occur with startling rapidity.

The crew of the yawl *Scylla* found just how important preparation and proper gear can be when a wave threw crewman Jack Weston overboard at midnight during the 1960 Bermuda Race. A quick-thinking companion immediately threw a life ring and light after Weston, but the gear fouled in the mizzen. Grabbing a spare floating strobe light, he succeeded in throwing it towards Weston, while simultaneously notifying the helmsman, who fixed the yacht's exact heading. Knowing the course they would have to return along, the crew struck sails and cranked the engine, only to find the battery dead. Again, forethought saved the day. A spare battery and jumper cables brought the engine to life. In less than an hour, Weston—who'd succeeded in swimming to the floating strobe—was rescued.

Even with the most careful precautions, going overboard is a constant threat aboard any yacht. Wearing harnesses, having high guard rails and proper nonskid all help, but provision must be made for recovery no matter what. To do this successfully, certain equipment must be kept aboard and kept in good order. This is one area where constant maintenance and checking are an absolute must. Lives depend upon it.

Even in a slight chop, it is difficult to spot someone in the water; in heavy seas, it is well-nigh impossible. Boat and victim are unlikely to remain on the wave crests for long. Assuming that the person fell overboard in less than perfect conditions—heavy weather—some sort of visual reference is needed to keep that soul in sight until the yacht can be maneuvered into a position favorable to pick-up.

Mastep's Man Overboard Recovery Equipment (MORE) system launches horseshoe, line and self-activating strobe, at the pull of a cord.

Undoubtedly, the best solution is a tall dan buoy attached to a horseshoe with a water-activated strobe light. Dan buoys should show at least 8 feet above the surface of the water, and be properly ballasted. They are not easy to stow, but the most logical place for them is lashed with very light breakaway twine to the backstay. When the horseshoe is launched, the dan buoy will break away and follow. A good addition is a reflective orange or yellow flag attached to the top of the shaft. The 8-foot height should be considered a minimum. In any seaway, the buoy will be easily obscured by the swell or wave tops, so the higher it is the better. Fiberglass is probably the best material for the dan buoy shaft since it can absorb shock; and closed-cell foam is best for the buoy proper.

The horseshoe should be attached to the dan buoy by a 10-foot length of spliced polypropylene line (⅜-inch diameter). The horseshoe proper must be made of closed-cell foam covered in flexible, plastic-coated cloth with strongly stitched attachment points for light, lines, whistles, etc. Furthermore, some means of securing the buoy around the wearer's trunk is necessary, preferably a short strap with a snap hook.

A plastic whistle should be attached as well as a self-activating strobe light. Guest, ACR and Plastimo make good strobe lights. These will automatically start flashing when salt water saturates a dissolving capsule in the mechanism, triggering the switch. Avoid flashing incandescent lights. They are not bright enough to be seen on a stormy night. A strobe can be sighted for some distance, and is designed to operate at near full power for an hour or more. The strobe, by the way, must be attached to the horseshoe with a lanyard, not glued in place. Otherwise, the chances are that it will land with the light facing down into the water, good for attracting sharks but not rescue. Also, when the light is attached to a lanyard, the victim will be able to hold the light aloft, greatly increasing the chances of being seen by his companions.

You should mount this entire conglomerate of life-sustaining apparatus to the stern rail (pushpit) of the yacht so that it is both secure and instantly releasable. Lashings will not do, use instead a specially designed holder for horseshoe, dan buoy and lines. Whistle, light and other signalling devices (dye marker, Skyblazer flares) should be secured to the horseshoe in a manner so as not to catch upon any deck fitting or the holder itself. The line between horseshoe and dan buoy must be coiled to run free and not hang-up on the holder. Finally, the holder should be mounted outside the pushpit, so the buoy need not be lifted over the rail.

Several quick-release holders are available, and have much to recommend them. With these—especially the MORE system—the whole kit springs overboard aft at the pull of a lanyard. The helmsman need not even turn around. Forespar and West Marine also make reliable systems.

Single-handers who manage to fall overboard have somewhat greater problems. Probably, the boat will be under control of self-steering gear or an autopilot, so it won't round up and it won't stop. Any single-hander should obviously be in a harness clipped to the jacklines, but if you do neglect this precaution, you must have devices at the ready to allow you to get back to the boat and regain the deck. A floating, trailing line at least 100 feet long, with a small float on the end, is the most obvious solution. However, assuming the yacht is charging along to windward at six knots, the chances of pulling yourself, fully-clothed, back to the boat are slight. Try pulling a bucket full of water aboard from a moving hull. A far better idea is to rig a trailing line which will also trip the self-steering gear, using a snap shackle with the line rove through a small block before running aft and overboard. This is the time and place where a permanently mounted stern ladder really comes into its own. By

The Mustang Thermofloat survival jacket is waterproof, bouyant and a good insulator. It can double survival time in frigid waters. Note the hooked-on neoprene shorts which help keep jacket from riding up.

no other means, unless you are the perfect athlete, will you be able to regain the security of the yacht.

Whether to wear a life jacket or not is a constant debate amongst sailors. Frankly, most don't. Complaints range from the fact that they are bulky, to the added weight, to the obstruction of movement. Certainly, wearing a personal flotation device (PFD) in heavy weather is a good idea.

The problem, is exacerbated by the fact that in the U.S., inflatable PFDs are not Coast Guard certified. Thus, even if you wear one, you are required to equip the yacht with approved-type solid foam-filled PFDs. This is not the case aboard airliners, of course, where CO_2 inflating PFDs are the norm, or in Europe where government-approved CO_2 PFDs are common. Inflatable devices are flat, flexible and compact. They can be topped-up by mouth inflation. However, they are prone to leaks and are not by U.S. standards truly "positive" flotation devices. Nevertheless, if checked regularly, they are a better solution to the restricted-movement problem than foam jackets. Reputable makers of PFDs include Mustang, Avon and Dunlop.

In cooler climes, a good flotation jacket (Coast Guard approved) is an ideal

The Bayleysuit is the ultimate in inflatable cold-water survival suits. Sailors in northern waters, especially single-handers, should consider it.

solution. These are lightweight, warm and quite comfortable, and have the advantage of serving as foul weather gear as well as a safety device. Most will support anyone in a head-back position. A good addition though, would be a crotch strap to prevent the jacket from riding up and hampering movement and, possibly, breathing.

A final wearable piece of safety gear for the man overboard is the so-called "survival suit". This is that clever bit of gear that makes you look like the Michelin Man. Obviously useful to the long-distance Arctic sailor, and not without possibilities for the single-hander in Northern waters, the survival suit consists of two layers of rubberized cloth bonded together. When you hit the water, you pull a cord, inflating, via a CO_2 canister, the inner space betwixt the two, and presto, you have both insulator and a flotation device. Its problems are sheer bulk and difficulty in getting into the thing, as well as expense. But if a solo circumnavigation is your plan, you should at least try one out. Bayleysuit, Mustang and Winel make good ones.

PUMPS AND PATCHES

A scared man with a bucket is the most effective pump, though the energy expended is disproportionate to the results. More efficient are diaphragm pumps. Three manufacturers distribute these worldwide, and their superb products can be recommended without reservation: Henderson, Whale (Munster-Simms) and Edson.

However, a pump is only as good as its capacity and ability to suck freely. One of the major problems with so many of the pumps installed as standard equipment on many yachts is their inability to move enough water fast.

The minimum capacity of any hand pump must be at least 25 gallons per minute. Anything less is an invitation to sinking. True, a smaller pump is admirable for clearing the bilges, but water enters at a remarkable rate once the watertight integrity of the hull has been broached.

This means that something on the order of a Whale 25 or the Edson pump is called for. Inlet and outlet hoses 2 inches in diameter will take almost anything which falls into the bilges.

In addition, the pump must be installed so that it can be operated by the helmsman while underway. Any installation must be watertight, through-deck and gasketed. Far too many installations mistakenly require the opening of a cockpit locker lid to operate the pump. This allows for the equalization of water in the boat, for whatever you pump out returns, as waves wash over the open lid!

Hoses must be long enough and double-clamped to the pump and hull outlet. The outlet hose must be looped above the waterline and discharge high enough on the hull to avoid backup. A neoprene flap mounted externally is a good idea. Inlet hoses can benefit from a strainer head or box and should be secured to the floor of the bilge with provision for quick dismounting for cleaning and repair.

All the above is well and good, but further provision must also be made for a second and even third pump mounted so they can be worked from below decks. All the criteria for mounting and operation remain the same.

Be sure that every pump is installed so that it can be comfortably worked either sitting or standing. Too often pumps are mounted in such a way that they can only be operated while you're stooping or crouching. Such a position can be cramping and eventually debilitating enough to impair your efficiency.

Another possibility is to install an engine-driven, high-capacity pump. This is a possibility, of course, only as long as the engine works. If the water level cuts the engine, this is not going to work. But, if you do install such a device, make sure that the capacity is as large as is possible: nothing under 25 to 30 gallons per minute. Considering that a 1-inch hole in the hull will let water enter at the rate of between 40 and 60 gallons per minute, you can see the reasoning behind this.

In fact, some sort of hull-patching device is about as necessary for the ocean cruiser or racer as is a pump. Umbrella patches, underwater epoxy, neoprene gaskets—none is foolproof, but at least one should be carried.

FIRE EXTINGUISHERS

Fire is the most dreaded catastrophe short of foundering. Considering the number of highly flammable materials aboard a modern yacht, the chances that a local blaze, say a galley fire, will spread are great. Obviously, every precaution must be taken to avoid fires in the first place—proper shut-off valves on stoves *and* tanks, more than adequate ventilation, fire retardant materials for curtains and cushion coverings, correct insulation for wiring and stove recesses and heaters.

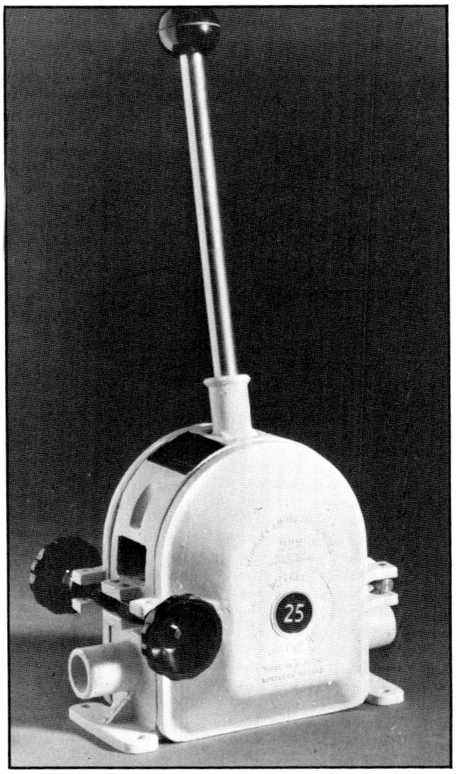

The Whale 25 bilge pump is a 30-gallons-per-minute, double-action pump which can be cleaned or disassembled with a twist of the wrist.

The Vetus gas detector warns of both vapor and smoke.

No matter what precautions are taken, however, the danger of fire is still present. A good alarm system, especially with propane stoves, is mandatory. Vetus and Super Sniffa make the best.

At least one fire extinguisher should be located in each compartment. Despite national differences in their contents, any fire extinguisher aboard must be capable of putting out electrical and chemical fires.

An EPIRB by ACR. Only the automatic, water-activated models are U.S. Coast Guard approved.

Halon automatic sprinkler systems are highly effective, though one point to remember is that such a system, if installed in the engine room, must have provision for instant engine shutdown. Otherwise, the Halon will be instantaneously sucked out by the diesel and the fire will reactivate.

All extinguishers must be mounted using quick-release brackets with free access. It is no use pinning one to the bulkhead right beside the stove. Don't put them into lockers, don't mount them in recesses, and don't mount them where the valves may be exposed to any stray knocks and bumps.

The largest handy capacity is the size to choose. For most purposes, the 10-pound size is the best choice. Be sure each extinguisher is charged and operative according to manufacturer's instructions and national authority regulations. A powder or chemical extinguisher will release its entire contents within a matter of seconds, so aim first, then release the lever. Do not attempt to save money on second-rate safety gear. You may never use it, but then again, it might just save your life and ship as soon as next weekend.

DISTRESS SIGNALS

If your vessel has become incapacitated or is foundering, or you are forced to take to the liferaft, you must employ some means of attracting the attention of potential rescuers. In such cases your radio may not be operable. For this reason, distress signalling equipment must be aboard every boat, no matter how close she may stay to shore.

The most effective, reliable and safest gear is some form—in fact, several forms—of visual signalling. The choices are dye markers, flags, flares, rockets, Very pistols (flare guns), smoke bombs and signal lamps. They all work, providing you know how to use them and someone is around to see them!

Too often, flares and distress signals are stored on board, updated regularly, but otherwise forgotten. Yet, in a real emergency, every member of the crew should know how to operate all distress signals on board quickly. This means drills and rehearsals. Trying to fire a parachute flare in heavy weather, under stress, is not child's play. It is a matter of the utmost seriousness. The chances of your having to do so are probably slim, but if and when the time comes, you must be prepared for the worst. You cannot, of course, set off pyrotechnics at the dock. But you can read every direction, and buy dummy flares to use for practice. This is worth the bother; it is not unknown for someone to set off a rocket downward, into the deck.

Powerful flares are perhaps the most effective visual signalling device available. Every few years, however, a yachting magazine or a government agency goes out and tests various flares and other visual signals. By and large, the results of these tests are appalling. Flares misfire, don't fire, can't be seen, sputter and scatter slag; smoke signals disperse even in a moderate breeze; mirrors don't focus light; and dyes cannot be seen for more than a few hundred yards.

As a seagoing person, you have little choice but to consider such findings, and then go out, at considerable expense, and buy an assortment of expendable flares for night and day use. A word of advice: if you can purchase SOLAS approved or commercial standard signals, do so. The SOLAS standard is much higher than the Coast Guard standards in the U.S. or those of the RYA in the U.K. (though they are not, of course, comparable organizations). Most manufacturers produce to several standards—Olin, Schermuly, Pains-Wessex, Smith & Wesson—and the higher the standards, the more reliable the device under extreme conditions.

For precise aim of the flare, a Very pistol is to be recommended. Some of the newer ones are plastic-metal combinations which can deform. Much better is the good old-fashioned variety, all-metal, which can be loaded with some rapidity. The type which must be unscrewed to load the cartridge is unsafe. No size cartridge smaller than 25 mm should be carried, twelve-gauge shells are being sold in vast quantities to a public unaware of their limited range and brightness. If you get 37 mm, all the better, especially offshore.

Other than flares, good signals include smoke bombs, dye markers, mirrors and radio transmitters. The two best are mirrors and EPIRBs (Emergency Position Indicating Radio Beacon). A well-designed signalling mirror can probably be seen from a greater distance and with more accuracy than any flare or smoke signal in daylight, provided you are sailing in sunshine. It is not subject to dispersal by wind and water and can be sent more or less where you want it. Bob Griffiths, certainly one of the most experienced blue water sailors of all time, used a mirror when wrecked in the Red Sea. Flares, smoke, everything else had failed to bring a response, even with ships steaming within a few miles. Finally, it was a makeshift mirror from the ship's head that did the trick.

EPIRBs are a more recent development and a more controversial one. These are being touted as the latest thing in lifesaving equipment. An EPIRB is a splendid device—it broadcasts on several frequencies, 121.5 and/or 243 MHz or 2182 kHz—and is compact, automatically activated, and can be afforded by almost everyone. The 2812 kHz type transmits on an international marine calling and distress frequency. This is monitored by large ships and Coast Guard stations. Very few aircraft can receive it, however, and if off the shipping routes, your chances of being intercepted are probably minimal.

The civilian aircraft frequency is 121.5 MHz and 243 MHz is used by military aircraft. These frequencies are of use for long ocean passages, but within soundings, very few aircraft will be listening, because they have switched to air traffic control frequencies. The EPIRB is *not* designed as an alerting device. For coastal passages with only occasional blue water forays, a good flare supply, or a VHF radio, is probably better.

Narco, Marconi and ACR all make reliable yacht EPIRBs. Marconi, in addition, makes one to SOLAS standard which is equipped with a manual generator. This means there will be no dead batteries to worry about, though the initial cost is greater than that of personal EPIRBs for a crew of six. If you are planning to cross oceans, by all means buy and maintain an EPIRB. In any place where aircraft fly, there is a good chance one will hear your call from as much as one hundred miles away.

The Atlantic foul weather suit—with its double-lapped seams, Velcro sealing tabs and PVC-coated fabric—is one of the finest suits made.

CLOTHING

Sun, rain, wind and cold all have their effect on safety and efficiency at sea. What you wear—or don't wear—will determine your comfort and well-being.

Certain basics apply everywhere. Every crew member needs a first-class set of foul weather gear. If nothing else, it makes a good windbreak. Having tried at least a dozen different makes and configurations over the years, I have developed a few rules to follow when buying 'oilies."

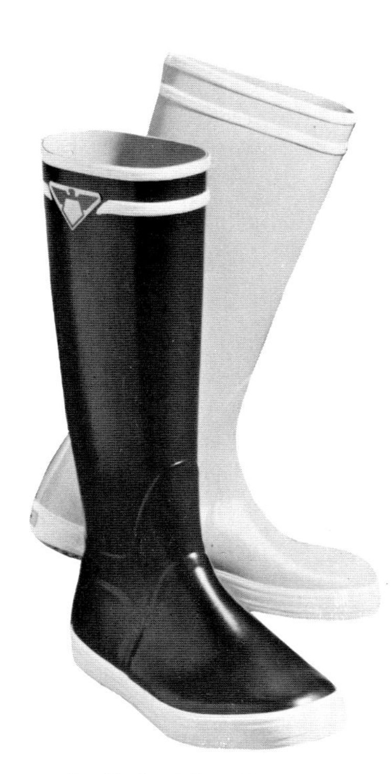

Romika boots from Germany. A proper boot should be knee-high and sized to allow double pairs of socks.

1. Make sure the suit is waterproof. This may sound obvious, but not only must the fabric exclude moisture, but more importantly, the seams and closures must do so as well. Seams should be taped and cemented. Front openings and cuffs must have overlapping flaps and strong zippers (Delrin or nylon are best). Drawstrings should be long enough to permit you to tie bows or knots with cramped, cold fingers.

2. Make sure the suit fits. Allow for at least two layers of heavy clothing underneath. The best time to buy foul weather gear is during the winter. Wear a heavy sweater to the chandlery. Make sure you can move freely, sit comfortably and stretch without tearing anything or binding.

3. Make sure you can do in it what you want. Movement and ease of entry are directly proportional to the type of sailing you'll do. A one-piece suit is fine for dinghy racing but the offshore sailor will probably want separate jacket and pants. Some sailors prefer anoraks. Pants are not very useful if only waist high. The ones which come to just under the armpit all around are the most useful, especially if it is not raining. They offer almost full protection with maximum ease of movement.

Foul weather gear comes in coated cotton, coated nylon and "breathable" coated nylon. It is available in heavyweight, lightweight, ordinary weight and super-lightweight cloths. Heavyweight offshore gear is best for all but the warmest climes. Sailing in Northern Europe can be cold even in midsummer; night sailing is cold amost anywhere. Furthermore, heavy-duty gear will stand much more abuse and resist tears better than lightweight suits. Coated cotton can be very comfortable, but it needs caring and airing. Polyurethane-coated nylon seems to fill the bill for most yachtsmen. The breathable stuff is great but is not made in a heavy enough cloth for really strenuous use.

Who makes it? Everyone. There are probably more manufacturers of sailing clothing than of any other sailing gear. The best are Henri-Lloyd, Atlantis, MacBean and Canor-Plarex. I've found that Henri-Lloyd has lasted longer than anything else. It can also deplete your pocketbook by almost as much as a Burberry trenchcoat. However, when you're offshore in a gale the last thing you want to think about is your wallet. Get the best and be comfortable.

FOOTWEAR

One of the marvelous things about sailing is the ease with which you can slip and slide about a deck—be it teak, Treadmaster or whatever. The main purpose of any sailing footwear is to lessen the chance of going overboard. The classic Topsiders, made by Sperry, are superb. The tread is incomparable. Good runners-up include Docksides by Sebago, and Dunlop and Eaton shoes. They all use decent tanned leather in a moccasin cut, with the soles attached to the moccasin bottoms. Docksides soles will last longer than Top-siders, but they are not as flexible and offer slightly less grip on a slippery deck.

Deck boots ought to come to just below the knee. Sperry makes the most widely available and the Dunlop boots are good, if you can find the kind sold to commercial fishermen. Specialty boots are made by Romika. Their dinghy racing boot is a splendid piece of podiatric engineering. The best boots have removable sole liners. A spare pair is a good idea for offshore since dry feet make for less hysterical sailors.

With shoes, any pair of thick socks works fine. Rubber boots deserve two pairs, because the wicking action of a second pair will keep your feet drier and warmer. Wool and cotton are good; an inner pair of silk socks, though expensive, is even better. Stay away from canvas or nylon deck shoes. They are always clammy and cold.

Chapter 8

THE BOSUN'S LOCKER

Whether you're planning a world cruise or a season of club races, an overall inspection of hull, rig and hardware should come before everything else on your agenda. If this seems like an overly cautious or time-consuming measure, remember that if you don't exorcise your fears before weighing anchor, you will carry them with you wherever you sail. More importantly, those fears may unfortunately turn out to have a basis in fact, and you may find yourself in real difficulty.

Inspecting and maintaining all the gear you carry on board is, of course, important. Earlier chapters have, for this reason, dealt with the maintenance of their respective types of equipment. In this chapter, though, we will consider the maintenance and repairs that assure the soundness of the boat's basic structure, at the same time recommending the best in tools and materials. We will also suggest the tool inventory you should carry to make sure you have the ability to make all crucial repairs at sea.

BOSUN'S TOOLBOX

Any mechanic worth his salt gripes about tools: about sockets that crack, wrenches that spread, screwdrivers that lose all semblance of a device supposed to turn screws into a hole.

What can you do to avoid or remedy the problem? The answer is simple. Buy the best, because the best is what the systems on your boat deserve. But you must also protect what you buy, just as scrupulously as you care for your crew, because one day you may badly need them all.

There are three major divisions of tools a ship's bosun needs: carpentry tools, mechanic's tools and rigging and sailmaker's tools. When planning your carpenter's toolbox, try to anticipate your real needs. If you spend the season near home, you won't need to carry a joiner's shop with you. Keep your toolbox simple and it will prove efficient.

The smart sailor can solve stowage problems by carrying a complete tool set in three small boxes. He can then have his important tools aboard without having to find space for a single monstrous box that can store tools of various sizes and shapes. Carpenter's tools, for example, are usually large. Those that are especially cumbersome—like saws, hammers and planes—can be organized neatly in a long, flat box, stowed efficiently beneath a fo'cs'l berth or up under the deck in the lazarette. The smaller mechanic's tools can be stowed inside a smaller box or boxes and made to live elsewhere—in a spot where a chunkier package is more appropriate—beside the engine, in the bilges or under a berth.

The size of your boat will determine the size of your tools, but you have to decide how much you are willing or able to spend for them. A fine crosscut saw, for example, can cost almost $100. Since virtually every manufacturer of tools makes good models and mediocre models, you should not just buy a name brand, even if the name is Stanley or Disston. Check to make sure that the tools are drop-forged steel, rather than cast or stamped metal. Cast tools break easily; stamped tools are filed to size by hand, so they are often ill fitting. If you seek a chisel, plane or screwdriver with a wooden handle make sure the wood used is a durable hardwood like beech, ash or boxwood. The wood must be closed-grained and free of knots. Tough plastic handles—made of cellulose acetate or polypropylene—withstand hammerblows well, but they are harder to grip than wood handles. For screwdrivers which may be used on the electrical system, however, the plastic handles are the better choice, because they are better insulators. Watch out for the novel hexagonal and octagonal handles though, as they make for uncomfortable and inefficient turning.

If you follow the above guidelines in buying tools made by Disston, Marples, Millers Falls, Record Ridgway, Sanderson Kayser, Spear & Jackson, Stanley, Henry Taylor or Wilkinson Sword, you'll be getting very fine tools indeed. If you are considering mail order, pick up a copy of Brookstone's catalog (in the U.S.). After you've spent a few winter's eves poring over this wonderful booklet, you may well be ready to buy a plane that is fine enough to serve as your morning razor. *WoodenBoat* magazine, too, contains both articles and advertisements, providing superb information about tool sources.

But remember that on a boat you must fit your needs to what you can carry, and in most cases that is very little. For simple woodworking, you should consider:

- Wood bits, ranging from ⅛ inch to 1 inch
- Set of combination (drill, counterbore, countersink) bits
- Hand-type twist drill or brace
- Claw hammer
- Ball-peen hammer
- 50-foot measuring tape
- Sharpening stone
- Crosscut saw
- Small pry bar or cat's paw
- ⅜- and ¾-inch chisels
- Sanding block and sandpaper
- Carpenter's all-purpose file
- 1- and 2-inch putty knives
- 8-inch plane

For more complicated jobs or large projects—especially if you plan to be away from port a long time—you should consider carrying power tools. If your boat has AC power capability, then using good-quality power tools will be no problem. Black & Decker, Bosch, Makita, Rockwell and Skil all make fine products, but whatever you buy protect it properly: Store power tools in plastic bags or tightly lidded plastic containers. Ordinary freezer jars or the flexible waterproof tubs made by companies like Tupperware work fine.

If you do use power tools—whether you're using ship's generator or shore power—equip the boat with Ground Fault Interruption. GFI protects the user of a plugged-in apparatus from becoming the shortest route to ground. The instant any current starts to stray out of an improperly grounded tool, the juice is shut off. You can buy GFI devices at many electrical supply houses. Consult an electrician for the best one near you. (Ordinary hardware stores seldom stock GFIs.) Remember that your boat *is* ground and that both of you will probably be wet—a perfect situation for a serious shock.

For those whose boats lack AC capability, several manufacturers build battery-powered tools. Black & Decker and Makita both make fine ⅜-inch power drills suitable for inclusion in your bosun's kit. Both work on rechargeable battery packs, and are strong and easy to use. Make sure you carry spare batteries, though, and bring your hand drill as a backup.

Because mechanics are often snobbish about their tools, there is a great variety of opinion concerning which companies make, in fact, the best mechanic's tools. Still, the consensus seems to settle on three major brands. Snap-On Tools is the name to be reckoned with, because they build the finest sockets, drives and wrenches available. S-K is also known as a manufacturer of high-quality tools that are available at slightly cheaper prices. Craftsman tools, made by Sears, Roebuck & Company, are pound-for-pound the best all-purpose medium-priced tools in the U.S. A fine U.K. manufacturer of nonspark mechanic's tools is Safety Tools.

Whatever brand you finally buy, insist on several things. First, your wrenches, sockets and drives must all be drop-forged steel or nonspark beryllium copper. The latter prevents stray sparks from igniting fumes in the bilges, but though beryllium copper tools are safer, they are also ten times as expensive as forged steel. Avoid the weaker stainless steel or cast tools. Second, your sockets must all be stout enough to face up to frozen nuts and overtight bolts. Thin-walled sockets might be fine for delicate engine work (in fact, some companies

The Black & Decker cordless rechargeable ⅜-inch drill is particularly useful aboard as it lessens the chance of accidental shock and allows greater access in tight places.

It comes with a recharging attachment (below) for the battery pack.

build them precisely for that purpose); but you'll be doing muscle-work for the most part, so get the beefier models available.

Set yourself up with the most flexible array of wrenches and sockets you can find. The key word is adaptability—the fewest number of wrenches that can do the greatest number of jobs. For instance, you might want to consider combination box-end and open-end wrenches, instead of a set of both. And buy a couple of extensions for your half-inch socket drive—with at least one that allows you to switch down to a ⅜-inch socket for tight work. Good starter sets are available from Brookstone, Sears or Stanley.

Multi-purpose tools can be handy, but avoid "magic" tools. Though double-ended screwdriver sets may seem like a good idea, they quickly slip, break and abrade into nothingness. Buy about half-a-dozen good drivers with sharp, well-machined heads and comfortable handles. Make sure to include Phillips heads in the lot.

Vise grips (or mole grips), too, are one of those tools that are sometimes handy, but don't think you can substitute them for the appropriate wrench when the time comes. If they slip, stripping the head of a bolt, you will soon be flinging them over the side.

The following is a list of mechanic's tools to include in your locker:

- Standard set of Allen wrenches
- ½-, ¾- and 1-inch cold chisels
- 1 pair slip-lock pliers
- 1 pair needle-nose pliers
- 1 side-cutter
- 1 hacksaw with spare blades
- 6 standard screwdrivers
- 2 Phillips-head screwdrivers
- Set of jeweler's screwdrivers
- Wire brush
- 8- and 10-inch adjustable wrenches
- 10 or 12 open-end/box-end wrenches
- Complete set of sockets with ½-inch drive; extensions and adapters for ⅜-inch drive; selected ⅜-inch sockets for working in tight spots
- 1 set metalworking drills
- Stilson wrench
- Assorted files
- Wire cutters or Felco cable cutters
- Hydrometer

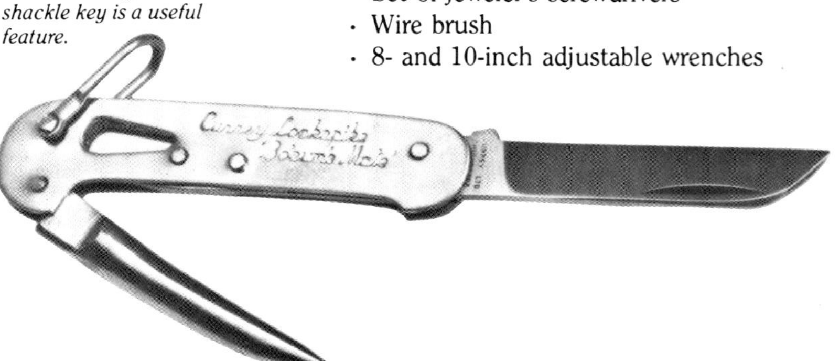

This Currey knife is a good all purpose crew's knife. Locking marlinspike is a must for safety, while the shackle key is a useful feature.

Since you are necessarily both mechanic and electrician on your vessel, make sure you can do simple wiring jobs with the tools at hand. Side-cutters are good for cutting wire; stripping will be possible with your basic seaman's knife; and crimping can be done with the needle-nose or standard pliers.

To test a circuit, however, you should have one standard electrician's tool: a multimeter, or VOM. This handy gadget provides you with a way to troubleshoot without feeling like shooting yourself. The ohmmeter lets you read the continuity of a circuit to determine if it is open, shorted or developing its proper resistance. The voltmeter reads the "live" voltage of a circuit directly. Many of these work with either AC or DC circuitry, but you will probably want one that serves only DC. In the U.S., go to Sears. They offer a fine, inexpensive line. For top-of-the-line gear, look into your local electrical supply house for a Triplett or Simpson unit. Bach-Simpson is a fine source in the U.K.

To complete your bosun's toolbox, you need sail-repair equipment. Even if your stitching technique won't win any prizes, you have to mend sails and rigging. The following is a list of essential rope- and sail-repair tools and materials:

- 6-inch scissors
- Sailmaker's wax
- Sailmaker's palm
- Sharp marlinespike
- Seam ripper
- Hot knife with spare tip (optional)
- Assorted weights of Dacron and nylon thread
- 8-10 spools waxed polyester and waxed hemp twine
- Needles: #13, #15, #17, #19

- Roll of light nylon ripstop tape
- Roll of 5-ounce Dacron tape, 6 inches wide
- Spool of tarred marline
- 25 feet siezing wire
- Several "D" or "O" rings
- Sailmaker's pliers
- Assorted weights of sailcloth
- Large spool of light, braided *parachute* cord
- Several rigger's awls
- Grommet set

Sail repair kits are fine as far as they go, but usually they do not provide enough for the ocean-going cruiser who is aiming at real self-sufficiency. Still, a good kit is a fine place to start the process of compiling your sail-repair gear. Moody Tools makes a good starter kit that includes a few needles, Dacron tape and polyester twine. Other manufacturers have kits with pretty much the same contents, and a few have palms and spikes included as well. Brookstone sells a palm-and-needle setup that is as good as they come. Your local sail loft should help you fill out the kit. One item—scissors—need not come from a specialty sail manufacturer. Clauss Cutlery makes some of the finest American scissors and shears; Wilkinson Sword manufactures fine ones in the U.K.

That you need a suitable sailor's knife goes without saying. Carry it with you at all times. One with a small spike for rope work is ideal, and it will prove even handier if it has a shackle-pin slot or "wrench" for those times you just can't get the shackle to let go. Ibberson and Captain Currey both make good ones.

One overall *caveat* applies to all kinds of tools: Keep moisture away from them. Stow all your tools in secure noncorrosive containers in a dry place. Another safeguard against corrosion is proper lubrication. Since most of your good tools are made of ordinary steel, make sure to spray them with WD-40 penetrating lubricant.

STRUCTURAL INSPECTION

If your boat is more than ten years old and she hasn't yet come under the careful eye of a qualified surveyor, get it surveyed before you weigh anchor again. The reason is simple. A good marine surveyor knows where, how and why to look at things you wouldn't dream of looking at. His report can be as vital a part of your ship's gear as any winch or backstay.

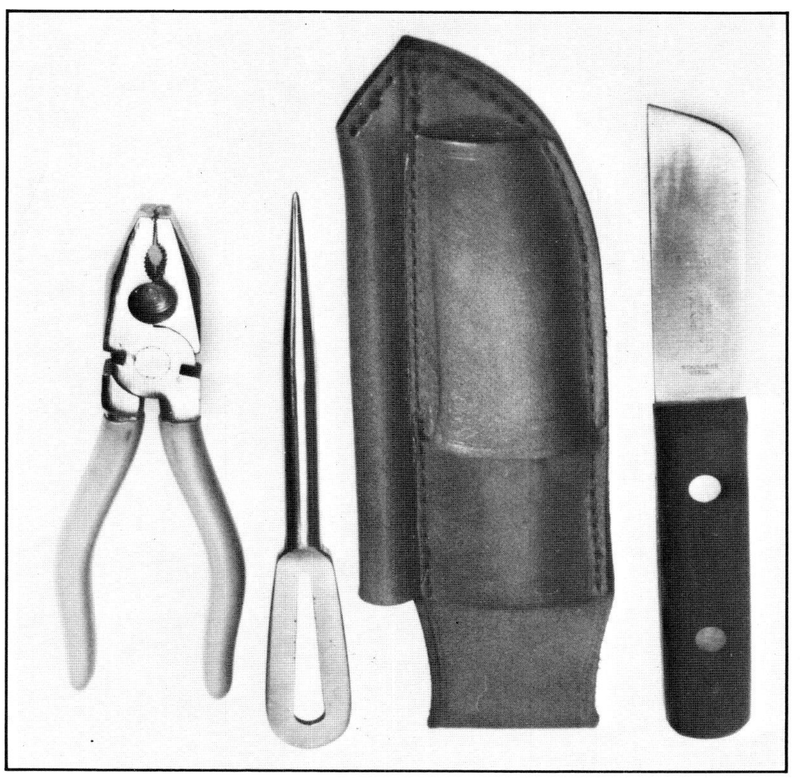

A complete set of rigger's tools in a handy belt sheath is almost a must for any serious voyager.

However, since there is no real reason to have a survey every year, you should be prepared to conduct your own inspection to make sure your boat is in top condition, following the orderly methods of the professional surveyor.

A surveyor's tools are simple. To begin with, you need only a note pad and pen. Devote a whole day to going over the boat. Then run through the list of problems you've located and determine what you're going to do about them.

Other tools you need are a sharp knife, a screwdriver and a flashlight. I also use a ⅜-inch chisel and a small plastic mallet, mostly for sounding the structural components of my wooden boat. A mallet is also handy for a fiberglass boat, since tapping with a knife or screwdriver handle won't always reveal the kind of problems—like delamination or core separation—that can occur within the layers of glass.

You might consider combining the surveyor's mallet with a hammer for your tool kit by buying a deadblow hammer. Made from a single piece of plastic, these hammers are tough enough to drive nails but soft enough for tapping on the hull. They never corrode, leave no mark and will not spark. Good ones are made by Stanley.

Wooden Hull

When inspecting a wooden boat, begin by sighting along the deckline, eyeballing the condition of the paint work and looking for discoloration from weeping fastenings.

As you step closer, poke at seams and then wiggle the prop shaft and rudder in order to feel for slop or play at the bearings. Check along the keel joint for signs of separation, unusual checking, or cracking. Check areas of stress—like those around the rudder post, at the garboards and at the bilges. Look at the zinc anodes. If any chalking or crumbling is present, brush it away to get a better look. If more than 30 percent of the zinc is wasted away, it needs to be replaced with a new zinc of the same rating. Examine the through-hull fittings for looseness or corrosion, and peel away some of the paint around them to examine the wood for discoloration that might indicate electrolytic damage.

In areas of stress, or wherever there is paint discoloration, loose bungs or weeping fastenings, pull some caulking, even if it looks good from the outside. Examine it for dampness or the beginnings of discoloration from water intrusion. Make a written note to replace any damaged caulking.

A Stanley deadblow hammer. These multi-purpose hammers make pounding less fatiguing, and they will not spark or corrode.

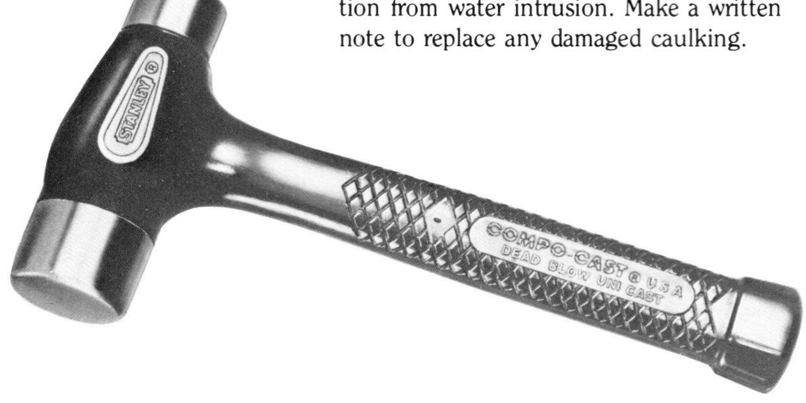

Pull any suspect fastenings from the areas mentioned above and examine them for discoloration or decay. Everdur screws, for example, will look dark or chalky-green if water has gotten at them. Other alloys can get chalky-white and pitted or take on a red cast, depending on whether they have corroded under the influence of galvanic action or because of oxidation. Note, again in writing, the need for replacement of any fastenings that look corroded. Also take care to replace the bungs in secure beddings of paint or sealer after you drive the screws back in.

Once every two years remove critical seams—at the garboard and the keel rabbet, for example. Renew these with fresh caulking, and work some red lead into them. The lead helps the caulking stick and protects metal parts.

After performing these basic exterior procedures, it's time to go below. Start at the stem and work aft, looking for three major things: water intrusion, which is seen as a dark streaking, discoloration or actual dampness; fastening failure, seen in bad rivet heads, sprung frames, corroded bolts; or structural failure, which can take the form of bulkhead separation, frame damage or rot. Check the following:

- Deck seams
- Sheer strake, around sheer clamp
- Chainplates
- Through-hulls
- Frame ends
- Stemhead
- Frame/floor joints
- Inner keel
- Mast step
- Transom edges
- Bulkhead/hull interfaces

Water intrusion in these areas calls for a probe with your knife (or chisel) to check for rot, especially where fresh water is suspected as the culprit. Using the mallet to tap lightly around fastenings in discolored areas will uncover any softness near the screw or bolt. A dull thud instead of a healthy pop indicates trouble. Note the extent of any rot damage. Later, you or your repairperson decide if replacement, sistering or simple chemical repairs are needed.

Now check the fastenings, searching for pulled rivet burrs, corroded keel bolts, loose nuts or weeping where fastenings should be. Note the type and size of fastener that needs replacing. If a fastening is loose due to rot, examine for a good spot to refasten, including it by name and position on your "rot repair" list.

Lastly, in each area open to your inspection, check for structural failure. Broken frames, cracked mast step, lifted floors, weak or shifted knees and clamps—all damage should be noted and specifically listed by name and location. The extent of repair needed will naturally depend on the extent of the damage, so be specific in your listings. You'll need detailed notations to help your memory later.

Fiberglass Hull

Compared to a wooden boat, a fiberglass boat is simple to inspect structurally. First of all, there are fewer members to check; second, there is a lot you simply cannot see. Bring your penknife and mallet, though, because what you can't see you may be able to hear by thumping about in the bilges.

The procedure to be followed is similar to the one used for a wooden boat. Begin by stepping back and eyeballing the hull to get a general feel for the overall picture. Check the zincs as suggested above, replacing them if they are badly wasted; check the other submerged metals extra closely if unusual zinc damage is noted. Peel away any flaking paint in order to look for the cause of the problem. Examine the rudder's post and check for binding or play that could indicate either bad bearings or distorted assembly. Work the propellor and shaft, looking for play at the stern bearing and spline.

In the bilges, check the following:

—Hull/deck joint: Check for moisture seepage; signs of deterioration in the seam (loss of sealant, loose fastenings); and corrosion of bolts or screws.

—Hull skin: Tap with the mallet around through-hulls and along the bilges; sound near the engine beds, where severe vibration might cause secondary bond failure; examine chainplates for seepage, corrosion and loose fastenings.

—Bulkhead/hull interfaces and glass-encapsulated stringers: Examine for failure of secondary glass bond, especially at main-strength bulkheads (forepeak, mast, aft end of cabin, rudder area); check for delamination by tapping with your mallet.

—Keel bolts: Check for looseness and corrosion; with the keel supported fully on the cradle, back off one or two of the bolts to examine the threads for distortion.

One important fact to note when you begin your survey is that many fiberglass boats have liners that obscure certain areas of the hull structure. If you have any problems inspecting vital hull areas, consider cutting out inspection points at strategic liner locations. Then you will have easy access for future inspections and repairs. You should consult your boat's builder before making such changes, however, just to make sure you're not severely weakening the liner, cutting into a wiring harness or sawing into a stringer.

Metal Hulls

On steel or aluminum boats, checking the zincs is crucial. Treat them as though they were the only thing between you and oblivion, and make sure you consult with a qualified expert when it's time to replace the anodes.

Spend time picking over any peeling or flaking paint on the hull, looking for corrosion underneath. Check all welded seams for signs of cracking, particularly in areas of high stress—near the rudder post, at the keel and at the turn of the bilge or chine. Use a wire brush to get down to bright metal under any bubbling or peeling, and check for pitting. Note whether the stricken area needs a new plate, or simply priming and a new coat of paint.

Below decks, you should examine a metal boat just as you would a fiberglass one. Fundamentally, this means you should look for frame separation, rust or corrosion around through-hulls and bonding cables, and cracking in welded seams. If your own inspection reveals any problems in framing or welds, consult a surveyor specializing in steel or aluminum boats

WOOD MAINTENANCE AND REPAIR

Because wood is the first and age-old material for boatbuilding, it has more lore and technique associated with it than any other material. And because wood is biodegradable, it also requires more maintenance. Fortunately, wooden boats are made up of thousands of component parts, so many repairs involve simply replacing the afflicted part or parts, leaving the rest of the structure alone.

Caulking

There are two types of caulking commonly used on carvel-planked boats: cotton and chemical (polysulfide or silicon rubber). Both work well, but one is not always a suitable replacement for the other. Because polysulfide and other chemical caulking must reside in a perfectly clean seam, it can be impossible to use it on an older boat whose planks have endured years of red lead, pitch, paint and other contaminants. Some planking, too, is unsuitable for use with chemical compounds: yellow pine and tamarack have unusually high resin contents which may weaken the bond of the flexible caulking materials.

Caulking is a delicate art. If you use too much cotton, the seams will spit it out; if you use too little, the hull will leak.

Before any caulking begins, make sure the new plank or section is fair with the old, using a foot-long jack plane. When it is fair, sand the plank and get ready to caulk.

Remove any debris or wood particles from the joint; then prepare your tools. You will need one or two caulking irons. For boats with relatively thin planking, use a 1/16-inch iron, but for thicker planking, you should have a ⅛-inch iron on hand, too. Cotton caulking is available at your chandlery.

Begin by neatly balling some lengths of cotton. Keep it clean. Start the caulking into the seam at one end, using a caulking hammer and iron. Work along slowly, being careful not to drive in too much. Work the cotton into the seam in loops—pulling it back on itself to produce a thickness appropriate for the seam section you're working on. Drive enough into the joint so that the plank will not force the caulking out when it swells in the water, but avoid overstuffing the seam. The idea is to produce a strand of caulking that lies against the plank edges, right in the middle of the seam, creating a slight depression in both the edges. Consult an experienced shipwright if you have any questions—every seam is different.

After initially working the caulking into the seam, go back over it and drive it home, leaving enough space on the outside of the seam for seam compound. When applying the compound, work it in with a 3-inch knife. Here is a good place to use polysulfide sealer. Boatlife makes a good one, available in both the U.S. and the U.K. Now you are ready to prime your surface, sand again and paint.

Polysulfide caulking is far easier to insert than traditional cotton caulking. Correct fit is not as crucial, and the material is so flexible that seams themselves, in effect, can control the amount of material they have in them. Still, if the seam spits out some caulking after the wood has dried out over the winter, you will need to replace it. That's one very good reason to keep any wooden boat in the water all winter.

If you've decided to replace old cotton with polysulfide, or if your new plank is a wood that—unlike resinous yellow pine or tamarack—can take the chemical adhesion, then follow these simple steps:

—Make sure the seams are thoroughly hooked-out and clean. If necessary, use an electric router on the seams, taking care to set up a guide on the outside of the adjacent planking against which to run the edge of the router. Use a small, tapered router bit, so the outside of the seam will be wider than the inner faces. Once routed, the seam should be primed with the material specified by the manufacturer of the chemical caulk you've chosen. Even oily woods like teak or Douglas fir—usually hard to use with polysulfides—can respond well if the proper primer is applied.

—Drive a single strand of cotton to the very bottom of the seam.

—Work the sealant into the seam, being careful to fill all voids entirely.

—Smooth, prime and paint.

Resins, Glues, Fillers

Many recent innovations in plastics technology help solve the wooden boat's repair problems. While this is true, you must remember that extensive use of synthetic materials can harm the overall integrity of a wooden boat. Why? Because wood breathes, moves, lives. If you put enough plastic in a wooden structure, the stresses become concentrated around the stiff, synthetic parts. Moreover, the boat will prove increasingly difficult to repair.

A friend who repairs Maine lobsterboats reported a striking example. In one such workhorse, he found extensive use of Git-Rot, a very effective rot-damage repair agent (when applied properly). The problem was that this old boat had so much Git-Rot in her that there was very little wood left. Her main timbers had practically been displaced by the plastic material.

When the shipwright tried to cut away some timbers for replacement, his saw blade dulled in the ossified wood. When he tried to remove fastenings, he found them permanently glued in place. The job became almost impossible. When he mentioned the cost of the work that would be necessary to make proper repairs, the boat's owner disappeared, never to return. The boat was broken up for firewood—as which it failed miserably. Apparently, Git-Rot is also an effective fire retardant.

Clearly, inorganic materials like plastics should not be used as major structural parts for traditionally built wooden vessels, except as glues, as local filler or for sheathing. The following is a list of some superior resinous materials that are suitable for repairing wooden boats:

—*Git-Rot,* made by Boatlife, is a superior material that, when used properly, can save lots of labor. It soaks into small sections of dry rot, displacing the soft wood with a hard, epoxy plastic. It is a two-part product. Mix according to instructions and pour into holes drilled at frequent intervals in the rotted section. Make sure that your holes cover the entire affected area. Dry the whole rotted area with a heat lamp or let the air dry it for a while before you begin pouring in the Git-Rot.

—*West System epoxy* is a fine laminating resin, made by Gougeon Brothers and distributed in the U.K. by Borden. Thickened slightly with powder filler, it is unsurpassed as a glue. When used unmixed, it soaks into wood surfaces like water, mummifying the fibers. As a filler—with lots of glass powder in the mix—its adhesion is still good, but it should be used only where there will be no flex in the filled joint.

—*Silicone sealant* is made by Dow Corning, Boatlife and others. Its flexibility makes it perfect for seams that swell and shrink—like those around deadlights and ports, along hatch slides and around engine instruments.

—*Polysulfide sealant* is an excellent material for caulking, filling deck seams and plugging screw holes. Boatlife's version of this compound is excellent; Rule Industries makes another good one.

—*Polyester fillers* come in two basic types. Boat Armor makes one that has strands of glass in it; the strands act as a matrix for holding the resin. Good and tough, this material can be difficult to get smooth because the glass strands cause an initial roughness that requires sanding. Buying strandless polyester resin (also available from Boat Armor) and thickening it with either glass powder or microballoons may be the best way to use polyester as a filler, since it is tough but easier to smooth.

—*Cluvit epoxy sealer* is a unique product that forms a very flexible, high-adhesion bond with wood. Because it is so flexible, it is the only epoxy suitable for filling and sealing deck leaks. Its only drawback is that it takes a relatively long time to cure.

Deck Seams or Canvas

There will inevitably come a time when you will be faced with the major job of replacing the caulking in your teak deck seams, or else removing and replacing the canvas coating on your painted deck or cabin top. As with many other areas of maintenance, modern technology has made the job easier than it was years ago, although it remains time-consuming.

Repairing deck seams in a laid-teak deck involves first hooking out the old caulking. Make sure to get it all out, as any left in the seam will spoil the adhesion of the new material.

Next, apply the new sealant carefully, working it into the seams with the pressure of the caulking gun and a 3-inch putty knife. Use one of the black polysulfides: Boatlife Life Calk is a good one, while Rule, Woolsey and International also make excellent compounds. Make sure to wipe away the excess immediately. Better yet, use masking tape on either side of the seams. When the application is done, allow the material to set thoroughly: the instructions on the can will suggest appropriate drying times. When cured, sand the material lightly to remove overspread.

Renewing old canvas, on the other hand, can be a brutal job, but take heart: once you've completed the work, you will never have to do it again, if you remove the canvas and convert to fiberglass.

An older deck that's seen its share of water working in under the canvas needs more than renewal; it needs refurbishing. Fiberglass, despite what some purists say is the most sensible way to go. Before you strip everything to begin work, make sure you make a "map" of the deck so that all fittings can be replaced in their original positions. Here, then, are the steps for making a brand new deck:

—Strip off all old canvas, including tacks and any paint or other adhesive underneath. Remove handrails, toerails and all deck fittings.

—Allow substrata to dry completely.

—Sand thoroughly.

—Find and repair any rotted spots or bad seams in the deck planking. Use Git-Rot for small punky spots, and replace any bad spots with new wood, fastening it securely to deck beams and/or adjacent planking. Use West laminating resin or another good marine epoxy for your gluing and filling operations. Boat Armor and Pettit also make fine epoxy resins. The object is to produce a deck that is dry and smooth enough to take its new covering.

—Buy enough sheets of ¼-inch exterior-grade plywood to cover the entire deck, and cut pieces to cover the deck right out to the sheer strake or cabin sides. When installing the plywood, bed it firmly in a thick wood glue like U.S. Plywood's Resorcinol, and fasten it with enough screws to hold the sheathing firmly in order to make a good glue bond. Once you have completed the sheathing, fill any gaps or seams with a hard polyester putty.

—Sand and smooth the entire sheathed surface.

—Now, fiberglass the raw plywood. Use 1.5-ounce mat and a flexible grade of resin from a distributor familiar with marine applications, like Defender Industries or Imperial Chemical Industries. Bring the mat right out to the sheer strake or cabin sides, leaving the overcut to be trimmed off later. You might want to staple the material as you work the resin into it, but this is not always necessary.

—Make sure to work all bubbles and wrinkles out of the mat as you apply the resin. If any imperfections remain after setup, grind them away and fill with polyester putty or resin that has been thickened with a powder filler.

—Replace all the fittings after priming the fiberglassed surface with a suitable primer. Also note that moldings and other deck features will probably have to be adjusted to accommodate the rise in deck level due to the plywood sheathing.

—Make sure there is no plywood edge exposed to the weather. Lap the glass over the edges if you can, installing well-bedded moldings where a glass overlap would be impossible. On the sheerline, for instance, the bedded rubrail should serve to seal the plywood deck edge.

The Scarph Joint

There will come a time when you will be faced with a noncritical piece of wood that has been damaged in only one small section. Toerails, coamings, hatch covers and solid spars are all frequently abused objects. When damage does occur, it is often possible to notch away the gouged or broken section and join a new piece of wood, or "Dutchman." To do this, though, you will need to adopt some form of the following procedure:

—If possible, remove the entire wooden structure that includes the affected area. Otherwise all your sawing must be done with the piece in place.

—Saw so that you excise the entire damaged area. If the top of a toerail is damaged, for example, use a powerful saber saw (one by Miller's Falls, Craftsman or Rockwell is worth having). Simply cut down across the bottom of the damage and back up again, making a roughly crescent-shaped hole.

—Now refine the joint. If the repair is cosmetic, just file or sand the cut square. Use the cut-out to pattern a new piece of stock. When done, the new piece should be fitted to the cut-out and adjusted.

—Glue the piece in with epoxy resin and fasten—with small wood screws or copper nails driven and countersunk into drilled holes—for curing.

—When cured, sand smooth and finish.

Critical structural scarphs—those below the waterline or subject to particular stress—follow a more stringent set of requirements. You will probably hire a boat carpenter to do such repairs, but the following is the basic procedure he should use. First of all, that joint must be cut out at an angle with both faces of the scarph perfectly smooth and fit true. The ratio of the length of the joint to the thickness of the wood should be 10 to 1. When joining the new piece, apply West laminating resin or other epoxy in its normal state to both glue faces and let it set for a few minutes, thus allowing it to work into the wood before the pieces are put together. The final glue application should be thickened with microballoons or other suitable powder. The joint is then made and clamped, but not so tight that the epoxy is forced to run wholesale from the glue line. The result is the best wood-to-wood glue joint possible.

FIBERGLASS REPAIR

When fiberglass first came on the scene almost thirty years ago, there were two questions raised in the minds of prospective buyers: how well would this untried resin/fiber composite wear, and how easily could it be repaired? It is now clear how long fiberglass lasts: virtually forever. And almost thirty years of experience have shown that patching and filling repairs are convenient and durable. A general description of one favored way of repairing a damaged hull is contained in the following section.

Fixing a Hole

Fiberglass repair requires some tools you may not have in your kit For example, for smoothing large, flat sections of material, you'll need a grooved laminating roller. For working in concave areas—along the fillets of a bulkhead joint or stringer—a small radius roller is also handy. Finally, a few cheap, expendable brushes are a must for working in tight spots.

You will also need a powerful rotary grinder or electric drill with a sanding pad. Aluminum oxide paper cuts best in heavy grinding. If the job is large, you may need to build a temporary mold or form. Cardboard or sheet metal is often best for this, but you will also need some kind of release agent for separating the form from the finally cured laminate. Mold-release wax is one type; another is mold-release film, which is a spray-on releasing agent. Allied Resins makes both types. Imperial Chemical Industries (ICI) is a good source in the U.K.

What follows is a method for applying a patch to a fiberglass hull. Note that the method will work for both plywood and cold-molded boats, as well as for emergency plate repairs to steel or aluminum.

—Cut away any frayed and rough fiberglass edges, enlarging the hole slightly and making it more regular in shape. If a stringer or bulkhead is involved, cut it away, too, making the hole fully accessible from the inside of the hull.

—Now prepare for application of fiberglass. Start by grinding the edges of the hole round. Then grind, chisel and sand an enlarged notch or step into the least accessible side of the hull—usually the inside.

—Tape a piece of flexible cardboard or sheet metal over the more accessible side, making sure it makes a fair curve with the rest of the hull. Against that form, from the inside, work in a mixture of finely cut cardboard scraps and a small amount of polyester resin. It will be removed later.

—Apply a layer or two of 10-ounce fiberglass cloth to the carved-out step on the inside of the hull. Allow it to cure.

—Now you can remove the form from the hull's good side, carefully chopping out the loose cardboard/resin mix.

—Grind a series of steps, in a concentric pattern, into the outside of the hull around the hole.

—Next, after thoroughly cleaning away any chips or dust from the cut-outs, apply a series of 10-ounce fiberglass cloth patches to the outside, setting one or two into each stepped cut-out. Finish the patch with one layer of 3-ounce mat. Make sure to build the outside surface of the patch up beyond the rest of the hull.

—Grind the patch on the good side, using ever finer weights of sandpaper. After grinding smooth, fill the imperfections with a mixture of resin and glass powder or microballoons.

—After dressing the patch with filler, allow to cure for at least 24 hours. Smooth the filled patch with the finest grade of sandpaper in your array.

—Using a gel coat repair kit (available in marine supply stores) or polyester resin pigmented to match your boat's gel coat, coat the finished surface. Both repair kits and pigmented resins can be obtained directly from fiberglass suppliers like Defender Industries or Imperial Chemical Industries (ICI). If you have trouble matching the gel coat pigment, consult your boat's builder, or paint the whole hull with one of the new linear polyurethanes.

Note that a bulkhead or stringer may be involved in the hull damage. If this is the case, repair the hull first; then use cardboard or sheet metal, in the same fashion as above, to fabricate a patch for the structural member. For a foam- or wood-filled stringer, cut away the damaged material, and put a wood or foam Dutchman in place, making sure it rests flush with the side of the hull; then glass as before, either using a form to deal with large areas or simply laying on the glass for small ones.

When applying glass cloth or mat, use stippling rollers, brushes or radius rollers. Have them all handy, because you'll be working fast. Make sure to work out all air bubbles and wrinkles in the cloth as soon as they appear. And don't try to take on too large a job at one time—if you find, for example, that one layer at a time is all you can install smoothly, then so be it. Grinding of each layer is permissible in preparation for the next.

Gel Coat Repairs

A more common condition on a fiberglass boat is some form of deterioration of the gel coat, the surface of the fiberglass laminate. The damage can appear as fine cracking or crazing of the surface, or as the kind of chipping and abrasion caused by knocking against pilings or other boats.

If you see localized crazing, call your builder. It might be due to unusual stress in that area caused by hull flexing. In such a case, professionals should be consulted before repairs are made.

With noncritical chipping or cracking, a gel coat repair is all that is called for. The following is a good procedure:

—Buy one of the gel coat repair kits available in your local marine supply store, or buy gel coat pigment and mix it with polyester resin according to manufacturer's instructions.
—Prepare the area to be repaired by gently gouging out the cracks or chips with a sharp awl or thin-bladed knife. Then lightly sand the area to be treated. Flush with acetone.
—Follow with a small amount of matched gel coat, building it up slightly higher than the original hull surface.
—Wet-sand the patch with fine paper until it is absolutely fair with the hull.
—Then buff with your grinder's buffer attachment, using grinding compound. Finish with fiberglass polish. Boat Armor makes several types of abrasive polish; fine pumice or automotive compound will work just as well.

A final note about fiberglass repair: When applying resin in an enclosed space, make sure to provide adequate ventilation. Open hatches and ports, and use a fan. Wear a respirator or filter mask to prevent yourself from inhaling the styrene vapors. When sanding fiberglass, wear a particle mask. Glass dust can be harmful to your health.

EMERGENCY HULL REPAIRS

During any long cruise offshore, you should be ready to repair structural damage to the boat. Here's where ingenuity, foresight and a good repair kit pay off.

The Repair Kit

Several major manufacturers put together emergency repair kits for boats, but most contain only enough material for small jobs. You will want to be more complete if you are going offshore. Your kit should contain the following:

- 2 quarts of underwater epoxy plus appropriate hardener
- 1 pound of cotton waste
- Various sizes of fiberglass scrap: 10-ounce cloth, 3-ounce mat, 24-ounce woven roving
- Polyester filler and hardener
- Two tubes silicone or polysulfide sealer
- Assorted nuts, bolts, sheet-metal screws, nails, seizing wire and parachute cord
- Shackles, turnbuckles, short lengths of chain and spare blocks, fitted to your particular boat
- Wooden dunnage: scraps of plywood, two-by-four pieces, battens and precut soft pine wedges

Fixing a Hole

When a boat is holed offshore, it is always wise to have one crew member stand by the life raft in case you should have to abandon ship quickly. The others must turn-to to fix the damage as quickly as possible.

If the hole is small—the result of a sprung or strained plank, sheered through-hull or collision with a reef or floating log—a repair with a "bandage" and underwater epoxy is often possible. If the damage is large, a crew must work quickly to plug the hole with dunnage, sails or cushions.

Imagine, for example—unpleasant as the scenario may be—that you hit a reef. A good emergency procedure to handle the situation follows: First, steer the boat clear of ground and get it laid-to. Water is flooding in faster than the pumps can handle it.

While one man stays by the liferaft, another is sent to fire-up the emergency engine-driven pump. At the same time that the other crew members man the hand pumps, the engine-driven unit is engaged through its belt-drive power takeoff. ITT-Jabsco pumps are excellent, since they can create suction of 90 gallons per minute.

The water is still rising, but at a less alarming rate. Now the crew finds the hole: 1 foot long, about 4 inches wide, jagged. The skipper orders cotton waste from the dunnage locker to be jammed into the hole from inside the boat.

Unbagging the storm jib and securing lines to all three corners, the crew quickly fashions a makeshift patch, throwing it over the side and pulling the lines snug to keep the sail bandage in place. With the leakage drastically reduced, the pump begins to reduce the bilge water.

Note that you can have a hull "bandage" made just for this purpose, instead of using the storm sail. Use a heavy weight of canvas, cut to about 6 feet square and set with stout grommets.

Now come more permanent repairs: with the bandage still in place, the skipper orders a piece of ¼-inch plywood cut to fit over the hole on the inside of the hull, and a corresponding piece to fit over the outside. If the scrap plywood is unavailable, the crew should use a piece of nonstructural joinery, like the bottom of a drawer or a thin plywood partition.

Underwater epoxy (Rule and Borden make good brands) is then worked into some dry cotton waste, and, when the plywood patches are ready, the soaked cloth is laid into the hole against the bandage. Handi-Wipes or other disposable towelling make a surprisingly good cotton filler. Now the plywood is blocked and braced against the inside of the hole. Bolt holes are then drilled from the inside and temporarily bunged.

A crew member next goes over the side with more epoxy and the other piece of plywood. Clipped securely into his safety harness, he removes the storm canvas and lays more epoxy-soaked rags into the patch, following quickly with the outer plywood patch. This patch must already have been drilled so its bolt holes line up with those on the inner patch. Bolts are then run through the hull from inside and taken up with nuts by the crewman in the water.

Obviously, this is a dangerous job for the man in the water, and it may make better sense to have several men working in shifts to complete the task. In some cases, water temperature or other factors may make any exterior repairs impossible to do. In such a case, leave the sail bandage in place, and simply keep the plywood or dunnage patch braced against the hull on the inside.

For smaller holes in a wood or fiberglass boat, repairs from the outside-in can work well. Again, underwater epoxy used along with Handi-Wipes, will help. A putty knife can wedge the resin-soaked waste into the void; nailing or screwing a light wood or sheet metal patch over it will help keep the emergency caulking in place while it cures.

PAINTS AND OTHER COATINGS

If technology has provided an ever-increasing range of choice for do-it-yourself repairs, it has also created confusion in other

TABLE 8-1
Average Paint Requirements

• This table shows how much paint is required to cover different areas on boats of all sizes. The quantities assume two coats of paint applied over an existing finish.

BOAT SIZE AND TYPE	Topside	Bottom	Boottop	Deck	Varnish	Interior
10′ Dinghy	1 qt.	1 pt.	—	—	1 qt.	—
14′ Rowboat	2 qt.	1 qt.	—	—	—	—
14′ Outboard	1 qt.	1 qt.	½ pt.	1 pt.	1 qt.	—
18′ Runabout	1 qt.	3 qt.	½ pt.	1 qt.	1 qt.	—
20′ Sailboat	2 qt.	3 qt.	½ pt.	3 qt.	2 qt.	—
24′ Runabout	2 qt.	3 qt.	½ pt.	1½ qt.	2 qt.	—
24′ Utility	2 qt.	3 qt.	½ pt.	1½ qt.	1 qt.	—
25′ Cruiser	3 qt.	3 qt.	1 pt.	2 qt.	2 qt.	2 qt.
32′ Cruiser	2 gal.	1½ gal.	1 pt.	2 qt.	3 qt.	2 qt.
36′ Sailboat	2 gal.	2 gal.	1 pt.	1 gal.	1 gal.	3 qt.
40′ Cruiser	2½ gal.	2 gal.	1 pt.	1½ gal.	1 gal.	1 gal.
60′ Yacht	4 gal.	5 gal.	1 qt.	3½ gal.	2½ gal.	2½ gal.

Source: Woolsey Marine Industries.

marine areas—particularly in the thousands of marine paints and coatings now available. Naturally each claims to be the best possible protection for your boat. But since the boat owner must decide which product is most appropriate for his specific needs, this section discusses and evaluates general classes of coatings, their uses and some of the superior brands available.

Bottom Paints

Different paints serve different functions and climates. If you race, a hard finish is best for the bottomsides, because it creates the least friction; if you cruise, however, a softer paint may be better. In addition, since the type of paint you use depends on where you sail, your choices are narrowed further. In northern waters, fouling problems are seasonal, while in the tropics, the problems are year-round. Clearly it is a good idea to consult boatmen experienced in your particular area before making a choice. Commercial fishermen, especially, can often offer well-tested suggestions.

The toxin found most often in antifouling paints is cuprous oxide. Such paints are effective in direct proportion to the content of this poison, the best containing more than 50 percent cuprous oxide by weight. Hard, racing coatings leach this toxin into the water, while softer paints gradually wear away, spilling their poison slowly. Hard paints—made by such fine firms as Woolsey and International—are epoxy based; softer ones use traditional tar or mineral spirit bases.

It is important to remember, however, that all cuprous-oxide paints are unsuitable for steel or aluminum boats, which must use some form of organo-tin (TBTO) paint instead. This is because copper sets up a galvanic reaction with most metal alloys, and thus can accelerate corrosion. The tin paints are good weed and algae inhibitors; though they are not as effective against barnacles as copper paints, the metal boat owner obviously has no choice but to use what is safe for the hull.

Before you select a bottom paint, read some labels and find out how much hull preparation is required. If you've got tar-based paint on the bottom and you want to cover it with a harder vinyl type, make sure you understand the extent of work required for the switch. You may change your mind when you find out you must take *all* existing paint off—with paint remover, sandpaper and elbow grease—before recoating.

Once you have a bottom paint that is compatible with the existing coating, you can begin work. Sand and lay on two coats. Do not thin the paint—you'll just dilute the poison—and make sure to follow manufacturer's guidelines regarding curing and launching times.

Rollers are the generally accepted tools for painting bottoms these days, but you'll still need brushes to do the detail work around hull fittings and rudder. If your boat is a centerboarder, work the paint up into the trunk with some carpeting tacked to a stick of appropriate length.

On new fiberglass bottoms, the mold-release wax must be removed completely with acetone. Then the surface must be primed with a brand of pre-etching primer or other coating compatible with the brand of paint you use. Priming metal hulls is a different matter, involving many coats of suitable primer.

Several manufacturers now offer bottom coatings that are supposed to last for more than one season. Applied in several layers of controlled thickness, they release their toxins gradually, stimulated by the mechanical action of water scrubbing against the hull. As the paint wears, it essentially cleans itself. The base coat finally shows through, signaling the owner that it is time to repaint. International Paint's Micron-22 is one paint of this type. It has been proven on dozens of ocean-going ships over the past several years. Some sources report running for three seasons on one paint job. The only drawback is that Micron-22 is very expensive and must be applied professionally with power spray equipment.

Topsides

Polyurethanes, epoxies, vinyls and alkyds are all options for the topsides. If you are concerned about initial cost, you should choose one of the excellent alkyd enamels for your topsides. Today's brands are all

TABLE 8-2
Choosing Abrasive Papers

Job	Sanding Method	Sanding Paper	Grit*
Old Paint and Varnish: Complete removal	Hand	Aluminum oxide cabinet paper	#60, #80, #100 open coat
	Oscillating power sander		
	Disk (Use with care) Lt. duty	Aluminum oxide disk	
	Disk (Use with care) Hvy. duty	Fiber disk	#24, #36, #40
	Belts	Aluminum oxide cloth	#24, #36, #40 open coat
Bare Wood Preparation: Preparation for paint or varnish	Hand	Aluminum oxide cloth	#60, #80, #100, #120 closed coat
	Oscillating power sander	Cabinet paper	#60, #80, #100, #120 open coat
	Disk with sponge-rubber pad	Aluminum oxide cloth	#60, #80, #100, #120 closed coat
	Belts		
Old Paint and Varnish: Preparation for recoat	Hand	No-load silicon carbide finishing paper	#100, #120, #150 open coat
	Oscillating power sander		
	Disk with sponge-rubber pad		
Sealer, Undercoater, Paint and Varnish	Hand	No-load silicon carbide finishing paper	#150, #180, #220 open coat
	Oscillating power sander		
	Disk with sponge-rubber pad		
Fiberglass: Preparation to paint	Oscillating power sander	No-load silicon carbide finishing paper	#80, #100 open coat

**A choice of three or four grits is given. For the average job, use the medium grit. Or start with coarse grit, finish with fine grit.*

Source: Pettit Paint Company

relatively hard, and they retain their gloss for up to three years. Application of these enamels is easy, since sanding is the only surface preparation necessary.

On the other hand, some sailors swear by one-part polyurethanes. They find the application every bit as simple as for alkyds. and feel that the extra cost is justified by the longer gloss retention. The one-part polyurethanes may last up to a full season longer than the alkyds.

Still other sailors prefer the newer two-part or "linear" polyurethanes. These paints form extremely hard, glossy surfaces and hold that gloss better than any other known coating. They are, however, both very expensive and difficult to apply. Newer, brushable versions—Awlgrip, Interthane (by International) and Durathane (by Pettit)—go a long way toward making amateur application easy, but spreading and drying problems still occur. Above all, keep in mind that you must work quickly, because the linear polyurethanes dry in a matter of minutes. Also, use primers specifically designed for those brands and, as always, follow manufacturer's recommendations in preparing the surface.

Painting metal boats should be left to the professionals. There are so many problems with corrosion and proper paint adhesion that each job is different, and each is too difficult for the average sailor.

Decks

The advice in the section on topsides also holds generally for decks, but the boat owner must also deal with the specific problems that decks present.

Some boats use paint with grit mixed in for the decks, to improve footing. For renewal of this grit texture, lay a coat of paint down, moving through the job section-by-section. After coating a manageable area, use a flour-sifter or jar to scatter sterile aquarium sand, ground walnut shells or microballoons over the tacky surface. Repeat the procedure. Coat and sprinkle areas you can manage. If you let the paint dry before you apply the grit, you will create an uneven texture in the final job. After applying the grit, add one coat of paint.

Interiors

Salt and spray corrode everywhere, so renew your interior paint every few years. Take care to sand thoroughly, and use a primer if one of the polyurethanes is to go on over older enamel.

On too many boats, interiors are heavy with the somber glow of teak. The cabin will look cooler and larger if broad surfaces —bulkheads, berth fronts and doors—are painted instead. The only difficulty is the psychological one of painting over teak, though if the surface is first sealed with a coat of varnish or shellac, you can easily remove the paint to virgin wood, if you change your mind.

Color schemes below can easily become garish. Keep overheads white or a pale, soft color: blue or green is coolest. In fact, unless you are prone to fits of constant repainting, keep all colors below decks as neutral as possible. Teak and mahogany, varnished or oiled make for attractive trim, though too much can make your boat seem like a panelled coffin.

On a wood boat, too much paint in the bilge is less than ideal, because it can keep the wood from breathing or trap moisture underneath it, leading to rot. Fiberglass boats, on the other hand *should* be painted in the bilge. For wood and fiberglass, the best solution is to use a specially designed bilge enamel and work it into all odd corners of the bilge.

Varnish and Teak Oil

Brightwork can be trouble if it is neglected for a year or two, especially if water has penetrated under the coating and discolored the wood. But when brightwork is well maintained, it adds immeasureably to your boat's beauty and value.

TABLE 8-3
Refinishing Fiberglass Topsides

E—Excellent
VG—Very Good
G—Good
F—Fair
*—Coverage per one coat

TYPE OF COATING	Applied by	Chemical & Salt Water Resistance	Scuff & Abrasive Resistance	Resistance to Fading & Chalking	Average Cover per Gallon*	Ease of Application	Notes
Polyester Surfacer/Gel Coat	Brush Spray	E	E	VG	150	Very Difficult	Applied surface must be sanded and polished
Linear Polyurethane	Spray Brush	E	VG	VG	300*	Difficult	Follow directions carefully, expensive
2-Component Epoxies	Brush, Roll Spray	E	VG	F	275*	Difficult	Avoid application on humid days
1-Component Polyurethane/Alkyds	Brush, Roll Spray	G	G	G	300*	Easy	Very good gloss
1-Component Epoxy/Alkyd	Brush Roll	G	F	G	275*	Easy	Avoid application on humid days
Automotive Acrylic Lacquer	Spray	E	F	E	100	Moderate	3 or 4 double coats using about 50/50 thinner
Alkyd Marine Paint	Brush, Roll Spray	F	F	F	300*	Easy	Least likely to succeed

There are several basic types of varnish on the market. Spar varnish is rapidly being replaced by tougher coatings like the polyurethanes or acrylics, but it is still the choice of many who love the mellow warmth it lends to wood. Moreover, it is easy to apply: wipe down darkened or damaged surfaces; simply sand and wipe with a tack rag; then put on a coat. Each successive coat should be treated the same way, sanding by hand or with a small orbital sander using light paper. Before applying each coat, take all the previous coat's gloss off with your sanding. The result will be mirror smooth.

One-part acrylics and polyurethanes are also superior coatings for wood. Make sure to use a marine-type synthetic, though, as some commercial brands are unsuitable for the tough conditions of sunlight and salt a boat experiences. One excellent coating of this type is Brite-Wood, by Cardel/Frismar. It is extremely glossy, holds its gloss well and is flexible. You can even use it to waterproof your charts! Other excellent coatings are made by International Paint Company.

You may also want to try one of the clear two-part linear polyurethanes as a varnish. Pettit makes a fine one called Crystal Clear Gloss. It is brushable, as are those made by International and Awlgrip. Note that these clear two-part polyurethanes can even be used on faded topsides or decks to restore something of the original high gloss.

There has been much talk of late regarding the use of traditional-looking oil finishes on natural wood. Oils do protect the wood better than varnishes, and they are far easier to maintain. Deks Olje—a fine oil product—comes in two finishes, gloss and matte. Whichever you choose, you will need to apply enough coats (at least six) to completely seal the wood. Still, the gloss coating is nowhere near as bright as even the dullest varnish. Tung oil and Boatlife's Teak Brite are other fine oils.

Of course, the use of varnish for finishing rails, hatches, coamings and decorative oddments on deck is traditional. However, if the yacht is to be moored in the Mediterranean or the Bahamas, it is well to consider the possibilities of foregoing the splendors of varnish for painted surfaces or even stainless steel railings and rubbing strakes. Not only will paint last longer in tropical conditions, but it is easier to apply, without the critical requirements of varnish, and certainly simpler to touch-up.

APPENDICES

Appendix A

EQUIPMENT SUPPLIERS

Manufacturers whose products are cited in *Under Sail* are listed in the following appendix:

ACR Electronics
3901 North 29th Avenue
P.O. Box 2148
Hollywood, FL 33022

Adler & Barbour Yacht Services
43 Lawton Street
New Rochelle, NY 10801

Aires Vane Gear
Northwood
Cowes
Isle of Wight
United Kingdom

Alden Electronic
1 Washington Street
Westboro, MA 01581

Alexander-Roberts Company
1851 Langley Avenue
Irvine, CA 92715

Alladin
ALH Incorporated
P.O. Box 7235
Nashville, TN 37210

Allied Resin
Weymouth Industrial Park
Pleasant Street
East Weymouth, MA 02189

American Bosch-AMBAC Industries
2664 Main Street
Springfield, MA 01107

American International Marine Corp.
P.O. Box 405, Department B1
Millersville, MD 21108

American La France
P.O. Box 6159
Charlottesville, VA 22906

Apelco
676 Island Pond Road
Manchester, NH 03103

Aptel Marine Division
APT Electronics Limited
Darwin Close
Reading
Berks RG2 OTB
United Kingdom

Aqualite
McMurdo Instrument Company
Rodney Road
Portsmouth PO4 8SG
United Kingdom

Aqua-Signal
P.O. Box 448540
D-2800 Bremen 44
West Germany

Aqua-Temp Corporation
421 North Line Street
Lansdale, PA 19446

Asimow Engineering Company
1818 Franklin Street
Santa Monica, CA 90404

Atkins & Hoyle
71 Portland Street
Toronto M5V 2M9
Canada

Atlantis Weathergear
Bay Street at the Waterfront
Sag Harbor, NY 11963

Atoms
28 Rue Smolett
06300 Nice
France

Auto-Helm
13375 Beach Avenue
Marina del Rey, CA 90291

Avon Inflatables Ltd.
Henely
Dyfed, South Wales
United Kingdom

Baby Blake
Blake & Sons
P.O. Box 15, Park Road
Gosport, Hants
United Kingdom

Barbarossa
Via Ceresio 12
Lomazzo, Como
Italy

Barient Company
4065 Campbell Avenue
Menlo Park, CA 94025

Barlow Marine USA
889 Production Place
Newport Beach, CA 92663

Bass Products
P.O. Box 901
Marblehead, MA 01945

Bayleysuit
900 South Fortuna Boulevard
Fortuna, CA 95540

Beaufort Air-Sea Equipment
#35 150 Milner Avenue
Scarborough, Ontario
Canada M1S 3R3

Black & Decker
Cannon Lane
Maidenhead
Berkshire SL6 3PD
United Kingdom
-or-
701 East Joppa Road
Towson, MD 21204

BMW
Montvale, NJ 07645
-or-
Ellesfield Avenue
Bracknell
Berks RG12 4TA
United Kingdom

Boat Armor Marine Products
Lan-O-Sheen
1 West Water Street
St. Paul, MN 55107

Boatlife
Life Industries
205 Sweet Hollow Road
Old Bethpage, NY 11804
-or-
75 High Street
Fareham
Hants PO16 7BG
United Kingdom

Bomar Inc.
Box 314
Charlestown, NH 03603

Borden Marine Products
11a Weston Grove Road
Southampton SO2 9EE
United Kingdom

Borg-Warner Corporation
South Aurora Street
Ithaca, NY 14850

Bosch Power Tools
P.O. Box 2217
Newbern, NC 28560

Brock-Seafarer
Electronic Laboratories
Fleet Lane
Poole
Dorset BH15 3BW
United Kingdom

Brookes & Gatehouse
Bath Road
Lymington, Hampshire
United Kingdom
-or-
154 East Boston Post Road
Mamaroneck, NY 10543

Brooks & Adams
Shady Lane, Kingstanding
Birmingham B44 9DX
United Kingdom

Henry Browne & Sons
Sestrel House
Loxford Road, Barking
Essex
United Kingdom

Browning Marine
P.O. Box 86
St. Charles, IL 60174

Bruce International
West Bay Street
P.O. Box N-7788
Nassau
Bahamas

Buck Algonquin Marine Hardware
Second & Columbia
Philadelphia, PA 19122

BUKH
South Western Marine Factors
43 Pottery Road
Poole
Dorset BH14 8RE
United Kingdom
-or-
Dave Stoll's Marine
2401 East Anaheim Street
Wilmington, CA 90748

Canadian Marconi Company
2442 Trenton Avenue
Montreal
Quebec
Canada

Canor Plarex
4200 23rd Avenue
West Seattle, WA 98199

Canpa Yacht Equipment
School Lane
Chandlers Ford Industries
East Leigh
Hants
United Kingdom

Captain Charles Currey Ltd.
Bosham
Chichester PO18 8ET
United Kingdom

Cardel Corporation
P.O. Box 456
Higganum, CT 06441

David Carne Productions
Seaway House
Commercial Road
Penryn
Cornwall
United Kingdom

Carniti
Oggonia
Italy

Cetec Benmar
3000 West Warner
Santa Ana, CA 92704

Cetrek Ltd.
Balena Close
Creekmoor, Poole
Dorset BH17 7DB
United Kingdom

Clamcleats Ltd.
Hertfordshire
United Kingdom

Clauss Cutlery
Fremont, OH 43420

Coast Navigation
1934 Lincoln Drive
Annapolis, MD 21401

Coastal Radio Ltd.
Westway
Chelmsford
Essex CM1 3BH
United Kingdom

Cole Hersee Company
20 Old Colony Avenue
Boston, MA 02127

Communication Associates Inc. (CAI)
200 McKay Road
Huntington Station, NY 11746

The Cordage Group Division
Columbian Rope Company
One Columbian Drive
Auburn, NY 13021

CQR Anchors
(See Simpson-Lawrence Ltd.)

Crewsaver Marine Equipment
Clarence Square
Mumby Road
Gosport
Hants PO12 1AQ
United Kingdom

Crosby Marine Refrigeration Systems
204 Second Avenue
St. Petersburg, FL 33701

Cummins Engine Company
1000 Fifth Street
Columbus, IN 47201

Danforth Division
Eastern Company
500 Riverside Industrial Park
Portland, ME 04103

Datamarine International
53 Portside Drive
Pocasset, MA 02559

Davis Instruments
642 143rd Avenue
P.O. Box 3157
San Leandro, CA 94578

Defender Industries
255 Main Street
New Rochelle, NY 10801

Demek
Delta Marine
70 Warwick Street
Birmingham B12 ONH
United Kingdom

W.H. Denouden (Vetus)
Fokkerstraat
Schiedam
Holland

Dickinson Marine Products
4300 11th Street NW
Seattle, WA 98107

Disston
Danville, VA 24543

R.L. Drake Company
540 Rochard Street
Miamisburg, OH 45342

Dunlop Tire and Rubber Company
Ryder Street
St. James's
London SW1Y 6TX
United Kingdom

Eberspacher
Eberspacherstrasse 24
D-7300 Esslingen
West Germany

Edson Corporation
492 Industrial Park Road
New Bedford, MA 02745

Elvstrom-USA (Suunto distrib.)
725 Boston Post Road
Guilford, CT 06437

Encron Energy Control Corporation
P.O. Box 127
1614 130th Avenue NE
Bellevue, WA 98009

Engel (Aqua-Marine)
381 Shirley Road
Southampton
Hants
United Kingdom

ENKES
7 Hawkes Street
Marblehead, MA 01945

Epsco Marine Division
411 Providence Highway
Westwood, MA 02090

Famet Marine
745 Second Avenue
Redwood City, CA 94603

Farymann Diesel
ENTEC
Box 189
Rahway, NJ 07065

Felco SA
2206 Les Geneveys
S/Coffiane
Switzerland

Fleet Marine Supply
1820 NE 146th Street
North Miami, FL 33181

Force Ten Marine Products
14749 Calvert Street
Van Nuys, CA 91411

K. Foreman Marine
Chapel Works
Braishfield
Romsey
Hants SO5 0PL
United Kingdom

Forespar
2672 Dow Avenue
Tustin, CA 92680

Francis
(See Simpson-Lawrence Ltd.)

Furuno
271 Harbor Way
South San Francisco, CA 94080
-or-
Second Floor
19 Park Street
Croydon CR0 1YF
United Kingdom

M.S. Gibb Ltd.
Warsash
Southampton S03
United Kingdom

Givens Associates
3198 Main Road
Tiverton, RI 02878

G & M Power Plant
White House Road
Ipswich
Suffolk 1P1 SLX
United Kingdom

Goiot SA
28 rue de Frère-Louis
44062 Nantes Cedex
France

Gougeon Brothers
705-06 Martin Street
Bay City, MI 48706
(See also Borden UK)

Groco
Gross Mechanical Labs
7240 Standard Drive
Hanover, MD 21076

The Grunert Company
195 Drum Point Road
Osbornville, NJ 08723

Guest Corporation
17 Culbro Drive
West Hartford, CT 06110

Jay Stuart Haft (CQR distributors)
8925 North Tennyson Drive
Milwaukee, WI 53217

Harken Yacht Fittings
1251 East Wisconsin Avenue
Pewaukee, WI 53072

Hasler Vane Gears
(See M.S. Gibb Ltd.)

Hasselfors Stainless Marine
Box 30-06
Ithaca, NY 14850

Peter Haward Ltd.
5 West Street
Abbotsbury
Weymouth, Dorset
United Kingdom

Henri-Lloyd
Bacon & Associates
112 West Street
P.O. Box 3150 B1
Annapolis, MD 21403

Hillerange
Seaward Products
1431 Portrero Avenue
El Monte, CA 91733

Jack Holt Ltd.
The Embankment
Putney
London SW15
United Kingdom
-or-
222 Severn Avenue
Annapolis, MD 21403

Homestrand
(See Kenyon Marine)

Honda Motors
100 West Alondra Boulevard
Gordena, CA 90247

Chellaram & Son
16-26 Banner Street
London EC1Y 8QE
United Kingdom

Hood Yacht Systems
Box 1049
Lime Street
Marblehead, MA 01945

Hurth
Carl Maschinen und Zahurad Fabrik
Holzstrasse 19
D-8000 Munchen 5
West Germany

Hydrovane Yacht Equipment
Woolverstone Marine
Ipswich
Suffolk
United Kingdom

Hynautic Inc.
1035 Old Venice Road
P.O. Box 668
Osprey, FL 33559

George Ibberson & Company
Violin Works
124 Scotland Street
S. Yorks S3 7DE
United Kingdom

Ideal Windlass Company
5810 Post Road
East Greenwich, RI 02818

Imperial Chemical Industries (ICI)
BIP Chemicals
P.O. Box 6
Popes Lane
Warley
West Midlands B69 4PD
United Kingdom

Inland Marine
79 East Jackson Street
Wilkes-Barre, PA 18701

Intech
282 Brokaw Road
Santa Clara, CA 95050

International Marine Instruments
40 Signal Road
Stamford, CT 06902

International Paint Company
P.O. Box 386
Union, NJ 07083
-or-
Henrietta House
9 Henrietta Place
London W1A 1AD
United Kingdom

Intermarine Electronics
Flowerfield Building 7
St. James, NY 11780

ITT Decca Marine
P.O. Box G
Palm Coast, FL 32037

ITT Jabsco Products
1485 Dale Way
Costa Mesa, CA 92626

International Yacht Equipment (IYE)
17-27 Kents Hill Road
South Benfleet
Essex
United Kingdom

C. Sherman Johnson Company
Industrial Park, Route 82
East Haddam, CT 06433

Keefe Manufacturing Company
P.O. Box 3418
150 Paul Drive
San Rafael, CA 94903

Kenyon Marine
P.O. Box 308
Guilford, CT 06437

Kleid Navigation
443 Ruane Street
Fairfield, CT 06430

Koolatron Industries
230 Bayview Drive
Barrie, Ontario L4N 4Y8
Canada

Lewmar Marine
Southmoor Lane
Havant
Hampshire PO9 1JJ
United Kingdom
-or-
Box 390
125 Wilbur Place
Bohemia, NY 11716

Lirakis Safety Harness
33 Howard Street
Newport, RI 02840

Lister Diesels
555 East 56th Highway
P.O. Box 386
Olathe, KS 66061
-or-
P.O. Box 1
Dursley
Glos GL11 4H5
United Kingdom

Lowrance Electronic
12000 East Skelly Drive
Tulsa, OK 74128

Loos & Company
54 Cableway
Pomfret, CT 06258

Paul E. Luke Inc.
Route 96
East Boothbay, ME 04544

Edward MacBean & Company
Woodilee Industries
Kirkintilloch
Glasgow G66 3UZ
Scotland

MacWhyte Wire Rope Company
2929 14th Avenue
Kenosha, WI 53141

Magnavox Marine Systems
2829 Maricopa Street
Torrance, CA 90503

Magnetic Components Ltd.
Falmouth
Cornwall
United Kingdom

Main Marine
North Barrack Road
Walmer, Deal
Kent
United Kingdom

Makita
John Harra Wood Supply
511 West 25th Street
New York, NY 10001
-or-
1 Finway
Dallow Road
Luton
Beds LU1 1TR
United Kingdom

Mansfield Sanitary
20 Wayne Street
Big Prairie, OH 44611

Marconi International Marine
Electra House
West Way
Chelmsford
Essex
United Kingdom

Marinaspec
Flint & Brown Ltd.
Chobbam, Woking
Surrey
United Kingdom
(See also Guest Corp. USA)

Mariner Company
1714 17th Street
Santa Monica, CA 90404

Marinetics Corporation
1638 Placentia Avenue
Costa Mesa, CA 92627

Marlow Ropes
South Road
Hailsham
Sussex BN27 3JS
United Kingdom

R.M. Marples & Son
Haven Works
Shillito Road
Parkstone Road, Poole
Dorset BH12 2BP
United Kingdom

Martec Engineering
2257 Gaylord Street
Long Beach, CA 90813

Mastep Ltd.
Waltham House
Town Cross Avenue
Bognor Regis
Sussex PO21 2DT
United Kingdom

Maxol
Sycamore Drive
Burnley
Lancashire
United Kingdom

Mercury Marine
1939 Pioneer Road
Fond du Lac, WI 54935

Merriman Holbrook
301 River Street
Grand River, OH 44045

Metal Marine Pilot
2119 Mildred Street
Tacoma, WA 98466

Microphor
P.O. Box 490
452 East Hill Road
Willits, CA 95490

Miller's Falls Company
57 Wells Street
Greenfield, MA 01301

Moody Tools
45 Dudley Street
P.O. Box 2248
Providence, RI 02905

Morrow Electronics
4740 Ridge Drive NE
E. Salem, OR 97303

Motorola/Modar Electronics
1313 East Algonquin Road
Schaumburg, IL 60196

Munster-Simms Engineering
Old Belfast Road
Bangor, County Down
Northern Ireland

Mustang Inc.
3810 Jacombs Road
Richmond
British Columbia V6V 1Y6
Canada

Narco Marine
Commerce Drive
Ft. Washington, PA 19034

Nashua Brass Company
45 East Hollis
Nashua, NH 03060

Navik
(See Plastimo)

Navtec Inc.
527 Great Road
Littleton, MA 01460

Navidyne Corporation
11824 Fishing Point Drive
Newport News, VA 23606

Neco Marine
Walton Road
Eastern Road
Portsmouth
United Kingdom
-or-
222 Severn Avenue
Annapolis, MD 21403

Newage Transmissions
Barlow Road
Coventry CV2 2LD
United Kingdom

Nexus Marine Systems
18 Corwin Street
Greenport, NY 11944

Nicro/Fico
2065 West Avenue 140th
San Leandro, CA 94577

Northern Radio Company
14975 Northeast 40th Street
Redmond, WA 98052

Northstar Marine
P.O. Box 95
Redondo Beach, CA 90277

Offshore Instruments
41 Birmingham Road
Cowes
Isle of Wight
United Kingdom

Olin Corporation
East Atlon, IL 62024

Optimus Inc.
12423 East Florence
Santa Fe Springs, CA 90670

Outboard Marine Corporation (OMC)
200 Sea-horse Drive
Waukegan, IL 60085
-or-
72 Pathoekeweg
B.8000 Brugge
Belgium

Pains-Wessex Ltd.
High Post
Salisbury
Wilts
United Kingdom

Palmer Johnson
61 Michigan Avenue
Sturgeon Bay, WI 54235

Perkins Engines
P.O. Box 697
32500 Van Born Road
Wayne, MI 48184

Perko
16940 N.W. 13th Avenue
P.O. Box 64000 D
Miami, FL 33164

J.H. Peters & Bey
D-2000 Hamburg-11
West Germany

Pettit Paint Company
36 Pine Street
Borough of Rockaway, NJ 07866

Plastimo
15 rue Ingenieur Verriere
P.O. Box 162
56104 Lorient
France

Proctor Masts
Duncan Road
Swanwick
Southampton
United Kingdom
-or-
2nd Street & Spa Creek
Annapolis, MD 21403

Q-Beam
Brinkmann Corp.
4215 McEwen Road
Dallas, TX 75234

Quantock Marine Enterprises
Church Street
Bridgewater
Somerset TA6 5AT
United Kingdom

Quartermaster
A.Q.M. Manufacturing Co.
High Orchard
Upton Bishop
Ross-on-Wye
Herefordshire HR9 7TT
United Kingdom

Raritan Engineering Co.
1025 North High Street
Millville, NJ 08332

Ratcliffe Marine Design
173 Washington Street
Pembroke, MA 02359

Ratelco
1260 Mercer Street
Seattle, WA 98109

Rauff & Sorensen
Fabrikstraken 13
DK-9230 Svenstrup
Denmark

Raytheon Company
Marine Products Division
676 Island Pond Road
Manchester, NH 03103

Record Ridgway Tools
Parkway Works
Sheffield S9 3BL
United Kingdom

Regency Electronics
7707 Records Street
Indianapolis, IN 46226

Regent Marine
1051 Clinton Street
Buffalo, NY 14206

Riebandt Vane Steering Gear
Madeira Marine & Manufacturing
P.O. Box 1218
Pinellas Park, FL 33565

Rieker Instrument Company
Sycamore & Mill Streets
P.O. Box 52
Clinton Heights, PA 19018

E.S. Ritchie & Sons
243 Oak Street
Pembroke, MA 02359

Rockwell International
400 North Lexington Avenue
Pittsburgh, PA 15208
-or-
430 Bath Road
Slough
Berks SL1 6BB
United Kingdom

Romika
Postfach 3330
Karl - Benz - Strasse
2-4 5500 Trier
West Germany

Ronstan Marine
P.O. Box 3449
Clearwater, FL 33515

Rostand Manufacturing Company
33 Railroad Avenue
Milford, CT 06460

Rule Paint & Chemical
Cape Ann Industrial Park
Gloucester, MA 01930

R.W.O. Marine Equipment
American International Marine
P.O. Box 405
Millersville, MD 21108

Sabb Dreadnought
Box 997
Carpinteria, CA 93013

Safe Flight Instrument Corp.
Westchester Airport
New King Street
White Plains, NY 10601

Safety Tools
Highlands Road
Shirley, Solihull
West Midlands B90 4NJ
United Kingdom

Sailomat Sweden AB
Hedvigsdalsvagen 26
Sollentuna S-19143
Sweden

Samson Ocean Systems
99 High Street
Boston, MA 02210

Sanderson Kayser
P.O. Box 6
Newhall Road
Sheffield
South Yorkshire S9 2SD
United Kingdom

Scatra AB
Box 2001
S-14902 Nynashamm
Sweden

Shaefer Marine
Industrial Park
New Bedford, MA 02745

Schermuly
Channel Marine
424 Margate Road
Ramsgate
Kent
United Kingdom

Schwing - Pilot
Schwing Hydraulic Electronik
Dorstener Strasse 428
D-4690 Herne 2
West Germany

Seagull Marine
1851 McGraw Avenue
Irvine, CA 92714

Sears, Roebuck & Company
4640 Roosevelt Boulevard
Philadelphia, PA 19132

Sebago
Westbrook, ME 04092

Sen-Dure Products
25 Moffitt Boulevard
Bay Shore, NY 11706

SGC Inc.
13737 Southeast 26th Street
Bellevue, WA 98005

Sharp & Company
Ramsgate Road
Sandwich
Kent CT13 9NP
United Kingdom

Signet Scientific Company
3401 Aerojet Avenue
El Monte, CA 91731

Silva
Instrumentverken AB
Kuskvagen 4
Sollentuna S-19147
Sweden
-or-
P.O. Box 966
Binghamton, NY 13902

Simpson Electric Company
853 Dundee
Elgin, IL 60120

Simpson-Lawrence Ltd.
218-288 Edmiston Drive
Glasgow G51 2YT
Scotland

Si-Tex
St. Petersburg/Clearwater Airport
P.O. Box 6700
Clearwater, FL 33518

S-K
Dresser Industries
3201 North Wolf Road
Franklin Park, IL 60131

Skil Power Tools
4801 West Peterson Avenue
Chicago, IL 60646
-or-
Fairacres Industrial Estate
Dedworth Road
Windsor
Berks SL4 1Q1
United Kingdom

Smith & Wesson
2100 Roosevelt Avenue
Springfield, MA 01101

Snap-On Tools
2801 80th Street
Kenosha, WI 53140
-or-
Derbyshire House
Lower Street
Kettering
Northants Kettering
United Kingdom

South Coast Rod Rigging
Sparkes Boatyard
Wittering Road
Hayling Island
Hampshire PO11 9SR
United Kingdom

Space Age Electronics
Spalding Hall
Victoria Road
Hendon
London NW4
United Kingdom

Spear & Jackson
St. Pauls Road
Wednesbury
Staffordshire WS10 9RA
United Kingdom

Sperry Top-Sider
960 Harrison Avenue
Boston, MA 02116

Standard Communications
P.O. Box 92151
Los Angeles, CA 90009

Stanley Tools
600 Myrtle Street
New Britain, CT 06050
-or-
Woodside
Sheffield
S. Yorks S3 9PD
United Kingdom

Stearn Sailing Systems
Box 111
Sturgeon Bay, WI 54235

Super Sniffa
Delmar
70 Warwick Street
Birmingham
United Kingdom

Surrette Storage Battery Company
8 Proctor Street
Salem, MA 01970

Survival & Safety Designs
1 Fifth Avenue
Oakland, CA 94606

Suunto
(See Elvstrom-USA)

Swift Instruments
952 Dorchester Avenue
Boston, MA 02125

Tamaya & Company
5-8, 3-Chome
Ginza
Chuo-Ku
Tokyo 104
Japan

Taylor Stoves
Telesonic Marine
60-62 Brunswick Centre
Marchmont Street
London WC1
United Kingdom

Henry Taylor Tools
The Forge
Lowther Road
Owlerton
Sheffield S6 2DR
United Kingdom

Terramar Industrial Ltd.
P.O. Box 114
Pelham, NY 10803

Texas Instruments
Marine Communications & Navigation
Box 226080 M/S 3107
Dallas, TX 75266

Thetford Corporation
P.O. Box 1285
Ann Arbor, MI 48106

Tiller Master
774 West 17th Street
Costa Mesa, CA 92627

Tilley Lamp Company
Dunmurray
Belfast
Northern Ireland

Triplett Corporation
286 Harmon Road
Bluffton, OH 45817

Universal Motors—Medalist
1552 Harrison Street
Oshkosh, WI 54901

Vecta
V - T Sales Corp.
5149 NE 12th Avenue
Ft. Lauderdale, FL 33334

Vetus
(See W.H. Denouden)

Volvo Penta
Building A
Volvo Drive
Rockleigh, NJ 07647
-or-
Otterspool Way
Watford
Herts WD2 8HW
United Kingdom

Wagner Engineering
40 Gostick Place
North Vancouver
British Columbia V7M 3G2
Canada

Thomas Walker & Sons
55 Oxford Street
Birmingham
United Kingdom

Wallis
Unit 39
South Hampshire Industrial Park
Totton
Southampton
United Kingdom

Weems & Plath
222 Severn Avenue
Annapolis, MD 21403

Wesmar
Box C 19074
905 Dexter Avenue
North Seattle, WA 98109

J.H. Westerbeke Co.
Leden Avenue
Avon Industrial Park
Avon, MA 02322

Whale Pumps
(See Munster-Simms)

Whistler Marine
410 Great Road
Littleton Common, MA 01460

Robert E. White Instruments
51 Commercial Wharf
Boston, MA 02110

Whitlock Marine Steering
Unit 7
Faldo Road
Barton-le-Clay
Beds
United Kingdom

Wichard
B.P. 139
63302 Thiers
France

Wilcox-Crittenden
Gulf & Western Manufacturing Co.
699 Middle Street
Middletown, CT 06457

Wilkinson Sword
Sword House
Totteridge Road
High Wycombe
Bucks HP13 6EJ
United Kingdom

Windpilot
John Adam
Ahrensburger Strasse 66
2000 Hamburg 70
West Germany

Winel of America
16014 Cowley Road
Grafton, OH 44044

Wishbone Marine Products
780 S.W. Ninth Terrace
Pompano Beach, FL 33060

Wood Freeman
(See Metal Marine Pilot)

Yacht Specialties Companies
1555 East St. Gertrude Place
Santa Ana, CA 92705

Carl Zeiss Inc.
444 Fifth Avenue
New York, NY 10018

Zodiac of North America
Box 400
Thompson Creek Road
Stevensville, MD 21666

Appendix B
NAVAL ARCHITECTS

The following is a list of leading naval architects around the world:

United States and Canada

John G. Alden Inc.
89 Commercial Wharf
Boston, MA 02110

Atkin & Co.
Box 5
Noroton, CT 06820

J.R. Benford & Assoc.
Box 399
Friday Harbor, WA 98250

Philip C. Bolger
250 Washington Street
Gloucester, MA 01930

John Brandlmayr Ltd.
200-4620 Sidney Street
Vancouver, B.C. V5N 5N8

Ted Brewer Yacht Designs Ltd.
217 Edith Point
Anacortes, WA 98221

Thomas P. Brittain
9957 Campus Way S.
Upper Marlboro, MD 20870

C&C Design Group
226 White Oaks Boulevard
Oakville, Ont. L6H 2B9

Richard D. Carlson
Box 310, Division Street
Sag Harbor, NY 11963

Cartwright Yachts
Box 308
Oriental, NC 28571

Chance & Company
Pratt Street
Essex, CT 06426

W.I.B. Crealock
Fiddler's Green Yacht Yard
1521 S. Hill Street
Oceanside, CA 92054

P.F. DeGrasse & Assoc.
3608 Coolheights Drive
Rancho Palos Verdes, CA 90274

Arthur Edmunds Inc.
2200 NE 52nd Street
Ft. Lauderdale, FL 33308

Eldredge-McInnis Inc.
57 Water Street, Box F
Hingham, MA 02043

Mark Ellis Design
335 Robinson Street
Oakville, Ont. L6J 141

Jules G. Fleder
Box 779-733
Summer Street
Stamford, CT 06904

Alan P. Gurney
121 E. 54th Street
New York, NY 10022

Ken Hankinson
Box 2551-G
La Habra, CA 90631

Robert B. Harris Ltd.
34 Coal Harbor Wharf
566 Cardero St.
Vancouver, B.C. V6G 2W6

Herreshoff Designs
18 Burnside Street
Bristol, RI 02809

Jacobs & Husby
344-B Rancheros Drive
San Marcos, CA 92069

Kaufman & Ladd Inc.
222 Severn Avenue
Annapolis, MD 21403

Scott Kaufman Yachts
219 E. 48th Street
New York, NY 10017

Bruce King Yacht Design
2230 Newport Boulevard
Newport Beach, CA 92663

C. William Lapworth Inc.
Box 1756
Newport Beach, CA 92663

Letcher Offshore Design
Box 104
Southwest Harbor, ME 04679

MacLear & Harris Inc.
28 W. 44th Street
New York, NY 10036

McCurdy & Rhodes Inc.
Box 206
Cold Spring Harbor, NY 11724

Roger Marshall Yacht Designs
Box 127-A
Jamestown, RI 02835

Edwin Monk & Son
Box 10397
Bainbridge Island, WA 98110

Gary W. Mull
1525 Lakeside Drive
Oakland, CA 94612

Nelson/Marek Yacht Design
2829 Canon Street
San Diego, CA 92106

Richard C. Newick
R.F.D.
Vineyard Haven, MA 02568

Payne & Franklin Inc.
31 Hazard Avenue
N. Kingstown, RI 02852

Robert H. Perry Yacht Designers
6400 Seaview Avenue NW
Seattle, WA 98107

Tom Potter & Assoc. Inc.
659-A Eldred Avenue
Jamestown, RI 02835

Raymond H. Richards
Box 3271
Newport Beach, CA 92663

Seaton-Neville
320 N. Bayshore Boulevard, Suite 206
Clearwater, FL 33519

Sparkman & Stephens Inc.
79 Madison Avenue
New York, NY 10016

Tanton Inc.
Box 270
Newport, RI

Charles W. Wittholz
100 Williamsburg Drive
Silver Spring, MD 20901

Arthur R. Wycoff
1550 Bunting Circle
Sanibel, FL 33957

Wylie Design Group
1924 Willow Street
Alameda, CA 94501

Nelson Zimmer
505 Maple Street
Marine City, MI 48039

United Kingdom

Ian L. Anderson
7 Hauley Road
Dartmouth
Devon

Robert Brasted
1 Navarino Court
High Street, Lymington
Hampshire SO4 9AE

Alan Buchanan & Partners Ltd.
Le Bourg Slip
St. Clement
Jersey C.1

Julian Everitt
Commercial Place
London NW1

Laurent Giles & Partners Ltd.
Quay Hill
Lymington
Hants SO4 9AR

Alan F. Hill
15 High Street
Burnham on Crouch
Essex CM0 8AG

Ron Holland Yacht Designs
Strand Farm House
Currabinny
Co. Cork, Ireland

Holman & Pye
21 City Road
West Mersea, Colchester
Essex CO5 8NE

Derek Kelsall
Sandwich Marina
Sandwich
Kent

Colin Mudie
Bywater Lodge
Pierside, Lymington
Hampshire SO4 8SB

Murray, Cormack Assocs.
Glade House
Hadlow
Kent TN11 0HZ

A. Mylne & Co.
6 Royal Terrace
Glasgow G3 7NT

Alan. M. Pape
"Haye"
Courtenay Close
East Looe
Cornwall PL13 1JK

Angus S. Primrose
Mercury Yacht Harbour
Hamble
Hant. SO3 5HR

Michael Pocock
Spring Corner
Lymington
Hant. SO4 9SP

Walter Rayner
21 Churchfield Road
Poole
Dorset BH15 2QL

Other
Amsterdam Naval Architecture
2 Herman Heyermans Weg
1077 WL Amsterdam
Box 7337
1007 JH Amsterdam
Holland

H.K. Bergmann
Oienkilen
1620 Gressvik
Norway

Bruce Farr Yacht Design
P.O. Box 2678
Auckland 1
New Zealand

Peter A. Ibold
Palais de La Scala
Av. Henry Dunant
MC Monte-Carlo
Monaco

Willem de Vries Lentsch
Van Eeghenstraat 94
Amsterdam
Holland

Lunstroo Custom Designs
Prins Hendrikkade 152
Amsterdam
Holland

Sciomachen
Via Algardi, 20
40128 Bologna
Italy

E.G. van de Stadt & Partners
Box 193
Wormerveer
Holland

F. de Voogt
H.W. de Voogt en Zoom C.V.
Zonnelaan 12-2012 TC
Haarlem
Holland

Appendix C
SAILMAKERS

The following is an international listing of leading sailmakers:

United States and Canada
Admiralty Sails
50 Crompton Avenue
E. Greenwich, RI 02818

Alan-Clarke Sailmakers Inc.
220 Route 25A
Northport, NY 11768

Anderson & Vining Sailmakers
155 Derby Street
Salem, MA 01970

Atlantic Sails
148 Middle Street
Portland, ME 04111

Blue Water Sails Ltd.
76 W. 6th Street
Vancouver, B.C.

E.S. Bohndell & Son
Commercial Street
Rockport, ME 04856

Boston Sails, Ltd.
120 Michigan
Point Edward, Ont.

Bowers Sails Inc.
14916 Minnetonka Boulevard
Minneapolis, MN 55343

Clark Sails
Dauntless Shipyard
37 Pratt Street
Essex, CT 06426

Competition Sails Inc.
1045 3rd Street South
St. Petersburg, FL 33701

Eastern Shore Sails
708 N. Section Street
Fairhope, AL 36532

John Eggers
1000 Highway #35
S. Amboy, NJ 08879

Skip Elliot Sailmakers
224¼ 21st Street
Newport Beach, CA 92663

Fogh Sails Ltd.
55 Ormshirk Avenue
Toronto, Ont.

Glencoe Sails Ltd.
539 King Street West
Toronto, Ont.

Haarstick Sailmakers
708 Willow Avenue
Ithaca, NY 14850

Harbor Sailmakers
Berth 41-A
Box 228
San Pedro, CA 90733

Hard Sails
204 Main Street
Islip, NY 11751
(and in CT and ME)

Hathaway, Reiser & Raymond Inc.
184 Selleck Street
Stamford, CT 06902

Hild Sails Inc.
225 Fordham Street
City Island, NY 10464

Hogshire Sailmakers Inc.
2401 Hampton Boulevard
Norfolk, VA 23517

Hood Sailmakers Inc.
Little Harbor Way
Marblehead, MA 01945

Horizon Sails
69 Jefferson Street
Stamford, CT 06902

Glen Housley Sailmakers
616 3rd Street
Annapolis, MD 21403

Jasper & Bailey Sailmakers
Brown & Howard's Wharf
Newport, RI 02840

Louis J. Larsen Inc.
40 Matinecock Avenue
Port Washington, NY 11050

Linsky Sails
3625 Colonial Avenue
Los Angeles, CA 90066

Mack-Shaw Sailmakers
100 Southwest 15th Street
Ft. Lauderdale, FL 33315

Maine Sail Co.
Cobb Road
Camden, ME 04843

Maken Sails
76 W. 6th Avenue
Vancouver, B.C.

Manchester Yacht Sails Inc.
Elm Street
P.O. Box P-203
South Dartmouth, MA 12748

Marblehead Sailmakers
89 Front Street
Marblehead, MA 01945

Marshall Sails
629 Terminal Way, #13
Costa Mesa, CA 92627

Mauna Lowa Sails
716-A Cooke Street
Honolulu, HI 96813

McKibbin Sails Inc.
1821 Reynolds Avenue
Irvine, CA 92714

Melges Sails Inc.
Zenda, WI 53195

Mitchell Sails
2670 Bridgeway
Sausalito, CA 94965

Murphy & Nye
2243 E. Elston Avenue
Chicago, IL 60614

Art Nelson Sailmakers
570 Auahi Street
Honolulu, HI 96813

Noank Sails
Box 492
6 Smith Street
Noank, CT 06340

Nootka Sailmakers
4401 Pacific Coast Highway East
Tacoma, CA 98424

North Sails
1111 E. Anchorage Lane
San Diego, CA 92106

Oakum Bay Sails Inc.
15 School Street
Marblehead, MA 01945

Obersheimer Sails
918 Main Street
Buffalo, NY 14202

Odyssey Sailmakers
2972 Century Place
Costa Mesa, CA 92626

O'Neill Sailmakers Inc.
193 Penn Avenue
Niantic, CT 06357

Percoco Sails Co.
2914 Bayport Boulevard
Seabrook, TX 77586

Ratsey & Lapthorn Inc.
East Schofield Street
City Island, NY 10464

Raudaschl Sails Canada Ltd.
7 Superior Avenue
Toronto, Ont.

Sailing Specialists
55 West Stark Street
Williams Bay
Milwaukee, WI 53192

Sailmakers Cooperative
Silver Street
Portland, ME 04101

Sailmakers Loft
Route 1
Box 525
Sumner, WA 98390

Sails USA Inc.
Silver Street
Box 542
Portland, ME 04112

Sails by Watts
21918 Harper Avenue
St. Clair Shores, MI 48080

San Pedro Sailmakers
511 West Santa Cruz
San Pedro, CA 90731

Franz Schattauer
6010 Seaview Avenue
Northwest Seattle, WA 98107

Schoonmaker/Campbell Sails
6400 Marine Drive
Long Beach, CA 90803

Paul Schreck & Co.
South Scenic Drive
Lillian, AL 36549

Seabrook Sail Shop
1909 Nickolson
Box 64
Seabrook, TX 77586

Shore Sails
1700 Niagara Street
Buffalo, NY 14207

Sobstad Sailmakers
Elm Street
Box 424
Old Saybrook, CT 06475

Spencer Sails
Mill Dam Road
Foot of Huntington Harbor
Box 583
Huntington, NY 11743

The Spinnaker Shop
Box 2776
Stanford, CA 94305

Stanton Sailmakers
4204 Gelncore Avenue
Marina del Rey, CA 90291

Starboard Sailmakers
2525½ Shelter Island Drive
San Diego, CA 92106

Peter M. Sutter Co.
Box 927
Sausalito, CA 94965

Taylor Sails
136 Adelaide Street East
Toronto, Ont.

Thomas Sailmakers
19106 Detroit Road
Cleveland, OH 44140

Thurston Sails Inc.
406-408 Water Street
Warren, RI 02885

Ulmer Sails
175 City Island Avenue
City Island, NY 10464

Vector Sails
2650 West Belden
Chicago, Il 60647

Wilson & Silsby
12 Atlantic Avenue
Marblehead, MA 01945

Yardarm Sailmakers Inc.
925 Webster
Needham, MA 02192

United Kingdom
Arun Sails
Fitzalan Road
Arandel
West Sussex

Bruce Banks Sails, Ltd.
372 Brook Lane
Sarisbury
Southampton SO3 6ZA

Bowker & Budd Ltd.
Brooks Lane
Bosham
Sussex

Cranfield Sails Ltd.
The Quay
Burnham on Crouch
Essex CMO BAZ

Jack Holt Sails Ltd.
The Embankment
Putney
London SW15

Hood Sailmakers
Bath Road
Lymington
Hants SD4 9RW

Jeckells & Son Ltd.
Wroxham, Norfolk & Lowestadt
Suffolk

Lucas Sails
Lucas & Son Ltd.
42 Broad Street
Portsmouth

McWilliam Sails
Vectis Yard
Cowes IOW

Miller & Whitworth Ltd.
Sustanum Works
East Street
Titchfield, Fareham
Hants

Oakley Sails Ltd.
Sustanum Works
East Street
Titchfield, Fareham
Hants

Ratsey & Lapthorn
34 Medina Road
Cowes IOW

Rockall Sails Ltd.
Bosham
Sussex

Team Sails Ltd.
The Retreat
Old Turnpike
Fareham
Hants

Other
Ahlstrom & Jornstedt
(Horizon Sails)
Lilla Skuggans Vag. 18
115 42 Stockholm
Sweden

Burke Sails
(Horizon Sails)
21 Higginbotham Road
Gladesville
N.S.W. 2111
Australia

Hood Sailmakers
326 Rt. de Turin
06300 Nice
France

Hood Sailmakers
Box 165
Milson's Pt.
N.S.W. 2061
Australia

McWilliam Sails
Crosshaven
County Cork
Ireland

North Sails
12 Polo Avenue
Monovale
N.S.W. 2103
Australia

Neil Pryde Ltd.
Box 9379
Kowloon City
Hong Kong

INDEX

M

N O

P

R

S

ACKNOWLEDGMENTS

The editors wish to thank the following companies and individuals for supplying photographs to *Under Sail:*

ACR Electronics, APT Electronics, Aqua-Temp Corporation, Arco USA, Atlantis Weathergear, Avon Inflatables, Barient Company, Barlow Marine, Black & Decker, Blake & Sons, BMW, Bomar, Red Boutilier, E.J. Bowman Ltd., Captain Charles Currey Ltd., Cetrek, Cross Power, Eberspacher, William Eickholt, M.S. Gibb Ltd., Goiot, Gori, Guest Corporation, Harken Yacht Fittings, Honda Motors, Hood Yacht Systems, Hynautic, ITT Decca Marine, ITT Jabsco Products, C. Sherman Johnson, Kenyon Marine, Koden, Koolatron Industries, Lectra/San, Lewmar Marine, Lirakis Safety Harness, Lo-Kata, Lowrance Electronic, Mariner Company, Marinetics, Marlow Ropes, Mercury Marine, Metal Marine Pilot, Morrow Electronics, Nautor Swan, Naivdyne Corporation, Navtec, Newage Transmissions, Nicro/ Fico, Outboard Marine Corporation (OMC), Perkins Engines, Richmond Ring, Romika, Scatra, Schaefer Marine, Seagull Marine, Sestrel, Simpson-Lawrence, Stanley Tools, Stearn Sailing Systems, Stowe Log, Surrette Storage Battery, Tamaya, Taylor Stoves, Texas Instruments, Tiller Master, Tilley Lamp Company, Vetus/Denouden, Volvo Penta, Wichard, Windex Wind Indicator, *Yachting World.*

Special thanks to Red Boutilier, *Yachting World* and Nautor Swan for chapter-opening pictures.

Thanks too to Ronstan Marine, Pettit Paint Company and Woolsey Marine Industries, for permission to reprint charts.